Cassius Dio and the Late Roman Republic

Historiography of Rome and Its Empire

Series Editors

Carsten Hjort Lange (*Aalborg, Denmark*)
Jesper Majbom Madsen (*SDU, Denmark*)

Editorial Board

Rhiannon Ash (*Oxford, UK*)
Christopher Baron (*Notre Dame, USA*)
Henning Börm (*Konstanz, Germany*)
Alain Gowing (*University of Washington, USA*)
Adam Kemezis (*Alberta, Canada*)
Christina S. Kraus (*Yale, USA*)
J. E. Lendon (*University of Virginia, USA*)
David Levene (*New York University, USA*)
Steve Mason (*Groningen, Netherlands*)
Josiah Osgood (*Georgetown, USA*)
John Rich (*Nottingham, UK*)
Federico Santangelo (*Newcastle, UK*)
Christopher Smith (*St Andrews, UK*)
Catherine Steel (*Glasgow, UK*)
Frederik J. Vervaet (*Melbourne, Australia*)
David Wardle (*Cape Town, South Africa*)
Johannes Wienand (*Braunschweig, Germany*)

VOLUME 4

The titles published in this series are listed at *brill.com/hre*

Cassius Dio and the Late Roman Republic

Edited by

Josiah Osgood
Christopher Baron

BRILL

LEIDEN | BOSTON

Cover Illustration: Vincenzo Camuccini (1771–1844), Assassination of Julius Caesar. Galleria Nazionale d'Arte Moderna. Photo Credit: Scala/Ministero per i Beni e le Attività culturali/Art Resource, NY. With permission.

Library of Congress Cataloging-in-Publication Data

Names: Osgood, Josiah, 1974– editor. | Baron, Christopher A., 1973– editor.
Title: Cassius Dio and the Late Roman Republic / edited by Josiah Osgood, Christopher Baron.
Description: Leiden ; Boston : Brill, [2019] | Series: Historiography of Rome and its Empire, ISSN 2468-2314 ; Volume 4 | Includes bibliographical references and index. |
Identifiers: LCCN 2019016583 (print) | LCCN 2019021607 (ebook) | ISBN 9789004405158 (E-book) | ISBN 9789004405059 (hardback : alk. paper)
Subjects: LCSH: Cassius Dio Cocceianus. Roman history. | Rome—History—Republic, 265-30 B.C.—Historiography.
Classification: LCC DG206.C38 (ebook) | LCC DG206.C38 C34 2019 (print) | DDC 937/.05072—dc23
LC record available at https://lccn.loc.gov/2019016583

Typeface for the Latin, Greek, and Cyrillic scripts: "Brill". See and download: brill.com/brill-typeface.

ISSN 2468-2314
ISBN 978-90-04-40505-9 (hardback)
ISBN 978-90-04-40515-8 (e-book)

Copyright 2019 by Koninklijke Brill NV, Leiden, The Netherlands.
Koninklijke Brill NV incorporates the imprints Brill, Brill Hes & De Graaf, Brill Nijhoff, Brill Rodopi, Brill Sense, Hotei Publishing, mentis Verlag, Verlag Ferdinand Schöningh and Wilhelm Fink Verlag.
All rights reserved. No part of this publication may be reproduced, translated, stored in a retrieval system, or transmitted in any form or by any means, electronic, mechanical, photocopying, recording or otherwise, without prior written permission from the publisher.
Authorization to photocopy items for internal or personal use is granted by Koninklijke Brill NV provided that the appropriate fees are paid directly to The Copyright Clearance Center, 222 Rosewood Drive, Suite 910, Danvers, MA 01923, USA. Fees are subject to change.

This book is printed on acid-free paper and produced in a sustainable manner.

Contents

Historiography of Rome and Its Empire Series   VII
Acknowledgments   VIII
Notes on Contributors   IX

1   Introduction: Cassius Dio and the Late Roman Republic   1
    Josiah Osgood and Christopher Baron

PART 1
Narrative Themes and Texture

2   Imperialism and the Crisis of the Roman Republic: Dio's View on Late Republican Conquests (Books 36–40)   19
    Estelle Bertrand

3   Electoral Bribery and the Challenge to the Authority of the Senate: Two Aspects of Dio's View of the Late Roman Republic (Books 36–40)   36
    Marianne Coudry

4   Wrinkles in Time: Chronological Ruptures in Cassius Dio's Narrative of the Late Republic   50
    Christopher Baron

5   Dio the Deviant: Comparing Dio's Late Republic and the Parallel Sources   72
    Mads Ortving Lindholmer

6   Cassius Dio and the Virtuous Roman   97
    Kathryn Welch

PART 2
Characters, Institutions, and Episodes

7   The Republican Dictatorship: an Imperial Perspective   131
    Christopher Burden-Strevens

8   Spectacle Entertainments in the Late Republican Books of Cassius Dio's
    Roman History   158
      Jesper Carlsen

9   Cassius Dio's Catiline: "A Name Greater Than His Deeds Deserved"   176
      Gianpaolo Urso

10 Dio and the Voice of the Sibyl   197
      Josiah Osgood

PART 3
Civil War and the Victory of Augustus

11 Responding to Civil War: M. Claudius Marcellus Aeserninus and
    M. Caelius Rufus in Cassius Dio, Book 42   217
      Andrew G. Scott

12 Cassius Dio on Sextus Pompeius and Late Republican Civil War   236
      Carsten Hjort Lange

13 Like Father Like Son: the Differences in How Dio Tells the Story of
    Julius Caesar and His More Successful Son   259
      Jesper Majbom Madsen

14 Towards the Conceptualization of Cassius Dio's Narration of the
    Early Career of Octavian   282
      Konstantin V. Markov

    Index   299

Historiography of Rome and Its Empire Series

Carsten H. Lange & Jesper M. Madsen

Brill's *Historiography of Rome and Its Empire* Series aims to gather innovative and outstanding contributions in order to identify debates and trends, and in order to help provide a better understanding of ancient historiography, as well as how to approach Roman history and historiography. We would particularly welcome proposals that look at both Roman and Greek writers, but are also happy to consider proposals which focus on individual writers, or individuals in the same tradition. It is timely and valuable to bring these trends and historical sources together by founding the Series, focusing mainly on the Republican period and the Principate, as well as the Later Roman Empire.

Historical writing about Rome in both Latin and Greek forms an integrated topic. There are two strands in ancient writing about the Romans and their empire: (a) the Romans' own tradition of histories of the deeds of the Roman people at home and at war, and (b) Greek historical responses, some developing their own models (Polybius, Josephus) and the others building on what both the Roman historians and earlier Greeks had written (Dionysius, Appian, Cassius Dio). Whereas older scholarship tended to privilege a small group of 'great historians' (the likes of Sallust, Livy, Tacitus), recent work has rightly brought out the diversity of the traditions and recognized that even 'minor' writers are worth exploring not just as sources, but for their own concerns and reinterpretation of their material (such as *The Fragments of the Roman Historians* (2013), and the collected volumes on Velleius Paterculus (Cowan 2011) and Appian (Welch 2015)). The study of these historiographical traditions is essential as a counterbalance to the traditional use of ancient authors as a handy resource, with scholars looking at isolated sections of their structure. This fragmentary use of the ancient evidence makes us forget to reflect on their work in its textual and contextual entirety.

Acknowledgments

The editors gratefully acknowledge the Danish Council for Independent Research and Georgetown University for funding of the 2017 conference at Georgetown's Villa Le Balze in Fiesole, Italy, from which this volume arose.

Anybody who has spent time at the Villa knows what care its staff puts into making visitors welcome and helping them get the most out of their stay in Fiesole. We warmly thank Fulvio Orsitto, Director of Villa Le Balze, Simona Mocali, Assistant Director of Villa Le Balze, and their colleagues for their warm embrace and superb organization. At Georgetown we also thank Chester Gillis, former Dean of the College, for his support and Christopher Brush, the Administrator of Classics, for help with logistics.

Carsten Hjort Lange and Jesper Majbom Madsen not only contributed papers to this volume; they also have helped us see it into publication. We are grateful to them and all of our contributors for the hard work they put into their papers and their promptness in meeting publication deadlines.

Finally, special thanks go to Brill's anonymous reviewer for helpful suggestions on the volume.

Notes on Contributors

Christopher Baron
is Associate Professor of Classics at the University of Notre Dame. He specializes in the study of the historical writing of ancient Greece and Rome as well as the history of the Greek world after Alexander. He is the author of *Timaeus of Tauromenium and Hellenistic Historiography* (2013) and General Editor of *The Herodotus Encyclopedia* (forthcoming). He is also currently at work on a survey of the Greek historians writing under the Roman Empire, from Dionysius to Eusebius.

Estelle Bertrand
is Associate Professor of Roman History at the University of Le Mans. She specializes in late Roman republican history and historiography (several articles). She is author, with Valérie Fromentin, of the edition-translation-commentary of Cassius Dio's *Roman History*, Books 45–46 and Book 47 in the Collection des Universités de France, Paris (2008 and 2014), and she was one of the directors of the French Cassius Dio Network (2011–2015) and co-edited the volume *Cassius Dion: nouvelles lectures* (2016, with several contributions). She is also interested in conceptions of time in the Roman empire and has published, with Rita Compatangelo-Soussignan, a volume on *Cycles de la Nature, Cycles de l'Histoire* (2015).

Christopher Burden-Strevens
is Lecturer in Ancient History at the University of Kent. He was awarded his PhD in 2015 as part of the *Fragments of the Republican Roman Orators* project under the supervision of Prof. Catherine Steel. Christopher has published several studies on Cassius Dio's narrative of the Republic, most recently "Reconstructing Republican Oratory in Cassius Dio's *Roman History*" (in *Reading Republican Oratory*, eds. C. Gray et al., 2018). With Mads Lindholmer he is co-editor of the recent volume, *Cassius Dio's Forgotten History of Early Rome* (2018) and is author of the forthcoming 2020 monograph, *Cassius Dio's Speeches and the Transformation of the Res Publica*. He is especially interested in all aspects of republican political history, currently the dictatorship in particular, and in ancient rhetoric (including political oratory and rhetoric in historiography).

Jesper Carlsen
teaches ancient history in the Department of History, University of Southern Denmark. Mostly a scholar of Roman social and economic history, he has also written extensively on Roman North Africa, gladiators, and Alexander the Great. He is the author of *Vilici and Roman Estate Managers until AD 284* (1995), *The Rise and Fall of a Roman Noble Family: The Domitii Ahenobarbi 196 BC–AD 68* (2006) and *Land and Labour: Studies in Roman Social and Economic History* (2013). He has edited the volumes *Alexander the Great: Myth and Reality* (1993), *Landuse in the Roman Empire* (1997), and *Agricoltura e scambi nell'Italia tardo-repubblicana* (2009). He also contributed to *Cassius Dio: Greek Intellectual and Roman Politician* (eds. C. H. Lange & J. M. Madsen, 2016).

Marianne Coudry
Professor Emeritus of Roman History, Université de Haute-Alsace, is a specialist of the Roman Senate of the mid- and late Republic (thesis in 1989 and many articles), and more generally of the political culture and society of the Roman Republic. She has recently co-edited a first volume on utopia in Greece and Rome, with Maria Teresa Schettino (*L'utopie politique et la cité idéale, Politica Antica* v, 2015), and a second is forthcoming. She has written on several Roman laws for the LEPOR database (URL: http://www.cn-telma.fr/lepor/). She is author, with Guy Lachenaud, of the edition-translation-commentary of Cassius Dio's *Roman History*, Books 36–37 and Books 38–39–40 in the Collection des Universités de France, Paris (2014 and 2011), and has written several contributions in *Cassius Dion: nouvelles lectures* (eds. V. Fromentin *et al.*, 2016).

Carsten Hjort Lange
Associate Professor, Aalborg University, is co-editor of Brill's *Historiography of Rome and Its Empire* Series and co-founder of two current international Networks: *Cassius Dio: Between History and Politics* (with Jesper M. Madsen, George Hinge, Adam Kemezis & Josiah Osgood) and *Internal War. Society, Social Order and Political Conflict in Antiquity* (with Johannes Wienand & Henning Börm). He is the author of two monographs: *Res Publica Constituta: Actium, Apollo and the Accomplishment of the Triumviral Assignment* (2009) and *Triumphs in the Age of Civil War: The Late Republic and the Adaptability of Triumphal Tradition* (2016). He has written articles on political and military history and has co-edited a volume on the Roman republican triumph with Frederik J. Vervaet (*The Roman Republican Triumph: Beyond the Spectacle*, 2014), as well as a volume on Cassius Dio (*Cassius Dio: Greek Intellectual and Roman Politician*, 2016) with Jesper M. Madsen.

NOTES ON CONTRIBUTORS   XI

Mads Ortving Lindholmer

is a PhD student at University of St Andrews where he is engaged in a project on the historical and literary development of the imperial *salutatio*. He received his MPhil from University of Glasgow with a thesis on Cassius Dio's late Republic and his BA from University of Southern Denmark. Lindholmer is co-editor of the recent volume entitled *Cassius Dio's Forgotten History of Early Rome* (2018), and he is also the author of several chapters and articles, especially on Cassius Dio. His research interests include the political history of the late Roman Republic and the Roman empire as well as imperial historiography.

Jesper Majbom Madsen

Associate Professor and Director of Teaching, University of Southern Denmark, is co-editor of Brill's *Historiography of Rome and its Empire* Series. He is the author of *Eager to Be Roman: Greek Response to Roman Rule in Pontus and Bithynia* (2009) and is the co-editor of *Roman Rule in Greek and Latin Writing: Double Vision* (2014) and *Cassius Dio: Greek Intellectual and Roman Politician* (2016). He has published a number of articles on emperor worship, lately "Cassius Dio and the Cult of Iulius and Roma at Ephesus and Nicaea (51.20.6–8)" (*Classical Quarterly* 66.1 [2016]). He is currently working on a monograph examining the Pompeian city-states in Pontos.

Konstantin V. Markov

Associate Professor, Lobachevsky State University of Nizhny Novgorod, is the author of a number of articles on Aelius Aristides, Cassius Dio, Flavius Philostratus, and Herodian. His research focuses on Roman historiography in general, as well as on imperial Roman political culture and the perception of Rome and the Roman empire by Second Sophistic authors. He has contributed to two volumes of the Russian translation of Cassius Dio's *Roman History*, Books 51–63 and 64–80 (2011 and 2014), and his work on the translation of Dio's Books 40–45 is in progress. He is currently working, jointly with Adam Kemezis and Prof. Alexander Makhlaiuk, on a collection of English translations of Soviet and Russian scholarship on Roman imperial historiography (under contract with Brill).

Josiah Osgood

is Chair and Professor of Classics at Georgetown University, where he has also served as Convener of the Faculty of Languages and Linguistics. He has published many articles and books on Roman history and Latin literature, including *Caesar's Legacy: Civil War and the Emergence of the Roman Empire* (2006),

Turia: A Roman Woman's Civil War (2014), and *Rome and the Making of a World State, 150 BCE–20 CE* (2018). He has also co-edited *The Alternative Augustan Age* (2019), a volume arising from a conference held at the Villa Vergiliana in Cuma, Italy in 2016. He is currently working on a book about Rome's destruction of Carthage.

Andrew G. Scott
is Assistant Professor of Classical Studies at Villanova University. His research focuses on the historiography of Severan Rome and the social history of ancient Sparta. He is the author of *Emperors and Usurpers: An Historical Commentary on Cassius Dio's Roman History, Books 79(78)–80(80) (217–229 A.D.)* (2018) and has recently published articles on various aspects of the histories of Cassius Dio and Herodian, as well as on the image of Spartan valor in various sources. He is currently working on a monograph on Cassius Dio's contemporary history (Books 73–80) and co-editing, with Carsten H. Lange, a volume entitled *Cassius Dio: The Impact of Violence, War, and Civil War*.

Gianpaolo Urso
is Marie Curie Fellow at the Catholic University of the Sacred Heart (Milan). He is the author of three monographs: *Taranto e gli xenikoi strategoi* (1998), *Cassio Dione e i magistrati. Le origini della repubblica nei frammenti della "Storia romana"* (2005), and *Cassio Dione e i sovversivi. La crisi della repubblica nei frammenti della "Storia romana"* (2013). He has published numerous papers on Roman republican history and on the Greek and Latin historiography of Rome. He has edited the proceedings of the international conferences of the Fondazione Niccolò Canussio (2000–2014, fourteen volumes) and has co-edited the collective volume *Cassius Dion: nouvelles lectures* (2016).

Kathryn Welch
is Associate Professor in the Department of Classics and Ancient History at the University of Sydney. She is the author of *Magnus Pius: Sextus Pompeius and the Transformation of the Roman Republic* (2012) and editor of *Appian's Roman History: Empire and Civil War* (2015). She is also co-editor, with Anton Powell, of *Julius Caesar as Artful Reporter: The War Commentaries as Political Instrument* (1998) and *Sextus Pompeius* (2002); with T. W. Hillard, of *Roman Crossings: Theory and Practice in the Roman Republic* (2005); with Kit Morrell and Josiah Osgood, of *The Alternative Augustan Age* (2019). Her main research interests include the transformation of politics and society at Rome in the first century BCE and the ways in which this upheaval was described in ancient narratives.

CHAPTER 1

Introduction: Cassius Dio and the Late Roman Republic

Josiah Osgood and Christopher Baron

1   Cassius Dio and the History of the Late Republic

Cassius Dio's *Roman History* is an essential, though often under-acknowledged, source for modern historians of the late Roman Republic.[1] Dio provides indispensable accounts of such major episodes as the passage of the *lex Gabinia* in 67 BCE empowering Pompey against the pirates, Julius Caesar's first consulship in 59 (38.1–11), and the series of honors voted to Caesar as dictator (43.14, 43.42–5, 44.4–8).[2] While we tend to rely less on Dio's account of the Gallic War, thanks to the survival of Caesar's own commentaries, for other campaigns he is the main source – Caesar's earlier war in Lusitania in 61 (37.47–8) and the war of Pomptinus (*pr.* 63) against the Allobroges in Gaul (37.37–48), to give two examples. Beyond narratives of specific events, Dio also provides important, sometimes unique, information on political and even social developments in the period. We hear much of electoral disorder and bribery, and, as Marianne Coudry shows in this volume, Dio sometimes is our most important source for laws against bribery. Jesper Carlsen, in his contribution, shows how much Dio has to say on gladiatorial contests, and the role of gladiators in political violence. Indeed, at numerous points Dio vividly depicts political violence in the city of Rome and the pressure exerted by the crowd. In addition to the events of Caesar's first consulship, one could mention events surrounding the trial of Gaius Rabirius in 63 (37.24–8), the wrangling of Clodius, Milo, and their supporters (39.17–21), the election of Pompey and Crassus to their second consulships in 55 and actions they undertook as consuls (39.17–21), or major unrest during the civil war between Caesar and Pompey (42.21–33).

---

1 His importance for understanding the Augustan principate – arguably even greater – is more widely acknowledged and discussed, e.g., Manuwald 1979; Rich 1989; Reinhold & Swan 1990. Note that it is only the Augustan books (50–6) that have been issued in the Penguin Classics series (Scott-Kilvert 1987); and also note the major commentaries on Augustan books of Rich 1990 and Swan 2004. Dio's triumviral narrative also received attention in Gowing 1992.
2 All subsequent dates in this chapter are BCE unless otherwise indicated. Translations of Dio are based on those of E. Cary in the Loeb Classical Library edition.

It is telling that Fergus Millar's recognition of Dio's value as a historian of the late Republic appears not in his important monograph of 1964, but in his much later *The Crowd in Rome in the Late Republic* (1998) – when Millar was actually writing republican history himself.[3] In the latter work, we hear of "Dio's excellent account of political exchanges in the early part of 59" (127) and "Dio's typically efficient summary of the legislation put forward by Clodius as tribune" (138). Writing of 55, Millar states: "Cassius Dio, describing the same events, gives a more detailed and circumstantial account, reflecting his much superior grasp of the Republican constitution and politics" (170–1).

This volume arises from a conference held at Georgetown's Villa Le Balze in Fiesole, Italy in May 2017 on Dio's treatment of the late Republic, one of a series sponsored by the Cassius Dio Research Network, a joint venture between the University of Southern Denmark, Aalborg University, Aarhus University, the University of Alberta, and Georgetown University. Contributors look in particular at the extant narrative covering events from the year 69 to the breakdown of relations between Caesar and the Senate in 50 (Books 36–40), but also the subsequent narrative of civil war and the final victory of Augustus, from 49 to 29 (Books 41–52).[4] Some write primarily as historians eager to use Dio as a source for their investigations; others have a deeper interest in Dio as a writer of history and his place in the historiographic tradition; some are particular experts on Dio and have, for example, contributed to major new editions of his work.[5] All share the view that both late republican history and Dio's *Roman History* are, in the end, better understood when approached in tandem, and collectively they make the case that more attention should be paid to Dio's account: indeed, in some cases, fresh analysis of key events or developments may find a more fruitful beginning with Dio than with Cicero.

The essays which follow repeatedly show that Dio reliably transmits precise historical details, sometimes otherwise unknown. The laws against bribery have already been mentioned. We can add details of the SCU and associated decrees, such as *hostis publicus* declarations (again noted by Coudry). In his

---

3 Millar's earlier assessment of the late republican books is fairly harsh (1964, 46–60). Lintott (1997), while recognizing Dio's importance for the writing of late republican history and arguing that Dio read widely and used a variety of sources, ultimately passes a rather negative verdict overall.

4 On Books 1–35 see, e.g., Simons 2009; Urso 2013; Burden-Strevens & Lindholmer 2018.

5 For this volume, it is especially important to note the editions of Lachenaud & Coudry 2011; Lachenaud & Coudry 2014; Fromentin & Bertrand 2008; Fromentin & Bertrand 2014. These, and other recent entries in the Budé series, have laid a foundation that all contributors to this volume build on. Also of major importance are many papers in Fromentin *et al.* 2016 cited throughout this volume and Lange & Madsen 2016.

contribution, Josiah Osgood shows that Dio has a well-informed account of Ptolemy XII's arrival in Rome in 57 and his struggle for reinstatement, and the unexpected role played by a Sibylline oracle made public in 56 by the tribune Gaius Cato. Osgood argues that modern historians have not focused on it sufficiently. In another paper, Christopher Burden-Strevens highlights Dio's unique emphasis on Pompey's refusal of a dictatorship in 53 and relates this to a "growing atmosphere of suspicion and concern about rumors of a dictatorship." Here, analysis of Dio alongside the evidence of Cicero's letters and contemporary coinage produces rich results.

Dio claims (fr. 1.2, 73[72].23.5) to have read nearly everything about the Romans written by anybody, and to have spent ten years taking notes for his *History* – without being granted a sabbatical, so far as we know. He certainly reveals familiarity with a range of earlier sources, mostly lost to us, as many papers in this volume show while not getting bogged down in the concerns of traditional *Quellenforschung*. Coudry makes a sharp contrast between Dio's account of the Senate's actions against Caesar in 49 (41.1–3) and that of Caesar himself in his *Civil War*. Andrew Scott treats Dio's alternative to the Caesarian account in *Bellum Alexandrinum* of conflict arising in 48 in Spain under the Caesarian governor Q. Cassius Longinus. Gianpaolo Urso uses Dio to reconstruct an alternative to both the Ciceronian and Sallustian portrayals of Catiline – and one different from the version that became canonical in the Augustan age. His paper recovers a time in the mid-40s when Catiline could be invoked positively. Kathryn Welch shows Dio unearthing, and re-presenting, a whole series of judgments of Roman statesmen made against Plato's formulation of the four cardinal virtues, including a particularly lively "virtues war" unleashed by Cicero in the 40s. In line with recent research, she shows that Dio's speeches – long dismissed as pure set-piece concoctions of the historian – are integral to his narrative and are in touch with discourses contemporary with their historical settings.[6] In sum, contributors suggest that Dio has distinctive interests in the light of which he shaped his own narrative, and so put his own gloss on episodes he found recounted in his sources, *but did not make it all up!*

This volume will be of use to working historians of the late Republic. It also breaks new ground by exploring in depth Dio's interest in framing larger historical interpretations and the implications of this for his narrative in detail. A major theme of the *Roman History* is the weakness of democracy. Democracy cannot, in Dio's view, cope with the military demands a world-wide empire imposes. And, as he pronounces in a famous disquisition at the beginning of Book 44 (1–2), in ruling so much of the world, in holding sway over so many

---

6   See, e.g., Burden-Strevens 2015; Burden-Strevens 2016; Kemezis 2016.

diverse peoples, in having men of such great wealth, the Romans found moderation nearly impossible. They lapsed into struggles over money and power.

When his narrative reached the year 29, Dio divided Rome's 725-year history up to that point into three phases: monarchic government (*monarchia*), republican government (*demokratia*), and *dynasteiai*; after Actium, "they began once again, strictly speaking, to be ruled by a monarch" (52.1.1). By *dynasteiai*, Adam Kemezis has argued, Dio means "a constant and largely uninterrupted succession of individual dynasts who may not always have full control of the political process, but whose power struggles still prevent its proper operation" (2014, 109).[7] Because of the loss of portions of his *History*, it is not clear when exactly Dio marks the slide from republican government into *dynasteiai*, but it is clear that we are in that mode from Book 36 on. The politicians we encounter, with the notable exception of Cato, try to advance their own power and to thwart competitors. They never act in the interest of ordinary citizens. The People and Senate try to assert authority – but it is increasingly in vain. As Burden-Strevens argues here, dictatorship – essentially a temporary monarchy – is a useful, even essential feature in the traditional republican constitution according to Dio, but it broke down in the wake of Sulla. So devastating is the competition of politics under *dynasteiai* that ultimately the whole system breaks down and no magistrates are left – just *anarchia* (40.46.3).

For Dio, the nature of a political regime dictates the behavior of those living under it. Under *dynasteiai*, acquisition of power is the goal, and essential to this is the acquisition of money – hence the heavy use of bribery repeatedly noted by the historian. Wars of conquest are undertaken primarily for personal gain, not collective necessity – and as Estelle Bertrand shows in her chapter on Dio's treatment of imperialism in the late republican books, *imperatores* become almost stereotypical figures, driven by ambition and lust for wealth. As Bertrand demonstrates, this helps to account for Dio's unique treatment of Q. Caecilius Metellus Creticus (*cos.* 69): while other sources record his cruelty, Dio charges him with a desire to establish *dynasteia* (36.18.1). And it helps to account for an intriguing feature of Dio's presentation of Julius Caesar: once Caesar is more or less established as monarch, his interest in wars of conquest slips away.

A consequence of all this is that while Dio has scathing remarks on the individual dynasts, he is actually less interested in individuals as such and sees

---

7   Kemezis' whole discussion (2014, 104–12) is important. Reinhold 1988, 169 glosses *dynasteiai* as "exceptional concentrations of personal power."

individual ambitions as less important.⁸ The dysfunctional republic creates Caesar, or Catiline, more than they create it. At key moments, Dio downplays individual personalities. The passage of the *lex Gabinia*, for instance, is less about the ambition of Pompey and more about the problems of running an empire – a struggle over what organ of government power should lie in. There are intense personal power struggles, but as Mads Ortving Lindholmer in particular argues in his chapter, such competition becomes almost institutionalized. At the same time, there are struggles between different organs of power, above all the Senate versus the dynasts. As Coudry puts it, the Senate's stand against Caesar in 49 is the powerful "climax of the ten years' fight between the Senate, as foremost element of the republican political system, and the dynasts, who have undermined it." Like Thucydides, Dio sees that under pressure, men are predictable in their behavior: "most men form both friendships and enmities with reference to others' power and their own advantage" (37.39.3). In Dio's presentation, as Scott writes, "human action constantly repeats itself, giving his history both a universal and static quality."⁹

Modern historians of course will not always agree with Dio's version of events or his interpretations. Famously, Gruen (1974) saw the late Republic coping rather well with its challenges until succumbing to a civil war brought on almost accidentally, while more recently Osgood (2018) has made a plea to focus less on breakdown and more on a series of innovations in the late Republic that made *pax Augusta* a possibility. Earlier, scholars such as Syme (1939) and Taylor (1949) played up personal struggles for power – exactly what contributors to this volume assert Dio saw as at best secondary.¹⁰ As long as Roman history is studied, these debates will continue. We assert here that Dio is a worthwhile interlocutor who offers valuable information, and his interpretations merit our attention, especially since they may draw on otherwise lost material.

We should also acknowledge his own vantage point in the early third century CE as a Greek intellectual and Roman senator.¹¹ Dio experienced the horrors of civil war – the steps it drove men to take – and could also look back at long periods of stability under monarchy. This profoundly shaped his political views. It gives his late republican and Augustan narrative a teleological

---

8   This is a theme running through the volume, and note also here the earlier study of Fechner 1986.
9   See further the brief but stimulating remarks of Reinhold 1988, 215–17.
10 But Syme did appreciate Dio's Thucydidean tone (1939, 154).
11 See now especially Lange & Madsen 2016.

quality that is not true to the actual experience of living through those years of Rome's history.[12] Yet in other ways his background and personality inform his *History*. As Carlsen notes in this volume, Dio had an antipathy for gladiatorial combat – the cost of games, and the allure they had for senators, who really should rise above it all – which owes something to the lavish spectacles of the imperial period and the performances of Commodus and Caracalla in particular. Marcus Aurelius, the paradigmatic good emperor for Dio, "disliked bloodshed so much that he even used to watch the gladiators fight, like athletes, without risking their lives"; and though he did give in to the people's demand to exhibit a lion that had been trained to kill men, Marcus himself refused to watch, and he would not manumit the lion's trainer (72[71].29.3–4). In some ways, Dio offers more of his opinions more obtrusively in his contemporary books – when he showcases his own life story – but careful attention to the late republican books can illuminate his perspectives.

2 Dio's Historiographic Choices

The papers in this volume not only use Dio to reinterpret Roman history, they also raise questions and reveal insights about Dio's historical method. Close examination of his account of the late Republic cannot help but shed light on the *Roman History* as a literary product, especially the structuring of its narrative. It is traditional to emphasize that the complexity of political and military developments in the late republican period creates challenges for the historian trying to organize and explain it all, especially one who had access to so many narratives and traditions. But these challenges are also opportunities for artistic effects. In writing his history, Dio relied on the annalistic tradition as a basic framework. But the final product is much more complicated than that, especially in the books examined in this volume.[13] A chronologically linear account organized around the annual election and office-holding of magistrates breaks down in various ways. To give one example noted by Coudry: after recounting the final years of Caesar's conquest of Gaul, Dio gives a general summary of concurrent events in Rome, commenting at one point, "During these same years, many tumults had occurred in the city, especially in the course of the elections" (40.45.1). The looser form the narrative takes here reinforces

---

12 This is a theme of many papers in Morrell, Welch, & Osgood forthcoming.
13 Rich 2016 argues for Dio's flexibility in his use of the annalistic method already in the now fragmentary Books 1–35. An important discussion of the late republican books is given in Bertrand, Coudry, & Fromentin 2016.

the sense of anarchy. Similarly, as Bertrand discusses, Dio at points offers continuous narratives of Pompey's and Caesar's wars of conquest that encompass more than one year – reflecting their extraordinary commands and attaching significance to them in the lead-up to civil war. To recount Caesar's activity in Gaul continuously across the consular years of 58 and 57 *and* across the end of Book 38 into Book 39 (38.31–39.5) is a special effect. Throughout the late republican books, as Christopher Baron shows in his chapter, we find Dio creating "wrinkles in time" – leaping forward (even to his own day) or looking back. This can help create a pregnant "moment": the extended account of Pompey's return from the East in Book 37 is a good example. Another is the famous account of the so-called Augustan settlement in Book 53.

Many earlier scholars considered Dio's management of time to be misleading, poor, or incompetent.[14] But if we recognize that Dio *chose* to organize his narrative in the way he did, interesting questions emerge. To pose just one here: why not simply follow a Polybian model, with a systematic arrangement of theaters of action within each consular year? Dio's decisions, one might respond, are surely meant to signal the breaking down of the Republic and its traditional system of magistrates, and to reflect the great wars of conquest. This becomes all the more true in the civil war books, where for long stretches the magisterial system ceases to function, or at least is a shadow of itself, and military campaigns were fought in multiple theaters across the entire Mediterranean world, sometimes taking on their own individual dynamic completely detached from events in the city of Rome. In short, Dio's bending of time highlights important moments, themes, and developments.

Dio also chooses to devote space to episodes and subjects that, given the vast amount of time he needs to cover, may seem odd. His lengthy speeches are notorious – but as new scholarship is showing (including papers in this volume), these often tie in with larger themes he is developing, such as the role of oratory in the failing Republic or the ethics of leadership.[15] Dio also allots space for his own direct commentaries on the political system – on favorite topics such as bribery, imperialism, and the virtues of monarchy. There are ethnographic digressions (on the Jews, 37.17; the Parthians, 40.14–15; the Dacians, 51.22.6–8), also scientific and antiquarian digressions (the days of the week, 37.18–19; the giraffe, 43.23.1–2; the calendar, 43.26; the topography of Baiae, 48.51), and tales of relatively minor figures. In his contribution, Scott studies the treatment of two such figures, Aeserninus and Caelius, and relates Dio's treatment of them to his great interest in civil war. Similarly, Carlsen ties the

---

14   See the discussion in Baron's paper in this volume.
15   See the works cited above, n. 6.

story of Antony's gladiators at Cyzicus (51.7.2–7) to the historian's Bithynian background. Contributors also sometimes highlight, and try to account for, Dio's omission of certain episodes, such as the Luca conference of 56 (Coudry), or his altering of chronology (Osgood, Urso). In general, more work remains to be done fully elucidating particular moments in the *Roman History* and studying recurring features of the narrative such as scientific digressions or portent lists.

This volume, as noted, treats the late republican books proper (36–40), but it also includes papers on the civil war books and the early career of Augustus (41–52). It is essential that these two portions of the *Roman History* be read together. There are significant continuities between them, and, more generally, the account of Augustus is a foil for the late republican narrative. As Jesper Majbom Madsen argues, Dio portrays Caesar as already holding monarchical power which can be legitimately passed on to his heir; yet, despite following similar paths to power, Caesar is depicted as self-serving, Augustus as a savior. Augustus starts as a dynast, but then breaks the whole system of *dynasteiai*; problems which proved so damaging under *dynasteiai*, such as bribery or rampant imperial expansion, find their solutions under *monarchia*. Augustus thus emerges, as Konstantin Markov shows in his paper, as the paradigmatic beneficial ruler.

One principle that has proven helpful to multiple papers is Christopher Pelling's notion of "biostructuring." The gradual introduction of a more biographical history – sections that follow the actions of one man – begins earlier than Octavian, at least with Julius Caesar, but even Pompey and Cicero can be seen in this light. The spotlight Dio shines on major figures (Catiline and Sextus Pompey could be added to this list, as several contributors show) helps point the way to the principate, eases the (narrative) transition from *dynasteiai* to monarchy, and explains Dio's views not just on why Augustus prevailed, but why the principate brought stability. As with the flexible use of the annalistic model, biostructuring, as Pelling writes, reveals "a wider historical vision here, and not at all an unrespectable one."[16]

The civil war books also affirm, once again, the importance of Dio's own experience with civil war and the Severan context in which he wrote. It bears noticing that while Dio devotes five books (36–40) to the twenty years from 69 to 50, his coverage of the civil war(s) from 49 to 29 then expands to fill twelve books (41–52). This slowing of the pace reflects, we believe, not only the crucial nature of these years for the formation of the empire Dio lived in, but also his hard-earned view that civil war places immense pressure on the institutions

---

16 Pelling 2006, 257–62 (quotation at 262); see also Coudry 2016.

and individuals of the governing class. Here, too, Dio had models to draw on from the historiographical tradition, most notably Thucydides' vivid portrayal of the breakdown of a society afflicted by *stasis*. On a literary level, echoes of Thucydides can add a sense of dread to Dio's narrative. And as Carsten Hjort Lange argues in his contribution, the Athenian historian also furnished Dio not just with language but with a conceptual framework for understanding human behavior during civil war. This influence from a classic Greek historiographical model, on material Dio had gathered from his wide reading in Greek and Latin authors and placed into a framework borrowed from the Roman tradition of historical writing, neatly epitomizes his accomplishment.

3 A Survey of This Volume

We have already signaled at least once each of the subsequent chapters in this volume. For the reader's convenience, we now summarize all of the papers in order. The volume is divided into three parts. Part 1 ("Narratives Themes and Texture") looks at some of Dio's main preoccupations across the late republican books (especially Books 36–40) as well as his structuring of the narrative. Part 2 ("Characters, Institutions, and Episodes") presents more focused case-studies of Dio's treatment of several political episodes as well as two institutions, the office of dictator and gladiatorial combat. Finally, Part 3 ("Civil War and the Victory of Augustus") highlights the importance of Dio's civil war narrative (Books 41–52), discussed above.

A pair of opening chapters reveal several of Dio's chief interests and their implications for his narrative. In "Imperialism and the Crisis of the Roman Republic," Estelle Bertrand shows how much attention Dio pays to Roman imperialism in Books 36–40. Wars of conquest, in Dio's view, were fought to advance individual politicians' power and increased rivalry and competition, making them fully a part of the politics of *dynasteiai*. Imperialism and the collapse of the Republic are closely intertwined. Dio's arrangement of his material reinforces the point: far from adhering to a simple annalistic framework, he uses such devices as multiple-year sections to suggest the breakdown of the republican system and foreshadow civil war. As dynast, Julius Caesar exemplifies Dio's harsh view of conquest, but then, as proto-monarch, he starts to take steps to rein in competition and expansion.

Marianne Coudry, in her chapter "Electoral Bribery and the Challenge to the Authority of the Senate," also focuses on Books 36–40 and once again shows how Dio's interest led him to make a careful selection of sources and ultimately to create a modified annalistic narrative. The historian is preoccupied with electoral disorder and bribery as symptoms of the failing *demokratia*, and he incorporates detailed accounts of bribery laws as well as more general reflection on the wrecking of republican magistracies. Dio also attaches particular importance to the Senate's increasing loss of control of both external and internal affairs – leading him to offer precise details of the Senate's actions and function. In Coudry's analysis, the breakdown of the Republic was for Dio a story less of power struggle (Caesarians vs. Pompeians, for example) and more of the destruction of institutions.

In "Wrinkles in Time: Chronological Ruptures in Cassius Dio's Narrative of the Late Republic," Christopher Baron deepens study of Dio's use of annalistic structure. While earlier scholarship harshly judged Dio's handling of chronology, Baron adds to recent reassessments, arguing that Dio's chronological scheme enhances larger themes – building up major moments by joining a series of events scattered across time, for instance, or slowing down the narrative in anticipation of a critical turning point, such as the assassination of Julius Caesar. Baron includes especially detailed analysis of Books 37, 43, and 48, revealing the elaborate narrative structure Dio achieves. An important conclusion is that Dio shows awareness of the chronological ruptures he creates – and this reinforces a major theme of the volume overall, that Dio put care into choosing to organize the narrative the way he did.

Complementing the earlier chapter of Coudry, Mads Ortving Lindholmer in "Dio the Deviant: Comparing Dio's Late Republic and the Parallel Sources" emphasizes that nearly institutionalized competition, rather than the individual faults of particular politicians, is the central factor in Dio's view of the breakdown of republican government. Lindholmer selects three episodes – Lucullus' loss of his command in the Third Mithridatic War, the passage of the *lex Gabinia*, and the Catilinarian conspiracy – and for each carefully compares Dio's treatment with that of other authors (the "parallel sources" of his title). This is a fruitful method that many other contributors to the volume invoke. Lindholmer shows that while other narratives are more character-driven, Dio's uses characters to illustrate the pervasive problem of competition. The story of the late Republic, for Dio, essentially lacks heroes – and, in a sense, villains.

That said, the ethics of leadership was a real concern of Dio, as Kathryn Welch shows in her chapter "Cassius Dio and the Virtuous Roman." Welch demonstrates how frequently Dio judges politicians against the rubric of the four cardinal virtues – wisdom, justice, courage, and temperance. Examples included Scipio Africanus, Hannibal, and Scipio Aemilianus. Late republican politicians (in particular Cicero, Julius Caesar, Marcus Agrippa, and Antony) fail in significant ways, creating a foil for Augustus. An achievement of Welch's paper is to show that while Dio's political views are very much in evidence in what he writes, his judgments are closely informed by views contemporaneous with the period he writes about. Welch suggests how Dio shapes his material, and how Dio can be used to help recover lost speeches and histories from a period of time when Augustus' ultimate victory and long years in power were not yet known and politicians argued over different paths forward for the Republic.

The next two chapters, the first in Part 2, offer case-studies of two institutions treated by Dio. In "The Republican Dictatorship: an Imperial Perspective," Christopher Burden-Strevens draws attention to Dio's interest in the dictatorship – part of his more general interest in the republican constitution. Burden-Strevens shows that for Dio, the dictatorship was an essential magistracy, and its failure is intertwined with the collapse of the Republic. A notable point in this chapter is Dio's distinctive treatment of Pompey's lack of interest in holding the dictatorship in 53. Burden-Strevens relates this to Dio's later treatment of Augustus – showing, once again, how the late republican and Augustan narratives reinforce one another. At the same time, Burden-Strevens also suggests that Dio's account of Pompey complements a contemporary debate on the dictatorship that can be recovered from Cicero as well as from coinage. Once again we see the distinctive value of the *Roman History* as a historical source.

Jesper Carlsen in "Spectacle Entertainments in the Late Republican Books of Cassius Dio's *Roman History*" looks at gladiatorial combats along with several other forms of public entertainment. Carlsen usefully highlights some of the pitfalls in trying to use Dio to write history. Scholarship on the Roman games treats Dio as a quarry for dozens of details without paying attention to their context in the *History*. While Dio is right to emphasize the importance of spectacles in the late Republic, his treatment also illustrates some of his own distinctive concerns as a third-century CE Roman senator who came from the Greek East, including the large sums spent on games in provincial cities – a problem flagged in the speech of Maecenas which Dio includes in Book 52.

A second pair of chapters in Part 2 turns to Dio's treatment of two episodes in political history and builds the case that Dio's narrative is well-informed and deserving of more attention by historians. Gianpaolo Urso, in "Cassius Dio's Catiline: 'A Name Greater than his Deeds Deserved,'" examines how Dio's account of the Catilinarian conspiracy diverges in many respects from the versions more familiar to us in Cicero and Sallust. The source Dio drew upon, contemporary with the late Republic and civil war period, emphasized the controversies that arose from Cicero's consulship already in 63. Rather than interpret Dio's choice not to follow Sallust as a poor decision, Urso calls attention to the "heterodox" details Dio preserves – including the notion of a "conspiracy of Lentulus" and accusations made by Antony in 44–43 that it was Cicero who had made Catiline hostile to the Republic. These are subtle hints that Dio made use of an array of sources, which has often been missed or downplayed by scholars assuming that his account is of less worth than others which survive.

Similar to Urso, Josiah Osgood in "Dio and the Voice of the Sibyl" demonstrates Dio's value to historians of the late Republic by investigating the sordid tale of Rome's attempts to restore King Ptolemy XII (Auletes) to Egypt in the 50s. Specifically, Osgood focuses on the role of the Sibylline oracle of 56 in Dio's account. In contrast to his other mentions of such oracles, Dio raises little doubt about this one. Overall, his narrative shows a good knowledge of events and is more balanced than modern accounts that have fixated on the authenticity of the oracle (though such balance is not evident in Dio's later discussion of Gabinius' actions and his trials in Rome). In Osgood's view, Dio's presentation adds a sense of dread to his narrative of Roman politics in the period while also underscoring some of his major themes, including the willingness of too-powerful politicians to neglect the wishes of Senate and People to the detriment of ordinary citizens.

Part 3 opens with Andrew Scott, "Responding to Civil War: M. Claudius Marcellus Aeserninus and M. Caelius Rufus in Cassius Dio, Book 42." Scott examines Dio's narrative of two episodes from 48 – an uprising in Spain, and Caelius' attempts at revolt in Italy – within the overall context of the civil war between Caesar and Pompey. Scott suggests that Dio specifically focuses on the figures of Marcellus and Caelius in order to highlight two possible responses to civil war (one ultimately successful, one not). Comparison with surviving sources demonstrates how Dio may have manipulated his source material in order to do so. Scott goes on to propose that Dio's narrative decisions here were informed by the experiences of his own time, as can be seen in a number of comparable passages from the contemporary portion of his history. He finds in Dio a fascination with survivors of such conflicts, as well as a conviction in the consistency of human nature.

Carsten Hjort Lange, "Cassius Dio on Sextus Pompeius and Late Republican Civil War," examines the phenomenon of defection and side-switching in Dio's civil war narratives. Lange focuses especially on Octavian ("young Caesar") and Sextus Pompey in 44–43 and in the circumstances surrounding the Treaty of Misenum in 39. For Dio, Sextus was one of the dynasts of the period: his goal was to be an equal partner in their "little cabal" and recover his father's patrimony. The application of modern political theory, including the concept of "balance of power," can help us see how alliances in a turbulent period formed and fragmented. Lange argues that in fact Dio takes a "realist" view of these affairs: the shifting alliances within the group are part of the game, and not (always) criticized by the historian. This investigation shows the value of thinking about Dio as a (historical) theorist of factions, *stasis*, and civil war, one who followed Thucydides' bleak view of human nature.

The final two papers treat Dio's portrayal of the two victors of the civil wars. In "Like Father Like Son: the Differences in How Dio Tells the Story of Julius Caesar and His More Successful Son," Jesper Majbom Madsen focuses on Dio's different approaches to and views of the reign and character of Julius Caesar and of Augustus: what made him depict Augustus as the selfless savior, while Caesar appears as the overambitious and power-hungry individual? For Dio, Caesar's dictatorship represented a much-needed turning point in the process towards monarchical rule – a first qualified attempt to end the political chaos of the late Republic. But Caesar was still a dynast, aiming above all at power for himself rather than acting in the best interests of the state. Although Dio had reservations concerning Octavian's role during the civil wars, overall he portrays both his reign and his ambitions much more positively. But, Madsen argues, Dio's contrasting accounts do more than celebrate Augustus for providing a more stable form of government: they also offer more general thoughts about what constituted the ideal form of constitution and how monarchical rule should be organized.

Finally, Konstantin Markov, "Towards the Conceptualization of Cassius Dio's Narration of the Early Career of Octavian," emphasizes the importance of Dio's view of human nature in his depiction of Caesar's heir. Scholars often dwell on the inconsistency of Dio's presentation: was the founder of the principate a ruthless and bloodthirsty opportunist, or the benevolent savior of Rome and sage architect of stable monarchy? Markov argues that Dio's views appear more complex but at the same time more consistent than is usually suggested. Octavian's behavior is what Dio would expect from a political leader in a time of civil war. The historian cannot ignore what his path to power was, but violent acts are inevitable in civil wars. More important are Dio's criteria for evaluation, in particular the strengthening of the state: it is the results that matter, not the means by which they are achieved. In the Augustan books Dio continues to emphasize the pragmatism of the founder of the principate and simultaneously pays attention to certain flaws of his rule and his person. In doing so, Dio enhances his own profile as a pragmatic historian writing in the tradition of Thucydides.

Bibliography

Bertrand E., Coudry, M., & Fromentin, V. (2016) "Temporalité historique et formes du récit. Les modalités de l'écriture dans les livres tardo-républicains", in V. Fromentin *et al.* (eds.), *Cassius Dion: nouvelles lectures* (Bordeaux): 303–16.

Burden-Strevens, C. (2015) *Cassius Dio's Speeches and the Collapse of the Roman Republic*, Dissertation: Glasgow.

Burden-Strevens, C. (2016) "Fictitious Speeches, Envy, and the Habituation to Authority: Writing the Collapse of the Roman Republic", in C. H. Lange & J. M. Madsen (eds.), *Cassius Dio: Greek Intellectual and Roman Politician* (Leiden & Boston): 193–216.

Burden-Strevens, C. & Lindholmer, M. (eds.) (2018) *Cassius Dio's Forgotten History of Early Rome: The 'Roman History' Books 1–21*, Leiden & Boston.

Coudry, M. (2016) "Figures et récit dans les livres républicains (livres 36 à 44)", in V. Fromentin *et al.* (eds.), *Cassius Dion: nouvelles lectures* (Bordeaux): 287–301.

Fechner, D. (1986) *Untersuchungen zu Cassius Dios Sicht der römischen Republik*, Hildesheim.

Fromentin, V. & Bertrand, E. (2008) *Dion Cassius: Histoire romaine, Livres 45 & 46*, Paris.

Fromentin, V. & Bertrand, E. (2014) *Dion Cassius: Histoire romaine, Livre 47*, Paris.

Fromentin, V. *et al.* (eds.) (2016) *Cassius Dion: nouvelles lectures*, Bordeaux.

Gowing, A. M. (1992) *The Triumviral Narratives of Appian and Cassius Dio*, Ann Arbor.

Gruen, E. S. (1974) *The Last Generation of the Roman Republic*, Berkeley.

Kemezis, A. (2014) *Greek Narratives of the Roman Empire under the Severans: Cassius Dio, Philostratus and Herodian*, Cambridge.

Kemezis, A. (2016) "Dio, Caesar and the Vesontio Mutineers (38.34–47): A Rhetoric of Lies", in C. H. Lange & J. M. Madsen (eds.), *Cassius Dio: Greek Intellectual and Roman Politician* (Leiden & Boston): 238–57.

Lachenaud, G. & Coudry, M. (2011) *Dion Cassius: Histoire romaine, Livres 38, 39 & 40*, Paris.

Lachenaud, G. & Coudry, M. (2014) *Dion Cassius: Histoire romaine, Livres 36 & 37*, Paris.

Lange, C. H. & Madsen, J. M. (eds.) (2016) *Cassius Dio: Greek Intellectual and Roman Politician*, Leiden & Boston.

Lintott, A. W. (1997) "Cassius Dio and the History of the Late Roman Republic", in *Aufstieg und Niedergang der römischen Welt* 2.34.3, 2497–523.

Manuwald, B. (1979) *Cassius Dio und Augustus: philologische Untersuchungen zu den Büchern 45–56 des dionischen Geschichtswerkes*, Wiesbaden.

Millar, F. (1964) *A Study of Cassius Dio*, Oxford.

Millar, F. (1998) *The Crowd in Rome in the Late Republic*, Ann Arbor.

Morrell, K., Osgood, J., & Welch, K. (eds.) (forthcoming) *The Alternative Augustan Age*, Oxford.

Osgood, J. (2018) *Rome and the Making of a World State, 150 BCE–20 CE*, Cambridge.
Pelling, C. (2006) "Breaking the Bounds: Writing about Julius Caesar", in B. McGing & J. Mossman (eds.), *The Limits of Ancient Biography* (Swansea): 255–80.
Reinhold, M. (1988) *From Republic to Principate: An Historical Commentary on Cassius Dio's Roman History Books 49–52 (36–29 B.C.)*, Atlanta.
Reinhold, M. & Swan, P. M. (1990) "Cassius Dio's Assessment of Augustus", in K. A. Raaflaub & M. Toher (eds.), *Between Republic and Empire: Interpretations of Augustus and His Principate* (Berkeley): 155–73.
Rich, J. (1989) "Dio on Augustus", in A. Cameron (ed.), *History as Text: The Writing of Ancient History* (London): 87–110.
Rich, J. W. (1990) *Cassius Dio: The Augustan Settlement (Roman History 53.1–55.9)*, Warminster.
Rich, J. (2016) "Annalistic Organization and Book Division in Dio's Books 1–35", in V. Fromentin *et al.* (eds.), *Cassius Dion: nouvelles lectures* (Bordeaux): 271–86.
Scott-Kilvert, I. (1987) *Cassius Dio, The Roman History: The Reign of Augustus*, London.
Simons, B. (2009). *Cassius Dio und die Römische Republik. Untersuchungen zum Bild des römischen Gemeinwesens in den Büchern 3–35 der Romaika*, Berlin.
Swan, P. M. (2004) *The Augustan Succession: An Historical Commentary on Cassius Dio's Roman History Books 55–56 (9 BC–AD 14)*, Oxford.
Syme, R. (1939) *The Roman Revolution*, Oxford.
Taylor, L. R. (1949) *Party Politics in the Age of Caesar*, Berkeley.
Urso, G. (2013) *Cassio Dione e i sovversivi. La crisi della repubblica nei frammenti della "Storia romana" (XXI–XXX)*, Milan.

PART 1

Narrative Themes and Texture

CHAPTER 2

Imperialism and the Crisis of the Roman Republic: Dio's View on Late Republican Conquests (Books 36–40)

Estelle Bertrand

Cassius Dio's *Roman History* has recently been the object of many new studies, which have demonstrated, building on Fergus Millar's illuminating thesis, how much the historiographical purpose of the work is connected to Roman political changes.[1] Indeed, in his narrative, Dio underlines each change of political regime with a discussion of the advantages and drawbacks of the new form of government. This is obviously the case with the famous Agrippa-Maecenas debate in Book 52, which concludes the narrative of the Roman Republic and opens the imperial books, and it also seems to be the case at the beginning of Book 3, which opened the republican cycle and included a speech, probably by Brutus, on the risks of political "*metabolai*."[2] This specific subordination of the whole narrative structure to the political shifts shows that, as is well known, political history takes precedence in Dio's project. This particular interest is also evidenced by the increase in the narrative concerning the late Roman Republic, as all scholars have come to recognize.[3] This increase is not an erroneous impression created by the fact that, in contrast with the rest of the work, substantial portions survive of the fourth, and all of the fifth, decades – the decades devoted to the last years of the Republic from the Social War up to the battle of Actium. In fact, the distribution of years per book in these decades really confirms the significant expansion of the narrative about this period of important political changes.[4]

---

1 This is the main trend of research on Dio's *Roman History*, as shown in the two recent volumes published by the French ANR team, Fromentin *et al.* 2016, and by its Danish counterpart, Lange & Madsen 2016, each with bibliographical review. Translations in this chapter are from the Loeb Classical Library, sometimes slightly modified.
2 Cass. Dio fr. 12.3a; on this speech, and its historiographical tradition, see Fromentin 2016, 184–5.
3 See recently Zecchini 2016, 118.
4 Bertrand 2015, 170; Rich 2016, 277.

Nevertheless, the importance Dio assigned to political history does not imply that he neglected military history, and it cannot be said that the historian had no interest in military events at all. The first reason why military events have to be included pertains to the annalistic global framework of the republican narrative, which leads Dio to correlate events *domi* with those *militiae*. But the annalistic model, which the author applies at his own discretion, is not the only cause of the inclusion of external events. Recent studies, especially by the French editors of Books 36 to 40, have shown that Roman imperialism is also a major topic in the *Roman History*, particularly in the late republican books.[5] This is not only because of the influence of Polybius and Livy,[6] Dio's probable historiographical models whose projects hinge on an overriding reflection about the reasons and consequences of Roman hegemony; it is also because, as we learn from at least two significant personal remarks in Books 44 and 47, Dio himself links the collapse of the Roman Republic to the growth of the Roman empire, which had reached an excessive size and could no longer be administered within the framework of the republican constitution.[7] In other words, according to Dio, the search for military glory had not only led to illegitimate wars which were of no benefit for the Romans, it also was a factor in the competition between republican dynasts, and finally a factor in internal strife and civil war.

Consequently, the great conquests, and conquerors, of the late Roman Republic are globally viewed in a negative light, and they are not so much an element of Roman history as evidence of political degradation.[8] In this global framework, the conquests of the republican dynasts – especially those

---

5   Lachenaud & Coudry 2014, l–lix; Bertrand 2016a.
6   This difficult question of Dio's alleged models has been explored in several chapters of Fromentin *et al.* 2016, among which see particularly Zecchini 2016 and De Franchis 2016.
7   Cass. Dio 44.2.4: πόλιν τε αὐτήν τε τηλικαύτην οὖσαν καὶ τοῦ τε καλλίστου τοῦ τε πλείστου τῆς ἐμφανοῦς οἰκουμένης ἄρχουσαν, καὶ πολλὰ μὲν ἀνθρώπων ἤθη καὶ διάφορα κεκτημένην πολλοὺς δὲ καὶ μεγάλους πλούτους ἔχουσαν, ταῖς τε πράξεσι καὶ ταῖς τύχαις παντοδαπαῖς καὶ ἰδίᾳ καὶ δημοσίᾳ χρωμένην, ἀδύνατον μὲν ἐν δημοκρατίᾳ σωφρονῆσαι, ἀδυνατώτερον δὲ μὴ σωφρονοῦσαν ὁμονοῆσαι. ("But for a city, not only so large in itself, but also ruling the finest and the greatest part of the known world, holding sway over men of many and diverse natures, possessing many men of great wealth, occupied with every imaginable pursuit, enjoying every imaginable fortune, both individually and collectively – for such a city, I say, to practice moderation under a democracy is impossible, and still more is it impossible for the people, unless moderation prevails, to be harmonious."). Cass. Dio 47.39.4–5: ὁμοφρονῆσαι μὲν γὰρ ἐν τῷ καθεστῶτι τρόπῳ τῆς πολιτείας οὐκέθ᾽ οἷοί τε ἦσαν – οὐ γὰρ ἔστιν ὅπως δημοκρατία ἄκρατος, ἐς τοσοῦτον ἀρχῆς ὄγκον προχωρήσασα, σωφρονῆσαι δύναται. ("For they were no longer capable of maintaining harmony in the established form of government. It is, of course, impossible for an unadulterated democracy that has grown to so proud an empire to exercise moderation.").
8   Lachenaud & Coudry 2014, lix.

of Pompey and Caesar, which occupy the main part of the fourth decade of Dio's *Roman History*, leading up to the civil war – as well as their narrative construction offer the opportunity, not yet completely explored, to understand Dio's criticism of the growing Roman hegemony during the republican era, and the complexity of the factors that led to the changes in the Roman constitution.

In this paper we shall try to explore the place that the late republican conquests – especially Caesar's – occupy in the narrative in order to show the complexity of Dio's enquiry into their role in the process of decline of the Roman Republic.

1 The Impact of External Events on the Late Republican Narrative

First, it is important to note that external events occupy a very significant place in the fourth decade, and this is particularly relevant to Books 36 to 40, which are preserved nearly in whole and cover the years 69 to 50 BC. Within the global annalistic framework, which is applied with "notable flexibility" in the so-called "republican" books, as recently demonstrated by Rich,[9] Dio's treatment of the external wars proceeds with narrative sections which cover several years (see Table 2.1). The wars conducted by Lucullus in the East in 69–67, Metellus' war against the Cretans in the same years, Pompey's campaign against piracy in 67, then against the king of Pontus, Mithridates, in 66–63, as well as the war conducted by Crassus against the Parthians in 54–53, all form ample narrative units which are more or less linked to sections devoted to internal affairs. Furthermore, in Books 38 to 40, events concerning Caesar's war in Gaul form the main element structuring the narrative, which from then on forgoes the year-by-year treatment.

This is not the first time Dio breaks with the annalistic narrative model: he had already applied this approach to the years 179 to 150 BC, with a view, it would seem, to condensing the narrative.[10] But in the fourth decade, his aim is quite different: in Books 36 to 40, external affairs are on the contrary dilated in sections which cover several years, and occupy more than half of the five books (157 chapters out of 291). In addition, we have to take into account the important developments on the debates and conflicts about external commands (21 chapters, among which 14 on the *lex Gabinia*),[11] and the discussions

---

9   Rich 2016, 286; see also Bertrand, Coudry, & Fromentin, 2016.
10 Rich 2016, 277.
11 See the second section of the Table.

TABLE 2.1 External affairs in Dio, Books 36–40, vs. Livy, *Per.* 98–108

Events away from Rome	Dio, Books 36–40 Book/chapters	Chapters per book	Livy, *Per.* 98–108 Books/sentences	Sentences per book	Dio // Livy
Lucullus' campaigns in Armenia and Mesopotamia (69–67 BC)	36.1–17	17	98.6; 9	2 / 9	31.5% // 22%
Metellus in Crete (69–67 BC)	36.17a–19	3	98.7 99.1, 4–6 100.3	98: 1 / 9 99: 4 / 6 100: 1 / 6	5.5 // 19.5%
Pompey's war against piracy (67 BC)	36.20–23, 37	4	99.3	1 / 6	7.5 // 16.5%
Pompey against Mithridates (66 BC)	36.45–54	10	100.1, 4–6	4 / 6	16% // 66%
	Book 36 => 34/54 63%		Books 98–100 => 13/21 61%		63% // 61%
Pompey's campaigns in East (65–63 BC)	37.1–7, 11–20	17	101.1–2, 4–6 102.1–4	101: 5 / 6 102: 4 / 7	29% // 70%
Pomptinus' operations against Allobroges (62–61 BC)	37.47–49.1	2	103.3	1 / 11	3.5 // 9%
Caesar in Lusitania (61–60 BC)	37.52–53	2	103.5	1 / 11	3.5% // 9%
	Book 37 => 21/58 36%		Books 101–3 => 11/24 58%		36% // 58%
Caesar's war in Gaul (58 BC)	38.31–50	20	103.10–11	2 / 11	40% // 16.5%
War in Gaul (57; 56–55 BC)	39.1–5, 40–54	39	104.1/2; 5; 8/9 105.5	5 / 9 105: 1 / 5	35% // 55.5%
War in Gaul (54–51 BC)	40.1–11, 31–43	24	106.4 107.6 108.4	106: 3 / 5 107: 2 / 6 108: 2 / 5	66% // 38.25%
Crassus' war against Parthians (54–53 BC)	40.12–30	19	106.5	1 / 5	28.5% // 20%
	Books 36–40 => 157 / 291 54%		Books 98–108 = 39 / 75 52%		54% // 52%

TABLE 2.1 External affairs in Dio, Books 36–40, vs. Livy, *Per.* 98–108 *(cont.)*

At Rome, laws about external commands	Book/ chapters	Chapters per book	Book/ sentences	Sentences per book		
lex Gabinia (67 BC)	36.23–36	14	99.3	1		
lex Manilia (66 BC)	36.42	1	100.1	1		
lex Vatinia (59 BC)	38.3	1				
Pompey's *cura annonae* (57 BC)	39.9	1	104.4	1		
lex Trebonia (55 BC)	39.33	1	105.3	1		
lex Pompeia (52 BC)	40.30; 46; 56	3				
	Books 36–40 => 21 / 291		Books 98–108 => 4 / 75		7 % // 5.5 %	

At Rome, honors and triumphs	Book/ chapters	Chapters per book	Book/ sentences	Sentences per book	
Pompey's honors (63)	37.21–23	3	103.12	1	
Pomptinus' triumph (54)	39.65	1			
	Books 36–40 => 4 / 291		Books 98–108 => 2 / 75		1.5 % // 2.5 %

External affairs away from Rome and at Rome	Books 36–40 => 182 / 291	Books 98–108 => 45 / 75	62.5 % // 60 %

of triumphal honors or awards (four chapters).[12] Put together, all these chapters relative to foreign policy, outside of Rome (157) as well as at Rome (25), add up to 62.5% of the material in Books 36 to 40. Taken along with the sections devoted to external military operations, these discussions of laws, triumphal honors, and the like help to focus attention on the growing links between external wars and political life: provincial administration, extraordinary commands owing to external risks, and competition for victory honors among *imperatores* appear therefore as an essential component of Dio's late republican history.

---

12 See the third section of the Table.

This is in part consistent with the tradition of Roman history writing, as the comparison with Livy seems to show,[13] but this plain linkage between internal and external matters and the importance granted to external policy evidences, nonetheless, the particular importance given these external affairs in Dio's history of the late Republic.

2 Political Competition and Conquests in the Late Republican History

Yet, in no way is this particular importance given to external conquests intended as a glorification of Roman hegemony or its actors.[14] On the contrary, according to Dio, the late republican wars are mostly undertaken for personal gain, no longer out of collective necessity. It should also be noted that in these books, Dio draws stereotyped portrayals of Roman *imperatores*: during their term of command, they all are driven by ambition, lust for glory and success. This stereotypical presentation is particularly glaring in the case of Metellus, victor over Crete, whom Dio accuses of wanting to establish *dynasteia* and of acting ruthlessly against the enemy while the other sources on this general only record his cruelty,[15] but the same tendency prevails for Lucullus, Pompey, Crassus, and indeed Caesar.[16]

---

13 Even if Livy's books on this period are preserved only in the form of brief summaries in the *Periochae*, we have nevertheless tried to compare, as Rich did for the whole republican period (Rich 2016, 277–8), the importance given in each work to external affairs: see the Table. Of course the accounts cannot be perfectly exact, because the sentences of the *Periochae* may not be entirely representative, but they can still give a rough idea and show that Dio's narrative is interested in external affairs as much as Livy's.

14 This is the very opposite of Appian, where the conquests are seen as an expression of Roman virtues: Price 2015, esp. 59; also Osgood 2015.

15 Cass. Dio 36.18.1: δυναστείας τε ἐρῶν καὶ τοῖς Κρησὶ τοῖς ὁμολογήσασιν αὐτῷ προσέβαλε, καὶ οὔτε τὰς σπονδὰς προτεινομένων σφῶν ἐφρόντιζε, κακῶσαί τε αὐτοὺς πρὶν τὸν Πομπήιον ἐπελθεῖν ἠπείγετο. ("In his eagerness for power he attacked even the Cretans who had come to terms with the other [Pompey], and heedless of their claim that there was a truce, hastened to do them injury before Pompey should come up.") Q. Caecilius Metellus, *cos.* 69, scored some important successes against the pirates in 68 (Liv. *Per.* 98–9): all the sources mention his cruelty, but not his ambition (Flor. 1.42.5; Val. Max. 7.6. ext. 1; Oros. 6.4.2; also Plut. *Pomp.* 29.2). An opposite tradition remembers the victories and triumph of the general (Cic. *Planc.* 27; Vell. Pat. 2.48.6), which are also attested by the honorary inscription from Paleokastro, one of the Cretan cities: Van Ooteghem 1967, 235.

16 Crassus: 40.12.1; Caesar: 37.52.1, 38.35.2; Bertrand 2016a, 694–5.

This reduction of the main late republican commanders to stereotyped warmongers in the fourth decade echoes the accusations spread by the enemies of Rome at the beginning of Book 36: when Lucullus was preparing the war against Mithridates, his enemies developed an active propaganda against him in order to persuade the Parthians to give them help and accused the Romans of *pleonexia*.[17] Clearly connected with Dio's portrayals of the Roman *imperatores*, this accusation is more than a mere commonplace cited in speeches of Rome's enemies in Roman historiography;[18] it is consistent with Dio's own analysis.

Indeed this topic of *pleonexia*, which Dio (36.1.2) ascribes to human nature and the accruing of possessions,[19] has clearly become the main component of late republican external policy. *Pleonexia* causes illegitimate wars or campaigns, rivalry between *imperatores*, and harm to Roman citizens, not to mention the damage to the defeated enemies. Lucullus is said to have been one of the best generals (στρατηγικότατος: 36.16.1), the first to cross the Taurus, but his successes were not fruitful and he was accused by the Romans of continuing the war for personal ends (36.2.1). In Book 37, Lucullus is finally described by Pompey as an example of military failure due to excessive ambition, an accusation which is nowhere else made in Greek or Roman historiography (37.7.2).

17 Cass Dio 36.1.2: καὶ τοὺς Ῥωμαίους διέβαλλον λέγοντες ὅτι, ἂν μονωθέντων σφῶν κρατήσωσι, καὶ ἐπ' ἐκεῖνον εὐθὺς ἐπιστρατεύσουσι· φύσει τε γὰρ πᾶν τὸ νικῶν ἄπληστον τῆς εὐπραγίας εἶναι καὶ μηδένα ὅρον τῆς πλεονεξίας ποιεῖσθαι, καὶ τούτους, ἅτε καὶ ἐν κράτει πολλῶν δὴ γεγονότας, οὐκ ἐθελήσειν αὐτοῦ ἀποσχέσθαι. ("And they also went to maligning the Romans, declaring that the latter, in case they conquered their present antagonists while these were left to fight single-handed, would immediately make a campaign against him. For every victorious force was inherently insatiate of success and set no bound to his greed [*pleonexia*]; and the Romans, who had won mastery over many, would not choose to leave him [the Parthian king] alone.")

18 The most famous quotation is of Mithridates' letter to Arsaces in Sallust's *Histories* (4.69.16–23 M): *Namque Romanis cum nationibus populis regibus cunctis una et ea vetus causa bellandi est: cupido profunda imperi et divitiarum* ("in fact, the Romans have one inveterate motive for making war on all peoples, nations, and kings: namely, a deep-seated desire for domination and for riches"). Cassius Dio alludes to this, mentioning an embassy to the Parthian king Arsaces (36.1.1). This is probably a literary reconstruction of the main themes of Mithridatic propaganda, also attested in Appian (*Mithr.* 98). Roman *pleonexia* also figures in the speech of Calgacus in Tac. *Agr.* 32; more examples and discussion in Madsen 2013, 312.

19 We also find the idea earlier in Dio's *Roman History*: at the beginning of the Second Punic War, the partisans of war against Carthage use this argument, apparently against the Carthaginians: fr. 55.1: ὅτι πέφυκε πᾶν τὸ ἀνθρώπειον δεσπόζειν τε ἐπιθυμεῖν τῶν ὑπεικόντων καὶ τῇ παρὰ τῆς τύχης ῥοπῇ κατὰ τῶν ἐθελοδουλούντων χρῆσθαι. ("All mankind is so constituted as to desire to lord it over such as yield, and to employ the turn of Fortune's scale against those who are willing to be enslaved.")

Some exceptions escape this wholesale indictment: C. Pomptinus, conqueror of the Allobroges in 62–61, is a rare figure exempted from any *cupido dominandi*: his campaigns were caused by an attack of the Gallic tribe in his province of Gallia Transalpina.[20] The narrative about Pomptinus is the most detailed we have: whereas, in the Livy summary, we find a short sentence about Pomptinus' successes against the Allobroges,[21] the account of these events occupies more than two chapters of Dio's Book 37 (47–49.1), otherwise mostly devoted to Pompey's campaigns in the East, and it includes many details: the names of his legates, the name of the leader of the rebellion (Catugnatus), topographical details otherwise not mentioned, and the name of the battle site. This segment offers an example of "traditional" provincial management, free from personal ambition, and Pomptinus' portrayal contrasts with that of the main dynasts, especially Caesar, who on the contrary wanted to conquer Gaul.[22] Through these contrasted portrayals, the historian highlights the overall degradation of the Republic's management of external affairs as well as the significant changes in mid-first century Roman imperialism.[23]

If Dio is critical of the individual motives which presided over late republican foreign policy, he is also critical of the consequences of Rome's late republican conquests.[24] Indeed Dio never offers a positive judgment of the results of the enlargement of the Roman empire. From the end of the Punic Wars onwards, Dio underlines the degradation of public life and the loss of ancestral traditions due to Rome's victories. The irruption of luxury in Rome after the victory over Antiochos in 189 BC led to moral degradation and decadence, but also to internal rivalry and jealousy towards some of the generals, namely the Scipios (fr. 64; fr. 63 = Zon. 9.20). This is much more the case in the sixties and fifties of the last century BC, when jealousy and rivalry between *imperatores*

---

20 Cass Dio 37.47.1: τῶν δὲ Ἀλλοβρίγων τὴν Γαλατίαν τὴν περὶ Νάρβωνα πορθούντων Γάιος Πομπτῖνος ὁ ἄρχων αὐτῆς τοὺς μὲν ὑποστρατήγους ἐπὶ τοὺς πολεμίους ἔπεμψεν. ("The Allobroges were devastating Gallia Narbonensis, and Gaius Pomptinus, the governor, sent his lieutenants against the enemy.")

21 Liv. Per. 103.3: *C. Pontinus praetor Allobrogas qui rebellaverant ad Solonem domuit*. ("Gaius Pomptinus the praetor subdued the rebellious Allobroges near Solo.")

22 The difference between the two generals was also underlined by Cicero, but in order to amplify Caesar's role: Cic. *Prov. Cons.* 32. We may add that in 39.65, Dio underlines at the very end of the book (as a conclusion?) the difficulties Pomptinus experienced in getting the triumph, as if evidence of the dynasts' monopolization of the triumphal honors at that time.

23 About this change, see Serrati 2013, esp. 163–6.

24 On this issue, see more arguments in Bertrand 2016a.

caused the increase of external commands, flouting ancestral tradition.[25] The topic of moral decadence, which is more or less a leitmotif of Latin historiography, since at least Sallust and Livy and probably even earlier,[26] is nevertheless noteworthy in the *Roman History*, because it is linked to a political periodization which is Dio's own, that is to say to the turning of the Republic into *dynasteiai*, an era (hard to date precisely) of personal powers which Dio places between the middle Republic and Augustan principate.[27]

In regard to this globally negative conception of late republican Roman conquests, the Pompeian and Caesarian conquests detailed in Books 36 to 40 deserve particular attention. What is obvious, besides the fact that they occupy nearly half of the narrative, is that the Pompeian and Caesarian external conquests clearly lead to civil war. Indeed, the external campaigns are in direct connection with events in Rome, and this connection allows the reader, as much as Dio's own explanations, to understand the process leading to civil war, which clearly constitutes the main topic of the subsequent fifth decade. In this regard, chapter 44 of Book 40 is particularly relevant. This chapter concludes the war in Gaul and represents a carefully prepared transition between external events and past and impending internal conflicts. Here, that is to say at the end of the war in Gaul, Dio does not mention any benefit of Caesar's successes, any more than the territorial expansion of the Roman empire, letting slip instead one short sentence about the brutal military occupation and the financial sanctions imposed on the Gauls.[28] But he dedicates a whole chapter to the political difficulties which Caesar is now experiencing: according to Roman law, after the end of his five-year command, he has to discharge his

---

25 On this topic in Dio, see Bertrand & Coudry 2016; these extraordinary commands in the late Republic were not so much monarchical forays as solutions allowed by the adaptability of the Roman constitution, but in fact they included the risk of a slide to monarchy: Hurlet 2010, 128–9.

26 In particular Sall. *Cat.* 11.5; Liv. 38.52.1, 39.6.4, but the topic appears earlier in Roman historiography, for the first time in the fragments of the *Annales* of Lucius Calpurnius Piso Frugi, about the victory over Perseus, according to Pliny the Elder, *HN* 17.244 (see Engels 2009, 863–6); on this theme in Dio, see Fechner 1986, esp. 136–50.

27 Cass. Dio 52.1.1. This particular characterization of the late republican history has been recently well expounded by Kemezis 2014, 104–12.

28 Cass. Dio 40.43.3: ἐκεῖνοί τε οὖν οὕτω κατελύσαντο, καὶ οἱ λοιποὶ μετὰ τοῦτο, οἱ μὲν ἑκούσιοι οἱ δὲ καὶ καταπολεμηθέντες, ἐχειρώθησαν, καὶ αὐτοὺς ὁ Καῖσαρ καὶ φρουραῖς καὶ δικαιώσεσι χρημάτων τε ἐσπράξεσι καὶ φόρων ἐπιτάξεσι τοὺς μὲν ἐταπείνωσε τοὺς δὲ ἡμέρωσε. ("So these foes became reconciled on these terms, and later the rest were subdued, some voluntarily and some when conquered in war; and Caesar by means of garrisons and punts and levies of money and assessments of tribute humbled some of them and tamed others.")

armies, but, as Dio explains, the political strife in Rome[29] and the growing power of Pompey prevent him from doing so. With this allusion to internal troubles, Dio seizes the opportunity to develop a section on domestic events. Accordingly, Dio condenses in fourteen chapters the internal affairs of the last three years in order to arrive, in chapter 60, at the upshot: Caesar decides not to dismiss his legions. This decision is precisely the reason why the Senate declares Caesar *hostis* and why the civil war gets started, as seen at the beginning of the following decade.[30]

Thus, in Books 36 to 40, the Pompeian and Caesarian conquests are not developed in order to illustrate the expansion of the Roman empire and to uphold the memory of the *imperatores*' successes, but to illustrate the excessive importance given victory on the battlefield in late republican political competition. This analysis – which, as noted above, is consistent with the turn to a breaking-up of the annalistic narrative and a switch mostly to alternating multiple-year sections – highlights the complexity of the causes of political change.

In regard to this analysis, the specific role of Caesar in the degradation of the Roman Republic deserves a fresh look. Indeed, on closer examination, the portrayal of Caesar as *imperator* proves much more complex than appears at first sight and seems to evolve according to the political transformation of late republican Rome.

3   Caesar: Late Republican Dynast?

In Books 36 to 40, the figure of Caesar appears as that of prominent dynast: he is one of the most ambitious generals, who is searching for glory in order to

---

29   Cass. Dio 40.44.1–2: καὶ οὐδεμίαν ἔτ' εὐπρεπῆ σκῆψιν πρὸς τὸ μὴ οὐ τά τε στρατόπεδα ἀφεῖναι καὶ ἰδιωτεῦσαι εἶχεν· ἐπεὶ δὲ τά τε ἐν τῷ ἄστει ἐστασιάζετο ... ("And he [Caesar] had no longer any plausible excuse for not disbanding his troops and returning to private life. But affairs in the city at this time **were in a state of turmoil** ...")

30   Cass. Dio 41.1–3. The chronology of the events of early January 49 BC is well established, especially thanks to the *Bellum Civile*: after stormy debates in the Senate, the vote of the *senatus consultum ultimum* and Caesar's *hostis* declaration occurred on January 7 (Caes. *B Civ.* 1.5; cf. Cic. *Fam.* 16.11.2); then, after he received the news from the tribunes Antony and Cassius, who, fearing for their life, had left Rome, Caesar entered Italy with his army, breaching the boundaries of his *provincia* (Cic. *Att.* 7.11.1, January 19; see Dio 41.4.1). See Wiseman 1994, 422–3; Allély 2012, 82–4. Of course, Dio follows this chronology, but the specific organization of external and internal events in Book 40 reveals his own perception of the causes of civil war.

establish his political power.³¹ This is particularly clear during his praetorship in Spain, when Dio says that Caesar engaged in warfare because he wanted a victory in order to gain the consulate (37.52.2). And in fact, he succeeded in being elected thanks to the fame his victories earned him (37.54.1). Later, after his consulship, he further undertook the war in Gaul because he wanted to achieve territorial conquest.³²

This overall framework of Caesarian conquest, driven by his personal thirst for power and leading to civil war, casts a shadow over his military valor, which, well-recorded in Roman history, Dio could hardly disregard.³³ As against his silence on Pompey's ambition to become a second Alexander,³⁴ Dio mentions several of Caesar's advances: he was first to cross the Rhine (39.50.1) and first to have fought the Britons (39.53.1). So the image of Caesar as a victorious general is quickly etched with symbolic new crossings, then rounded off with the place allocated to him in the process of Roman imperialism. Caesar is the only one of the late republican generals to have given a speech on Roman imperialism, the famous Vesontio speech before his troops in 58 BC, whose particular length is highly relevant to the place Dio allocates to Caesar.³⁵

But although they are mentioned many times, Caesar's discoveries and his role as a conqueror are not greatly emphasized. The speech about Roman imperialism is annihilated by the contradiction Dio mentions between Caesar's personal ambitions in the Gallic campaign and his justification of Roman imperialism on the basis of collective necessity.³⁶ We find also many other allusions to *imperatores*' successes: for example, Lucullus too was said to be first to cross the Taurus during the war against Mithridates (36.16.1), an accomplishment which is in Plutarch's *Life of Lucullus* (46.3) but omitted by Appian (*Mithr.* 90).³⁷ Caesar's discoveries in Britain were also surpassed by his successors.³⁸ So in Books 36–40, Caesar's portrayal as a conqueror, while generally similar to the rest of the literary tradition, is tarnished. Furthermore, even if

---

31 Urso (2016, 29) has noted that the term *dynasteia* is most often applied to Caesar in the *Roman History*.
32 Cass. Dio 38.31.1 (as shown also by Kemezis 2016, 244).
33 Geiger 1975.
34 His ambition is undoubted, see Villani 2013.
35 The speech is much more developed in Book 38 (chapters 36–46) than in Caesar's *Commentarii* (*B Civ.* 1.40): Gabba 1955, 305–6; Lachenaud & Coudry 2011, lxii.
36 See, on this speech and its interpretation, Kemezis 2016.
37 Appian on the contrary says that the war was ended without any firm success: *Mithr.* 91.
38 The insular nature of Britain was recognized not by Caesar, but by Agricola, during the campaigns of 74 to 78 AD (as repeated in Book 66: 66.20.1), and again in Dio's own time, by Septimius Severus during his campaign against the Caledonians in 211 AD (as restated in Book 77[76].12). On this topic, see Bertrand 2016b, 723.

he really succeeded in external wars, crossing new boundaries, these successes were a factor of internal crisis, as indeed were also those of the other Roman generals, and they led to civil war. Caesar's campaigns, exactly like those of the late republican dynasts, grew the Roman empire to an excessive size, which the republican regime was no longer able to control. In this regard, it is not an accident that Dio's reflections on the links between the excessive expansion of the Roman empire and the ruin of the Republic are inserted precisely after these campaigns and their following internal conflicts, in Book 44 and Book 47:[39] Caesar completed the process of Roman expansion, and so doing, was one of the main actors in the collapse of the Republic.

But Caesar's figure undergoes a notable evolution between the fourth and fifth decades: his thirst for military victory seems to restrict itself to the competition with other dynasts during the sixties and fifties. We find no more allusions to Caesar's military ambition in Dio's narrative after Pharsalus: in Book 42, the conflict with the king of Pontus, Pharnaces, in 47 BC, is minutely explained: for Dio, it is the civil war troubles – the *stasis* – which give Pharnaces the opportunity to attack Roman possessions and constrain Caesar to undertake a campaign, a point of view rather different from other sources (42.45.1–2).[40] In Book 43, reporting the Parthian campaign, which, according to the tradition, Caesar was preparing in 44 BC, Dio is the only ancient source to explain that the war was decided by the Roman people – who wanted to avenge Crassus – not by Caesar's ambition (contrary to nearly the whole tradition).[41] Furthermore, within all the Caesarian laws alluded to in Book 43, after Caesar returned to Rome, Dio chooses to mention the *lex Julia* of 46 BC, which restricted the praetorian provincial commands to one year, and those of the consular commands to two years, in order, according to the author's own

---

39   Quoted above, n. 7.
40   Liv. *Per.* 113.4 gives scant information and does not mention any cause for war; Plut. *Caes.* 50.1 writes that Pharnaces was insatiable in his quest for victory, and makes no mention of the civil war.
41   Cass. Dio 43.51.1: πράττοντος δὲ αὐτοῦ ταῦτα ἐπιθυμία τε πᾶσι τοῖς Ῥωμαίοις ὁμοίως ἐσῆλθε τιμωρῆσαι τῷ τε Κράσσῳ καὶ τοῖς σὺν αὐτῷ φθαρεῖσι, καὶ ἐλπὶς τότε, εἴπερ ποτέ, τοὺς Πάρθους καταστρέψασθαι. τόν τε οὖν πόλεμον τῷ Καίσαρι ὁμοθυμαδὸν ἐψηφίσαντο, καὶ τὴν παρασκευὴν αὐτοῦ πολλὴν ἐποιοῦντο. ("But while Caesar was thus engaged, a longing came over all the Romans alike to avenge Crassus and those who had perished with him, and they felt some hope of subjugating the Parthians then, if ever. They unanimously voted the command of the war to Caesar, and made ample provision for it.") Cf. Plut. *Caes.* 58.4–7; App. *B Civ.* 2.111: in both sources, ambition is the main factor in this project, and Cicero attests that it was Caesar's project: Cic. *Att.* 13.27.1; see Malitz 1984; Sommer 2010, 126–8.

comment, to prevent any gain of power.⁴² To the best of our knowledge, Dio is the only historian who mentions this law. It is not an accident: as we know, Dio is particularly attentive to the necessity of controlling provincial commands, as can be seen especially in the advice of Maecenas to Augustus (52.20.4).

Mentioning this specific law, Dio gives Caesar a significant part in the process of devising a new form of government – the only one capable of putting an end to the destructive rivalry between external commands. The part Dio gives Caesar here is consistent with the evolution of Dio's assessment of Caesar's power in the following books, in other words the evolution from *dynasteia* to *monarchia*.⁴³ This change appears clearly at the end of Book 43, where Caesar becomes authentically a monarch in Dio's point of view;⁴⁴ from now on, Dio's narrative turns into the imperial narrative he adopts later in the principate books, a (so-called) "biostructuring" history.⁴⁵ This is clear in Book 44, entirely devoted to Caesar's death: general reflection, negative *omina*, senatorial honors as causes of jealousy and plots, and funeral are laid out as in the case of

---

42 Cass. Dio 43.25.3: ὅτι τε αὐτὸς πολλοῖς τῶν Γαλατῶν ἐφεξῆς ἔτεσιν ἄρξας ἔς τε τὴν ἐπιθυμίαν ἀπ' αὐτοῦ τῆς δυναστείας μᾶλλον προήχθη καὶ ἐς τὴν παρασκευὴν τῆς ἰσχύος ἐπηυξήθη, κατέκλεισε νόμῳ τοὺς μὲν ἐστρατηγηκότας ἐπ' ἐνιαυτὸν τοὺς δὲ ὑπατευκότας ἐπὶ δύο ἔτη κατὰ τὸ ἑξῆς ἄρχειν, καὶ μηδενὶ τὸ παράπαν ἐπὶ πλεῖον ἡγεμονίαν τινὰ ἔχειν ἐξεῖναι. ("Again, since it was by ruling the Gauls for many years in succession that he himself had conceived a greater desire for dominion and had increased the equipment of his force, he limited by law the term of propraetors to one year, and that of proconsuls to two consecutive years, and enacted that no one whatever should be allowed to hold any command for a longer time.")

43 As shown by Carsana 2016, 552–4, especially about Caesar's political power. See also the paper of Madsen in this volume.

44 Cass. Dio 43.45.1: ἕτερα δὲ δὴ τοιάδε ἐψηφίσαντο δι' ὧν καὶ μόναρχον αὐτὸν ἄντικρυς ἀπέδειξαν. ("But the Senate passed the following decrees besides, by which they declared him a monarch out and out.") The first time the term occurs in connection with Caesar's ambition is during the war against Pompey (41.24.3, alluding to Caesar's dream of power), but it really names Caesar's power only here, after Munda, in 45 BC. The historical chronology of Caesar's alleged monarchical project in the last months of his life has been much discussed, just as it is debated whether Caesar really wanted to be a king, but what is quite certain is that, if this project existed, it was not earlier than 45 BC (for the chronology, mostly based on a numismatic study, see Alföldy 1953; for an accurate study of the concession of honors and their place in Caesar's monarchical project, see Ferrary 2010).

45 Pelling 2006, 258: by "biostructuring" history, Pelling means that Dio sees late republican history as dominated by great men; even if this structure is not complete, strictly speaking, before the political beginnings of the young Caesar, in Book 45, "this shift towards biostructuring events remains interesting and expressive": especially in Book 43, Roman events are more and more directly connected to Caesar's biography.

later emperors, especially Augustus (Book 56).[46] This mutation of Caesar into a monarchical figure is also evidenced, after his death, by the section – the most detailed we have – which Dio devotes to the divinization of Caesar during the Triumvirate in Book 47.[47]

4   Conclusion

To conclude, Dio's analysis of the late republican crisis evinces an interesting complexity, in that he clearly links the excessive expansion of the empire to political change. In Books 36 to 40, the conquests, specifically those of Pompey and Caesar, occupy a major place in the narrative, within sections where they connect with political events in a manner which makes clear their role in the start of the civil war.

In this regard, the figure of Caesar as a conqueror is also complex: on the one hand, he is the author of important conquests and discoveries, but these conquests are due to his thirst for glory, and they are lessened by later achievements. Besides, they allowed him to gain political power and caused civil war. Thus, he is one of those last republican dynasts who contributed to the excessive expansion of the Roman empire and consequently to the ruin of the Republic. On the other hand, he also tried to control the provincial governorships in order to curb competition, as Dio is at pains to point out.

Moreover, between the fourth and the fifth decades, Caesar's figure evolves, and he is portrayed also as one of the actors of a new form of government, the *monarchia*, the only regime capable of controlling the risk of territorial expansion, in other words of preserving political and social order. His portrayal as a conqueror is therefore consistent with his rise to power in the fourth and fifth decades of the *Roman History*, that is to say from *dynasteia* to *monarchia*, which is one of the most important political analyses concerning the late Roman Republic in Dio's project.

---

46   Augustus' death forms the main part of Book 56, and is presented in a similar order, if not exactly the same: negative *omina* (29); death (30); Livia suspected of having poisoned her husband (30); funeral and various speeches (34–45); honors (46–7).

47   If these elements are not sufficient to assert that Dio considers Caesar as the first monarch *stricto sensu*, as do the biographers Suetonius and Plutarch (on this imperial historiography about Caesar, see Geiger 1975), his role in the advent of the monarchical regime is nevertheless obvious.

Bibliography

Alföldy, A. (1953) *Studien über Caesars Monarchie*, Lund.
Allély, A. (2012) *La déclaration d'hostis sous la République romaine*, Bordeaux.
Bertrand, E. (2015) "Cassius Dion et les cycles de l'histoire: du *topos* littéraire à la réflexion historique", in E. Bertrand & R. Compatangelo-Soussignan (eds.), *Cycles de la Nature, Cycles de l'Histoire. De la découverte des météores à la fin de l'Age d'Or* (Bordeaux): 163–72.
Bertrand, E. (2016a) "Point de vue de Cassius Dion sur l'impérialisme romain", in V. Fromentin *et al.* (eds.), *Cassius Dion: nouvelles lectures* (Bordeaux): 679–99.
Bertrand, E. (2016b) "L'empire de Cassius Dion: géographie et *imperium Romanum* dans l'*Histoire romaine*", in V. Fromentin *et al.* (eds.), *Cassius Dion: nouvelles lectures* (Bordeaux): 701–24.
Bertrand, E. & Coudry, M. (2016) "De Pompée à Auguste: les mutations de l'*imperium militiae*. 2. Un traitement particulier dans l'*Histoire romaine* de Dion", in V. Fromentin *et al.* (eds.), *Cassius Dion: nouvelles lectures* (Bordeaux): 595–608.
Bertrand, E., Coudry, M., & Fromentin, V. (2016) "Temporalité historique et formes du récit. Les modalités de l'écriture dans les livres tardo-républicains", in V. Fromentin *et al.* (eds.), *Cassius Dion: nouvelles lectures* (Bordeaux): 303–16.
Botermann, H. (2002) "*Gallia pacata – perpetua pax*. Die Eroberung Galliens und der 'gerechte Krieg'", in J. Spiegel (ed.), *Res publica reperta. Zur Verfassung und Gesellschaft der römischen Republik und des frühen Prinzipat. Festschrift für J. Bleicken zum 75. Geburtstag* (Stuttgart): 279–96.
Carsana, C. (2016) "La teoria delle forme di governo: il punto di vista di Cassio Dione sui poteri di Cesare", in V. Fromentin *et al.* (eds.), *Cassius Dion: nouvelles lectures* (Bordeaux): 545–58.
De Franchis, M. (2016) "Tite-Live, modèle de Cassius Dion ou contre-modèle?", in V. Fromentin *et al.* (eds.), *Cassius Dion: nouvelles lectures* (Bordeaux): 191–204.
Engels, D. (2009) "Déterminisme historique et perceptions de déchéance sous la république tardive et le principat", *Latomus* 68, 859–94.
Fechner, D. (1986) *Untersuchungen zu Cassius Dios Sicht der römischen Republik*, Hildesheim.
Ferrary, J.-L. (2010) "A propos des pouvoirs et des honneurs décernés à César entre 48 et 44", in G. Urso (ed.), *Cesare precursore o visionario? Atti del Convegno internazionale, Cividale del Friuli, 17–19 settembre 2009* (Pisa): 9–30.
Fromentin, V. (2016) "Denys d'Halicarnasse, source et modèle de Cassius Dion?", in V. Fromentin *et al.* (eds.), *Cassius Dion: nouvelles lectures* (Bordeaux): 179–90.
Fromentin, V. *et al.* (eds.) (2016) *Cassius Dion: nouvelles lectures*, Bordeaux.
Gabba, E. (1955) "Cassio Dione e l'imperialismo difensivo", *Rivista storica italiana* 67, 301–11.

Geiger, J. (1975) "Zum Bild Julius Caesars in der römischen Kaiserzeit", *Historia* 24, 444–53.

Hurlet, F. (2010) "Pouvoirs extraordinaires et tromperie. La tentation de la monarchie à la fin de la République romaine", in A. J. Turner, J. H. Kim On Chong-Gossard, & F. J. Vervaet (eds.), *Private and Public Lies: The Discourse of Despotism and Deceit in the Graeco-Roman World* (Leiden & Boston): 107–30.

Kemezis, A. (2014) *Greek Narratives of the Roman Empire under the Severans: Cassius Dio, Philostratus and Herodian*, Cambridge.

Kemezis, A. (2016) "Dio, Caesar and the Vesontio Mutineers (38.34–47): A Rhetoric of Lies", in C. H. Lange & J. M. Madsen (eds.), *Cassius Dio: Greek Intellectual and Roman Politician* (Leiden & Boston): 238–57.

Lachenaud, G. & Coudry, M. (2011) *Dion Cassius: Histoire romaine, Livres 38, 39 & 40*, Paris.

Lachenaud, G. & Coudry, M. (2014) *Dion Cassius: Histoire romaine, Livres 36 & 37*, Paris.

Lange, C. H. & Madsen, J. M. (eds.) (2016) *Cassius Dio: Greek Intellectual and Roman Politician*, Leiden & Boston.

Madsen, J. (2013) "The Provincialisation of Rome", in D. Hoyos (ed.), *A Companion to Roman Imperialism* (Leiden & Boston): 305–18.

Malitz, J. (1984) "Caesars Partherkrieg", *Historia* 33, 21–59.

Osgood, J. (2015) "*Breviarium totius imperii*: The Background of Appian's *Roman History*", in K. Welch (ed.), *Appian's Roman History: Empire and Civil War* (Swansea): 23–44.

Pelling, C. (2006) "Breaking the Bounds: Writing about Julius Caesar", in B. McGing & J. Mossman (eds.), *The Limits of Ancient Biography* (Swansea): 255–80.

Price, J. J. (2015) "Thucydidean *Stasis* and the Roman Empire in Appian's Interpretation of History", in K. Welch (ed.), *Appian's Roman History: Empire and Civil War* (Swansea): 45–64.

Rich, J. (2016) "Annalistic Organization and Book Division in Dio's Books 1–35", in V. Fromentin *et al.* (eds.), *Cassius Dion: nouvelles lectures* (Bordeaux): 271–86.

Serrati, J. (2013) "Imperialism and the Fall of the Republic: *post hoc ergo propter hoc*?", in D. Hoyos (ed.), *A Companion to Roman Imperialism* (Leiden & Boston): 155–68.

Sommer, M. (2010) "Le ragioni della guerra: Roma, i Parti e l'ultimo imperativo di Cesare", in G. Urso (ed.), *Cesare precursore o visionario? Atti del Convegno internazionale, Cividale del Friuli, 17–19 settembre 2009* (Pisa): 123–40.

Urso, G. (2016) "Cassius Dio's Sulla: *Exemplum* of Cruelty and Republican Dictator", in C. H. Lange & J. M. Madsen (eds.), *Cassius Dio: Greek Intellectual and Roman Politician* (Leiden & Boston): 13–32.

Van Ooteghem, J. (1967) *Les Caecilii Metelli de la République*, Bruxelles.

Villani, D. (2013) "Entre *imitatio Alexandri* et *imitatio Herculis*: Pompée et l'universalisme romain", *Pallas* 90, 335–50.

Wiseman, T. P. (1994) "Caesar, Pompey and Rome, 59–50 B.C.", in *The Cambridge Ancient History* (2nd ed.): Vol. 9, 368–423.

Zecchini, G. (2016) "Cassius Dion et l'historiographie de son temps", in V. Fromentin et al. (eds.), *Cassius Dion: nouvelles lectures* (Bordeaux): 113–24.

CHAPTER 3

Electoral Bribery and the Challenge to the Authority of the Senate: Two Aspects of Dio's View of the Late Roman Republic (Books 36–40)

Marianne Coudry

Dio's narrative of Rome's political life in his preserved "republican books" (36–40), which describe the twenty last years of the Republic before the outbreak of the civil war between Caesar and Pompey, in 49 BC, reveals some striking peculiarities. One of the most noticeable is the contrast between two kinds of passages: some provide very precise information, mostly institutional, with sometimes personal commentary added by Dio, for instance about Rabirius' trial in 63 (37.26–8); other passages instead are surprisingly brief, or even completely silent, on important facts which other ancient authors do mention, sometimes at length. One well-known example is the conference held in Luca in 56, when Pompey, Crassus, and Caesar planned with their followers the distribution of magistracies and provinces for the next years: Dio omits it,[1] but on the other hand he gives a very detailed and unique account of how the senators fought against the management of the consulship and the other magistracies by Pompey and Crassus in 55 (39.28–30) – which was the mere application of the Luca agreement. His presentation of both moments is probably linked, as if Dio found the latter details more appropriate to make the event understandable for his readers than mentioning the conference itself: such a device testifies to his originality in presenting the political issues of the late Republic. Another example, usually neglected, is the senatorial meetings of the end of 50, when Caesar attempted through his agent, the tribune Curio, to negotiate his candidacy to the consulship: Plutarch and Appian give a detailed report, but Dio does not.[2] Instead he provides the fullest preserved description of the senatorial gatherings of the first days of 49, which opened the civil war. These omissions are clearly not the result of Dio's ignorance or careless gathering of information: they reveal deliberate choices, which in turn

---

[1] As Rich 1989, 93–4 underlined, deeming this omission was quite deliberate. Note that translations of Dio in this paper are taken most often from the Loeb Classical Library edition.
[2] Plut. *Caes.* 30, *Pomp.* 58.4–10; App. *B Civ.* 2.9–31.

shed light on Dio's general ideas about the late Roman Republic, mainly how the stability of the political system was challenged by powerful dynasts.

Pointing out these sorts of peculiarities in Books 36 to 40 invites us to proceed further, and to investigate how far, in some specific passages, Dio deviates from other streams of the tradition, to try to understand why he made such choices among his sources, to wonder how they contribute to a coherent and articulated depiction of Rome's political evolution, and, in short, to analyze how he built such a narrative – which also implies identifying the shortcomings of his *History*. With this objective in mind, I focus on two specific topics, electoral bribery and the power of the Senate, although there are others similarly important in Dio's republican books: the decline or perversion of some of the magistracies, like the censorship and consulship, or the damaging action of the tribunes, or the growing disorder in popular assemblies.[3] The choice of the topic of electoral bribery, *ambitus*, better allows one to highlight Dio's originality: the wealth and quality of his information, his long-term reflections, his specific judgments.[4] As for the topic of the Senate's *auctoritas*, it deserves attention for the same reasons, but also on other grounds: because it was central to Cicero, too, either as a leading actor at some important moments such as his consulship, when he faced Catiline's conspiracy, or as a hopeless witness resigned to the weakening of traditional institutions, as during Caesar's consulship. We may try to see how close are Dio's analyses to Cicero's on these matters.

1 Electoral Bribery as a Fatal Weakness of the Late Republic

Dio's concern about bribery must be set in the frame of his conception of democracy, which, in Book 36, he places in Catulus' mouth in the narrative of the vote of the *lex Gabinia* that provided Pompey with a completely unusual command to crush piracy in the Mediterranean Sea.[5] Catulus, one of the most prominent senators of the time, voices the ideas of those who vigorously oppose Gabinius' proposal. In a long speech uttered before the popular assembly, he tries to prevent its voting, and makes use of arguments taken from political theory, pretending that the command proposed for Pompey was basically a

---

3 Some of them are treated in Fromentin *et al.* 2016. See also Lachenaud & Coudry 2011, lxxii–lxxiv, lxxvi–lxxx.

4 Although electoral bribery in late republican Rome has been the subject of numerous studies, among which see Yakobson 1999 and Rosillo López 2010, chap. 2, Dio's contribution to our information is generally underestimated.

5 See Coudry 2016.

violation of the rules of democracy. He explains that democracy implies that everyone has access to public functions – "that is *demokratia*" – and must take a share in them – "that is *isomoiria*" (36.32.1).[6] In other words, elections and free competition for magistracies are a necessary condition for the working of the republican system, and Pompey's command is a dangerous infringement of this principle.[7] That special background must be remembered when we consider the subsequent passages dealing with electoral corruption, which Dio considers as part of a wider phenomenon, the harm to the republican system of magistracies.

The first passage to examine deals with the issuing of the *lex Calpurnia de ambitu* in 67, included in a series of events of domestic politics recorded together for that year, separate from the vote of *lex Gabinia*. What is striking is the very detailed account provided by Dio, actually the best preserved on the law:[8] first the context, increasing electoral corruption after the exclusion, during the *lectio* of 70, of a high number of senators, eager to recover their senatorial status and rank through election; then the action of the consuls; the insistence of the senators to have them elaborate a suitable proposal; and the harsh subsequent conflict with tribune C. Cornelius (36.38–9). The other information we get about this law comes from Asconius' commentary on Cicero's defense of Cornelius when he was tried, but, significantly, his account does not focus on the law as much as Dio's.[9] The most interesting element in Dio's record is the detailed report of the action of the senators, presented as the real promoters of the proposal, which aimed at replacing a more severe one initially brought forth by the tribune Cornelius (36.38.4–5):

Ἡ γὰρ βουλὴ συνιδοῦσα ὅτι τὸ μὲν ὑπερβάλλον τῶν τιμωρημάτων ἐν μὲν ταῖς ἀπειλαῖς ἔκπληξιν ἔχει οὔτε τοὺς κατηγορήσοντας οὔτε τοὺς καταψηφιουμένους τῶν ὑπαιτίων, ἅτε καὶ ἀνηκέστων αὐτῶν ὄντων, ῥᾳδίως εὑρίσκει, τὸ δὲ δὴ μέτριον ἔς τε τὰς κατηγορίας συχνοὺς προάγει καὶ τὰς καταψηφίσεις οὐκ ἀποτρέπει, μεταρρυθμίσαι πῃ τὴν εἰσήγησιν αὐτοῦ καὶ τοῖς ὑπάτοις νομοθετῆσαι αὐτὴν ἐκέλευσεν.

---

[6] We should be aware that this commonplace definition of democracy, put forward in Catulus' speech as a positive political ideal, is criticized by Dio as misleading in his well-known repudiation of Caesar's murder and comparison between democracy and monarchy (44.2.1).

[7] On Catulus' speech, see Coudry 2015. Dio's view of competition as a main feature of the republican political system has been explored by Lindholmer 2016.

[8] See Ferrary 2001, 165–7.

[9] And this difference is still present in modern literature about Cornelius' tribunate (McDonald 1929 being more confident in Dio's account than Griffin 1973).

The Senate, realizing that while excessive punishments have some deterrent force as threats, yet men are not then easily found to accuse or condemn those on trial, since the latter will be in desperate danger, whereas moderation encourages many to accusations and does not prevent condemnations, was desirous of modifying his proposition somehow, and bade the consuls frame it as a law.

We may wonder if this passage does not echo the senatorial debate itself, or at least part of it, maybe the *sententia* which won the day. Anyway it testifies to Dio's interest in the managing of electoral corruption at that time.

Something else deserves notice: the law is not just presented as an important event of this year, and the first one to be recorded at that. It is part of a set of decisions involving corruption in general, as Dio frames it: "In sum, the Romans were so concerned at that time to prevent corruption (τὸ μηδὲν δωροδοκεῖσθαι) that ..." (36.40.3). And he gives a variety of information about different people concerned by corruption as provincial governors in these years. These few chapters (36.38–40) form a unit, the topic of which is corruption in general, inserted in the annalistic narrative. This is a literary device that is not very frequent in Dio's republican books, and it reveals his concern for this problem. Moreover, by concluding the discussion with a eulogy of Lucullus' integrity, he brings together two different kinds of remarks about corruption, in a rather unusual blending: strictly institutional on the one side, moralizing on the other.

Electoral bribery appears again in the narrative of the year 66. It is presented as the cause of the events usually called Catiline's first conspiracy (36.44.3–5), a rather confused question, on which Dio's account, however, is not original, except in its insistence on the efficiency of the Senate's action.[10] Dio is original, instead, about the beginnings of Catiline's conspiracy in 63: although Catiline's repeated failures in consular elections are mentioned in a large part of the tradition (Sall. *Cat.* 26.5; Asc. 83C, App. *B Civ.* 2.2), only in Dio's *History* is the *lex Tullia de ambitu* presented as the starting point of Catiline's action. This new law was designed, Dio says, to prevent Catiline's schemes of bribery, and so incited Catiline, well aware of the fact, to plot the murder of Cicero and some other nobles (37.29.1–2). The next step is the consular elections themselves: defeated again, Catiline "no longer directed his plot in secret or against Cicero and his adherents only, but against the whole commonwealth (πᾶν τὸ κοινόν)" (37.30.1). So, Dio's narrative of the outbreak of Catiline's

---

10 Although some of the information he provides may be inaccurate (see Lachenaud & Coudry 2011, 78 n. 212).

conspiracy highlights specific, individual moments which carefully underline the relation between *ambitus* and unrest.

But the question surfaces again, on a much broader scale, in the years 53 and 52, which appear in Dio's narrative as the climax of *ambitus*. The topic is prominent in the five chapters describing the political situation, when the narrative comes back to the city of Rome after the conclusion of the Gallic war (40.45–50). And, quite unusually, the events of both years are mingled: at this point, Dio deliberately puts aside the annalistic principle, and chooses instead a thematic one. His first words sound like a warning to his audience: "During these same years many tumults had occurred in the city, especially in connection with the elections" (40.45.1). And he repeatedly mentions frantic corruption and violence exerted without any limit by competitors, which lead to anarchy, in the root sense of the word: lack of magistrates to take care of the city (40.46.3, 40.50.3). The most complete description is given as an introduction to the narrative of Clodius' murder on the Via Appia (40.48.1):

> Τοιαύτης οὖν τότε τῆς ἐν τῷ ἄστει καταστάσεως οὔσης, καὶ μηδενὸς τοῖς πράγμασιν ἐπιτεταγμένου, σφαγαὶ καθ' ἑκάστην ἡμέραν ὡς εἰπεῖν ἐγίγνοντο, τάς τε ἀρχαιρεσίας, καίτοι σπεύδοντες ἐπὶ τὰς ἀρχὰς καὶ δεκασμοῖς καὶ φόνοις δι' αὐτὰς χρώμενοι, οὐκ ἐπετέλουν.

> Such being the state of things in the city at that time, with no one in charge of affairs, murders occurred practically every day, and they could not hold the elections, although men were eager to win the offices and employed bribery and assassination to secure them.

Such a picture is also to be found in other sources, mostly Appian (*B Civ.* 2.19), but the specificity of Dio's account is his insistence on the topic, and his adding unique information, not to be found elsewhere. One example is a proposal made by the tribunes of the plebs to reinstate an old magistracy, the tribunate with consular power, in use at a time when plebeians were refused access to the consulship, "so that more magistrates might be elected" (40.45.4). This precision allows us to illuminate the link between the widespread electoral corruption of these years and the inadequacy of the system of magistracies which made access to the consulship so difficult for more and more numerous *praetorii*. This is a situation that modern specialists have long acknowledged,[11] but which only Dio, among ancient authors, has underlined. And this is very

---

11   See e.g. Yakobson 1999, 145–7.

typical of his conception of the politics of the late Republic: *ambitus*, in his eyes, is more an institutional than a moral problem.

The appeal made to Pompey to overcome this crisis, which had culminated in the murder of Clodius and the subsequent disorders, and his designation as consul without colleague, resulted in his proposing a series of laws, well attested in the tradition, but which Dio, once again, presents along very specific lines. Pompey's *lex de ambitu*[12] is described in much detail, in a whole chapter (40.52), which is quite unusual, with no parallels found elsewhere.[13] More interesting: in contrast to the whole tradition, which either alludes to the satisfaction of the senators (App. *B Civ.* 2.25: they praised him for having restored the *politeia*), or directly eulogizes Pompey's efficiency in stopping *ambitus* (Vell. 2.47.3; Plut. *Pomp.* 55.11; Plin. *Pan.* 29.1), Dio's statement is clearly critical. He admits that many culprits were convicted, which sounds like praise of the law, but he also mentions how Pompey himself undermined his accomplishment in allowing some to escape punishment (40.55.1–2).[14]

With the beginning of the civil war, the dictatorship of Caesar, the Triumvirate and further civil war, elections could no longer be held according to the rules, and various devices were found to fill the magistracies. But Dio's concern for *ambitus* does not disappear altogether. It meets its last expression in the Augustan books, in contexts which are either narratives of political events, or general reflections. To the first kind belongs the precise and vivid description of the violent unrest (στάσις) aroused by consular elections in 22 BC (54.6.1–4), after Augustus had, the year before, resigned the consulship "so that as many as possible might become consuls" (53.32.3). Dio's comment on the riot caused by rivalry between the candidates is unambiguous: "Thus they gave a further proof that they could not survive under a democratic government (ἀδύνατον ἦν δημοκρατουμένους σφᾶς σωθῆναι)." The same thing happened again at the beginning of 19 BC, but the event is allowed only a brief mention in Dio's narrative (54.10.1), as is the law *de ambitu* which Augustus shaped the year after (54.16.1), and the new conditions he laid down in 8 BC after all the magistrates elected had been accused of bribery (55.5.3).

In other passages of the Augustan books, the topic of *ambitus* is embedded in general reflections about the new regime. First, it finds a place in Maecenas' speech, about the choice of officials for a monarch: "Those to whom any task

---

12 See Ferrary 2001, 189–96.
13 Asconius, in the *argumentum* of Cicero's *Pro Milone* (36C, 39C), gives some precise details of the law, but not a coherent account.
14 The same kind of criticism had been uttered by Dio about Pompey and Crassus' laws against bribery in 55 (39.37.1).

was entrusted would be appointed because of their merit (ἀπ' ἀρετῆς) and not as the result of the lot or rivalry for office (κλήρῳ καὶ σπουδαρχίᾳ)" (52.15.3). And later in Augustus' funeral eulogy (56.40.4), where Tiberius praises Augustus because:

> τό τε ἀξίωμα τῶν ἀρχαιρεσιῶν αὐτῷ [sc. τῷ δήμῳ] ἐτήρησε, κἀν ταύταις τὸ φιλότιμον ἀντὶ τοῦ φιλονείκου σφᾶς ἐξεπαίδευσε, κἀν τῶν σπουδαρχιῶν αὐτῶν τὸ πλεονεκτικὸν ἐκκόψας τὸ εὔδοξον αὐτοῖς ἀντέδωκε.

> He preserved for them [the People] the dignity of the elections; and at these elections he inculcated in the citizens the love of honor rather than the love of party strife, and eliminating the element of greed from their office-seeking, he put in its place the regard for reputation.

Unsurprisingly, Dio's concern for the topic of electoral bribery appears again, in both these passages, as part of his more general interest in the system of magistracies and the rules on which it is based, an interest colored by a moral conception. Moreover, such a policy, assigned to Augustus, of retaining elections as a method to provide governing elites, while freeing them from bribery, is an important element of Dio's picture of the ideal imperial regime – although he does not conceal the difficulties Augustus had to face in this matter. It is one of the reasons for his praise of Augustus as a model for the kind of regime he conceives as an ideal for Rome, a mix of monarchy and democracy.[15] This was a regime in which he could himself find his own place and legitimacy as a senator, selected through election, and whose promotion was achieved on this basis, as his multiple consulships testify, especially the second one when he had the emperor as his colleague. So, his interest in *ambitus* in the late Republic seems clearly connected both with his theoretical reflection on the regimes – Republic and principate – and with his experience as a Severan senator.

2   The Breakdown of the *auctoritas* of the Senate

Dio's description of the Senate's guidance of politics in the late Republic is no less rooted in his general reflection about the Roman *politeia* than his depiction of *ambitus*. It is a fact that, among numerous passages devoted to recounting the harsh conflicts opposing such or such a political leader to the senators as a whole, some are nothing more than description of the actions

---

15   See the very convincing analysis of Coltelloni-Trannoy 2016.

and counter-actions of both sides, as for instance the tribune Gabinius, acting for Pompey's sake, and arousing violent reaction against his proposal to create for Pompey an extraordinary command to crush piracy (36.23–4), or Crassus and Pompey secretly maneuvering to be elected consuls in 56 and driving the senators to violent although ineffective indignation (39.28–30). But from time to time the narrative goes further, and Dio explicitly presents the events as revealing something crucial on the level of institutional realities of the moment.

This appears in full light when he records Rabirius' trial in 63 (37.26–8), a strange judicial operation generally considered[16] as a maneuver initiated by Caesar to enhance his popularity, by attacking an old and obscure senator, Rabirius, who had taken part in the repression of the *seditio* of Saturninus ordered by the Senate nearly forty years before, in 100. Dio's presentation of the trial is very clear-cut (37.26.1–2):

> ὅ τε γὰρ Σατουρνῖνος πρὸ ἔξ που καὶ τριάκοντα ἐτῶν ἐτεθνήκει, καὶ τὰ κατὰ τὸν πόλεμον τὸν πρὸς αὐτὸν οἱ ὕπατοι τότε παρὰ τῆς βουλῆς προσετετάχατο, ὥστε ἡ γερουσία ἄκυρος ἐκ τοῦ δικαστηρίου ἐκείνου τῶν ψηφισμάτων ἐγίγνετο. κἀκ τούτου πᾶς ὁ κόσμος τῆς πολιτείας ἐταράττετο.

> Saturninus had been killed thirty-six years earlier, and the fight waged against him by the consuls of the period had been at the direction of the Senate. Hence, as a result of the proposed trial, the Senate would lose authority to enforce its decrees. In consequence, the whole order of the constitution would be disturbed.

Dio is clearly alluding first to the so-called *senatus consultum ultimum* (SCU) voted in 100, which directed the consuls to "take care that no harm came to the city," as the usual formulation held, and secondly to Catiline's conspiracy which he will relate a few chapters later. He intends to suggest to his audience that Rabirius' trial helped to stimulate those people who defied the Senate and weakened its capacity to defend the Republic by such decrees. As a matter of fact, among our sources about the SCU and associated decrees, such as the *hostis publicus* declarations, Dio's republican books provide the most rich and precise material we have left for the last years of the Republic (67 to 40 BC), if we except Cicero himself.[17] This alone deserves notice, for this kind of decree, voted in contexts of dire political crisis, was a test of the Senate's authority.

---

16 See e.g. Gruen 1974, 78–80, 277–9. Caesar's backing is stated by Suetonius (*Iul.* 12).
17 See the tables in Allély 2012, 150–1.

For this reason, Dio's narrative of Catiline's conspiracy (37.29–36) requires closer examination: the way he records how the plans and actions of the Catilinarians were counteracted is revealing of his view of the Senate's function. His account, which is particularly precise, stands clearly apart from others:[18] while Sallust, and even more Velleius, Plutarch, and Appian put Cicero front and center and record how the Romans were grateful to him, Dio systematically minimizes his action: he even falsely ascribes Catiline's flight from Rome to a *senatus consultum*, not to Cicero's *First Catilinarian*.[19] He emphasizes instead the numerous and effective decrees voted by the Senate. Remarkably, some of these are known only through his account, such as the proclamation of a *tumultus*, or the posting of garrisons inside the city (37.31.1, 3). The only effective action recognized as Cicero's is the catching of the Allobroges' ambassadors and the disclosure of the conspiracy in the Senate (37.34.1–2). Proceeding along the same lines, Dio also insists on the decrees voted a little later to protect Cicero against those (most notably the tribune Metellus Nepos) who attacked the execution of Lentulus and his accomplices decided in December 63 – a decision not mentioned anywhere else (37.42.3).

The meaning of his narrative in unambiguous: under these circumstances, when "Catiline no longer directed his plot in secret or against Cicero and his adherents only, but against the whole city (πᾶν τὸ κοινόν)" (37.30.1), it is the Senate who ensured its safety. Logically, in this perspective, the real target of the violent criticisms aroused against the execution of Lentulus is the Senate, too, and not Cicero, as was maintained: "Cicero came near being tried for the killing of Lentulus and the other prisoners. This charge, though technically brought against him, was really directed against the Senate" (37.42.1–2). Such is Dio's view when he concludes the narrative of the conspiracy, and he expresses it again later, when he explains the aims of Clodius' law of 58 directed against those who had put to death citizens without a popular trial, as Cicero had done (38.14.5):

ἔφερε μὲν γὰρ καὶ ἐπὶ πᾶσαν τὴν βουλήν, ὅτι τοῖς τε ὑπάτοις τὴν φυλακὴν τῆς πόλεως, δι' ἧσπερ καὶ τὰ τοιαῦτα σφίσι ποιεῖν ἐξὸν ἐγίγνετο, προσετετάχει, καὶ μετὰ τοῦτο καὶ τοῦ Λεντούλου καὶ τῶν ἄλλων τῶν τότε θανατωθέντων κατεψήφιστο.

---

18 See Lachenaud & Coudry 2014, lxv–lxviii (Notice) and 161–71 (Notes on the text). Also see the paper of Urso in this volume.

19 Dio writes (37.33.1): "The Senate voted that Catiline should leave the city."

It brought within its scope, indeed, the entire Senate, because the Senate had charged the consuls with the protection of the city, by which act it was permitted them to take such steps, and afterwards had condemned Lentulus and the others who were put to death at that time.

Only in his description of the senatorial meetings of January 49, on the eve of the civil war, will Dio give as many details about the proceedings and decisions of the Senate. And again this appears as deliberate: for him, it is the moment when the Senate gathers all its strength to resist Caesar's menace, and fails. Between these two events, he points the stages of the Senate's weakening. First comes Caesar's consulship in 59 and the vote of his agrarian law against the will of the senators (38.2–3). Then comes Pompey and Crassus' joint consulship in 55 and the ineffectiveness of the Senate's action against their managing of elections and provincial commands (39.28–33) – a point he decided to set out with many details, probably because he interpreted it as the result of the conference in Luca which he omitted. And finally there is Pompey's third consulship in 52: a pragmatic solution and a last resource to the crisis resulting from *ambitus* that culminated in Clodius' murder (40.50).

The famous senatorial meetings of the first days of 49 thus appear as the last step of this evolution, the ultimate attempt of the senators to resist the power of the dynasts which ruined the Senate's authority in the state. Strikingly, Dio's record is, after Caesar's own, the most detailed we get, and putting both side by side is very revealing of their opposite interpretations. Caesar's opening chapters of his *Bellum Civile* (1.1–5) are a violent attack on the obstinate refusal of the consuls and the Pompeian senators to consider his (pretended) offers of peace. So, Caesar records on one side their menacing speeches, on the other side the moderate propositions which they disregard, and finally the harsh decisions (supposedly) voted against the Caesarian tribunes Antony and Cassius, and the SCU. Dio's narrative (41.1–3) is quite different. It reports the successive moments of the senatorial meeting (which lasted several days): how the consuls resisted the tribunes who wanted Caesar's letter to be read in the Senate, but had to yield; how they organized a vote on Caesar's propositions, not according to the usual practice of individual answer, but by *discessio*, walking to one side or the other of the room; how the result – that Caesar should lay down his command – was made ineffective by a veto of the tribunes; how the senators still had their decision written down (so it became a *senatus auctoritas* instead of a *senatus consultum*) and how the veto was discussed; how the tribunes protested and left the Senate-house; and finally how the SCU was voted. Dio even adds the vote of the *tumultus* and of the warning to Caesar that he would be declared *hostis publicus* if he did not abide to the Senate's decisions.

The peculiarity of this narrative is its exactness: the stages of the deliberation are very clearly described, with unusually numerous details, so that the uncommon character of some of the proceedings are made conspicuous – the *discessio*, the writing down of the *auctoritas senatus*. And the meaning of this report seems clear: on Dio's view, this senatorial meeting is the climax of the ten years' fight between the Senate, as foremost element of the republican political system, and the dynasts, who have undermined it. The consuls and the senators gather all the available means to resist Caesar's menace. By describing them, and letting his audience understand how ineffective they will probably be, Dio underlines that the breakdown of the Republic is not a matter of power (Caesarians versus Pompeians, as in Caesar's narrative), but of wrecked institutions. This is probably why he did not describe the senatorial meetings of the end of 50, when the senators already tried to reject Caesar's demands, as we noticed: he chose early 49, instead, as the most significant according to his view of turning points in the history of Rome.

3   Conclusion

To sum up the main results of this analysis of Dio's picture of the place of *ambitus* and of the authority of the Senate in late republican Roman politics, three points might be stressed.

First, concerning these topics, his narrative usually offers details more precise and accurate than what we read in other accounts, sometimes even unique – a fact which reveals his particular interest for such matters. Thus our knowledge of the laws aiming against electoral bribery (the *lex Calpurnia* of 67, the *lex Tullia* of 63, and especially the *lex Pompeia* of 52) relies deeply on his *History*. The same is true about the electoral disorder of the years 53–52, the variety of decrees produced by the Senate to stop the effects of Catiline's conspiracy, or the vicissitudes of the Senate meetings of January 49.

Second, Dio often provides original views on the events, obviously resulting from a careful choice of information among his sources. Very interesting, for instance, is his use or disuse of Cicero's writings concerning Rabirius' trial: both authors consider that the *res publica* is in danger (Cass. Dio 37.26.2; Cic. *Rab. perd.* 5, 35), but Cicero is not as clear-cut as Dio on the question put at stake by the trial – was it by the Senate's authority or the magistrates' authority that Saturninus was put down?[20] The same happens for Catiline's conspiracy: again, both consider that the *res publica* is in danger, but Cicero's action during the fight against the Catilinarians is minimized by Dio, as if he disregarded the Catilinarian orations. And in his record of the senatorial meeting on December 5, Dio pictures Cicero as urging the execution of Lentulus and his fellows "by exciting and terrifying the senators" (37.35.4). Cicero himself pretended to be the obedient instrument of the Senate, in his last Catilinarian oration (*Cat.* 4.24), and later, when he came back from exile (*Dom.* 94) or even in 55 (*Pis.* 14) – yet it must be acknowledged that Dio, in the so-called consolation of Philiscus, does put this idea in Philiscus' mouth (38.25.2, 4). However, Dio's view of the position and function of the Senate in the republican regime is in entire agreement with Cicero's, as is expressed in his well-known general statements in *Pro Sestio* (137), *De re publica* (2.56), and *De legibus* (3.28).[21]

An inescapable effect of Dio's choices is his shortcomings: for instance the social background of Catiline's accomplices, so important in Cicero and Sallust's eyes, is completely omitted, and their aims are rather approximately described – or even falsely described, for instance distribution of lands (37.30.2). But this should rather be understood as a logical consequence of the general purpose of his *History*, a large-scale work shaped to provide an understanding of historical change ascribed to a selection of actors and events.

All this – and here we come to our last point – is the result of his wide historical reflection, which creates relationships between facts not evidently connected, as for instance the fight against bribery and the formation of Catiline's conspiracy, but which also provides a coherent understanding of the late Republic, with clear-cut phases and well-identified turning points. Such are the vote of the *lex Gabinia* in 67 for external policy – from now on the Senate lost control over the great wars and the management of empire[22] – and the establishment of the so-called "First Triumvirate" in 60 – for then, it lost control of domestic policy as well. This chronological scheme can be noticed for the two topics we investigated: after 60, bribery becomes overwhelming, and is no longer seriously opposed; and for the Senate's authority, Caesar's consulship of 59 is the first lost battle. It should be noted that this choice of 60–59 as turning point in the political history of late republican Rome is not original: it was first

---

20 Both Senate's and magistrates' authority: *Rab. perd.* 2–3. Only the consuls' authority when he argues that Rabirius was but obeying their orders: *Rab. perd.* 23, 27, 31, 34. But the reverse five years later: *senatus auctoritas* (*Pis.* 4).
21 See Ferrary 1982, 743–8; Mitchell 1971; Mitchell 1991, 52–6, 61–2; Bonnefond-Coudry 1989, 11–14.
22 I have tried to demonstrate that this choice was an original view of Dio: Coudry 2016.

expressed by the contemporary witnesses, and became from Augustus' time on the standard view.[23] But in Dio's *History* it becomes a very effective tool to build a coherent narrative of the fall of the Republic. The important idea behind all this is that the breakdown of the Republic is a history of changing institutions, as Fechner had already stated in his book of 1986, not (or less so, anyway) of moral decay.

Bibliography

Allély, A. (2012) *La déclaration d'hostis sous la République romaine*, Bordeaux.

Bonnefond-Coudry, M. (1989) *Le Sénat de la République romaine, de la guerre d'Hannibal à Auguste: pratiques délibératives et prise de décision*, Rome.

Coltelloni-Trannoy, M. (2016) "La πολιτεία impériale d'après Cassius Dion (livres 52–59)", in V. Fromentin *et al.* (eds.), *Cassius Dion: nouvelles lectures* (Bordeaux): 559–66.

Coudry, M. (2015) "Cassius Dion et les magistratures de la République romaine: le discours de Catulus contre la *rogatio Gabinia* (36, 31–36)", *Cahiers Glotz* 26, 43–65.

Coudry, M. (2016) "Cassius Dio on Pompey's Extraordinary Commands", in C. H. Lange & J. M. Madsen (eds.), *Cassius Dio: Greek Intellectual and Roman Politician* (Leiden & Boston): 33–50.

Fechner, D. (1986) *Untersuchungen zu Cassius Dios Sicht der römischen Republik*, Hildesheim.

Ferrary, J.-L. (1982) "Le idee politiche a Roma nell'epoca Repubblicana", in L. Firpo (ed.), *Storia delle idee politiche, economiche e sociali* (Torino): 723–804.

Ferrary, J.-L. (2001) "La législation *'de ambitu'* de Sylla à Auguste", in *Iuris vincula. Studi in onore di Mario Talamanca*, III (Napoli): 159–98.

Fromentin, V. *et al.* (eds.) (2016) *Cassius Dion: nouvelles lectures*, Bordeaux.

Griffin, M. (1973) "The Tribunate of Cornelius", *Journal of Roman Studies* 63, 196–213.

Gruen, E. S. (1974) *The Last Generation of the Roman Republic*, Berkeley.

Lachenaud G. & Coudry M. (2011) *Dion Cassius: Histoire romaine, Livres 38, 39 & 40*, Paris.

Lachenaud G. & Coudry M. (2014) *Dion Cassius: Histoire romaine, Livres 36 & 37*, Paris.

Lindholmer, M. (2016) *Cassius Dio, Competition and the Decline of the Roman Republic*, MPhil Thesis: Glasgow.

Lintott, A. W. (1971) "Lucan and the History of the Civil War", *Classical Quarterly* 21, 488–505.

McDonald, W. (1929) "The Tribunate of Cornelius", *Classical Quarterly* 23, 196–208.

Mitchell, T. N. (1971) "Cicero and the senatus consultum ultimum", *Historia* 20, 47–61.

---

23 As well noticed by Lintott 1971, 494.

Mitchell, T. N. (1991) *Cicero, the Senior Statesman*, New Haven & London.
Rich, J. (1989) "Dio on Augustus", in A. Cameron (ed.), *History as Text: The Writing of Ancient History* (London): 87–110.
Rosillo López, C. (2010) *La corruption à la fin de la République romaine (IIe–Ier s. av. J.-C.). Aspects politiques et financiers*, Stuttgart.
Yakobson, A. (1999) *Elections and Electioneering in Rome: A Study in the Political System of the Late Republic*, Stuttgart.

CHAPTER 4

Wrinkles in Time: Chronological Ruptures in Cassius Dio's Narrative of the Late Republic

Christopher Baron

1   Introduction and Terminology

Cassius Dio's fifth decade covers the years 49–31 BCE, from Julius Caesar's crossing of the Rubicon to the victory of Caesar's heir at Actium. In how many different ways could a Roman historian choose to narrate these eighteen momentous and complex years? An annalistic structure breaks down quickly, as many commentators on Dio have pointed out. This is due both to the pressure of historical events themselves – consuls chosen for multiple years ahead of time, the holding of extraordinary powers, and battles between Roman legions rather than against foreign enemies – and also to authorial decision, as Dio uses Julius Caesar and then Octavian to usher in a more "biographical principle" of organization. Nonetheless, even without the consular year as a guide, the historian could choose to proceed as close to the actual chronology as possible (à la Thucydides or Polybius), taking into account the different theaters of action within each year. Dio's procedure in his presentation of the late Republic and civil wars (Books 36–50) has received scholarly attention, partially because it is not entirely obvious which procedure he has chosen. There is a chronological narrative thread, and the beginnings of consular years are still marked; but Dio also strays from this structure in striking ways.

An excellent article by Estelle Bertrand, Marianne Coudry, and Valérie Fromentin (2016) has recently outlined, for Books 36 through 51, some of the ways in which Dio breaks the annalistic structure beyond just the concern for matching a new year with a new narrative unit. They emphasize two points: 1) these are narrative *choices* on Dio's part, and 2) these ruptures showcase certain themes which Dio wishes to highlight concerning the fall of the Republic.[1] In this essay, I want to continue this investigation in further detail at the narratological level, looking for ruptures or – in some cases, since they are

---

1   See also Lindholmer forthcoming; Rich 2016 analyzes the evidence for annalistic structure in the fragmentary Books 1–35.

softer and more subtle – what we might call *wrinkles* in the chronological flow. To illustrate the notion, I begin with two items from the opening of Book 48, in the aftermath of the battles at Philippi in 42 BCE (48.1.1 and 2):

> ὁ μὲν οὖν Βροῦτος καὶ Κάσσιος οὕτως ἀπώλοντο, τοῖς ξίφεσιν οἷς τὸν Καίσαρα ἀπεχρήσαντο σφαγέντες· οἵ τε ἄλλοι οἱ τῆς ἐπ' αὐτὸν ἐπιβουλῆς μετασχόντες, **οἱ μὲν πρότερον, οἱ δὲ τότε, οἱ δὲ μετὰ ταῦτα**, πλὴν πάνυ ὀλίγων, ἐφθάρησαν …

> Thus Brutus and Cassius perished, slain by the swords with which they had murdered Caesar; and also the others who had shared in the plot against him were all, except a very few, destroyed, **some before this, some at this time, and some subsequently**.[2]

> ὁ δὲ δὴ Καῖσαρ καὶ ὁ Ἀντώνιος τοῦ μὲν Λεπίδου **παραχρῆμα**, ἅτε μὴ συννικήσαντός σφισιν, ἐπλεονέκτησαν, **ἔμελλον** δὲ καὶ ἐπ' ἀλλήλους **οὐκ ἐς μακρὰν** τρέψεσθαι· χαλεπὸν γὰρ ἄνδρας τρεῖς ἢ καὶ δύο ὁμοτίμους, ἐγκρατεῖς τηλικούτων ἐκ πολέμου πραγμάτων γενομένους, ὁμονοῆσαι.

> As for Caesar and Antony, on the other hand, they secured an advantage over Lepidus **for the moment**, because he had not shared the victory with them; yet **they were destined before long** to turn against each other. For it is a difficult matter for three men, or even two, who are equal in rank and as a result of war have gained control over such vast interests, to be of one accord.

The first sentence of Book 48 takes a specific moment in time (a single historical event, the deaths of Brutus and Cassius at Philippi) and links it to the past, to the present, and to the future; in addition, the reference to the swords which slew Caesar provides a glance even further back in time. The second sentence attaches, to a brief interpretative statement on the historian's part, a foreshadowing of events which still lie in the future of the narrative (but which are already known to the reader). Thus, immediately after the pivotal battles at Philippi, and at the beginning of a new book, Dio offers two very brief chronological ruptures – wrinkles, given the succinct nature of the first, and the way in which the second nests itself within the author's more general

---

2 All translations are taken from the Loeb Classical Library edition (Earnest Cary), unless noted.

statements.³ These have the effect of keeping the larger span of Roman historical time before the eyes of his readers and encouraging them to see underlying causes and the ramifications of watershed events. This reminder of past, present, and future within the time of the narrative by necessity also returns Dio's contemporary reader to consciousness of his or her own time, the end point of Dio's work.

The field of narratology has developed a useful terminology for classifying and thinking about these chronological ruptures.⁴ **Analepsis** is a movement backward in time/narrative, **prolepsis** a movement forward. These can be **internal**, that is, they can refer backward or forward to events *within* the period treated by the historian's narrative; or they can be **external**, referring to events *outside/beyond* that period. There are no external analepses in Dio's narrative with which we need to concern ourselves (reference to events before the founding of Rome). External prolepses, in the case of Dio's *Roman History*, could be complicated, if one were to take his end point of 229 CE as the strict narratological terminus; but for present purposes, I will treat any reference Dio makes to customs, titles, buildings, etc. as they exist in his own day as an external prolepsis. Finally, an author can pause the narrative in order to discuss a topic without reference to a specific time, or in which a specific time is unimportant: a "timeless" excursus or digression.⁵

As an indication of the intricacies we can find in Dio's narrative, consider the graphic analysis of Book 47 (Table 4.1).⁶ This book is well-known for its long internal analepsis on the activities of Brutus and Cassius in the East between the Ides of March 44 BCE and the battles at Philippi in October 42. In the previous three books, plus the first nineteen chapters of Book 47, Dio has focused on the course of events at Rome during that two-and-a-half-year period. But, before narrating the conflict at Philippi which brings Book 47 to a close, he

---

3   The balance of the period as a whole may, for a Greek reader, have further softened these glances forward and back: the first wrinkle, signaled by μέν/δέ/δέ, occurs within the major μέν clause, so that the reader still awaits the corresponding δέ; the second wrinkle falls at roughly the same position in its clause, though not syntactically parallel.

4   The most important model for narratological analysis of ancient literature has been that of Genette 1980; within Classics, the work of Irene de Jong has been fundamental. For introductory discussions and short treatments of individual ancient authors, see de Jong, Nünlist, & Bowie 2004; de Jong & Nünlist 2007; Rood 1998 offers an extended treatment of Thucydides.

5   The introductory material in de Jong, Nünlist, & Bowie 2004 contains a useful glossary (xv–xviii). I use "'timeless' digression" rather than "static" or "dynamic description," partially to avoid concern over how to distinguish static vs. dynamic. It should also be noted that there may often be some overlap between external prolepsis and "timeless" digression.

6   See Fromentin & Bertrand 2014, xi–xvi, for analysis of the structure of Book 47.

devotes twelve or sixteen chapters (depending on where one draws the line) to the deeds of Brutus and Cassius in the East within that same time frame. Furthermore, within this analeptic section there are further analepses in which Dio explains the genesis of the situation in each theater of the war: brief references to Crassus' campaign against the Parthians and to the aftermath of the battle of Pharsalus, a longer account of Caecilius Bassus in Syria, and another short explanation of Dolabella's position. In the midst of the Bassus analepsis, Dio jumps even further back in time to the activities of Lucullus and Crassus in the East – an analepsis within an analepsis within an analepsis, worthy of the 2010 film *Inception* with its multiple levels of intricately nested dreamscapes. Just as importantly, the table also reveals that, even outside of the well-known Brutus and Cassius "digression," Dio engages in a great deal of chronological shifting in Book 47. There are multiple analepses and prolepses, including an external prolepsis which attributes a custom still practiced in Dio's day to the triumvirs' first year in office; and two "timeless" digressions momentarily bring the narrative to a halt.[7]

TABLE 4.1   Narratological analysis of Cassius Dio, *Roman History* Book 47

1–19 Triumvirs enter Rome (Nov. 43 BCE) **(MS)**
   1, portents for each of the triumvirs: those for Lepidus and Antony occurred before they entered Italy **(AN)**, while Octavian's occurred immediately after the pact had been agreed to
   3.1–5.2, references to the proscriptions of Sulla **(AN)** for comparison
   3.3, Dio notes he is unable to find **(EP)** the reason for only the two white tablets in this proscription
   7.3, proof of Octavian's lack of cruelty: when he broke off and ruled alone, he did nothing like this **(IP)**
   8.3–4, description of Antony and Fulvia's treatment of Cicero's head **(IP)**; his murder occurs three chapters later, at 11.1–2
   12.1–2, brief analepsis **(AN)** to set up Sextus Pompey in Sicily (a safe haven for the proscribed)
   15.4, last note in year 43: the triumvirs did everything as they wished, so that "Caesar's monarchy **(AN)** seemed like gold"

---

7   Cf. Hidber 2004, 197–8: he lists references to Dio's own day, but misses several from these books. The list in Millar 1964, 211–13, differs in some places.

TABLE 4.1　Narratological analysis of Cassius Dio, *Roman History* Book 47 (*cont.*)

16.1, consuls of 42 BCE **(MS)**
　NB the murders and noteworthy stories of the proscriptions have all been narrated under 43 BCE (chs. 9–10); at the beginning of 42 BCE, we get information on the auctioning of property (and greed), and honors for Julius Caesar (chs. 18–19) **(TD)**
18.3, at the beginning of year, the triumvirs took an oath to consider all Julius Caesar's acts binding, τοῦτο καὶ νῦν … γίγνεται **(EP)**
　20–36, Brutus and Cassius in the East (44–42 BCE) **(AN)**
　　21.2–3, brief references to Crassus and Pharsalus **(AN²)**, explaining why Cassius and Brutus found supporters
　　21–5, Brutus in Greece, Macedonia, and Asia
　　26–31, Cassius in Asia and Syria
　　　26.3–27.5, analepsis **(AN²)** to set up the situation in Syria (Bassus)
　　　　27.3, cross-references even further back to Lucullus and Crassus **(AN³)**
　　　29.1, brief analepsis on Dolabella **(AN²)**
　　　29–31, multiple concurrent narratives: Cassius, Dolabella, Cimber and Tarsus
　　32–4, Brutus and Cassius against Rhodes and Lycia; patching up differences
　　35, Brutus and Cassius move against Norbanus and Saxa in northern Greece
　　　35.3, Symbolon **(TD)** near Mt. Pangaion
36, the narrative threads come back together **(MS)** when Norbanus and Saxa send a request for help to the triumvirs in Italy (cf. 32.3–4)
37–49, Battle of Philippi (Oct. 42 BCE) **(MS)**
　39, Dio's comments on the momentousness of this battle: the end of Republican freedom **(IP)**
　40–1, reinforced by portents and omens, "both before and after" (40.7) **(AN/IP)**
　49.2–4, end of book: note on the fate of Brutus; Caesar's assassins who survived made their way later to Sextus Pompey **(IP)**

(MS)　main story (or narrative thread)
(AN)　analepsis, **(AN²)** analepsis within analepsis, **(AN³)** still further within analepsis
(IP)　internal prolepsis
(EP)　external prolepsis
(TD)　"timeless" digression (or static/dynamic description)

2   Scholarly Judgments on Dio's Treatment of Time

The chronological structure of Dio's narrative, as we can view it in the extant books, has of course received the attention of scholars for a long time. Until very recently, their judgment has been mostly critical, usually faulting Dio for presenting an unclear and inaccurate chronology of events which impedes recognition of their temporal and causal relationships. In 1899, Eduard Schwartz dedicated four columns of his Pauly-Wissowa entry on Dio to such criticism, lamenting the "false connections and confusion" sometimes created by Dio's willingness to forgo strict annalistic structure. For his prime example, Schwartz turns to the treatment of Brutus and Cassius in Book 47, noting its "destruction of synchronisms" and thus of "historical connections."[8] Schwartz seems to see Dio being influenced by a theory of historical writing which prioritizes narrative over details – needless to say, the completely wrong approach in the German scholar's view. Sixty-five years later, Fergus Millar devoted five pages to the same passage of Dio. While Millar can be read as treating Dio more sympathetically, the overall assessment remains critical: pointing out the ways in which Dio's narrative fails to make connections between events in Rome and the East, how it must be supplemented from our other evidence in order to understand what's going on, as well as a couple chronological errors committed by Dio. If anything, Millar damns Dio with faint praise:

> The narrative is straightforward and, within the limits of its style, accurate ... There are no formal indications of chronology; the whole section is treated as an excursus; and the consuls, Dio's normal method of dating, are not given here as they are in the main narrative. A number of dates are indicated implicitly, by the connexions with contemporary events already narrated. But it is hard to believe that Dio's readers, or hearers, could have known (if they cared) what year the narrative had reached unless they already had a considerable acquaintance with the period.[9]

---

8 Schwartz 1899, 1688: "... unter dieser Zerreissung der Synchronismen die Erkenntnis der historischen Zusammenhänge auf das empfindlichste leidet ..." ("under this laceration of the synchronisms, the knowledge of the historical connections suffers at its most delicate point").

9 Millar 1964, 57–8: note the interesting aside in the last sentence, betraying acknowledgment of the different expectations brought to the historical text by ancient vs. modern readers.

Millar at least recognizes that the section on Brutus and Cassius is presented as an excursus, but he fails to fully appreciate that special status when he goes on to complain that Dio does not use his primary method of dating there. A bit further on, we find some telling language on Millar's part as he discusses Dio's treatment of Cassius in Syria:

> The situation here [47.26.1] needed some explanation [as Dio himself notes] … and *Dio was forced to go back* and cover the military history of the province [Syria] from 46 BC onwards – thus having in effect an excursus within an excursus.[10]

Dio *was forced* to embark upon a chronological digression – as if he found a pre-existing narrative and then manipulated it as best he could, perhaps *too* cleverly. Both Schwartz and Millar operate under a two-part assumption: 1) Dio's "normal" procedure was straightforward annalistic; and 2) that was the correct way to write history, or at least the most amenable to the reader's comprehension of events.

A generation later, Alain Gowing still followed the same basic approach. Dio's "usual procedure" was annalistic, at least until he began to recount events in the aftermath of Caesar's assassination. In these books (44–9), Gowing finds that Dio in general organizes his narrative around a specific event.

> All of these books are broken up by occasional digressions, such as 47.20–34 where he diverts to Brutus and Cassius in the East in preparation for his account of the battles at Philippi. *The need for such digressions usually results from Dio's preoccupation with Octavian.* Thus it often happens that material is placed out of chronological order (or occasionally compressed at first and expanded later) to be brought in only when it becomes relevant to Octavian. This frequently results in an erroneous impression of cause and result and a rather unsatisfactory sense of the relationship of events abroad to those in Italy.[11]

---

10 Millar 1964, 58–9 (italics mine). The same notion is reflected in Millar's conclusion (60): "Dio did no more, and tried to do no more, than write down 'what happened' in each area in succession, in correct style and easily digestible form." But at the beginning of the section, Millar had pointed out how no other ancient author chooses such an arrangement for this period.

11 Gowing 1992, 34–5 (italics mine).

Here we find a little more recognition of Dio's own input into the shape taken by his work: Gowing implies, at least, that *Dio* decided to focus on Octavian. But there is still a sense that the historian did not realize, or was caught unawares by, the next step such a focus would necessitate, which was a chronological digression that negatively impacted the reader's comprehension of events.

As recently as two decades ago, with the publication of the *Aufstieg und Niedergang der römischen Welt* volume in which Dio appeared, the traditional negative evaluation of Dio's chronological arrangement largely persisted, though cast in a new form. Andrew Lintott argued that the consular year was, in fact, "not a structural principle of" the *Roman History*, and that Dio rather composed using a thematic approach. Once again, the Brutus and Cassius section of Book 47 serves as the classic example. Despite his new claim, Lintott still finds the results sorely lacking. He blames an ill-suited Herodotean model of following a story through to its end, combined with the richness of material for this period, for producing sections which would seem "to have been written by a second-rate compiler of *annales* rather than a man committed to pragmatic history and the lessons provided by general historical themes."[12] And once again, we find language implying that Dio's narrative had control over him, rather than vice versa: sometimes, if there is a danger of things getting too out of balance, Dio "*resorts to brief annalistic reports* to bring the reader up to date"; "... [o]n the whole, thanks to the *references to the consuls which are slipped in*, we can be reasonably sure to which year each event is assigned, although the overall structure is based on topic."[13] This still assumes that the correct way to write history is purely annalistically, and that Dio's consul references are afterthoughts. Lintott admits as much, parenthetically: "(One must concede that Dio probably did not worry about chronology on what was for him so small a scale ...)."[14]

---

12   Lintott 1997, 2504–8, quote on 2508.
13   Lintott 1997, 2504 (first quotation) and 2508 (second quotation), all italics mine.
14   Lintott 1997, 2509. Swan in the same volume seems trapped by this traditional viewpoint. He begins by claiming that Dio's "end chapters" which round out consular years in the annalistic tradition do not represent "a scholarly or literary product of his own" or respect for tradition (only one in four years have them), but are "fragments" from his annalistic source(s) (1997, 2539). But Swan goes on to argue that Dio did not want to interrupt "the complex empire-wide narrative of civil and external strife that he had written spanning events of these two years," that is, 41 and 40 BCE (48.32.1–33.5). But how is such a narrative not "a literary product of [Dio's] own"?

So, in ninety-eight years of scholarship, it may appear that not much had changed. But already in the 1990s, a new approach was taking shape. We can glimpse an early instance of it in the introduction to the Budé volume for Books 48 and 49 of the *Roman History*. On Book 48, which also features a series of analeptic excurses in many different theaters of action (including Perusia and Sicily) leading up to the pact of Misenum, Freyburger and Roddaz begin by stating that Dio seems *too* attached to the annalistic tradition. But they go on to make an important new claim: that his purpose here is "to show the complexity of the situation and the simultaneity of the events in a great variety of geographical locations."[15] In other words, Dio's analepses do not reveal carelessness or confusion on the author's part, or previously neglected notes inserted after the fact, or the clumsy stitching together of multiple sources.[16] The claim that Dio was an author in control of his material informs my approach to the analyses which follows.

3   Analysis 1: Book 37

My first detailed example comes from Book 37, specifically, a passage in the middle of the book (chapters 20–3) in which Dio breaks the chronological thread of the annalistic structure by discussing Pompey's decision ultimately to give up his extraordinary powers (Table 4.2). As we will see, this chronological wrinkle, though serving essentially as a prolepsis, does not signal itself as such until the end; it incorporates analeptic features; and it is preceded by "timeless" digressions which enhance the narrative suspense it creates.

---

15   Freyburger & Roddaz 1994, xxii ("Quoique conscient des limites de la méthode annalistique, Dion semble trop attaché à cette tradition des historiens anciens pour y renoncer. Il souhaite au contraire bien montrer la complexité des situations et la concomitance des événements dont la localisation géographique est fort variée.") Cf. Hose 1994, 440–1; Juntunen 2013, 467–8.

16   See now the introductory "Notice" in Fromentin & Bertrand 2014, where the original nature of Dio's composition is emphasized (e.g. p. viii); in their view, "les choix narratifs de Dion … sont dictés par une interprétation personnelle des événements" (xii). See also Scott in this volume, who argues that "Dio has selected and arranged his material in a way that reflects the concerns of his own times and that does not likely mirror what he found in his source material."

TABLE 4.2 Narratological analysis of Cassius Dio, *Roman History* Book 37

1–7 Pompey in the East (65 BCE) **(MS)**
[there is a gap in text after chapter 7 – Xiphilinus preserves some matters from 64 BCE, Pompey still in East **(IP)**]
8–9 Julius Caesar's magnificent show as aedile, other end-of-year matters
10 Dio passes quickly over 64 BCE **(MS)**
   just notes two important events, including the death of Catiline **(IP)**
11–14 Mithridates' end (63 BCE) **(MS)**
15–16 Pompey in the East **(MS)**
   15.1, Arabians are now subjects of Rome **(EP)**
   17, digression on the Jews **(TD)**
      18–19, digression on calling the days of the week after the planets **(TD)**
   20–3, discussion of Pompey's decision to give up his powers **(IP – see 24.1)**
      20.2, the nations in Asia to whom he gave laws still use them **(EP)**
      20.3, "a deed forever worthy of admiration" **(IP²)**
      21.3, he added no name to his own, other than Magnus, which he had already obtained **(AN)**
      20–1 *passim*, many honors were voted him in his absence **(both AN and IP, of a sort)**
      22.1, Julius Caesar re-introduced **(AN)**
   22.4, Cato now for the first time came forward to oppose Pompey's honors
      23.1, all that happened while he was gone; but when he came home, no more honors were added, at Pompey's insistence **(IP)**
      24.1, "These things happened over the course of time" (μέν) **(IP)**, τότε δέ Rome was at peace
   24, rationale and procedure for the *augurium salutis* **(TD)**
25–7 general civil disturbances, especially trial of Rabirius **(MS)**
   28, digression on the military flag **(TD)** ending with ἔτι καὶ νῦν **(EP)**
29–38 Catiline **(MS)**
   36.4, the sacrifice and festival voted in thanks of the conspirators' execution "had never happened before from any such cause" **(TD/AN)**
39–41 Catiline's end (62 BCE) **(MS)**
42–4 further political machinations of that year (Cicero, Pompey, Caesar)
45 Clodius and Caesar's wife
46 acquittal of Clodius, other events in the city of 61 BCE **(MS)**
47–8 conflict with Allobroges in Gaul
49–50 Pompey returns to Italy, appoints consuls, but fails in his plans (60 BCE) **(MS)**
51 other events in the city that year

TABLE 4.2 Narratological analysis of Cassius Dio, *Roman History* Book 37 *(cont.)*

52–3 Caesar provokes conflict as praetor in Lusitania in order to gain glory
    52.2, Caesar's dream at Gades, statue of Alexander **(AN)**
54–8 formation of so-called First Triumvirate, instigated by Caesar's wish to be elected consul immediately
    58.2–4, portents of future disaster **(IP)**

(MS)   main story (or narrative thread)
(AN)   analepsis, **(AN²)** analepsis within analepsis, **(AN³)** still further within analepsis
(IP)   internal prolepsis
(EP)   external prolepsis
(TD)   "timeless" digression (or static/dynamic description)

While chapters 20–3 of Book 37 are concerned with Pompey's return to Italy, the narrative flow is actually stopped beginning at chapter 17, which is a "timeless" digression on the Jews. In fact, we can even go further back: before recounting the death of Mithridates in chapters 11–14, Dio moves the annalistic narrative forward rapidly, writing that there were few events of note in 64 BCE, but two amazing ones, one of which is the acquittal of Catiline (37.10). One effect of this maneuver on Dio's part is that the Catilinarian affair is blended with the death of Mithridates, implying that Catiline stepped into the position of Rome's greatest enemy once Mithridates was dead.[17]

With the Pontic regions subdued, Pompey turns his attention to Aretas, king of the Arabians (37.15.1). Dio mentions that the Arabians whom Pompey attacked are now subjects of Rome (thus an external prolepsis). Pompey's next target was Syrian Palestine and the Jews who lived there (37.15.2–16.4), from which arises the digression on that people (chapter 17); this is followed by a two-chapter digression (18–19) on the practice of calling the days of the week after the planets (connected to the main story by the fact that "the day of Saturn," i.e. the Sabbath, plays a role in Pompey's capture of Jerusalem). All of this creates a substantial narrative pause. Remember the situation: Mithridates is dead, but Pompey retains his extraordinary command, huge army, and vast resources, and must decide whether and how to return to Italy. A little like Pompey, the reader, too, is waiting to see what happens.[18] This sus-

17   Bertrand, Coudry, & Fromentin 2016, 307.
18   Although Dio has not yet set up the situation as such in his narrative before the Jewish digression – this does not occur until chapter 20 – most contemporary Roman readers

pense is broken, or apparently so, at the beginning of chapter 20, where Dio states that Pompey, when he had arranged all these things, returned to Pontus, then Asia, Greece, and Italy. But this turns out to be an internal prolepsis, rather than the main narrative thread, since Dio now launches into an excursus on Pompey (chapters 20–3).

Within the Pompey excursus, we have instances of three types of chronological rupture: analepsis, internal prolepsis, external prolepsis; there is also an emphasis on "firsts." We also find what we might call a self-referential analepsis: a comment referring back not so much to a prior event in the narrative as to the earlier narrative itself. The excursus begins with an external prolepsis, as Dio remarks that the nations in Asia to whom Pompey gave laws still use them today (δεῦρο, 37.20.2). As we will see, another reference to Dio's own time occurs soon after the Pompey excursus ends, perhaps bracketing this discussion of Pompey and his decision in a way that brings the readers' consciousness back to their own time. Next comes the main thrust of the digression, which appears as an internal prolepsis and, in a sense, a timeless memorial: Pompey's (eventual) choice to lay down his power was "a deed forever worthy of admiration" (37.20.3). The temporal shifting is enhanced early in the next chapter when Dio notes that Pompey added no name to his own, though he could have, except for Magnus – "which, of course, he had gained even before these achievements" in the East (37.21.3, internal analepsis). Throughout these two chapters, Dio notes that many honors were voted to Pompey in his absence. These statements can be seen as fulfilling all three temporal possibilities: since Dio has already told us how this affair ends, they are in that sense analeptic; since this turns out to be a chronological digression, however, these notes about honors voted to Pompey over the course of 63–61 BCE are also proleptic (since Dio in fact gets to those points in time later on); and within the excursus itself, they provide a narrative backbone, moving the account along as far as Dio is willing to take it here. Next, in chapter 22, two of the prominent characters of the late republican narrative appear: Julius Caesar, whom Dio introduces as if he is now going to become a major player (he has in fact already appeared), and Cato the Younger, who Dio says now for the first time came forward in order to oppose Pompey's honors. In fact, most of the chapter consists of a glowing commendation of Cato's character.[19]

were presumably familiar enough with the course of events to know what lay ahead. Pompey himself has been sufficiently highlighted by Dio in Book 36 to make him the narrative thread.

19 Coudry 2016, 290, notes that Cato's initial portrait here (37.22) is repeated almost word-for-word at his death (43.11.6). Perhaps the latter then serves to create a wrinkle in time without actually interrupting the narrative: the attentive or inquisitive reader of the latter

At last, in chapter 23, Dio begins to make it clear that this whole discussion of Pompey has, in fact, been a chronological digression: "They gave these things to Pompey while he was away, but nothing when he had returned."[20] This too can be seen as fulfilling varied narratological functions: "when he had returned" points us to the future, but Dio has already taken us there. Finally, at 24.1 Dio smoothes out the wrinkle he has created:

> καὶ ταῦτα μὲν ἀνὰ χρόνον ἐγένετο, τότε δὲ οἱ Ῥωμαῖοι πολέμων ἀνάπαυσιν τὸν λοιπὸν τοῦ ἔτους χρόνον ἔσχον, ὥστε καὶ τὸ οἰώνισμα τὸ τῆς ὑγιείας ὠνομασμένον διὰ πάνυ πολλοῦ ποιῆσαι.
>
> All this took place **in the course of time**. **Temporarily** the Romans had a respite from war for **the remainder of the year**, so that they even held the so-called *augurium salutis* **after a very long interval**.

Only here, at the end of the chronological digression, does Dio state explicitly that it has in fact been that. When added to the previous two digressions, we end up with seven chapters in which the narrative pauses (while we, with Dio, jump forward in time and then back again). As if to emphasize that fact, Dio lards this first sentence of chapter 24 with words and expressions related to time. The reference to "the remainder of the year" appears to bring us back to the annalistic track, but in fact the rest of the chapter presents yet another "timeless" digression, as Dio explains the rationale and procedure of the *augurium salutis*. The following fourteen chapters (25–38) narrate events at Rome in 63 BCE, most notably the Catilinarian affair.

Consider what Lintott has to say about Dio's procedure here:

> [Dio] seems to have conceived the Mithridatic campaigns culminating in Pompey's triumphal return as a separate unit which he wished to highlight, while important features of the domestic political background, even for example the *lex Manilia*, were left to find their place in the notes of events at Rome. Later, when he wrote up his notes on various themes, there were not enough indications of time in his material on Pompey in the East for him to make satisfactory links with his material on Rome.[21]

---

passage is taken from 46 BCE back to the late 60s for a moment. Cf. also Dio's remarks on the hypocrisy of Caesar's tears over Pompey's head (42.8.2–3), given his prior actions (commented on by Coudry, p. 296).

20   Cass. Dio 37.23.1: ἀπόντι μὲν δὴ οὖν αὐτῷ ταῦτ' ἔδοσαν, ἐλθόντι δὲ οὐδέν (my translation).
21   Lintott 1997, 2510–11.

Lintott is quite correct that Dio considered Pompey's defeat of Mithridates and his return to Rome as a narrative unit which he was unwilling to break up. But rather than read this as Dio being careless in his note-taking, or misunderstanding the history of the late Republic, it makes more sense to see these wrinkles in time as a way for Dio to highlight this crucial "moment," which was not a single event but a series of decisions and developments – military, political, social, diplomatic – over the course of three years, a process whose ultimate outcome would have enormous consequences for the Republic.[22] Dio could have narrated all this in annalistic fashion as it occurred, in 62 and 61 BCE, or he could have saved it all for Pompey's actual return to Italy. But he chose not to do so: instead, the achronic presentation of Pompey in Book 37 is surrounded by and infused with further chronological ruptures.[23] It is important to point out that Dio was well aware of the wrinkle he had created: later in the same book he twice notes that Pompey was still in Asia in 62 BCE (37.43.1, 44.3), and at 37.49.1 he finally narrates Pompey's return to Italy. In fact, the rest of Book 37 (after chapter 38) moves very quickly through three years' worth of events: from the resolution of the Catilinarian conspiracy to the formation of the so-called First Triumvirate. There is an interesting analepsis near the end of the book (37.52.2): Caesar's dream at Gades and his reaction to seeing a statue of Alexander, while serving as quaestor in 69. Dio places it here, while Caesar is propraetor in Lusitania and just before his deal with Pompey and Crassus, rather than earlier.[24] This authorial choice serves as the culmination of Caesar's numerous but, as of yet, passing mentions in Book 37 (22.1, 37, 44.1–2), in which he is always plotting, laying the groundwork for his own dominance.

4 Analysis 2: Book 43

The other book I would like to look at in detail is 43, one that has not received as much attention for its chronological structuring, in part I imagine because

---

22 Juntunen 2013, 467, also comments on Dio's occasional practice of describing future events in order "to give further emphasis to a point."

23 See Bertrand in this volume, on Dio's narrative construction of large units, specifically Books 36–40, in which he begins to eschew an annalistic treatment; rather, after concentrating on external affairs in Books 38–40, near the end of Book 40 he reviews events at Rome over that period.

24 We lack the beginning of Book 36, where Dio treats events of 69 BCE. Though theoretically possible, it is highly unlikely that he narrated Caesar's time as quaestor in Gades at that point.

there is no lengthy narrative unit that breaks obviously from the main thread. The book begins (Table 4.3) in 46 BCE with Caesar in Africa; the Battle of Thapsus and the suicides of Scipio and Cato are wrapped up in the first twelve chapters, at which point Dio follows Caesar back to Rome, marking the occasion in chapter 13 with comments on the dictator's policy of clemency. We then get a description of the scene in Rome, Caesar's speech to the Senate, and the celebration of his quadruple triumph.

Chapter 22 opens with some subtle touches:

> τὰς μὲν δὴ οὖν ἄλλας τῶν νικητηρίων ἡμέρας ὥς που ἐνενόμιστο διήγαγε· τῇ δὲ τελευταίᾳ ἐπειδὴ ἐκ τοῦ δείπνου ἐγένοντο, ἔς τε τὴν ἑαυτοῦ ἀγορὰν ἐσῆλθε βλαύτας ὑποδεδεμένος καὶ ἄνθεσι παντοδαποῖς ἐστεφανωμένος, καὶ ἐκεῖθεν οἴκαδε παντὸς μὲν ὡς εἰπεῖν τοῦ δήμου παραπέμποντος αὐτόν, πολλῶν δὲ ἐλεφάντων λαμπάδας φερόντων ἐκομίσθη. τὴν γὰρ ἀγορὰν τὴν ἀπ' αὐτοῦ κεκλημένην **κατεσκεύαστο**· καὶ ἔστι μὲν περικαλλεστέρα τῆς Ῥωμαίας, τὸ δὲ ἀξίωμα τὸ ἐκείνης ἐπηύξησεν, ὥστε καὶ μεγάλην αὐτὴν ὀνομάζεσθαι.

> The first days of the triumph he [sc. Caesar] passed as was customary, but on the last day, **after they had finished dinner, he entered his own forum** wearing slippers and garlanded with all kinds of flowers; thence he proceeded homeward with practically the entire populace escorting him, while many elephants carried torches. For **he had had the forum built** which was called after himself, and it is distinctly more beautiful than the Roman Forum; yet it had increased the reputation of the other so that that was called the Great Forum.[25]

Dio begins with remarkable apparent nonchalance: "after they had finished dinner, he entered his own forum." Initially, the historian continues to describe that evening's events; but then he pauses, with a *gar* clause, to explain that Caesar "had had the forum built which was called after himself." Dio then switches to the present tense and his own day, remarking on the status of this forum and of the Roman Forum, now called "Great." This is the first of seven such external prolepses in the rest of Book 43 (twenty-nine chapters).[26]

Dio continues with his description of the festivities at Rome, in the course of which he offers up a "timeless" digression on the giraffe (καμηλοπάρδαλις,

---

25   Cass. Dio 43.22.1–2, slightly adapted from Cary.
26   See Pelling 2006, 271 n. 21. These are: 24.2 (silk canopy at gladiatorial contests), 26.1 (the Julian calendar), 44.2–3 and 4–5 (*Imperator* as name and title), 46.5–6 (the practice of naming suffect consuls), 49.1 (position of the Rostra), 51.3 (*aediles Cereales*).

brought to the city now by Caesar for the first time), as well as two mentions of customs introduced by Caesar which still exist in Dio's day: the silk canopy at the gladiatorial contests (a barbarian custom that has come down "*even* to our time") and the reform of the calendar, which receives a short chapter of its own (26). Throughout this section there is a noticeable increase in narratorial interventions such as "I will record/omit." Chapters 28–40 of Book 43 cover events surrounding the Battle of Munda in Spain and carry the narrative into 45 BCE. As with many of the military campaigns in these books, this unit contains an analepsis to set up the situation in that theater, tracing the actions of Gnaeus Pompey over the previous year or so (43.29–30).

After describing the death of Gnaeus Pompey and one of his lieutenants after the battle, Dio marks the transition to Caesar's triumphant return to Rome with his own comments on what was to come: "Caesar, too, would doubtless have chosen to fall there, at the hands of those who were still resisting and amid the glory of war, in preference to the fate he met not long afterward ..."[27] Dio then notes the omen of the palm shoot at the site of the Battle of Munda, which (in hindsight) concerned not Caesar but his young grand-nephew Octavius; but, Dio says, "as Caesar did not know this ... he showed no moderation, but was filled with arrogance, as if immortal" (43.41.3). Here, the knowledge possessed by the author is both passed on to the reader and explicitly denied to the protagonist, thus heightening the pathos of the moment – one of the interesting ways in which historical narrative, where the reader knows the ending, must employ different techniques from fiction.

TABLE 4.3   Narratological analysis of Cassius Dio, *Roman History* Book 43

1–9 Julius Caesar in Africa (46 BCE) **(MS)**
    9.4, the region we call Africa **(EP)**
    9.5, Scipio flees and commits suicide **(IP)**
10–12 death of Cato, resolution of African affairs
13 Dio comments on Caesar's policy of clemency
    13.4, reference to Caesar's later *Anticato* in response to Cicero **(IP)**
14–27 Caesar in Rome: speech, triumph
    22, the Forum Iulium: Caesar enters "his own forum"; then Dio explains that he had had it built **(AN)**
    23, Dio will pass over many spectacles, but he will record the καμηλοπάρδαλις **(TD)**

---

27   Cass. Dio 43.41.1: εἵλετο δ' ἂν καὶ ὁ Καῖσαρ ἐκεῖ που πρός τε τῶν ἔτι ἀνθεστηκότων καὶ ἐν τῇ τοῦ πολέμου δόξῃ πεπτωκέναι μᾶλλον ἢ ὅπερ οὐκ ἐς μακρὰν ἔπαθεν....

TABLE 4.3 Narratological analysis of Cassius Dio, *Roman History* Book 43 *(cont.)*

> 24.2, Caesar also introduced a silk canopy at the gladiatorial contests, a barbarian custom that has comedown "even to us" for the luxury of women **(EP)**
> 26, he established the calendar as it currently stands **(EP)**

28–40 Caesar and his forces in Spain (Munda)
> 29–31.1, analepsis to set up situation in Spain (Cn. Pompey) **(AN)**
> 33.1 transition to 45 BCE **(MS)**
>> 41, Caesar would no doubt rather have died in Spain than suffer the fate which soon awaited him; the omen of the palm shoot was directed toward Octavian rather than him **(IP)**

42–6 triumphs and honors for Caesar in Rome
> 43.2–5, Caesar had always been too concerned about his appearance; quips from Sulla and Cicero **(AN)**, concluded by narratorial explanation for this digression
> 44.2–3, invention of *Imperator* as a sort of personal name, τὸ καὶ νῦν ... **(EP)**
> 44.4–5, explanation of current custom regarding title *Imperator*, granted again to a victorious emperor **(EP)**
> 45.4, the statue of Caesar next to those of the kings and Brutus provoked the plot against him **(IP)**

46.1 Dio notes that not all this happened "on one day"
> 46.2–6, first time a replacement consul was named for someone who withdrew before end of year; comment on current custom, as well as what his practice will be in the narrative going forward **(EP)**

47–51 further arrangements by Caesar in 45 and beginning of 44 BCE (introduced at 49.1) **(MS)**
> 49.1, rostra moved back to its current position **(EP)**
> 49.2, Caesar never finished theater, it was later completed by Augustus **(IP)**
> 50.3–5, refounding of Carthage and Corinth, which had been laid to ruins **(AN)**
> 51.3, two plebeian aediles given title *Cereales*, a custom καὶ ἐς τόδε **(EP)**
> 51.4–5, among the praetors for the year was Publius Ventidius, who had fought against Rome in the Social War **(AN)**, been captured and led in triumph, but later pardoned, entered the Senate, and eventually conquered the Parthians and held a triumph over them **(IP)**
> 51 *passim*, emphasis on the arrangements for future years which Caesar made **(IP)**

(MS) main story (or narrative thread)
(AN) analepsis, **(AN²)** analepsis within analepsis, **(AN³)** still further within analepsis
(IP) internal prolepsis
(EP) external prolepsis
(TD) "timeless" digression (or static/dynamic description)

The rest of Book 43 consists of two sections: one on Caesar's additional triumph and honors in Rome (chapters 42–6), and one on his further arrangements and projects at the end of 45 BCE and the beginning of 44 (chapters 47–51). Here we find a fascinating mix of analepses, internal prolepses, and external prolepses as Dio moves the narrative slowly toward the fateful day to which he has just alerted the reader (and which is not actually narrated until the next book):[28]

- 43.43.2–5: When the issue of Caesar's being overly concerned about his appearance arises, Dio embarks on a sort of review of Caesar's lifetime of fashion choices, which ends with quips from Sulla and Cicero about this "ill-girt fellow." Dio explicitly comments on his digression here, saying that he has inserted it so that no one will be ignorant of the stories told about Caesar – perhaps another way of foreshadowing his imminent disappearance from the narrative.
- 43.44: Dio describes the Senate's granting the title *imperator* to Caesar as a name – emphasizing the break with tradition and the flattery involved – as well as how the title functions in his own day.
- 43.45.4: A brief internal prolepsis again points forward to the conspiracy against the dictator, in connection with the statue of Caesar being placed next to those of the kings and L. Junius Brutus.
- 43.49.1–2: This alternation – of current customs which began with Caesar, followed by internal prolepses – is repeated twice more. The first pair, here, refers to Augustus, who finished the theater begun by Caesar.
- 43.50: Sandwiched between those pairs is an analeptic chapter, of a sort. Dio notes that some people compared Caesar's laws and extension of the pomerium to the actions of Sulla, but that Caesar prided himself on his clemency in opposition to Sulla's famous cruelty. This evocation of the earlier dictator (the second in this book, after 43.43.4) is followed by another source of pride for Caesar: the re-founding of Carthage and Corinth. Dio highlights these cities' reappearance in the narrative with a rhetorical asyndeton, calling them πόλεις ἀρχαίας λαμπρὰς ἐπισήμους ἀπολωλυίας ("cities ancient, brilliant, famous,

---

28 See Pelling 2006, 257–62 on Dio's use of "biostructuring," that is, the employment of biographical details to create a larger structure for the historical narrative, and especially to close off narrative "rings"; at pp. 258–9 Pelling discusses the end of Book 43. Coudry 2016 examines the possibility of extending the "biographical principle" of the imperial books to those of the late Republic.

destroyed," 50.4), and claiming that Caesar not only refounded those cities but did so "in memory of their former inhabitants."
- 43.51.3–5: Finally, the figure of Publius Ventidius receives special attention almost at the very end of the book, via the same sort of alternation as at 43.49.1–2. The reason for his appearance is his selection as praetor – amazing, since he had been captured by the Romans during the Social War and paraded in the triumph of Pompeius Strabo, only to be released and later enrolled in the Senate. After this analepsis, Dio goes on to allude to Ventidius later celebrating his own triumph over the Parthians (in 39 BCE), thus completing the circle of Fortune. It is interesting, however, that Dio himself does not comment on this irony or the vicissitudes of Fortune here, leaving the narrative to speak for itself. At the same time, the combination of analepsis and prolepsis as Book 43 comes to a close pulls readers up from the details and encourages them to consider the broader span of events.[29]

Book 44 then begins with two chapters on the heinousness of Caesar's murder and the impossibility of moderate democracy in a city as powerful as Rome. Given the various theaters of action and the number of important precedents for the future monarchy established by Caesar, Dio in Book 43 has many reasons to be moving around in time. As a sort of proto-emperor, Caesar makes for a good foil with Augustus and subsequent *principes*. His clemency invited not just the explicit comparison with Sulla (above), but also implicitly with Augustus and even Septimius Severus. Creating these chronological wrinkles just before Caesar's assassination – a key moment for the structure of Dio's work (and any student of Roman history) – increases suspense and adds to the weight of his history, in a similar fashion to his delaying of Pompey's return to Italy.

5   Conclusion

A concern for keeping the overarching narrative of Roman history as a whole in the reader's mind may help explain many of the decisions Dio made concerning the chronological structure of his work. To return to where I started,

---

29   Cf. Bertrand, Coudry, & Fromentin 2016, 312–14, who note a number of political themes (especially that of *pleonexia*) highlighted by Dio's *achronie*, which moves the reader's attention from the short-term to the long-term processes of Roman history.

with Book 48, after the opening chapters pointing to past, present, and future, Dio covers events of 41 to 38 BCE within a fairly clear annalistic framework: new consuls are introduced in chapters 4, 15, 34, and 43. But even this basic presentation can be adjusted in subtle ways. The consular year of 40 BCE enters the narrative as follows (48.15.1):

ἐκείνης δ'οὖν ἐπί τε Γναίου Καλουίνου δεύτερον καὶ ἐπ' Ἀσινίου Πωλίωνος ὑπάτων ἁλούσης καὶ τἆλλα τὰ ἐν τῇ Ἰταλίᾳ, τὰ μὲν βίᾳ τὰ δὲ ἐθελοντί, τῷ Καίσαρι προσεχώρησε.

After the capture of Perusia in the consulship of Gnaeus Calvinus (who was serving for the second time) and Asinius Pollio, the other places in Italy also went over to Caesar, partly as the result of force and partly of their own accord.

The new consuls are subordinated to a genitive absolute, as if to reflect their separation from the real historical action. More bluntly, when introducing the consuls of 41 BCE, Dio writes that "Publius Servilius and Lucius Antonius became consuls in name, but in reality it was Antonius and Fulvia."[30] As in previous books, even while maintaining the annalistic framework, Dio uses chronological ruptures to mark the breakdown of the republican system. Between chapters 15 and 27 of Book 48, the events of 40 BCE are narrated; but only four chapters in that stretch are actually devoted to that year. The rest consist of analeptic presentations of events in three different theaters (Sicily, Africa, and Parthia/Syria), the last one containing a further analepsis to explain how Labienus ended up leading Parthians to war against Romans. This is all preceded by a prolepsis instigated by mention of the flight of Livia and her child, the future emperor Tiberius, from Italy under Octavian's rule. Here, Dio does explicitly comment on the "most paradoxical nature" of events – that these two, at that time in flight from Octavian, would one day be the most important components of the imperial family.[31]

---

30   Cass. Dio 48.4.1: ... ὀνόματι μὲν ὅ τε Σερουίλιος ὁ Πούπλιος καὶ ὁ Ἀντώνιος ὁ Λούκιος, ἔργῳ δὲ οὗτός τε καὶ ἡ Φουλουία ὑπάτευσαν.

31   Cass. Dio 48.15.4: ὥστε καὶ τοῦτο ἐν τοῖς παραδοξοτάτοις συμβῆναι· ἥ τε γὰρ Λιουία αὕτη ἡ τὸν Καίσαρα τότε φυγοῦσα μετὰ ταῦτα αὐτῷ ἐγήματο, καὶ ὁ Τιβέριος οὗτος ὁ σὺν τοῖς τοκεῦσι τότε ἐκδρὰς τὴν αὐτοκράτορα ἀρχὴν αὐτοῦ διεδέξατο. ("This, again, was one of the strangest whims of fate; for this Livia, who then fled from Caesar, later on was married to him, and this Tiberius, who then took flight with his parents, succeeded Caesar in the office of emperor.")

Scholars have often deemed such a narrative structure scattered and unfocused. But when we are faced with sections of narrative which seem confused (or confusing) and out of order, it might help to set aside our own concern with chronological precision (perhaps a bias resulting from awarding pride of place to institutional and legal history) and to examine other possibilities of arrangement. As the inheritor of a double historiographical tradition – Greek and Roman – Dio had numerous options available to him. He was also writing for an audience that knew how the story of the late Republic ended and, most likely, that had greater familiarity with cultural and institutional details than we do, despite the separation of 250 years. Finally, Dio was faced with a mass of often conflicting material which may, itself, not have been overly concerned with exact synchronisms between events in different theaters of action. Sometimes, the quickest route between two points was not a straight line.[32]

Bibliography

Bertrand, E., Coudry, M., & Fromentin, V. (2016) "Temporalité historique et formes du récit. Les modalités de l'écriture dans les livres tardo-républicains", in V. Fromentin *et al.* (eds.), *Cassius Dion: nouvelles lectures* (Bordeaux): 303–16.

Coudry, M. (2016) "Figures et récit dans les livres républicains (livres 36 à 44)", in V. Fromentin *et al.* (eds.), *Cassius Dion: nouvelles lectures* (Bordeaux): 287–301.

de Jong, I. J. F. & Nünlist, R. (eds.) (2007) *Time in Ancient Greek Literature* (Studies in Ancient Greek Narrative, Volume 2), Leiden & Boston.

de Jong, I. J. F., Nünlist, R., & Bowie, A. (eds.) (2004) *Narrators, Narratees, and Narratives in Ancient Greek Literature* (Studies in Ancient Greek Narrative, Volume 1), Leiden & Boston.

Freyburger, M.-L. & Roddaz, J.-M. (1994) *Dion Cassius: Histoire romaine, Livres 48 & 49*, Paris.

Fromentin, V. & Bertrand, E. (2014) *Dion Cassius: Histoire romaine, Livre 47*, Paris.

Genette, G. (1980) *Narrative Discourse: An Essay in Method*, translated by J. E. Lewin, Ithaca, NY.

Gowing, A. M. (1992) *The Triumviral Narratives of Appian and Cassius Dio*, Ann Arbor.

---

32 I would like to thank above all Josiah Osgood, for his comments and encouragement on early drafts of this paper; also the organizers and members of the Cassius Dio Network, whose knowledge of and enthusiasm for the historian have made this project so enjoyable and enriching.

Hidber, T. (2004) "Cassius Dio", in I. J. F. de Jong, R. Nünlist, & A. Bowie (eds.), *Narrators, Narratees, and Narratives in Ancient Greek Literature* (Leiden & Boston): 187–99.

Hose, M. (1994) *Erneuerung der Vergangenheit: die Historiker im Imperium Romanum von Florus bis Cassius Dio*, Stuttgart.

Juntunen, K. (2013) "The Lost Books of Cassius Dio", *Chiron* 43, 459–86.

Lindholmer, M. (forthcoming) "Exploiting Conventions: Dio's Late Republic and the Annalistic Tradition", in C. H. Lange & J. M. Madsen (eds.), *Cassius Dio the Historian: Methods and Approaches* (Leiden & Boston).

Lintott, A. W. (1997) "Cassius Dio and the History of the Late Roman Republic", in *Aufstieg und Niedergang der römischen Welt* 2.34.3: 2497–523.

Millar, F. (1964) *A Study of Cassius Dio*, Oxford.

Pelling, C. (2006) "Breaking the Bounds: Writing about Julius Caesar", in B. McGing & J. Mossman (eds.), *The Limits of Ancient Biography* (Swansea): 255–80.

Rich, J. (2016) "Annalistic Organization and Book Division in Dio's Books 1–35", in V. Fromentin *et al.* (eds.), *Cassius Dion: nouvelles lectures* (Bordeaux): 271–86.

Rood, T. (1998) *Thucydides: Narrative and Explanation*, Oxford.

Schwartz, E. (1899) "Cassius (40)", in A. Pauly, G. Wissowa, & W. Kroll (eds.), *Realencyclopädie der classischen Altertumswissenschaft* (Stuttgart): III/2, 1684–722.

Swan, P. M. (1997) "How Cassius Dio Composed his Augustan Books: Four Studies", in *Aufstieg und Niedergang der römischen Welt* 2.34.3, 2524–57.

CHAPTER 5

Dio the Deviant: Comparing Dio's Late Republic and the Parallel Sources

Mads Ortving Lindholmer

Dio has traditionally been seen as an unoriginal source for the late Republic; despite important revisions, this conclusion continues to permeate even newer scholarship.[1] This is seen clearly in the argument of Rees from 2011, namely that Dio differs from the parallel sources, "if he differs at all, only in the *intensity* of his account."[2] This assertion is echoed in other recent works[3] although no detailed comparison of Dio's account of the late Republic with the parallel sources has emerged on which to base this argument. Indeed, no author in the recent edited volumes on Dio focuses directly on Dio and the sources for the late Republic, despite the inclusion of a number of chapters devoted to *Quellenforschung*.[4]

In this chapter, I will explore the relationship between Dio and the other sources for the late Republic. It is important to underline that I will not focus on traditional *Quellenforschung*, as the main objective is not to identify the source or sources that Dio used for his narrative but rather to explore what Dio's deviations and parallels in relation to other sources can tell us about his interpretative framework for the late Republic. In contrast to the widely-held view that Dio was unoriginal,[5] I will argue that he is distinctive, both on a detailed level and in his grander interpretation of the late Republic, and that his consistent deviations from the parallel sources aim to present political competition as the central destructive factor of the late Republic.[6] This political competition is institutional in the sense that it emerges from the institutional

---

1 I would like to thank Christopher Baron and Josiah Osgood for their valuable comments and suggestions for improving this chapter. I am also grateful to Josiah Osgood for inviting me to the wonderful conference in Fiesole from which this volume emerged.
2 Rees 2011, 4.
3 Lintott 1997, 2498–501; Sion-Jenkis 2000, 184–5; Kemezis 2014, 103.
4 Fromentin *et al.* 2016; Lange & Madsen 2016a. See e.g. Westall 2016 in the latter volume.
5 See e.g. Millar 1964, 46; Rees 2011, 4; Kemezis 2014, 93.
6 For this argument, see also Lindholmer 2016; 2018a; 2018c; forthcoming b.

setup of the Republic with its unavoidable competition for offices and prestige.[7] The institutional character of this problem is evidenced in Dio's consistent portrayals of all players as engaged in this destructive competition.[8] It is thus not tied merely to a few problematic individuals but is a pervasive institutional problem. As I have argued elsewhere, problematic competition had existed since the dawn of Dio's Republic, in contrast to the idealized accounts of the early and mid-Republic in other authors.[9] However, it is only in the late Republic, due to the emergence of empire and the influx of resources, that this competition becomes fundamentally destructive in Dio.[10] Dio's central distinguishing feature, then, is that he focuses on the institutional problems of the Roman political world, whereas the parallel sources present a character-driven narrative where the individual is at the center. These institutional problems revolve around the political competition that was an integral part of the republican system. Through these conclusions, I will furthermore argue that traditional *Quellenforschung* attempting to reconstruct lost sources on the basis of Dio is problematic.

However, *Quellenforschung* in fact constitutes a significant part of the research on Dio's republican books so far: Schwartz argued that Dio relied substantially on Livy for the Republic and Augustan age,[11] but in 1979 Manuwald severely undermined the widespread support enjoyed by Schwartz's conclusion,[12] and the previous consensus on this point does indeed appear surprising in view of the meager summaries of Livy's account available for comparison. Dio's use of the contemporary historians Aufidius Bassus, Cremutius Cordus, Asinius Pollio, Aelius Tubero, and Sallust (i.e., his *Histories*) has also received scholarly attention, but no sizeable parts of their works, even

---

7   On Dio's focus on institutional problems, see also Coudry in this volume, who argues that Dio conceives of *ambitus* as an institutional rather than a moral problem. Hinard 2005 also notes Dio's interest in institutional matters but does not explore Dio's broader political interpretations.

8   Dio asserts that only Cato took part in public life without an eye to personal gain: 37.57.3. See, however, also Dio's praise of Catulus: 36.30.5.

9   Lindholmer 2018a.

10 The importance of empire in this transformation is, for example, clearly set out in the speech of Maecenas where Dio writes that "ever since we were led outside the peninsula and crossed over to many continents and many islands, filling the whole sea and the whole earth with our name and power, nothing good has been our lot" (ἀφ' οὗ δὲ ἔξω αὐτῆς ἐξήχθημεν, καὶ ἐπὶ πολλὰ καὶ τῶν ἠπείρων καὶ τῶν νήσων ἐπεραιώθημεν, καὶ πᾶσαν μὲν τὴν θάλασσαν πᾶσαν δὲ τὴν γῆν καὶ τοῦ ὀνόματος καὶ τῆς δυνάμεως ἡμῶν ἐνεπλήσαμεν, οὐδενὸς χρηστοῦ μετεσχήκαμεν, 52.16.2). For this problem of institutional competition in Dio, see especially Lindholmer 2016; 2018a; 2018c; forthcoming b.

11 Schwartz 1899, 1697–714. For previous works see Haupt 1882; 1884.

12 Manuwald 1979, 168 and *passim*.

in epitomated form, survive and the conclusions therefore stand on rather shaky ground.[13] The wider reasons behind Dio's choices are, however, left untouched by most scholars of traditional *Quellenforschung*.

Through a focus on Lucullus' command, the *lex Gabinia*, and the Catilinarian conspiracy, I will, by contrast, argue that Dio deviated from a dominant tradition seen in the parallel sources in order to emphasize the destructiveness of institutional competition and the consequent untenability of the late Republic. I have chosen these portions of Dio's work as they represent both internal and external matters and both longer and shorter stretches of narrative. The consistency of Dio's focus on institutional competition across these different narratives is, therefore, all the more striking and cannot be dismissed as merely connected to a single part of the narrative or interpretation. The main sources chosen for comparison are Appian, Plutarch, Velleius, and Sallust and to a lesser extent Livy's *Periochae*, in addition to Suetonius who touches upon the period in his biography of Julius Caesar. In relation to the *Periochae*, it is of course important to remember that it only preserves a tiny part of Livy's original narrative. However, it might still give an impression of Livy's basic presentation of key events which can then be compared to Dio. This selection also carries with it the exclusion of other authors of which Orosius, Florus, Valerius Maximus, and Cicero should be mentioned. However, the former two mainly touch upon the foreign wars of Rome without according much attention to the part of Lucullus' campaigns that survive in Dio, whereas the writings of the latter two are not structured as historical narratives. These four sources are consequently ill-suited to be compared to Dio's narrative of the events chosen here.

1   Lucullus and His Command

The narrative surrounding the removal of Lucullus from his command in the Third Mithridatic War is central in Dio's Book 36 and covers the first seventeen chapters. Dio thus accords the event far more attention than the parallel sources and also has a decidedly different focus: whereas the parallel sources focus on Lucullus the individual from a moral perspective, Dio uses Lucullus to explore the problems of political competition. Furthermore, Dio includes unique narrative material concerning the highly destructive competition among the generals, competition which allowed Rome's enemies easy successes. The

---

13   Aufidius Bassus: Marx 1933, 325–6; Levi 1937; Townend 1961, 232; Manuwald 1979, 258. Cordus: Millar 1964, 85; Swan 1987, 286. Pollio: Micalella 1896; Sordi 1971, 170–2; Lintott 1997, 2519–20. Tubero: Zecchini 1978. Sallust's *Histories*: Haupt 1882, 143–6. For a newer treatment, see now Westall 2016.

narrative surrounding Lucullus' command has thus been purposefully shaped to focus on the destructiveness of institutional competition, in contrast to the parallel sources.

This is clearly seen from a brief overview of the different sources: Appian largely ignores Lucullus' command, and the other sources treat it far more briefly than Dio. In one perspective, seen in Velleius, Lucullus is disinclined to end the war because "he was a victim to the love of money (*pecuniae pellebatur cupidine*)"[14] and hereafter the power-hungry Pompey takes over.[15] Velleius furthermore judges Lucullus harshly as he relinquishes his command: "he was the first to set the example for our present lavish extravagance" (*profusae huius ... luxuriae primus auctor fuit*).[16] This is clearly in line with Velleius' view of the Republic as degenerating into luxury; he ignores the political realm and only devotes a single chapter to the event. In a contrasting perspective, seen in Plutarch and the Livian *Periochae*, Lucullus is a glorious general, robbed of his victory by the immoral and mutinying soldiers.[17] Fortune, Lucullus' own failings, and the envy of the popular leaders are all mentioned by Plutarch,[18] but the most important immediate factor is instead Clodius, who incites the soldiers to mutiny and who "most of all vitiated (τὸ μάλιστα ... διειργασμένον) the undertakings of Lucullus."[19] The *Periochae* seems in agreement with Plutarch, as it argues that "a mutiny of the soldiers ... kept Lucullus from pursuing Mithridates and Tigranes and obtaining the ultimate victory."[20] These sources, then, focus on the individuals Lucullus, Clodius, and Pompey, while the political institutions of Rome are mostly ignored.

Dio's focus, on the other hand, is on the broader functioning of Roman politics, particularly the connection between competition and foreign commands. However, he does not neglect the individuals and their actions but instead uses these to present his interpretation. This is seen in the beginning of Dio's narrative where Lucullus is removed after he failed to follow up a victory over Tigranes: "Because of this he was charged *by the citizens, as well as others* (παρά τε τοῖς ἄλλοις καὶ παρὰ τοῖς πολίταις) with refusing to end the war, in order that he might retain his command (ἀρχή) a longer time."[21] It is

---

14   Vell. Pat. 2.33.1.
15   Vell. Pat. 2.33.2.
16   Vell. Pat. 2.33.4.
17   Liv. *Per.* 98; Plut. *Luc.* 19, 34.5.
18   Plut. *Luc.* 33.
19   Plut. *Luc.* 34.1.
20   Liv. *Per.* 98. Adapted from Schlesinger 1959.
21   Cass. Dio 36.2.1 (my emphasis). All translations of Dio are from Cary 1914–1927, and for other quoted authors, I have likewise used the Loeb Classical Library. Any adaptations of the translations have been noted.

noteworthy that the alleged object of Lucullus' desire is not money, as in Velleius' account, but rather the perpetuation of power which has convincingly been shown by Christopher Burden-Strevens to be a central problem in Dio's account of the late Republic.[22] Lucullus is thus indeed problematic himself in Dio's version, but this is not couched in typical *Dekadenz* rhetoric as seen in Velleius and his focus on luxury and money. The narrative centers rather on the problematic functioning of competition where Lucullus and the other late republican generals, especially Pompey and Caesar, cling to commands, which was a central challenge to the authority of the Senate in Dio's late Republic. That the accusation against Lucullus can be made convincingly by a broad spectrum of individuals, "citizens as well as others" as Dio puts it, furthers the critique of the late Republic.

Dio's narrative again deviates from the parallel sources' in his treatment of Clodius and in fact describes two mutinies. The first is at Nisibis where he echoes Plutarch and blames Clodius and his "innate love of revolution"[23] for the mutiny. Dio's is the only account to emphasize the perfidy that Clodius the mutineer was married to Lucullus' sister.[24] Dio then comments on the second mutiny:

> ἐταράχθησαν δὲ καὶ τότε ἄλλως τε καὶ ἐπειδὴ τὸν Ἀκίλιον τὸν ὕπατον, ὅς τῷ Λουκούλλῳ διάδοχος δι' ἅπερ εἶπον ἐξεπέμφθη, πλησιάζοντα ἐπύθοντο· ἐν γὰρ ὀλιγωρίᾳ αὐτὸν ... ἐποιοῦντο.

> At this time, however, they became turbulent again, largely because they heard that Acilius, the consul, who had been sent out to relieve Lucullus for the reasons mentioned, was drawing near, and they accordingly regarded Lucullus with contempt.[25]

Whereas Plutarch blames Clodius for the single mutiny he records, Dio asserts that the political machinations in Rome directed against Lucullus are the real cause of his trouble, and Dio underlines the importance of this factor by the emphatic particle -περ, attached to the relative pronoun. It is thus the constant competition, manifested both by Lucullus' ambition and the rivalrous attack on him from Rome, which creates the problems in Dio's account – a noteworthy contrast to the character-driven narratives of the parallel sources.

---

22   Burden-Strevens 2015, 162–80; Burden-Strevens 2016, 3–11. See also Eckstein 2004, 279–88.
23   Cass. Dio 36.14.4.
24   Cass. Dio 36.14.4.
25   Cass. Dio 36.14.4.

This institutional focus is again seen in Dio's detailed description of intense egoistical competition within the group of generals sent to relieve Lucullus, and it is important to note that this narrative element is only found in Dio. Lucullus is here undecided as to his next step because he is unaided by his rival generals, and Dio emphasizes the perplexity of Lucullus in this situation.[26] Marcius Rex, who had been consul the year before and was on his way to Cilicia, declines Lucullus' request for aid on "the pretext (πρόσχημα)"[27] that his soldiers refused to follow him. Dio underlines the falseness of this by his use of πρόσχημα and even tells us that the main mutineer, Clodius, after he had fled the army of Lucullus, was welcomed and put in command of the fleet by Marcius because of their relation by marriage.[28] This is an important critique from Dio as Marcius here puts family relations and the competition with Lucullus above the interests of the Republic. After the soldiers of Lucullus deserted *en masse*, he also desisted from protecting Roman lands as his replacement Acilius was drawing near.[29] Furthermore, Acilius too is roundly criticized, as Dio writes that he delayed his arrival after realizing that it was now too late to rob Lucullus of his victory.[30] The result of this egoistical competition is devastating and immediate: "the soldiers of Mithridates won back almost all his domain and caused great havoc in Cappadocia."[31] Dio's narrative is here distinctive, as the focus is no longer on the incompetence or pyrrhic greatness of Lucullus but instead on the destructive functioning of institutional competition which severely undermines Rome's interests. As a consequence of this competition, Mithridates is given easy successes and the mutineer Clodius is rewarded with a command. Here Dio's narrative of the events breaks off and leaves the reader with a forceful reminder of the dangers of excessive competition.

This unique narrative of competition is far too complex to have been invented, and Dio thus shows himself to be a careful selector of material as the narrative facilitates the presentation of institutional competition as the central problem of the late Republic. In conclusion, Dio does have similarities with the other authors, but his institutional focus and criticisms are clearly different from the parallel sources, and he even includes unique narrative material as support. Dio's account is not bereft of the exploration of individuals found in the parallel evidence. However, this element is not an end in itself but rather a

---

26   Cass. Dio 36.23.3. Adapted from Cary 1914–1927.
27   Cass. Dio 36.17.2.
28   Cass. Dio 36.17.2.
29   Cass. Dio 36.17.2.
30   Cass. Dio 36.17.1. Adapted from Cary 1914–1927.
31   Cass. Dio 36.17.1.

means to communicate and strengthen Dio's critique of the political system of Rome which is his main area of investigation. Furthermore, Dio describes every single general above as engaged in destructive competition and thereby portrays this as an institutional problem rather than connected to a few individuals.

2 The *lex Gabinia*

The narrative surrounding the *lex Gabinia* constitutes the first treatment of internal politics in Rome in Dio's Book 36, and the law stands as the central internal event of the book given that fourteen whole chapters are devoted to it. Dio again here deviates significantly from the tradition seen in the parallel sources in his focus on institutional competition. In contrast to the parallel sources, Dio is not merely interested in Pompey but rather deviates purposefully to portray every single player as engaged in selfish competition. Through this, Dio again portrays the competition as an institutional problem rather than connected to individuals. It is a narrative essentially without heroes.[32]

Dio is also distinctive through the sheer length of his narrative. The other sources treat this event far more superficially. Appian does not include the enactment of the *lex Gabinia* itself, while Livy's account of the lead-up to this law is not incorporated in the *Periochae*.[33] Velleius does include the *lex* and continues his focus on the individual: he criticizes the immense power given to Pompey but asserts that a similar grant of power had been accorded Antonius (in 74), which had caused no nervousness in Rome: "sometimes the personality (*persona*) of the recipient of such power, just as it renders the precedent more or less dangerous, increases or diminishes its invidiousness."[34] The importance of the individual thus dominates the political institutions. The significant factor here is, therefore, Pompey's character and the more minor figure of Gabinius is consequently ignored. Plutarch echoes Velleius in his focus on Pompey, unsurprisingly given his biographical structure, and also merely mentions Gabinius as proposer of the *lex*. He does note that Gabinius is the intimate of Pompey but no collusion is suggested.[35] However, in contrast to Velleius, Plutarch asserts that the populace supported the law and even acted threateningly.

---

32   One of the very few exceptions is Catulus whom I treat below.
33   Liv. *Per.* 99.
34   Vell. Pat. 2.31.4.
35   Plut. *Pomp.* 25.2.

Dio first of all deviates from the tradition in giving by far the fullest treatment of the event, illustrating it through speeches given to Pompey, Gabinius, and Catulus.[36] This indicates the enormous importance with which Dio invested this event, which is a testament to his institutional focus; the significance of the *lex Gabinia* is inherently institutional in nature as it breaks the constitutional norms of Rome and creates a dangerous precedent. To Dio, furthermore, the *lex* is also a product of the problematic political competition in the late Republic, as an ambitious dynast with the support of the people is able to trump the Senate and the upright but unavailing Catulus, and push through the first of the deeply problematic extraordinary commands. Pompey is of course important here, but Dio rather focuses on the changing balance of power between ambitious individuals and the Senate, which is both a cause and a result of the problematic institutional competition. The *lex Gabinia*, in short, is central to Dio's narrative of the end of the Republic because of its long-term consequences for the political system[37] rather than for Pompey personally.

This significance of the *lex Gabinia* to Dio's work is further supported when contrasted with the comparatively meager space, merely two chapters, devoted to the later *lex Manilia*. This indicates that Dio had already made his exploration of the problematic extraordinary commands in the narrative surrounding the *lex Gabinia* and saw another grand exposition as superfluous. Plutarch and Velleius, by contrast, give roughly equal space to the laws but never appear interested in the wider political ramifications of Pompey's great power. Dio is thus singularly interested in the institutional and constitutional ramifications of the *lex*,[38] and presents it as the outcome of political competition. This is seen in Dio's portrait of an ambitious Pompey craving the command, which stands in contrast to the narratives of Plutarch and Velleius where Pompey is wholly passive and, in Plutarch's account, even withdraws on the day of the vote.[39] Dio comments:

---

36   On the speeches, see now Burden-Strevens 2015, 167–72, 215–20; Burden-Strevens 2016.

37   Coudry 2016. For similar arguments, see Bertrand & Coudry 2016. See also Burden-Strevens (2015, 167–72; 2016, 193–203, 208–9) who underlines the importance of the *lex* to Dio's historical interpretation. *Contra* Rodgers 2008 who asserts that the speeches connected to this *lex* "serve his philosophical or moralizing agenda better than they serve history" (297). She sees Dio's focus on the *lex Gabinia* as an understandable mistake for a historian with careless chronology and a poor understanding of the Republic (306–8).

38   Dio's interest in constitutional matters is often noted but not explained. See e.g. Fechner 1986, 8–9; Hinard 1999, 431; 2005, 271; Lachenaud & Coudry 2011, lxviii.

39   Plut. *Pomp.* 26.1.

ὁ Πομπήιος ἐπιθυμῶν μὲν πάνυ ἄρξαι, καὶ ἤδη γε ὑπό τε τῆς ἑαυτοῦ φιλοτιμίας καὶ ὑπὸ τῆς τοῦ δήμου σπουδῆς οὐδὲ τιμὴν ἔτι τοῦτο, ἀλλ᾽ ἀτιμίαν τὸ μὴ τυχεῖν αὐτοῦ νομίζων εἶναι, τὴν δὲ ἀντίταξιν τῶν δυνατῶν ὁρῶν, ἠβουλήθη δοκεῖν ἀναγκάζεσθαι. ἦν μὲν γὰρ καὶ ἄλλως ὡς ἥκιστα προσποιούμενος ἐπιθυμεῖν ὧν ἤθελε· τότε δὲ καὶ μᾶλλον, διά τε τὸ ἐπίφθονον … ἐπλάττετο.

Pompey, who was very eager to command, and because of his own ambition and the zeal of the populace no longer now so much regarded this commission as an honor as the failure to win it a disgrace, when he saw the opposition of the *optimates*, desired to appear forced to accept. He was always in the habit of pretending as far as possible not to desire the things he really wished, and on this occasion did so more than ever, because of the jealousy that would follow.[40]

Pompey here clearly lusts duplicitously for power, and the competition itself in fact causes further degeneration as Pompey is forced to employ duplicity to avoid φθόνος. While Velleius and Plutarch portrayed Pompey as passive, Dio seems to have rejected this portrayal of Pompey in order to continue his distinctive presentation of Roman politics where all actors compete egoistically for their own good. This fundamental problem is also highlighted by Dio's previous narrative of Lucullus' command and his subsequent description of the senators and Gabinius in relation to the *lex Gabinia*.

Dio again deviates significantly in his portrayal of Gabinius, who was completely ignored in Velleius and Plutarch. An example of this is that Gabinius is given a whole speech that is even longer than Pompey's, and the two speeches in fact function in tandem as a duplicitous *recusatio* in order to avoid φθόνος. Moreover, and very importantly, Dio is the only source to explicitly suggest the possibility that Pompey had spurred Gabinius on to make this proposal, which fits with his picture of the ambitious general.[41] Dio does also mention another possibility, namely that Gabinius was trying to ingratiate himself with Pompey, but this still remains unique in the source tradition and functions equally well in Dio's critique of the egoistically ambitious politicians of the late Republic.[42] Furthermore, it is also only Dio who criticizes Gabinius, and he does so forcefully by saying that he was "not prompted by any love of the common welfare, for he was a most base fellow (κάκιστος … ἀνήρ)."[43] This critique appears banal

---

40 Cass. Dio 36.24.5–6.
41 Cass. Dio 36.23.4.
42 Cass. Dio 36.23.4.
43 Cass. Dio 36.23.4.

and could feature in any of the other sources. However, in Dio's narrative it becomes a continuation of his focus on egoistical competition which is permeating and destroying the Republic: Gabinius in Dio is centrally important to the enactment of this deeply problematic law but acts self-interestedly. Gabinius thus demonstrates that the degraded competition was not merely due to the dynasts but rather permeated the Roman political world; his personal failings are not an individual problem but instead characteristic of Rome as a whole. Indeed, Dio comments in Book 37 that only Cato was selflessly involved in politics,[44] which again shows Dio's focus on the degeneration of institutional competition.

Another important contrast to Velleius and Plutarch is Dio's view of the Senate. Velleius writes that the *optimates* advised against the command "but sane advice succumbed to impulse."[45] Plutarch has a similar narrative as the Senate vehemently opposed the *lex* since "such unlimited and absolute power, while it was greater than envy (μεῖζον μὲν φθόνου), was yet a thing to be feared (φόβου)."[46] Dio, on the contrary, is far more critical of the Senate: "that body preferred to suffer anything whatever at the hands of the freebooters rather than put so great a command into Pompey's hands; in fact they came near slaying Gabinius in the very Senate-house (ἐν αὐτῷ τῷ συνεδρίῳ)."[47] Firstly, the Senate is not opposed to the command in itself, as they are in Plutarch, but rather to the increase of Pompey's power, and they self-interestedly put their enmity above the good of Rome in stark contrast to the positively described Senate in Velleius. The constant egoistical competition and a consequently dysfunctional Senate thus preclude solutions to the piracy problem. Secondly, the senators are uniquely violent in Dio's narrative[48] as he is the only one to assert that they almost killed Gabinius, and through αὐτῷ in ἐν αὐτῷ τῷ συνεδρίῳ, Dio emphasizes that this even took place in the Senate-house. Dio's use of violence to create his negative picture of late republican competition is further seen in his presentation of the violent populace. Plutarch also includes this factor but whereas the people in his account come close to attacking one senator,[49] in Dio the people "rush upon them [the senators] as they sat assembled; and if

---

44 Cass. Dio 37.57.3.
45 Vell. Pat. 2.31.4.
46 Plut. *Pomp.* 25.3–4. Adapted from Perrin 1914–1926.
47 Cass. Dio 36.24.1.
48 This is typical also for Dio's account of the earlier Republic: Libourel 1968; 1974; Lange 2018; Lindholmer 2018a. For Dio's rejection of the common idealization of the earlier Republic, see also Lindholmer 2018b, 579–88. For Dio's early and mid-Republic more broadly, see Burden-Strevens & Lindholmer 2018.
49 Plut. *Pomp.* 25.4.

the senators had not gotten out of the way, they would certainly have killed them."[50] Dio thus increases the violence as all the senators are at risk here and they even have to flee to save their lives. Furthermore, Pompey is highly popular among the people and they hereby become a tool used to force the Senate's acceptance of the *lex Gabinia*. This use of the people and their forceful violence by Pompey's camp against the Senate exemplifies the new distribution of power in Dio's late Republic, where individuals could in fact overpower the Senate through the help of the people, which exacerbates institutional competition. Ambitious politicians, here personified by Pompey, have through the people and their violence gained sufficient unconstitutional power that the Senate is overwhelmed and the traditional constitutional constraints broken via the extraordinary command.[51] Dio has thus again through deviations put institutional competition at the heart of his account.

Dio's account is of course not completely unique or fabricated as most main elements and several details are identical in the other sources. However, Dio presents and embellishes his material in a wholly different way, as both Gabinius and Pompey are self-serving and mendacious, and the latter's ambition is the central driving force. The presentation of the Senate as also engaged in selfish competition again portrays this competition as an institutional problem since all players partake. Dio thus switches away from the individual that is so important in Velleius and Plutarch and focuses on the political institutions. Individuals are not neglected, but they are used to communicate and strengthen Dio's critique of the political system and the destructive role of competition in a way that is unique in the source tradition.

In contrast to the events surrounding Lucullus, it seems that at least some of Dio's deviations originate in embellishments: the explanation of the motivations of Gabinius, Pompey, and the Senate appears to be Dio's own work. It is, on the other hand, harder to determine the origins of the unique account of violence and the suggestion of collusion between Gabinius and Pompey. However, given that I am not attempting to identify Dio's source(s), these considerations are of secondary importance. What is important, instead, is the clear picture that Dio has here again manipulated and selected his material to create a narrative where the political institutions and the destructiveness of competition take center stage. The focus on institutional competition is furthermore notably identical to Dio's narrative surrounding Lucullus' command, which suggests that this problem, in Dio's eyes, was pervasive both among the generals in the provinces and in Rome itself. These parallels suggest that Dio

---

50   Cass. Dio 36.24.2.
51   See also e.g. Cass. Dio 38.1–8.

made his narrative choices based on a premeditated interpretative framework that governed his work. It thus seems that Dio attempted to present an institutional explanation for the problems of the late Republic where competition stood at the center.

3   The Catilinarian Conspiracy

This institutional perspective and the consistent deviations from the parallel sources are likewise seen in relation to the Catilinarian conspiracy of 63. The parallel sources are again focused mainly on Catiline and depict him as a madman who was inherently destined for the conspiracy. In Dio, by contrast, Catiline's conspiracy is portrayed as the result of uncontrollable institutional competition, while his moral degeneracy is not in focus. The second major area of deviation in Dio is the portrayal of Cicero: Dio rejects the heroic depiction of the parallel sources since this would have undermined his institutional approach.[52] The Catilinarian conspiracy, then, is used by Dio to present his interpretation of the fall of the Republic centered on institutional competition.

This is a central event in the historiography of the late Republic and, not surprisingly, all of our sources treat it to some extent. The narratives are often complex and I will not here follow them minutely but instead focus on the main aspects and on points where Dio deviates from the tradition preserved in the parallel sources. Sallust's *Bellum Catilinae* is our most thorough treatment, and here we are told that Catiline's corrupt character played a fundamental role in the conspiracy. This corruption is an integral part of Catiline as he had "an evil and depraved nature ... His disordered mind ever craved the monstrous, incredible, gigantic ... He was spurred on, also, by the corruption of the public morals, which were being ruined by two great evils of an opposite character, extravagance and avarice."[53] The ensuing conspiracy is, then, a natural consequence of Catiline's nature: "Catiline formed the plan of overthrowing the government ... because his own debt was enormous in all parts of the world ... There was no army in Italy ... this was his golden opportunity."[54] The general moral degeneration is important, but the individual here again plays a central role as Catiline's personal corruption is key in the creation of the plot. This explanation is inserted even before the so-called first Catilinarian conspir-

---

52   Both Coudry and Urso in this volume also rightly emphasize Dio's originality in relation to the causes for the Catilinarian conspiracy and Cicero's role in it.
53   Sall. *Cat.* 5.1–8.
54   Sall. *Cat.* 16.4.

acy of 66, thereby heightening the importance of Catiline's natural corruption. Cicero, on the other hand, is the main hero of the narrative, continuously frustrating Catiline's designs and earning high praise from the people.

Velleius' short work is far briefer but also praises Cicero for detecting the conspiracy by his "extraordinary courage, firmness, and careful vigilance."[55] "Catiline," Velleius writes, "was driven from the city by fear of the authority of the consul [i.e. Cicero]."[56] However, the wider political causes or consequences are non-existent – in a continuation of Velleius' previously seen focus. In the Livian *Periochae*, Cicero is again the savior of Rome: "This conspiracy was extirpated by the energy of Marcus Tullius Cicero."[57] Appian gives a fairly full narrative that mirrors Sallust's, explaining the conspiracy as natural to Catiline and portraying Cicero as the hero: "Catiline was ... a madman ... He had reduced himself to poverty in order to gratify his ambition, but still he was courted by the powerful, both men and women, and he became a candidate for the consulship as a step leading to absolute power ... Cicero, the most eloquent orator and rhetorician of the period, was chosen instead."[58] Appian's narrative thus also revolves around individuals, especially the madman Catiline. Lastly, this picture is seen in Plutarch as well, who also underlines the degenerate state of society: "matters needed only a slight impulse to disturb them, and it was in the power of any bold man to overthrow the commonwealth, which of itself was in a diseased condition. However, Catiline wished to obtain first a strong base of operations."[59] We are again lacking a definite starting point for the idea of a conspiracy as this is the first we hear of any plans on the part of Catiline. The biography of Cicero is by far the fullest treatment of the conspiracy by Plutarch, and Cicero is of course the central hero. The general acceptance among the sources of Cicero's heroic role and of Catiline's inherent corruption is at least in part the product of the use of Cicero's speeches as source material by Sallust and subsequent historians. In conclusion, all the parallel sources focus persistently on Cicero and Catiline as the two central characters who drive the narrative forward.

Dio gives many of the same details as the parallel sources but deviates in two main areas, namely the origins of the conspiracy and the treatment of Cicero. Before the second conspiracy, Catiline had been described once by Dio in relation to the so-called first conspiracy, but Dio there merely calls him "very

---

55   Vell. Pat. 2.34.3.
56   Vell. Pat. 2.34.4.
57   Liv. *Per.* 102.
58   App. *B Civ.* 2.2.
59   Plut. *Cic.* 10.5–11.1.

bold (θρασύτατος)" without elaborating.[60] It is instead a surprising acquittal, which Dio places in 63, for his deeds under Sulla that spurs Catiline on:

> τοῦτό τε οὖν παρὰ δόξαν τοῖς πολλοῖς ἐχώρησε ... ἐπὶ τοῖς αὐτοῖς ἐκείνοις αἰτίαν ... λαβὼν ἀπελύθη. καὶ δὴ καὶ ἐκ τούτου χείρων τε πολὺ ἐγένετο, καὶ διὰ τοῦτο καὶ ἀπώλετο· τοῦ γὰρ δὴ Κικέρωνος τοῦ Μάρκου μετὰ Γαΐου Ἀντωνίου ὑπατεύσαντος ... ἐπεχείρησεν ἐκεῖνος τήν τε πολιτείαν νεωτερίζειν καὶ τοὺς συμμάχους ἐπ' αὐτῇ συνιστὰς ἐς φόβον σφᾶς οὐ σμικροῦ πολέμου ἐνέβαλεν.
>
> This matter, then, turned out contrary to most people's expectation ... [Catiline], although charged with the same crimes as the others ... was acquitted. And from this very circumstance he became far worse and even lost his life as a result. For, when Marcus Cicero had become consul with Gaius Antonius ... Catiline undertook to set up a new government, and by banding together the allies against the state threw the people into fear of a mighty conflict.[61]

Strikingly, Catiline's acquittal in a trial that is unattested in the other narratives[62] is the direct cause for the Catilinarian conspiracy. Dio hereby focuses far less on the personal immorality of Catiline. He is neither a madman nor inherently destined for revolution. Instead, Dio gives the impression that it was only from the year 63 that Catiline started forming his plans. Furthermore, in the context of the problematic late Republic, the unexpected result of Catiline's trial suggests foul play and becomes part of Dio's presentation of an inherently malfunctioning Rome. Rather than Catiline's corrupted morals, then, it is the dysfunctional Republic that creates the conspiracy.

The above quotation about Catiline is inserted by Dio as a summary of the conspiracy but in the subsequent more detailed narrative, he again deviates from the source tradition in telling ways. Cicero is the main mover behind a severer punishment for bribery, the *lex Tullia de ambitu*:

> τοῦτ' οὖν καὶ ἐκεῖνος δι' ἑαυτόν, ὅπερ που καὶ ἀληθὲς ἦν, ἐγνῶσθαι νομίσας ἐπεχείρησε μέν, χεῖρά τινα παρασκευάσας, τὸν Κικέρωνα καὶ ἄλλους τινὰς τῶν πρώτων ἐν αὐταῖς ταῖς ἀρχαιρεσίαις, ἵν' ὕπατος εὐθὺς χειροτονηθῇ, φονεῦσαι ...

---

60   Cass. Dio 36.44.4.
61   Cass. Dio 37.10.3–4.
62   The trial is of course attested in other sources, such as Asconius' commentary, but Dio's is the only *narrative* to include this element.

> Catiline, accordingly, believed that this decree had been passed on his account, as was indeed the case; and so, after collecting a small band, he attempted to slay Cicero and some others of the foremost men on the very day of the election, in order that he might immediately be chosen as consul.[63]

This narrative is again completely unique to Dio and gives the lead-up to the actual conspiracy a decidedly different flavor, as Dio puts political competition center stage. The Senate attempts to correct the problematic bribery, part of the destructive late republican competition, but through this in fact spurs Catiline on to take even more extreme measures in his quest to become consul. Dio has hereby again included a deviation that allows him to highlight the destructiveness of competition in the late Republic, and he even indicates that this problem is unsolvable since the seemingly positive law rather makes Catiline's competitive behavior even more extreme. This whole situation is borne out of the republican institutional competition for offices, but the competition has here turned destructive and uncontrollable. An important reason for this is the weakness of the Senate and traditional authority, and the excessive power of ambitious individuals, as exemplified in this situation where the Senate's attempts are characteristically futile and result in the imminent collection of a personal army by Catiline.

However, before this, Catiline fails miserably in both plot and elections: "new consuls were chosen, and Catiline no longer directed his plot in secret or against Cicero and his adherents only, but against the whole commonwealth."[64] In Sallust, Plutarch, and Appian, Catiline is a corrupted madman, and his desire for revolution and outrages far precedes the actual conspiracy of 63. In Dio, on the other hand, the so-called first conspiracy is consciously played down and the catalyst for the second conspiracy instead consists of institutional problems in the shape of the seemingly corrupt courts, the futile senatorial attempt to rectify the problematic excessive bribery, and, lastly, destructive competition in the consular elections. Dio does also incorporate Catiline's moral degeneration but he uses it to focalize his critique of the functioning of political competition. This competition provides the concrete cause for the conspiracy rather than an inherent moral failing in Catiline, as in the other sources. This seems a difference of prioritization: especially Sallust, Velleius, and Plutarch but also Appian explore the individual, Catiline, as their main theme and use the political situation around the Catilinarian conspiracy to do so. Dio, by contrast,

---

63   Cass. Dio 37.29.2.
64   Cass. Dio 37.30.1.

uses the individual as a tool to explore the political problems of Rome. The main difference in the two versions of the origins of the conspiracy thus seems to be one of priority and perspective.

The second major area of deviation in Dio's account is the role played by Cicero. Dio includes the well-known assassination plot against Cicero from 63 where the consul was supposed to be killed in his house.[65] However, Dio's is the only narrative to include another previous assassination plot against Cicero which the latter exposes.[66] Afterwards, Cicero is disbelieved in the Senate:

(οὔτε γὰρ πιθανὰ ἐξηγγελκέναι καὶ διὰ τὴν ἑαυτοῦ ἔχθραν καταψεύδεσθαι τῶν ἀνδρῶν ὑπωπτεύθη), ἐφοβήθη ἅτε καὶ προσπαρωξυγκὼς τὸν Κατιλίναν.

His announcement was not regarded as credible and he was suspected of having uttered false charges against the men because of personal enmity, [and] Cicero became frightened, now that he had given Catiline additional provocation.[67]

This frightened Cicero stands in sharp contrast to the hero of the parallel sources, and it is significant that the suspicion of egoistical rivalry undermines Cicero's effort to help the state. This suspicion is again representative of the institutional problem of constant and pervasive egoistical competition for offices in Dio's late Republic where no one works for the state, which precludes the possibility of assistance or corrections. Thus, the alternative depiction of Cicero supports the creation of this representation of republican politics. This negative description of Cicero is highly consistent as Dio often posits an alternative cause when the former achieves a success. An example is Cicero exposing another plot on his life while consul: it was divulged since Cicero, "being a man of great influence, and one who gained many followers through his speeches, either by conciliation or by intimidation (ἐκφοβῶν), had many men to report such occurrences to him."[68] It is not Cicero himself but his helpers who uncover the conspiracy, and his great rhetoric, extolled by Appian and Velleius,[69] is here cast in a decidedly less flattering light as a tool for political competition. This portrayal of rhetoric is representative of Dio's

---

65 Cass. Dio 37.32.4. See also e.g. Plut. Cic. 16.1. Sallust places unspecified "plots" in 63: Cat. 26.
66 Cass. Dio 37.29.2.
67 Cass. Dio 37.29.3.
68 Cass. Dio 37.33.1.
69 App. B Civ. 2.2; Vell. Pat. 2.34.3.

late Republic where it is often exploited by mendacious dynasts to further their political aims.[70]

Even Cicero's grand exploit of thwarting Catiline's main plot is partly undermined: "the statue of Jupiter was set up on the Capitol ... For these seers [i.e. the ones instructing the statue to be set up] had decided that some conspiracy would be brought to light by the erection of the statue, and ... its setting up coincided with the discovery of the conspirators."[71] Dio here selectively includes a typical annalistic element in order to undermine Cicero's claim to have protected the city.[72] Dio's is also the only narrative to portray Catiline's flight from Rome as the result of a vote in the Senate rather than due to Cicero's *First Catilinarian*, as asserted by the parallel sources.[73] Furthermore, in the other accounts of the Catilinarian conspiracy, Cicero is extolled as the savior of Rome[74] and even called "father of his country"[75] by the people in Appian and Plutarch. Dio, on the other hand, mentions several times the anger of the populace towards Cicero since he had the conspirators killed unlawfully[76] and because of his boastfulness: "[Cicero] certainly did take great pleasure not only in being praised by others but also in extolling himself ... [Cicero] added to his oath the statement that he had saved the city; and for this he incurred much greater hatred."[77]

Cicero is hereby transformed in Dio from the masterful rhetorician and "father of his country" to a boastful and hated figure. This is not "a failure, perhaps the most complete of his History."[78] Rather, it furthers Dio's overall picture of the thoroughly problematic republican competition where rhetoric becomes a political weapon and no one, except Cato, works for the common good. Essentially, the portrayal of Cicero demonstrates Dio's skillful and selective use of the then-available source material, perhaps including imperial anti-Ciceronian literature,[79] in order to support his interpretation of the Republic – an interpretation that has no space for a heroic Cicero. Just as in the case of the origins of the conspiracy, Dio here emerges as a careful selector and manipulator of sources who had an interpretative framework with

---

70   Burden-Strevens 2015, 214–29; Kemezis 2016.
71   Cass. Dio 37.34.3–4.
72   On Dio's use of the annalistic tradition, see Rich 2016; Lindholmer forthcoming a.
73   Cass. Dio 37.33.1; Sall. *Cat.* 31.6; Vell. Pat. 2.34.4.
74   Sall. *Cat.* 48.1.
75   App. *B Civ.* 2.7; Plut. *Cic.* 23.6, 24.1.
76   Cass. Dio 37.38.1. See also 38.12.4–7 for a very similar evaluation of Cicero.
77   Cass. Dio 37.38.2.
78   Millar 1964, 55.
79   For an overview, see Gowing 2013.

political competition at its center, which informed his approach to Roman history. Dio's narrative of the Catilinarian conspiracy is thus again distinctive. He switches the focus from the moral degeneracy of Catiline and the heroics of Cicero, and rather concentrates on the problem of political competition which in his narrative actually creates the conspiracy. Overall, then, Dio deviates purposefully from the source tradition in his narrative of the Catilinarian conspiracy with the aim of highlighting the problems of institutional competition. Furthermore, Dio again portrays everyone as involved in this destructive competition which hereby becomes an institutional problem. This presentation of all players as involved in destructive competition is strikingly similar to Dio's accounts of Lucullus' command and the *lex Gabinia*, which reveals an important unity in the functioning of this competition across different parts of the narrative.

4 Conclusion

In this chapter, I have shown how Dio deviates significantly from the tradition preserved in the parallel sources in his treatment of Lucullus' command, the *lex Gabinia*, and the Catilinarian conspiracy in order to present and strengthen an interpretation of the fall of the Republic where institutional competition is the central destructive driving force.[80] Dio consistently portrays all players as involved in selfish competition, and the problem of competition hereby becomes institutional rather than merely connected to individuals. Dio's narrative is practically devoid of heroes. One notable aspect here is the consistency with which Dio's narrative deviates from the parallel source material, which shows that Dio was neither following any of the sources extant today nor the lost portion of Livy, as far as we can tell from the *Periochae*. However, the narrative elements unique to Dio are too complicated to be explained away by embellishments or invention alone and thus demonstrate a careful selection process of the available material in order to communicate and strengthen Dio's interpretation. This would only be further evidenced if one examined other parts of the narrative. An example is Caesar's agrarian reforms in Book 38 where Dio, in contrast to all other sources, focuses on the necessity of the reforms and portrays all players, including the Senate, as acting selfishly, while the parallel sources merely focus on Caesar's negatively portrayed

---

80 For more on this argument, see Lindholmer 2016; 2018a; 2018c; forthcoming b.

ambition and the valiant but futile attempts by the Senate to oppose him.[81] The same picture emerges when examining Caesar's military campaigns. The parallel sources focus on the greatness of Caesar the general, whereas Dio detracts from the importance of Caesar and presents these campaigns as the manifestation of a malfunctioning imperialism that is exploited by ambitious generals.[82] Dio does mention the problematic import of Asiatic luxury[83] but this theme never becomes central in his narrative, in sharp contrast to Sallust and Velleius,[84] as he rather focuses on institutional problems centered on competition.

The consistent presentation of all parties involved as engaged in egoistic competition in the narratives of the above events gives the problematic competition an institutional character since it is not tied to any individual. This underlines Dio's institutional approach to republican history: institutional competition had become fundamentally destructive as a consequence of empire at the start of the late Republic and the actions of individuals had little influence on the workings of this pervasive problem. Thus, the problematic competition functioned essentially in the same way throughout Dio's late Republic and does not appear to have been affected significantly by the normally asserted turning points. Dio does of course accord importance to select turning points, such as the *lex Gabinia*, but this should not obscure the striking continuity of the functioning of destructive competition.[85] This lack of change in the destructive functioning of institutional competition also creates an impression of Dio's late Republic as inherently unworkable. This impression is further supported by Dio's incorporation of problematic institutional competition right from the very dawn of the Republic, in sharp contrast to the idealized narratives of the early and mid-Republic in Livy and Dionysius.[86] Thus, Dio essentially presents a Republic that contained the seeds of its own destruction from the start, in the shape of institutional competition. Once Rome attained its empire, the competition spiraled out of control and nothing in Dio's late

---

81   Cass. Dio 38.1–7. App. *B Civ.* 2.11; Liv. *Per.* 103; Plut. *Caes.* 14.2, 14.9–12; Suet. *Caes.* 20; Vell. Pat. 2.44.4.
82   On Dio's treatment of Caesar compared to the parallel sources, see Lindholmer forthcoming c.
83   Cass. Dio fr. 64.
84   Hortensius is e.g. the only general in Dio's extant Republic to turn down a command because of a preference for the luxury of Rome. All other generals happily exploit these commands for their own benefit, as exemplified in the above section on Lucullus and his command.
85   Partly *contra* Coudry in this volume, who views different late republican turning points as decisive.
86   Lindholmer 2018a.

Republic appears to fundamentally affect its functioning. In this distinctive and original perspective, Pompey, Caesar, and the other dynasts become mere manifestations of the institutional problem of political competition. This detracts from the importance of these individuals and suggests that institutional political competition is the essential cause for the fall of Dio's Republic – in sharp contrast to the parallel sources.[87]

One might object that Dio's supposed originality is due to a source that is today no longer extant. However, Dio insists that he had read practically everything written about the Romans[88] and that he had spent ten years taking notes,[89] which, despite the possibility of distortion as part of self-presentation, undermines the idea that Dio's work is the result of a single or a few unknown sources. Furthermore, while our knowledge of ancient working methods remains hazy,[90] Nissen's Law – namely that ancient historians followed a single source for stretches of narrative, which is often implicitly presumed in *Quellenforschung* – appears decidedly unlikely to apply here, since Dio's deviations are highly consistent and thoroughly informed by his own overall aims. This undermines the idea that Dio's originality derives from a single completely unknown source.[91] Several unknown sources could be another, albeit speculative, possibility, and the sources available to Dio were surely far more numerous than what survives today. However, scrolls were too large and impractical to allow a historian to work directly from several sources at the same time. Lucian, in his work on history writing, suggests instead that writers should compose an *aide-memoire* (ὑπόμνημα) of their material[92] and it seems an attractive hypothesis that Dio followed this model.[93] The ὑπόμνημα would provide Dio information from a wide array of sources without the impracticalities, thereby freeing the historian from the dependence on a single or perhaps two sources, which the consistent deviations from the parallel evidence suggest was necessary.[94]

Moreover, the parallel sources show a noteworthy unity in the themes they choose to emphasize which are decidedly different from Dio's. This suggests that Dio, the latest of these writers, was not working from a hypothetical source

---

87   For this argument, see Lindholmer forthcoming b.
88   Cass. Dio fr. 1.2.
89   Cass. Dio 73.23.5.
90   For Dio's working method, see Millar 1964, 32–40; Pelling 1979, 92–5; Rich 1989, 89–92; Mallan 2014, 760 n. 8; Burden-Strevens 2015, 44–6.
91   This is the suggestion of Libourel 1968 and 1974 for the early Republic.
92   Luc. *Hist. Conscr.* 48; Burden-Strevens 2015, 44–5.
93   *Contra* Millar 1964, 33.
94   So Rich 1989, 89–92 for the Augustan age.

tradition that was available to his predecessors. Thus, the hypothetical source furnishing Dio with his deviations would necessarily have been written in the mere half a century between Appian and Dio. If such a source had existed, it is also doubtful whether Dio would even have chosen to write such a full account of the late Republic since another, newly written work would have fulfilled this niche. In short, Dio's consistent and calculated deviations cannot be explained away by a hypothetical and speculative source, and are instead a manifestation of his interpretative framework centered on competition.

This independent framework makes Dio's work impractical for reconstructing older sources and undermines conventional *Quellenforschung* attempting to identify Dio's main source, which still constitutes an important part of scholarly work[95] – arguably a significant factor in the traditional reluctance to ascribe such a framework to the historian. This is not to argue that all *Quellenforschung* should be abandoned. Urso has demonstrated the rewards to be reaped from locating the traditions, rather than the individual authors, from which Dio worked.[96] This undermining of traditional *Quellenforschung* is further exacerbated by the comparisons in this chapter which show Dio's institutionally and politically focused framework to be very different in scope from the other sources where the individual is the main area of interest and driver of the narrative. Dio, by contrast, uses the individual as a tool in his critique of the institutional functioning of the late Republic which is his most important arena of investigation. This chapter has also shown how Dio consistently and in a sophisticated manner highlights destructive competition in his narrative of the late Republic by presenting an alternative portrait compared to other authors. The parallel sources occasionally deal with political problems as well but fail to invest them with the broader political significance of Dio's narrative. The dissimilarities can of course partly be explained by a variation in the available source material or by generic differences between the authors. However, these aspects cannot account for the fact that Dio's narrative is so consistently different and constantly furthers the same institutional explanation. Instead, the consistency of Dio's deviations suggests the presence of an interpretative framework focused on institutional competition, which undermines the older views of Dio as a simple historian[97] while also weakening the moral strand of

---

95 Even as recent as Schettino 2006; Simons 2009; Westall 2016.
96 Urso 2005; 2011; 2018; and in this volume.
97 Millar 1964, 46; Lintott 1997, 2514–17.

scholarship illustrated by, for example, Kuhn-Chen and Rees.[98] Furthermore, it also challenges the still widespread view that Dio was unoriginal.[99]

In conclusion, Dio employed a highly selective use of the available sources to create a distinctive account of central episodes of the late Republic, where the fundamental institutional problem of political competition takes center stage and the importance of individuals is downplayed.[100] Modern scholarship on the late Republic has likewise often sought to avoid the common focus of ancient historiography on individuals and concentrated on institutional aspects instead.[101] Through his focus on institutional competition rather than on individuals, Dio is thus in fact the ancient source that most closely resembles modern perspectives on the fall of the Republic. Consequently, modern criticisms of Dio's understanding of the Republic appear excessive,[102] and it seems that modern scholars would gain from according Dio's distinctive interpretation attention in its own right.

Bibliography

Bertrand, E. & Coudry, M. (2016) "De Pompée à Auguste: les mutations de l'imperium militiae 2. Un traitement particulier dans l'Histoire romaine de Dion", in V. Fromentin *et al.* (eds.), *Cassius Dion: nouvelles lectures* (Bordeaux): 595–608.

Brunt, P. A. (1986) *Social Conflicts in the Roman Republic*, London.

Burden-Strevens, C. (2015) *Cassius Dio's Speeches and the Collapse of the Roman Republic*. Dissertation: Glasgow.

Burden-Strevens, C. (2016) "Fictitious Speeches, Envy, and the Habituation to Authority: Writing the Collapse of the Roman Republic", in C. H. Lange & J. M. Madsen (eds.), *Cassius Dio: Greek Intellectual and Roman Politician* (Leiden & Boston): 193–216.

Burden-Strevens C. & Lindholmer, M. (eds.) (2018) *Cassius Dio's Forgotten History of Early Rome: The 'Roman History' Books 1–21*, Leiden & Boston.

---

98   Kuhn-Chen 2002, 243–6; Rees 2011. Also *contra* Hose 1994, 436 and partly Sion-Jenkis 2000, 184–5.
99   Millar 1964, 46; Rees 2011, 4; Kemezis 2014, 93.
100 The institutional focus of Dio demonstrated above furthermore resonates with Lange and Madsen's brief recent suggestion (2016b, 2–3) that Dio approaches Roman history in a structural fashion.
101 Meier (1966) sees a crisis without alternative, at least for the period from 49; Brunt (1986) argues for social conflicts; Millar (1998) concentrates on the People; Steel (2013) focuses on the Senate.
102 E.g. Schwartz 1899, 1690–1; Millar 1964, 47–9; Lintott 1997, 2514–17.

Cary, E. (1914–1927) *Cassius Dio: Roman History* (9 vols.), London.

Coudry, M. (2016) "Cassius Dio on Pompey's Extraordinary Commands", in C. H. Lange & J. M. Madsen (eds.), *Cassius Dio: Greek Intellectual and Roman Politician* (Leiden & Boston): 33–50.

Eckstein, A. (2004) "From the Historical Caesar to the Spectre of Caesarism: The Imperial Administrator as Internal Threat", in P. Baehr & M. Richter (eds.), *Dictatorship in History and Theory* (Cambridge): 279–98.

Fechner, D. (1986) *Untersuchungen zu Cassius Dios Sicht der römischen Republik*, Hildesheim.

Fromentin, V. *et al.* (eds.) (2016) *Cassius Dion: nouvelles lectures*, Bordeaux.

Gowing, A. (2013) "Tully's Boat: Responses to Cicero in the Imperial Period", in C. Steel (ed.), *The Cambridge Companion to Cicero* (Cambridge): 233–50.

Haupt, H. (1882) "Jahresberichte. Dio Cassius", *Philologus* 41, 140–58.

Haupt, H. (1884) "Jahresberichte. Dio Cassius", *Philologus* 43, 678–701.

Hinard, F. (1999) "Dion Cassius et l'abdication de Sylla", *Revue des études anciennes* 101, 427–32.

Hinard, F. (2005) "Dion Cassius et les institutions de la république romaine", in L. Troiani & G. Zecchini (eds.), *La cultura storica nei primi due secoli dell' impero romano* (Rome): 261–81.

Hose, M. (1994) *Erneuerung der Vergangenheit: die Historiker im Imperium Romanum von Florus bis Cassius Dio*, Stuttgart.

Kemezis, A. (2014) *Greek Narratives of the Roman Empire under the Severans: Cassius Dio, Philostratus and Herodian*, Cambridge.

Kemezis, A. (2016) "Dio, Caesar and the Vesontio Mutineers (38.34–47): A Rhetoric of Lies", in C. H. Lange & J. M. Madsen (eds.), *Cassius Dio: Greek Intellectual and Roman Politician* (Leiden & Boston): 238–57.

Kuhn-Chen, B. (2002) *Geschichtskonzeption griechischer Historiker in 2. und 3. Jahrhundert n. Chr.: Untersuchungen zu den Werken von Appian, Cassius Dio und Herodian*, Frankfurt am Main.

Lachenaud, G. & Coudry, M. (eds.) (2011) *Dion Cassius: Histoire romaine. Livres 38, 39 & 40*, Paris.

Lange, C. H. (2018) "Cassius Dio on Violence, *Stasis*, and Civil War: The Early Years", in C. Burden-Strevens & M. Lindholmer (eds.), *Cassius Dio's Forgotten History of Early Rome: The 'Roman History' Books 1–21* (Leiden & Boston): 165–89.

Lange, C. H. & Madsen, J. M. (eds.) (2016a) *Cassius Dio: Greek Intellectual and Roman Politician*, Leiden & Boston.

Lange, C. H. & Madsen, J. M. (2016b) "Between History and Politics", in C. H. Lange & J. M. Madsen (eds.), *Cassius Dio: Greek Intellectual and Roman Politician* (Leiden & Boston): 1–12.

Levi, M. (1937) "Dopo Azio: Appunti sulle fonti augustee: Dione Cassio", *Athenaeum* 15, 3–25.

Libourel, J. (1968) *Dio Cassius on the Early Roman Republic*. Dissertation: University of California.

Libourel, J. (1974) "An Unusual Annalistic Source Used by Dio Cassius", *American Journal of Philology* 95/4, 383–93.

Lindholmer, M. (2016) *Cassius Dio, Competition and the Decline of the Roman Republic*. MPhil Thesis: Glasgow.

Lindholmer, M. (2018a) "Breaking the Idealistic Paradigm: Competition in Dio's Earlier Republic", in C. Burden-Strevens & M. Lindholmer (eds.), *Cassius Dio's Forgotten History of Early Rome: The 'Roman History' Books 1–21* (Leiden & Boston): 190–214.

Lindholmer, M. (2018b) "Cassius Dio and the 'Age of Δυναστεία'", *Greek, Roman, and Byzantine Studies* 58/4, 561–90.

Lindholmer, M. (2018c) "Reading Diachronically: A New Reading of Book 36 of Cassius Dio's Roman History", *Histos* 12, 139–68.

Lindholmer, M. (forthcoming a) "Exploiting Conventions: Dio's Late Republic and the Annalistic Tradition", in C. H. Lange & J. M. Madsen (eds.), *Cassius Dio the Historian: Methods and Approaches* (Leiden & Boston).

Lindholmer, M. (forthcoming b) "The Fall of Cassius Dio's Roman Republic", *Klio*.

Lindholmer, M. (forthcoming c) "The Role of Caesar's Wars in Dio's Late Republic", in C. H. Lange & A. Scott (eds.), *Cassius Dio: The Impact of Violence, War, and Civil War* (Leiden & Boston).

Lintott, A. W. (1997) "Cassius Dio and the History of the Late Roman Republic", *Aufstieg und Niedergang der römischen Welt* 2.34.3, 2497–523.

Mallan, C. (2014) "The Rape of Lucretia in Cassius Dio's *Roman History*", *The Classical Quarterly* 64/2, 758–71.

Manuwald, B. (1979) *Cassius Dio und Augustus: philologische Untersuchungen zu den Büchern 45–56 des dionischen Geschichtswerkes*, Wiesbaden.

Marx, F. (1933) "Die Quelle der Germanenkriege bei Tacitus und Dio", *Klio* 26, 321–9.

Meier, C. (1966) *Res publica amissa: eine Studie zu Verfassung und Geschichte der späten römischen Republik*, Wiesbaden.

Micalella, A. (1896) *La fonte di Dione Cassio per le guerre galliche di Cesare*, Lecce.

Millar, F. (1964) *A Study of Cassius Dio*, Oxford.

Millar, F. (1998) *The Crowd in Rome in the Late Republic*, Ann Arbor.

Pelling, C. (1979) "Plutarch's Method of Work in the Roman Lives", *Journal of Hellenic Studies* 99, 74–96.

Perrin, B. (1914–1926) *Plutarch's Lives* (11 vols.), London.

Rees, W. (2011) *Cassius Dio, Human Nature and the Late Roman Republic*. Dissertation: Oxford.

Rich, J. (1989) "Dio on Augustus", in A. Cameron (ed.), *History as Text: The Writing of Ancient History* (London): 87–110.

Rich, J. W. (2016) "Annalistic Organization and Book Division in Dio's Books 1–35", in V. Fromentin *et al.* (eds.), *Cassius Dion: nouvelles lectures* (Bordeaux): 271–86.

Rodgers, B. S. (2008) "Catulus' Speech in Cassius Dio 36.31–36", *Greek, Roman, and Byzantine Studies* 48, 295–318.

Schettino, M. (2006) "L'histoire archaïque de Rome dans les fragments de Dion Cassius", in E. Caire & S. Pittia (eds.), *Guerre et diplomatie romaines* (Aix-en-Provence): 61–75.

Schlesinger, A. (1959) *Livy: History of Rome. Vol. 14*, London.

Schwartz, E. (1899) "Cassius (40)", in A. Pauly, G. Wissowa, & W. Kroll (eds.), *Realencyclopädie der classischen Altertumswissenschaft* (Stuttgart): III/2, 1684–722.

Simons, B. (2009) *Cassius Dio und die Römische Republik. Untersuchungen zum Bild des römischen Gemeinwesens in den Büchern 3–35 der Romaika*, Berlin.

Sion-Jenkis, K. (2000) *Von der Republik zum Prinzipat: Ursachen für den Verfassungswandel in Rom im historischen Denken der Antike*, Stuttgart.

Sordi, M. (1971) "Cassio Dione e il VII libro del *De Bello Gallico* di Cesare", in L. Ferrero (ed.), *Studi di Storiografia Antica in Memoria di L. Ferrero* (Turin): 167–83.

Steel, C. (2013) *The End of the Roman Republic, 146 to 44 BC: Conquest and Crisis*, Edinburgh.

Swan, P. (1987) "Cassius Dio on Augustus: A Poverty of Annalistic Sources?", *Phoenix* 41/3, 272–91.

Townend, G. (1961) "The Post of *ab epistulis* in the Second Century", *Historia* 10/3, 375–81.

Urso, G. (2005) *Cassio Dione e i magistrati. Le origini della repubblica nei frammenti della Storia romana*, Milan.

Urso, G. (2011) "The Origin of the Consulship in Cassius Dio's Roman History", in H. Beck *et al.* (eds.), *Consuls and Res Publica: Holding High Office in the Roman Republic* (Cambridge): 41–60.

Urso, G. (2018) "Cassio Dione e le fonti pre-liviane: una versione alternativa dei primi secoli di Roma", in C. Burden-Strevens & M. Lindholmer (eds.), *Cassius Dio's Forgotten History of Early Rome: The 'Roman History' Books 1–21* (Leiden & Boston): 53–75.

Westall, R. (2016) "The Sources of Cassius Dio for the Roman Civil Wars of 49–30 BC," in C. H. Lange & J. M. Madsen (eds.), *Cassius Dio: Greek Intellectual and Roman Politician* (Leiden & Boston): 51–75.

Zecchini, G. (1978) *Cassio Dione e la guerra gallica di Cesare*, Milan.

CHAPTER 6

Cassius Dio and the Virtuous Roman

Kathryn Welch

Recent studies of Cassius Dio demonstrate his sensitivity to the political discourses current in the times about which he wrote even while he was also deeply immersed in the concerns of his own day.[1] One of those discourses was the role of individual character in maintaining stable and effective government.[2] Dio did not subscribe to a view, common among the Romans, of a balanced constitution destroyed by a descent into immorality for which monarchy became an eventual if regrettable solution. Rather, he was suspicious from the outset of participatory government where good and bad men competed for power.[3] Monarchy, he thought, was better and fairer, but his monarchs were held to a high standard of decency, even if he recognized that even good monarchs slipped from time to time and that the exigencies of leadership led to some awful decisions.[4] Individual qualities were therefore something that Dio considered carefully as he recorded century after century of Roman history.[5]

With this issue in mind, my paper highlights the moments when Dio used a specific set of criteria, the four cardinal virtues of wisdom, justice, courage, and temperance, to assess quality of character. The scheme itself went back to Plato,[6] but the Stoics adopted it and, eventually, it found its way into Roman politics through the influence of men such as Panaetius of Rhodes, Blossius of

---

1   I would like to thank Josiah Osgood for the invitation to present this paper to the Cassius Dio Network at Fiesole in 2017 and again for his helpful interventions, and those of Chris Baron, as editors. Kit Morrell, Gianpaolo Urso, Christopher Burden-Strevens, Roger Pitcher, and Hannah Mitchell also assisted greatly with the development of the arguments I present here. They should not be held responsible for any shortcomings. Thanks are due too to the lively audiences at Fiesole and at the Macquarie University SPQR meeting of November 2018 for their probing questions and comments. Translations are those of Cary (Loeb Classical Library), adapted where necessary, unless otherwise stated.
2   See in particular the collection of essays in Burden-Strevens & Lindholmer 2018 and the references to earlier literature they provide.
3   Madsen 2018 demonstrates this attitude across Dio's surviving work, with special reference to his treatment of the early Republic.
4   Jones 2016, 297–8; Madsen 2016, 140–9.
5   Madsen 2016, 142–3.
6   Plato *Rep.* 4.427e–435c, 441c–443c.

Cumae, Posidonius of Apamea, and P. Rutilius Rufus.[7] In 44–43 BCE, Cicero expanded and Romanized the scheme in his *De officiis*, a work which was in large part an adaptation of Panaetius' Περὶ τοῦ καθήκοντος ("On the Appropriate").[8] Cicero's treatment both signified and encouraged a general habit that moved the scheme well beyond philosophy and into mainstream political rhetoric. Eventually, a different but related quartet of virtues was inscribed on the golden shield that honored Rome's new *princeps* Augustus and at the same time reminded him of his role as a citizen. The scheme was less frequently used thereafter, and later *principes* justified their position by means of a far more general list of qualities.[9]

Dio did not ascribe to a particular philosophical school, but he was familiar with philosophical language and ideas and included recognizable philosophical tropes.[10] In what survives of the *Roman History*, the four virtues first appear in fragments pertaining to individuals from the third and second centuries BCE, then in several episodes from his account of the first century BCE, and finally in two Augustan settings. In each case, his usage corresponds to the ways in which the scheme was configured in contemporary discourse. Thus, it seems probable that Dio did not create the terms of the assessment, nor did he select for himself the individuals who are judged by these criteria. To a large extent, such associations had already become canonical. Rather, it appears that he used existing examples as a significant strand in a broader discussion about good and bad leadership and, in the end, to demonstrate the superiority of well-managed monarchy as a system of government.[11]

---

7   On the Stoics' interpretation of the virtues, Long 1996. On their competing interpretations of the Platonic quartet, Schofield 2013. On Stoic philosophy and Roman politics, see especially Capelle 1932; Strasburger 1965; Erskine 1990; Griffin & Barnes 1997; Barnes & Griffin 1999; Stone 2008; Simons 2009; Baronowski 2011, 21–5; Morrell 2017.

8   Cic. *Off.* 1.8–10. On the relationship between Panaetius' work and Cicero's, see Griffin's introduction to Atkins' commentary and translation (1991, xix–xxi); Dyck 1995, 17–18; Kries 2003.

9   Fears 1977 and 1981; Wallace-Hadrill 1981; Welch forthcoming a. Simons (2009, 290) notes the difference between Dio's characterizations of the emperors and the "stoischen Informanten" of the earlier books.

10 Madsen 2016, 152. Jones (2016, 299–300) points out that Dio's interest in Plato's philosophy is part of his self-presentation as an educated teacher.

11 Simons 2009, 299.

1   The Very Model of a Roman Stoic: Four Virtues in the Fragments of
     Dio's Early Books

Various character assessments from Dio's republican books are known to us only because the Constantinian excerptor included them in his collection *De virtutibus et vitiis*.[12] Of these, Dio describes only five individuals in terms of the four virtues, including C. Fabricius Luscinus (cos. 282), M. Claudius Marcellus (consul for the first time in 222 and for the last in 210), P. Cornelius Scipio Africanus (cos. 205, 194), L. Aemilius Paulus (cos. 182, 168), and his son P. Scipio Aemilianus (cos. 147, 134).[13] Other Romans (for example L. Quinctius Cincinnatus, M. Furius Camillus, and Q. Fabius Maximus Rullianus) are deemed virtuous, but the Stoic scheme plays no obvious role in Dio's evaluation.[14]

These five men do not exhibit the four virtues in the same way, but the correspondences are strong enough to see them as a distinct group. The first, Fabricius, is "most incorruptible" (ἀδωρότατος), astute in his judgment of character, willing to put the good of the community ahead of personal enmity, and able to overcome jealousy.[15] Dio implies his courage by equating him with the military expert (but not-virtuous) Rufinus.[16] We thus have justice, wisdom, moderation, and courage. His overall excellence is highlighted in overtly Stoic terms (fr. 40.2):

---

12   Mallan 2018 and Fromentin 2018 offer a detailed treatment of Dio's text and its relationship to the Constantinian excerptors, Zonaras, and Xiphilinus. Coudry 2018 provides a comprehensive assessment of Dio's treatment of "great men" in his early books.
13   Simons 2009, 188–279; Kemezis 2014, 106.
14   Madsen 2018, 108–11. Cincinnatus is known for his "moderation" (σωφροσύνη) and outstanding "bravery" (ἀρετή); the Faliscans found Camillus to be righteous and god-fearing (fr. 24.3: οὔγε καὶ πολεμίου οὕτω δικαίου ἐπεπείραντο). In the context of the Gallic disaster, he is law-abiding, scrupulous, and patriotic (fr. 25.7: οὕτω γάρ που νόμιμος ἀκριβής τε ἀνὴρ ἐγένετο ὥστε καὶ ἐν τηλικούτῳ τῆς πατρίδος), and Rullianus, like Fabricius, supported the advancement of his personal enemy, L. Papirius Cursor (fr. 36.26).
15   Cass. Dio fr. 40.1–2. For a full treatment of Dio's assessment of Fabricius, see Coudry 2018, 147–53, especially 150 where she remarks that Dio's Fabricius looks more like a Stoic than a statesman. See also Madsen 2018, 111–12 on Fabricius' honesty.
16   Other authors recognize Fabricius' qualities, but in a general manner. Aulus Gellius (*NA* 4.8.1) sets Fabricius up as a military hero, calling him "a man of great glory and great deeds" (*magna gloria vir magnisque rebus gestis*) but does not reference Stoic thought so overtly.

φιλόπολίς τε γὰρ ἀκριβῶς ὤν, καὶ οὐκ ἐπὶ προσχήματι ἀρετὴν ἀσκῶν, ἐν τῷ ἴσῳ τό τε ὑφ' ἑαυτοῦ καὶ τὸ δι' ἑτέρου τινός, κἂν διάφορός οἱ ᾖ ...

Since he loved his city keenly and did not practice excellence for outward appearance, he thought it a matter of indifference whether the state was benefited by him or by some other man ...

The great Marcellus is also explicitly endowed with the four virtues (fr. 57.31). He has "courage" (ἀνδρεία), "temperance" (σωφροσύνη), and "justice" (δικαιοσύνη), though this is tempered by his refusal to control his troops in victory. His wisdom is obliquely included in that his lenience functions as a mechanism for drawing some communities towards the Romans and away from Hannibal.

The elder Africanus "had splendid native ability supplemented by an excellent education" (ἦν καὶ φύσεως ἀρετῇ κράτιστος καὶ παιδείᾳ λογιμώτατος). Both these elements make him "noble-minded" (μεγαλόφρων), suggesting a sense of justice and generosity, and a "great achiever" (μεγαλοπράγμων), suggesting his bravery on the battlefield (fr. 57.38). Wisdom is affirmed via the superlatives that describe Scipio's natural talent and learning, justice (both deliberative and distributive) and courage are asserted in his capacity for great deeds, and temperance lurks behind the assertion that he is driven by "steadfast intention" (ἐχέγγυῃ διανοίᾳ) rather than "empty pride" (κενὸν αὔχημα).[17]

Dio's Paulus is more complicated (fr. 67). He is a good general and, like Fabricius, "incorruptible" (ἀδωρότατος), implying his sense of justice. He is also "measured" (μέτριος), "most shrewd" (εὐβουλότατος), and brave. Along with the cardinal four, he is also said to be "most fortunate" (εὐτυχέστατος) in prosecuting warfare. His reputation for good fortune might have been tempered if Dio had generalized: when both his younger sons died around the time of his triumph, Paulus became a byword for misfortune.[18] Dio's Paulus also is somewhat too inclined to exhibit the slippery virtue of generosity: he favors his victorious soldiers over his victims. Unlike Marcellus, who is also overly forbearing towards his soldiers, there is no suggestion that Paulus uses lenience as a strategy.

Dio credits Aemilianus with all four virtues in high degree (fr. 70.4). He is excellent in his ability to plan and (as a result) to make quick decisions under pressure (ἄριστος μὲν ἦν ἐκ πλείονος τὸ δέον ἐκφροντίσαι, ἄριστος δὲ καὶ ἐκ τοῦ

---

17   The excerptor says that Scipio has the "greatest nobility of mind, and of language as well" (τό τε φρόνημα καὶ τὸ τῆς γνώμης καὶ τὸ τῶν λόγων). For a full treatment of Dio's view of Africanus, see Simons 2009, 200–40.
18   Polyb. 18.35; Liv. 45.40. Paulus' change in fortune, Val. Max. 5.10.2: "first the most fortunate and then the least lucky" (*nunc felicissimi nunc miserrimi*). Also Plut. *Aem. Paul.* 31–6.

παραχρῆμα τὸ κατεπεῖγον ἐρευνῆσαι). His experience in decision-making and his thoughtfulness allow him to accomplish his objectives "safely" (ἀσφαλῶς), pointing to a prudence that reduces a dependence on good fortune (fr. 70.5). Similarly, Aemilianus is "brave" (τολμητής) rather than rash (fr. 70.5). "In an amazing way" (τὰ μάλιστα ἄν τις αὐτοῦ θαυμάσειεν), he can move between planning and execution, between the realm of the general and the realm of the soldier (fr. 70.6). We see ability to plan re-emerge at fr. 70.8, where Aemilianus' providence is also stressed. Dio then moves to his capacity for justice (fr. 70.7). Aemilianus "kept faith scrupulously" (τὴν πιστότητα ... ἀκριβῆ ἐκέκτητο) with friends and enemies, Romans and foreigners alike. This passion for rectitude had practical value as it won many individuals and cities over to his side. Finally, Dio expounds on Aemilianus' temperance, expressed both as "moderation" (μετριότης) and "reasonableness" (ἐπιείκεια). He is thus both measured and reasonable. As in the case of Fabricius, Aemilianus' virtue places him beyond the reach of normal human envy (fr. 70.9). Dio provides much more extensive detail about each of Aemilianus' virtues than he does in the previous character assessments, but there is considerable consistency in the vocabulary and conceptual framework in all the Roman character assessments.

The peculiarity of these five descriptions is further highlighted by a comparison with three non-Romans, Hannibal, Massinissa, and Viriathus, who share some of these qualities but not all four. Dio's Hannibal is intelligent, trustworthy, and brave, but lacks temperance when crossed, and his wisdom is manifested in his cunning and cynicism rather than his use of it for any higher purpose (fr. 54.1–3):[19]

> συνεῖναί τε γὰρ ὀξύτατα καὶ ἐκφροντίσαι πάνθ' ὅσα ἐνεθυμεῖτο τάχιστα ἐδύνατο· καίτοι πέφυκεν ὡς πλήθει τὸ μὲν βέβαιον ἐκ βραδυτῆτος, τὸ δὲ ὀξύρροπον ἐκ τάχους διανοίας ὑπάρχειν. ποριμώτατος τε γὰρ ἐκ τοῦ ὑπογυωτάτου καὶ διαρκέστατος ἐς τὸ φερεγγυώτατον ἦν·[20] τό τε ἀεὶ παρὸν ἀσφαλῶς διετίθετο καὶ τὸ μέλλον ἰσχυρῶς προενόει, βουλευτής τε τοῦ συνήθους ἱκανώτατος καὶ εἰκαστὴς τοῦ παραδόξου ἀκριβέστατος γενόμενος, ἀφ' ὧν τό τε ἤδη προσπῖπτόν οἱ ἑτοιμότατα καὶ δι' ἐλαχίστου καθίστατο, καὶ τὸ μέλλον ἐκ πολλοῦ τοῖς λογισμοῖς προλαμβάνων ὡς καὶ παρὸν διεσκόπει.

---

19 On literary descriptions of Hannibal's character and the high degree of intertextuality they contain, see, for example, Moore 2010. Jones 2016 considers the role of *paideia* in later parts of Dio's history.

20 ποριμώτατος is Foster's emendation for κ ... ώτατος.

> He could comprehend matters most clearly and plan out most promptly every project that he conceived, notwithstanding the fact that, as a rule, sureness is the result of deliberation and instability the result of a hasty disposition. He was most resourceful in the most sudden emergency, and most steadfast to the point of utter trustworthiness. Not only did he safely handle the affair of the moment, but he accurately read the future beforehand; he proved himself a most capable counsellor in ordinary events and a most accurate judge of the unusual. By these powers he not only handled the situation immediately confronting him most readily and in the briefest time, but also by calculation anticipated the future afar off and considered it as though it were actually present.

Massinissa (fr. 57.50) and Viriathus (fr. 73) receive shorter treatment. Massinissa could successfully plan and execute war and was outstanding in "trustworthiness" (πίστις), despite being a normally "untrustworthy" (ἄπιστος) Numidian! Dio's treatment of these figures shows some Stoic influence and some similarity in vocabulary with his five Romans, but, like Cincinnatus and Camillus, they do not possess all four cardinal virtues.[21]

Lintott (1997, 2500) rightly suggests that Dio's description of Hannibal, along with that of Aemilianus, relies heavily on Thucydides' portrait of Themistocles (1.138.3). All three know how to make the best decisions under pressure and are outstanding in their foresight.[22] However, Dio goes further than Thucydides' summary, which concentrates mainly on Themistocles' "sagacity" (σύνεσις). Dio's Hannibal has this same quality (fr. 54.1–9), but he also has physical strength which, like his mental capacity, results from a combination of natural talent, training, and experience. The emphasis on "training" (παιδεία), both Punic and Greek, presents another departure from Thucydides, who stipulates that Themistocles' talents were not assisted by any training. However, Dio's Hannibal is not a good Stoic either. His fundamentally pessimistic view of humankind enables him to forestall plots and to stay ahead of both his friends and enemies. If people choose not to follow him, they could find themselves victims of his φρόνημα, a word that can mean arrogance as well as strength of mind, and Dio surely intends to imply the former at this point. Thus, moderation is also missing from the portrait.

---

21 Simons 2009, 188–99, 273–9. On the Stoic overtones in Appian's characterization of Africanus, Viriathus, and Aemilianus in the *Iberike*, Gómez Espelosín 1993, 424.

22 There are more Thucydidean overtones in Aemilianus' precaution in the face of danger (Thuc. 2.11.4–5, Cass. Dio 21.70.4).

Simons has suggested that in forming all these portraits, Dio combined material from the philosopher-historian Posidonius with the work of a historian like Valerius Antias or Claudius Quadrigarius.[23] Posidonius might well be the source for some of this discourse. We know that he wrote about Scipio Africanus and M. Marcellus.[24] However, especially with respect to Aemilianus, the record is more complicated. Polybius, for example, was a personal acquaintance whose assessment (32.9–16) also portrays Aemilianus as possessing exactly the same virtues.[25] We know that Polybius also wrote favorably about Aemilianus' behavior at the sack of Carthage in 146, stressing his "human empathy" (φιλανθρωπία) even at the moment of the city's destruction.[26] The Sicilian author Diodorus (36.26–7) even references Polybius at this point. Simons rejects Polybius as a source for Dio because he sees Dio presenting a portrait of someone seeking excellence for its own sake. This would make him a better Stoic than the man Polybius describes. He merely desired a reputation for excellence.[27] The passage in Dio also fails to refer to the examples that both Polybius and Diodorus offer to demonstrate Aemilianus' virtue. This point is well made.

Simons must be right to link all these portraits to an early first-century author. In relating Aemilianus' conquest of Carthage, Dio closely follows the character assessment of someone who argued for, and even reinforced, the Stoicizing terms of Polybius' ideal.[28] Whoever it was might also be responsible for Dio's philosophically-inspired hostility towards Tiberius Gracchus.[29] At the same time, Dio has added his own stamp to the material. In the case of Africanus and the non-Romans, he stresses "training" (παιδεία) more than a Stoic might have.[30]

---

23 Simons 2009, 271.
24 Posidonius on Africanus: Kidd 1999, 339; Marcellus: Kidd 1999, 332–6.
25 Polyb. 31.29.1–7. See also Diod. 31.27.8.
26 Baronowski 2011, 2.
27 Simons 2009, 260–2. Diodorus must be using Polybius in his character sketch at 31.26–7. He references Polybius himself, and the language as well as the information closely matches Polybius' description.
28 Dio himself is aware of negative assessments of Aemilianus. See, for example, fr. 84.1, where Dio acknowledges the charge of "ambition" (φιλοτιμία). Even at this point, however, Dio says that his enemies recognized his patriotism ("they saw he was valuable to the state," χρήσιμόν τε γὰρ πρὸς τὰ κοινὰ ἑώρων).
29 Cass. Dio fr. 83.1: "and when once he had turned aside from what was best, he drifted, quite in spite of himself, into what was worst" (καὶ ἐπειδὴ ἅπαξ ἔξω τοῦ βελτίστου παρετράπη, καὶ ἄκων ἐς τὸ κάκιστον ἐξώκειλε). Lange 2018, 183–4.
30 Simons (2009, 195, 208–9) draws attention to the importance of education ("Erziehung") for Posidonius (frs. 176, 148 Edelstein & Kidd). However, with respect to Hannibal and Viriathus, Dio emphasizes the lessons from non-Hellenic and real-life experience rather

Even so, Posidonius is only one of several possibilities. Aemilianus' own association with Stoicism and his friendship with several Stoics will have had an impact on various treatments. According to Cicero (*Off.* 2.76), Panaetius of Rhodes, who travelled with Aemilianus, is said to have praised him as "self-controlled" (*abstinens*);[31] Cicero himself offered a positive assessment and frequently drew attention to his Stoic connections. P. Rutilius Rufus (c. 160–after 78), another adherent of Stoicism, was a contemporary of and known to both Aemilianus, Panaetius, and Posidonius. Although it is hard to know exactly who said what about Aemilianus, it is clear that many contemporaries had a view and that they were not in agreement. There was one issue which might have aroused criticism. Aemilianus was the destroyer of Numantia as well as Carthage. At least one author was hostile to Aemilianus and used Stoic terms in the critique. As Tweedie (2015, 181–2) demonstrates, we can compare Aemilianus' character in three works by Appian – the *Punica*, *Iberike*, and *Civil Wars* – and find differences that must reflect the different attitudes of his sources. In the *Punica* (almost certainly based on Polybius), Aemilianus possesses virtue, especially that of φιλανθρωπία, while in the *Iberike*, Aemilianus is expressly denied the same virtue in the conquest of Numantia. Tweedie argues that P. Rutilius Rufus is the most likely source for the less favorable view. Rutilius was present at Numantia, and, if he is the source, his negative view was based on personal interaction.[32] By contrast, they might have agreed (though not everyone did) with his lackluster defense of the actions of his controversial cousin, Tiberius Gracchus.[33]

What should be recognized is that this is a highly selective list. The specific virtues and their repeated appearance suggest that descriptions of these five Romans owe their terms to at least one Stoicizing writer who treated the third and second centuries, but also that Dio has selected and adapted that material in line with his own preoccupations.

---

than philosophical *paideia*. The failed *paideia* of Tiberius Gracchus (fr. 83.1) looks rather different. Here we might well have a case of Posidonius, Rutilius, or another Stoicizing conservative writer suggesting that Gracchus was educated in Stoic precepts, but that they did not prevail over his ambition (Rees 2011, 16–17). On the competition between Greek philosophical *paideia* and Roman *disciplina*, Gildenhard 2007, 97–106.

31   Posidonius himself is the source for Aemilianus and Panaetius' joint travels to Alexandria on a diplomatic mission to Ptolemy VIII. See Kidd 1999, 32 T7 (T10A Jac.); Athenaeus 12.549D–E. (NB Athenaeus confuses Posidonius with Panaetius).

32   Tweedie 2015, 172. Strasburger (1965, 40) proposes Posidonius as the source of ambivalence rather than Rutilius.

33   Plutarch (*Apophth. Scip. Min.* 23 = *Mor.* 201F) and Appian (*B Civ.* 1.19) both record hostility towards Aemilianus after Tiberius Gracchus' death (Beness 2005).

2 Cicero in Exile

As we might expect, Cicero's virtues also come under Dio's scrutiny but via a convoluted path. The first instance is when Cicero encounters Philiscus during his exile.[34] The meeting is otherwise unattested and scholars, with good reason, have supposed that the story is pure fiction.[35] Rees, as part of his study of human nature in Dio, argues that the dialogue displays close affinity with Ciceronian language and ideas and there is a slim possibility that Philiscus actually existed.[36] Whether that is correct or not, its particular use of the cardinal virtues suggests that if Dio did not create the episode he seized upon it in order to highlight his judgment that Cicero was a weak politician and a failed philosopher.[37]

In Dio's narrative, Philiscus, on meeting Cicero, immediately berates him for failing to accept his exile with the equanimity of someone who has not only previously displayed "prudence" (φρόνησις) and "wisdom" (σοφία) but also enjoyed the best "training" (παιδεία).[38] Philiscus then goes through each of the four virtues, commenting on Cicero's attainment in each case. He also returns to the idea that upbringing is the basis for wisdom, as we saw with Hannibal and Viriathus.

Wisdom comes first in the list (38.22.1–2). Philiscus perceives that Cicero is "most sagacious" (φρονιμώτατος), a quality evidenced in Cicero's ability to lead the state out of danger. Next (38.22.2), Cicero is commended as "most just" (δικαιότατος), and again the evidence is plain: Cicero had taken care to defend his *patria* and his friends against their enemies. This is high praise, and suspiciously different from Dio's normal hostility. Dio more than once calls Cicero a "turncoat" (αὐτόμολος).[39] Cicero is also praised for his "moderation" (σωφροσύνη), although Philiscus' reasoning is rather vague at this point

---

34 For a full discussion, Rees 2011, 163–80.

35 Simons 2009, 16, referring to 38.28.1, calls the exchange "einen philosophisch anmutenden Dialog." Kemezis (2014, Appendix 1) suggests that the episode acts as a *consolatio ad Dionem* following Dio's own exile in 229. Jones (2016, 300) highlights the many Platonic resonances in the episode.

36 Rees 2011, 164–170.

37 In the case of M. Porcius Cato (as Martin Stone observed [see n. 86 below]), Dio acknowledges the four virtues but in four different contexts: purity (37.57.3); equity (38.3.1); integrity (39.22.4); general excellence (42.13.2); intelligence (σύνεσις) (42.57.2). On Dio's treatment of Cato, see also Mallan 2016, 261–2; Madsen 2018, 116. On Cato's adherence to Stoicism, Morrell 2017, esp. 98–128, with notes to previous studies.

38 Cass. Dio 38.18.1–3.

39 Cass. Dio 36.44.2, 39.63.5, 46.3.4. On Dio's view of Cicero, Millar 1961, 15–16; Lintott 1997, 2514–18; Rees 2011, 102–16.

(38.22.3). Then Philiscus expresses surprise that a man so well versed in three virtues should be so deficient in the fourth (38.22.4–5):

> οὕτω δὲ δὴ τούτων ἐχόντων ἐγὼ μέν σε καὶ ἀνδρειότατον ᾤμην εἶναι, τοσαύτῃ μὲν ῥώμῃ διανοίας τοσαύτῃ δὲ καὶ ἰσχύι λόγων χρώμενον· (5) σὺ δέ, ὡς ἔοικας, αὐτὸς ἑαυτοῦ, ἐκπλαγεὶς ὅτι παρά τε τὴν ἐλπίδα καὶ παρὰ τὴν ἀξίαν ἔπταισας, παρῄρησαί τι τοῦ σφόδρα ἀνδρείου.
>
> This being the case, I, for my part, supposed you were also very brave, enjoying, as you did, such force of intellect and such power of oratory. But it seems that, startled out of yourself through having failed contrary to your hopes and deserts, you have fallen a little short of true courage.

There is perhaps a little more to this part of the dialogue. Rees makes the point (2011, 179) that "[Philiscus] associates Cicero with good motives, many of which Cicero has claimed for himself, in a way that allows Dio to impress upon the reader what things Cicero fell short in." I agree, but the effect calls into question not just Cicero's courage, which is clearly lacking, but also the other virtues of wisdom, justice, and temperance that Philiscus so generously assigns to him. Can they be truly present, or does a failure in courage give the lie to the other three, especially temperance? Cicero has been anything but moderate in Dio's narrative.[40] If, as Rees suggests, the story was adapted rather than invented, then Dio has at very least used it to reinforce his treatment of a character whose opinions and self-justifications he refused to accept.

3   The Virtuous Caesar?

Dio's treatment of the virtues of Gaius Julius Caesar raises equally interesting but different questions.[41] General acknowledgment of Caesar's qualities is spread throughout the narrative. At Placentia, for example, Caesar is assigned the role of a moral instructor more intent on moderating his soldiers' behavior than calling out their general disobedience (41.27.2).[42] There is emphasis on

---

40 On Cicero's corrosive "free speech" (*parrhesia*), see Mallan 2016.
41 A full study of this topic is beyond the scope of this paper. What follows attempts to open up discussion of Dio's nuanced treatment of Caesar's virtues, especially when the four are ascribed in one context.
42 Fantham (1985, 120) calls Dio's version a "long moralizing speech … that would certainly have bored any self-respecting legionary into violence or despair." Chrissanthos (2001, 65) ascribes the view to Pollio.

the importance of ethical behavior at this point, especially when fighting in a civil conflict (41.32–3). At other times, Dio stresses Caesar's bravery, goodness, and humanity,[43] and, above all, his "reasonableness" (ἐπιείκεια), the term he consistently uses to translate the Latin *clementia*.[44] However, Dio also shows us many of Caesar's less admirable traits, especially when he describes Caesar's lack of moderation at the end of the year 45.[45] Burden-Strevens (2015, 95–102) argues that even when Dio includes praise of Caesar, usually in direct speech, the surrounding context undermines the claims of the speaker and gives the lie to Caesar's reputation. In one vital passage where Caesar dispenses clemency after the battle of Thapsus, Dio demonstrates this measured and subtle attitude rather than the positive assurances recorded by more partisan authors.[46] The two appearances of Caesar with the four virtues should be read against this complicated assessment.

Directly upon his return from the African campaign, Dio's Caesar delivers a speech in the Senate in which he claims that moderation will be the hallmark of his new role as consul and dictator.[47] The speech itself is designed to win the "good will" (εὔνοια) of anyone who was afraid or suspicious ("fearing his power and suspicious of his proud bearing," τήν τε δύναμιν αὐτοῦ φοβουμένους καὶ τὸ φρόνημα ὑποτοπουμένους).[48] What follows is a claim to all four cardinal virtues.

In the first place, "Caesar" states (43.15.7) that his motivation in undertaking the war was limited. He wished (reasonably in his view) only to punish and rebuke only those opponents who had attacked him (ὥστε πάντας μὲν τοὺς ἀντιπολεμήσαντας κολάσασθαι πάντας δὲ τοὺς ἀντιστασιάσαντας νουθετῆσαι), to "play the role of an honest man safely" (ἀνδραγαθίζεσθαι ἀσφαλῶς), and to attain "prosperity with glory" (εὐτυχεῖν εὐκλεῶς). The speech thus opens with a display of temperance, in his terms.

---

43   For example, at 43.50.2 there is reference to Caesar's reputation for bravery and goodness: "he gained a great reputation not only for bravery but also for goodness" (οὐκ ἐπ' ἀνδρείᾳ μόνον ἀλλὰ καὶ ἐπὶ χρηστότητι ἰσχυρῶς εὐδοκίμησεν).

44   Cass. Dio 44.6.4, 8.1. See also Plut. *Caes.* 57.4 and the Greek translation of *RGDA* 34.2.

45   Cass. Dio 43.41.3; Welch 2012, 112–13.

46   Dio 43.12–14. For a succinct and useful comparison of divergent reports, Pelling 2011b, 404–8. Holmes, famous for his outright partisanship, calls Dio a "malignant historian" precisely because he adopts a measured approach to Caesar at this point (1923, 266).

47   Cass. Dio 43.15–18. The speech has drawn very little attention. Millar (1961, 12–13), in keeping with his general view, suggests that it has very little to do with Caesar and relates very closely to Dio's own situation. Burden-Strevens (2015, 95–102) does much more to show how the speech functions within the narrative.

48   The vocabulary at 43.15.1 recalls Dio's description of Hannibal's "arrogance" (φρόνημα) (fr. 54, quoted above). Overt comparison of Caesar and Hannibal is a significant feature of an anti-Caesar tradition (Ahl 1972; Vessey 1982).

"Caesar" then recognizes the justice embedded in living up to his earlier promises of clemency (43.16.1). He raises the examples of Marius, Cinna, and Sulla, who promised fair treatment but did the exact opposite (43.15.3). By contrast, "Caesar" presents himself as the "good" (καλός) and "just" (δίκαιος) man. The theme of the proper use of victory then moves delicately to wisdom: the greater the share of "heaven-granted" (ἐκ τοῦ δαιμονίου) talent, the greater the responsibility there was to make use of it "more prudently" (εὐβουλότερον). Then moderation appears more openly. "Success" (εὐπραγία) needs "temperance" (σωφροσύνη) and "authority" (ἐξουσία) must be "measured" (μετριάσασα). There is no real need to articulate courage. The whole speech rests on the audience's awareness of Caesar's unrelenting military victories. "Caesar" is pledging to display the remaining three virtues to the same degree because success is nothing "without moral excellence" (χωρὶς ἀρετῆς). Virtue, he says, ensures that one will be loved in life and will attain genuine commendation after death (43.16.3). Dio must have been aware of the irony in this statement, both in the occasional lack of temperance he notes in Caesar and in the violence that would soon end his spectacular career.

Caesar with four virtues makes another appearance via direct speech later in the narrative. Dio, along with Appian (*B Civ*. 2.144–6), puts a long oration into the mouth of Marcus Antonius on the occasion of Caesar's funeral (44.36–49).[49] Over many chapters, Antonius extols Caesar's virtues, claiming his "excellence" (ἀρετή) eight times within the speech. Once again, we get a combination of innate mental sharpness and training, which together formed the cleverness we have already observed in other contexts (44.38.6–8). Indeed, Caesar had all the cognitive skills one could wish for. He was also generous but a fair manager (44.39); thus, beneficence (*liberalitas*) is kept in proper check. Caesar's clemency (44.39.4) comes next. In fact, his capacity for goodness was so intense that he failed to see evil in others (44.39.5), suggesting a very un-Caesar-like naiveté. Antonius then moves on to Caesar's public service (44.40), where both justice and courage are on display. The descriptions are sanitized in the extreme. Comparison of Caesar's praetorship with that given in Dio's narrative (37.52–4), for example, reveals two very different versions.[50] Caesar's courage then comes into focus, via a description of the Gallic campaigns (44.43–4). His sorrow at the misfortune of civil war (44.44.3–4) and his clemency in the aftermath (44.45) again underpin a reputation for moderation. This is more than

---

49 Scholarship on Antonius' funeral speech is extensive. See, for example, Kennedy 1968; Gowing 1992, 228–34; Hölkeskamp 2013, 11–13; Mahy 2013, 331, 339–40; Setaioli 2017. Very few take time to consider Dio's contribution.
50 On the comparison, see Burden-Strevens 2015, 226.

just clemency, however. Caesar's ability to withstand the lure of Alexandria and its luxurious lifestyle is a true victory for temperance (44.46.1–3). As if his reputation for saving Romans in his own civil war was not enough, he is also credited with saving the survivors from the wars with Lepidus and Sertorius (44.47.6). The last chapter (44.49) draws all his virtues and offices together to underline the heinous nature of the conspiracy to kill him.

The speech has been dismissed as a standard funeral oration created by Dio himself.[51] Burden-Strevens, however, notes its essential role in the text, especially in that it answers (and defeats) Cicero's proposal for an amnesty. And, in Dio's hands it is obvious political spin: at each point the image of Caesar it presents runs completely counter to the figure that Dio presents elsewhere.[52] Dio's Caesar, it seems, is not as virtuous as Antonius claims.

How much of this panegyric comes from Caesar's own context and how much, as is usually assumed, is Dio's creation? Although, as we shall see, it is not inconceivable that Antonius at some point might have praised Caesar against the template of the four virtues, there are signs that in this form it cannot be what it purports to be. In the first place, it seems to know Antonius' future reputation. Reference to virtue in the face of the fleshpots of Alexandria is particularly ironic (44.46.2), as is an ability to control one's inclination to *liberalitas*, two temptations to which Antonius himself famously yielded. Yet judging Caesar against the cardinal virtues *was* a contemporary strategy which Cicero, for one, employed during Caesar's lifetime and in scathing terms after his death.[53] In the speech *Pro Marcello*, Cicero expresses the same view of glory that Dio has Caesar purport in his speech to the Senate.[54] At the end of the *Second Philippic*, when comparing the virtues of Caesar with Antonius' deficiencies, Cicero says that Caesar had all the virtues, even if in perverted

---

51   Kennedy states (1968, 102), "Dio's speech need not be considered since it bears little resemblance to the rest of the evidence and is clearly a product of the historian himself." Gowing (1992, 230), citing Schwartz, notes the philosophical overtones in Dio's direct speech.

52   Burden-Strevens 2015, 96–7, 223–9. I thank him for making me reconsider this speech and for many other valuable observations on a draft of this paper.

53   Cicero's "praise" is best exemplified in *Pro Rege Deiotaro* (e.g. 34: "We saw a leader who was not only not a tyrant but most merciful in his victory," *non modo non tyrannum, sed clementissimum in victoria ducem vidimus*), delivered at the end of 45.

54   Cic. *Marc.* 8–9, 26; Welch 2012, 309. The sentiment appears again in Dio as part of the younger Caesar's speech to the Senate on 13 January 27 (53.8.1–3; Galinsky 1996, 73; Welch 2012, 309–10). In addition, Cicero develops the theme that supernatural forces rather than human decisions were to blame for the outbreak of civil war in the speeches he delivers in 46–45, a theme explored also in Caesar's alleged speech to the Senate.

or lesser form,[55] but his famous *clementia* was a sham, simply a strategy for establishing his corrosive power ("He won over his own men with rewards and his enemies with the image of clemency," *suos praemiis, adversarios clementiae specie devinxerat*). In the *De officiis*, a work written alongside the *Second Philippic*, Cicero overtly criticizes Caesar for lacking the virtue of justice, thereby rendering all his acknowledged talents destructive rather than a cause for praise.[56] Later, Velleius, strangely, reflects this judgment, although his obvious intention is to praise, not criticize (Vell. Pat. 2.41.1–2):

> *hic nobilissima Iuliorum genitus familia et, quod inter omnis antiquitatis studiosos constabat, ab Anchise ac Venere deducens genus, forma omnium civium excellentissimus, vigore animi acerrimus, munificentia effusissimus, animo super humanam et naturam et fidem evectus, magnitudine cogitationum, celeritate bellandi, patientia periculorum Magno illi Alexandro, sed sobrio neque iracundo simillimus, qui denique semper et cibo et somno in vitam, non in voluptatem uteretur …*

Caesar was descended from the very noble and, it is generally agreed, very ancient family of the Julii, tracing his line back to Anchises and Venus. Preeminent among all his fellow citizens for his good looks, he was possessed of a very keen and vigorous intellect and extreme generosity, and his courage transcended human nature and surpassed human belief. In the magnitude of his projects, in the speed of his military action, and in resolve in the face of danger, he most resembled the famous Alexander the Great, but a sober Alexander and not one given to anger; he was, in fact, a man who employed food and sleep to sustain life, not for pleasure.[57]

In many ways, Velleius' description maps onto Dio's. Velleius presents Caesar as smart, generous, and courageous. His temperance is also manifest. Justice is the problem. Caesar is *effusissimus* in his liberality, but there is no hint of deliberative justice. Given Velleius' overt intention to praise Caesar, it cannot be that he himself has decided to omit "the mistress and queen of the virtues" (Atkins 1990).[58] Velleius appears to be reproducing praise which contains a sub-text of criticism that he has not picked up.

---

55 *Phil.* 2.116; Stone 2008, 227–8.
56 Especially at *Off.* 3.82–5, but also at *Off.* 2.23. Dyck 1996, 395, 406, 575–6, 603–8.
57 Translation from Yardley & Barrett 2011. On Velleius' treatment of Caesar, Pelling 2011a.
58 Atkins 1990 examines the role of deliberative justice in Cicero's *De officiis*. As she points out (1990, 258–63), justice controls the treatise just as it is the fundamental basis for *societas* (1990, 263). Its absence from Velleius' praise of Caesar is striking.

It is no stretch to think that Caesar's defenders responded to such assessments with material that stressed the full gamut of Caesar's virtues, including deliberative justice, and that Dio, with heavy irony, draws on this tradition. If so, both speeches perhaps arise out of the lively discourse about Caesar's character that started before his death and continued for several generations, which Dio, on seeing the potential for irony, seized and then developed with great enthusiasm. That it is his own composition remains a distinct possibility, but, even if so, it draws upon an established habit of praising or criticizing this divisive and contested figure in terms of his measure against the cardinal virtues.

4   Calenus versus Cicero: a Contest in Virtue

Dio presents the virtues of both Antonius and Cicero in direct competition in a long speech assigned to Quintus Fufius Calenus. Its role is to answer Dio's version of Cicero's rhetorical attack on Antonius in late 44 and early 43. The circumstances are artificial, and even the content of the speech has little to do with its dramatic context.[59] Although it is normally read against the *Philippics*, the terms of the speech align far better with the *De officiis*.[60]

The first unambiguous indication of a virtue-for-virtue contest is provided at 46.3.4. The major challenge involves justice, as it does in *De officiis* (*Off.* 1.20–60). Cicero is called "untrustworthy by nature" (ἄπιστος φύσει). He is a troublemaker who lacks *gravitas* and is well-deserving of the name of "turncoat" (αὐτόμολος) which, as we have seen, Dio has already used in the context of 66 (36.44.2). Cicero's history of failing to act justly continues in the next chapter, where he is called a "cheat and charlatan" (γόης καὶ μάγος) who could not operate in any society governed by "concord" (ὁμονοία).[61] A voice for hire by the guilty as well as the innocent (46.7.1), driven by jealousy of everyone who rose above him (46.8.3), Cicero was too afraid to challenge Caesar when such a challenge might have made a real difference. Antonius, in fact, should not have

---

59 On the speech of Q. Fufius Calenus in context, see Millar 1961, 19–22; Stone 1999, 54; Rees 2011, 149–62; Burden-Strevens 2015, 64–70; Fomin 2016, 231–2.

60 Stone 2008, 237. Dio's Calenus shows some connection to other anti-Ciceronian invectives, including the Pseudo-Sallustian invectives and two letters attributed to Marcus Brutus, but they are not framed within the terms of the cardinal virtues.

61 Cass. Dio 46.4.1, also 46.12.3. The criticism is meant to catch the attention of the reader, especially given Cicero's published views on *concordia* as the foundation of the *res publica*. Important too is the setting: Dio (wrongly) places the debate in the Temple of Concord.

to apologize for Caesar's recognition of his "excellence" (ἀρετή).⁶² Antonius, on the other hand, says Calenus, could admonish the all-powerful dictator. This is the lesson of the Lupercalia, when he prevented Caesar from making himself King of the Roman People.⁶³

Calenus' Antonius is a paragon of virtue. He manifestly demonstrates his capacity for prudence, justice (both deliberative and distributive), courage, and temperance, while Cicero's whole career is testament to his injustice, stupidity, cowardice, and unawareness of what is either fitting or temperate.⁶⁴ Antonius' courage and prudence can be seen in his giving an issue serious consideration before either acting or speaking:⁶⁵ having made it his business to ascertain Caesar's intentions, he utilizes the force of place (the Roman Forum), the audience (the Roman People), and the right occasion (the Lupercalia) to achieve the right outcome. The envious assassins and their leader Cicero offer nothing but discord and violence, but Antonius would have prevented Caesar from going too far in the first place.⁶⁶ Words such as "most wise" (σοφώτατα), "in complete safety" (ἀσφαλέστατα), and "most intelligently" (φρονιμώτατα) demonstrate how his refined sense of justice and courage are tempered by excellent good sense and reasonableness.

Cicero emerges as Antonius' exact opposite, with any suggestion of virtue inviting heavy sarcasm. His demonstrated deficiencies should have made him ashamed to criticize Antonius, whose response to Caesar was measured and sensible. Cicero is accused of sexual intemperance because he married a young girl (in fact his ward) for her money, while carrying on an affair with Caerellia, a woman much older than himself (46.18.3–4). He does not know how to raise his son, who is drunk more often than sober, and his relationship with both Terentia and Tullia further reveals his deviance from accepted social norms.⁶⁷

---

62 Cass. Dio 46.13.2–3: ὅτι ἐφοβοῦ νὴ Δία. εἶτα σὺ μὲν τότε σιωπήσας συγγνώμης διὰ τὴν δειλίαν τεύξῃ, οὗτος δὲ ὅτι σοῦ προετιμήθη, δίκην διὰ τὴν ἀρετὴν ὑφέξει; ("Because, by Jupiter, you were afraid. Shall you, then, who were silent at the time, obtain pardon for your cowardice, and shall he, because he was preferred over you, submit to punishment for his virtue?")

63 Cass. Dio 46.17–19. NB 46.17.5: "And [Antonius] convinced [Caesar] of his error most cleverly and restrained him most prudently, until, abashed and afraid, he would not accept either the name of king or the diadem" (καὶ ἐξήλεγξε σοφώτατα καὶ ἐπέσχεν ἀσφαλέστατα, ὥστε καὶ αἰδεσθέντα καὶ φοβηθέντα μήτε τὸ ὄνομα τὸ τοῦ βασιλέως μήτε τὸ διάδημα).

64 Stone 2008, 230–3.

65 Cass. Dio 46.19.4: "having seen clearly" (ἀκριβῶς εἰδώς).

66 Cass. Dio 46.19. On the source tradition for the Lupercalia, Welwei 1967; Weinstock 1971, 331–40; Pelling 1988, 146–7.

67 For a discussion of Cicero's relationship with Tullia, see Treggiari 2002, 69–73. On Marcus Junior and inebriation: Sen. Suas. 7.13; Sen. Ben. 4.31; Plin. HN 14.147; Wright 1997, 53–9.

Worse still, Cicero *pretends* to be an upright citizen, but the whole city knows otherwise. Cicero has no right to lecture Antonius (or anyone else) on appropriate behavior. Damningly, although Calenus does not say so, some will have known that Cicero's own philosophical treatise poses hypocrisy as worse than almost any other fault.[68]

The contest over courage mostly emphasizes Cicero's implicit and explicit cowardice. According to Calenus, Cicero trembles whenever he appears in court (46.7.2–4); he would not stand up to the dictator Caesar, but, with Caesar dead, will accuse Antonius of wrong-doing for actions taken on Caesar's watch (46.15.2). A review of Cicero's career shows him fearing Antonius' lictors in 47 (46.16.5), running away from his trial in 58 (46.21.2), accepting Antonius' provincial assignments of November 44, and then objecting after Antonius was out of the way (46.23.4–5).

Neither does Cicero know how to receive a favor, and so he fails in either giving or receiving *liberalitas*. The strongest expression of this can be found at 46.22.2–3, just before Calenus accuses Cicero of being the *auctor* of a conspiracy in which he was too cowardly to take an active part:[69]

> ... ἀντὶ δὲ τῆς ἀχαριστίας ἧς ἐκείνου κατηγορεῖς, αὐτὸν μὴ ἀδικεῖν τοὺς εὐεργέτας. ἓν γάρ τοι καὶ τοῦτο τῶν κακῶν τῶν ἐμφύτων αὐτῷ ἐστιν, ὅτι μισεῖ μάλιστα πάντων τούς τι αὐτὸν εὖ πεποιηκότας, καὶ τῶν μὲν ἄλλων ἀεί τινας θεραπεύει, τούτοις δὲ ἐπιβουλεύει.

> ... instead of accusing him of ingratitude, cease from wronging your benefactors! For this, I must tell you, is one of Cicero's inherent defects, that he hates above all others those who have done him any kindness, and that while he is always fawning upon men of the other kind, yet he keeps plotting against these.

The historical Cicero discusses this very charge at length in the *Second Philippic*. He argues that he owed nothing either to Caesar or Antonius, who should not have been in a position to harm him in the first place.[70] In general, Cicero found it hard to be enthusiastic about the virtue of *liberalitas*, and Antonius'

---

68   Cass. Dio 46.18. On hypocrisy, compare 46.16.4 with *Off.* 1.41.
69   On Cicero as *auctor* of the conspiracy, Cass. Dio 46.22.3–5; *Phil.* 2.25–8; Ramsey 2003, 198–205. On envy and resentment as important themes for Dio, Burden-Strevens 2015, esp. 180–92.
70   Cic. *Phil.* 2.5. See also *Phil.* 1.11; Ramsey 2003, 167–9.

positive reputation for it caused him particular anxiety. He deals with it by calling it *largitio*, and thus turning it into a vice.⁷¹

Apart from judging Cicero by his own treatise on virtue, Calenus' speech reflects *De officiis* in other, rather surprising, ways. Cicero chooses *decorum* ("seemliness") as a Latin equivalent to the Greek concept τὸ πρέπον, the ordering aspect of temperance.⁷² The concept encompasses physical as well as moral beauty.⁷³ When Dio has Calenus criticize Cicero's appearance and actions as not appropriate for a person of his age and status, the terms of the criticism reflect Cicero's conceptualization.⁷⁴ For example, Cicero is accused of trying to hide his legs, because they are ugly; he is too interested in his hair (46.18.2–3); his voice trembles with fear and almost disappears.⁷⁵

More than any other episode involving the cardinal virtues, the Calenus speech allows us to see how Dio manipulates his source material to make a point that has little to do with the surrounding narrative and everything to do with his wish to make a clear judgment of character. He situates the speech within the vigorous senatorial debates of early January 43 over whether Antonius was a public enemy or not. Unlike the speech that Appian gives to Lucius Calpurnius Piso for the same occasion, its content bears little connection to that context.⁷⁶ Moreover, whereas the long speech that Dio gives to Cicero at the end of Book 45 draws on several of the *Philippics*,⁷⁷ Calenus' case concentrates on Antonius' career to the point of the Lupercalia in February 44, and only briefly draws attention to the eventful months following Caesar's assassination. Even linguistic echoes with the *Second Philippic* are few and limited.⁷⁸ Thus, while there is considerable overlap in subject matter, actual direct engagement is not nearly as apparent as the manifest interaction between Cicero's *Philippics* and Dio's "Cicero" speech in Book 45.

The terms in which Calenus frames Antonius' demonstration of prudence are also quite specific, and even puzzling. Calenus openly admits that Caesar

---

71 Stone 2008, 232–3.
72 Cic. *Off.* 1.93; Walsh 2000, xx; Stone 2008, 218. Schofield (2012) provides an extended discussion on the adaptation of temperance for new conditions in the *De Officiis*.
73 Cic. *Off.* 1.96–131.
74 Cic. *Off.* 1.127 on true modesty; 1.130 on appropriate male dignity; 1.131 on an appropriate manner of walking.
75 Compare Cic. *Off.* 1.132–3, 136 with Cass. Dio 46.7.2.
76 App. *B Civ*. 3.54–60; on speeches in Dio, Gowing 1992, 236–7; on Piso, van der Blom 2013, 313.
77 Fromentin & Bertrand 2008, xxiii–xxviii; Burden-Strevens 2015, 59–64.
78 Fromentin & Bertrand 2008, xxviii–xxxii; Burden-Strevens 2015, 66. Relevant correspondences include Cass. Dio 46.20.1 = *Phil*. 2.11; 46.20.1 = 2.16; 36.20.3–5 = 2.18; 46.22.3 = 2.27; 46.22.4 = 2.28; 46.22.5 = 2.4; 46.22.6 = 2.5.

was aiming at tyranny and that Antonius was right to pull him back from the brink (46.19.8–20.1):

> τὰ μὲν οὖν Ἀντωνίου ἔργα σοι ταῦτά ἐστιν, οὐ σκέλος ἄλλως κατάξαντος ἵνα αὐτὸς φύγῃ, οὐδὲ χεῖρα κατακαύσαντος ἵνα Πορσένναν φοβήσῃ, ἀλλὰ τὴν τυραννίδα τὴν τοῦ Καίσαρος σοφίᾳ καὶ περιτεχνήσει, καὶ ὑπὲρ τὸ δόρυ τὸ Δεκί[μ]ου καὶ ὑπὲρ τὸ ξίφος τὸ Βρούτου, παύσαντος. σὺ δ', ὦ Κικέρων, τί ἐν τῇ ὑπατείᾳ σου οὐχ ὅτι σοφὸν ἢ ἀγαθόν, ἀλλ' οὐ καὶ τιμωρίας τῆς μεγίστης ἄξιον ἔπραξας;

> Here, then, you have the deeds of Antonius; he did not break a leg in a vain attempt to make his own escape, nor burn off a hand in order to frighten Porsenna, but *by his cleverness and consummate skill*, which were of more avail than the spear of Deci[m]us or the sword of Brutus, he *put an end to the tyranny of Caesar*. But as for you, Cicero, what did you accomplish in your consulship that was not deserving of the greatest punishment instead of being wise and good?

This is not the Antonius we meet in Appian, or even in the *Thirteenth Philippic*. Rather, it bears a close relationship to the Antonius who abolished the title of dictator and who courted the good opinion of a large number of senators before the younger Caesar arrived and changed politics forever.[79] "Yes," he might have said, "Caesar needed to be stopped, and my shaming him into refusing a crown at the Lupercalia went a long way to reining him in; assassinating him, on the other hand, was as unjust and stupid as it was unnecessary." This is a thoroughly *republican* Antonius.[80] To borrow a term from musicology, the *tessitura* of the speech connects it not to early 43, by which stage Antonius had come forward as Caesar's avenger and therefore was no longer likely to criticize him, but to the months leading up to and including the opening of his fight with Cicero in September 44.[81] The Calenus speech presents an Antonius

---

79 *Phil.* 1.3, 5.10; Frisch 1946, 66; Ramsey 2010, 89–90; Halfmann 2011, 68; Ferriès 2012, 56.
80 Stone 2008, 237, drawing particular attention to Cass. Dio 46.22.6, where Antonius' behavior after Caesar's assassination is "republican," not "tyrannical." A concentration on Cicero's treatment of P. Lentulus Sura in 63 also connects the speech to Antonius, his stepson (46.2.3, 46.20.3–5).
81 Antonius' role as avenger was deliberately obfuscated by the younger Caesar who for political reasons could not afford to share the honor. Syme (1939, 205–9, 215) is well aware of it. For an extended study of the implications of Antonius' claims, see Welch 2014; 2019; forthcoming b.

that cannot be found in the rest of Dio's narrative and yet one who closely corresponds to the character that Cicero is at such pains to defeat in 44 and 43.

5   Antonius and His Lost Virtues

Unlike other authors, Dio has little to say about Antonius' virtues in the many books that cover the period of his ascendancy.[82] In the lead-up to the battle of Actium, however, he has the younger Caesar tell the soldiers that they have nothing to fear. Antonius might have once been formidable, but a descent into effeminacy has left him a shadow of his former self (50.27.6–7):

> τί τις ἂν αὐτοῦ φοβηθείη; τὴν ἀκμὴν τοῦ σώματος; ἀλλὰ παρήβηκε καὶ ἐκτεθήλυνται. τὴν ῥώμην τῆς γνώμης; ἀλλὰ γυναικίζει καὶ ἐκκεκιναίδισται. τὴν εὐσέβειαν τὴν πρὸς τοὺς θεοὺς ἡμῶν; ἀλλὰ πολεμεῖ καὶ ἐκείνοις καὶ τῇ πατρίδι. τὴν πιστότητα τὴν πρὸς τοὺς συμμάχους; καὶ τίς οὐκ οἶδεν ὅπως τὸν Ἀρμένιον ἐξαπατήσας ἔδησε; τὴν [δὲ] ἐπιείκειαν τὴν πρὸς τοὺς φίλους; καὶ τίς οὐχ ἑόρακε τοὺς ὑπ' αὐτοῦ κακῶς ἀπολωλότας; τὴν εὐδοξίαν τὴν παρὰ τοῖς στρατιώταις; καὶ τίς οὐχὶ καὶ ἐκείνων αὐτοῦ κατέγνωκε;

> What is there about him that anyone should dread? His strength of body? But he has passed his prime and become effeminate. His strength of mind? But he plays the woman and has worn himself out with unnatural lust. His piety toward our gods? But he is at war with them as well as with his country. His faithfulness to his allies? But who does not know how he deceived and imprisoned the Armenian? His reasonableness towards his friends? But who has not seen the men who have miserably perished at his hands? His reputation with the soldiers? But who even of them has not condemned him?

Antonius' physical strength comes first, mental strength second, duty third, *fides* fourth, and reasonableness last. In each case the virtue is denied. The younger Caesar asserts that circumstances have robbed Antonius of all these qualities, but this is to say that he once had them. The evidence for his debilitation comes from the fact of his relationship with Cleopatra, his failure in Parthia, and his treatment of Artavasdes of Armenia, whom he tricked into surrender and humiliation.

---

82   On the tradition of Antonius' virtues (as opposed to his vices) in other authors, Welch forthcoming c.

Also significant is the addition of a virtue that Dio has not previously connected to the quartet, that of εὐσέβεια ("sense of reverence"), a common translation of *pietas*. The limiting expression in the younger Caesar's speech, moreover, specifies that the *pietas* that Antonius has betrayed is towards the gods and the fatherland, exactly the same specification as would be found on the *clupeus virtutis* presented to the newly named Augustus on 16 January 27.[83] Furthermore, instead of "temperance" (σωφροσύνη), the younger Caesar refers to Antonius' lack of "reasonableness" (ἐπιείκεια) which, as we have seen, Dio uses to translate the Latin *clementia*. Dio's direct speech again references the exact political rhetoric of its original historical context.

A similar idea of Antonius' dissipated virtue re-emerges in Dio's summary of Antonius' character at the moment of his death in 30 (51.15.2):[84]

> ὁ μὲν συνεῖναί τε τὸ δέον οὐδενὸς ἥσσων ἐγένετο καὶ πολλὰ ἀφρόνως ἔπραξεν, ἀνδρείᾳ τε ἔν τισι διέπρεψε καὶ ὑπὸ δειλίας συχνὰ ἐσφάλη, τῇ τε μεγαλοψυχίᾳ καὶ τῇ δουλοπρεπείᾳ ἐξ ἴσου ἐχρῆτο, καί τά τε ἀλλότρια ἥρπαζε καὶ τὰ οἰκεῖα προΐετο, ἠλέει τε ἀλόγως συχνοὺς καὶ ἐκόλαζεν ἀδίκως πλείονας.

> [Antonius] had no equal in comprehending what was needed, yet he committed many acts of folly. He at times distinguished himself for bravery, yet frequently failed through cowardice. He was characterized equally by greatness of soul and by servility of mind. He would plunder the property of others and would squander his own. He showed compassion to a large number unexpectedly and punished even more without justice.

The language is very familiar. Antonius has "intelligence" (σύνεσις) but it is negated by his stupidity. His acknowledged "courage" (ἀνδρεία) has descended into the cowardice that led to his downfall. He was "great-souled" (μεγαλόψυχος) but displays a "slavish spirit" (δουλοπρέπεια). He gives much, but he takes much. He is often clement, but more often arbitrarily cruel. In other words, Dio summarizes Antonius as possessing all four virtues but having them cancelled out by a precisely corresponding vice.

---

83   Welch (2012, 304–12; forthcoming a) argues that the golden shield presented to the newly-named Augustus on 16 January 27 originally represented a different philosophy and intention from the *corona civica* awarded on 13 January and only later became inextricably linked to it.
84   Welch 2012, 142–53, 218–30.

Dio's summary of Cleopatra's character, juxtaposed with that of Antonius, remains general.[85] His assessment of Antonius, however, reflects a story of the loss of each of the cardinal virtues. The contrast is stark. Antonius is a figure normally noted for his vices, and yet Dio associates him with the cardinal virtues in four different contexts and in four very different modes. In my own view, it is extremely unlikely that our author went to the trouble of creating each episode with such incredible precision of detail and close reference to what was a fast-moving political situation. As in each case studied so far, with the possible exception of the Philiscus dialogue, it is more probable that the basis already existed, and he crafted each episode to suit his narrative purpose.

6   Agrippa the Enigma

Even the Philiscus dialogue, however, looks less of a Dionian invention when it is compared with Dio's obituary for Marcus Agrippa.[86] There are strong affinities also between the obituary for Agrippa and that for Antonius, studied above. Agrippa died unexpectedly in 12 BCE (54.28.3). After describing his funeral, Dio gives a short but rich assessment in terms that are both familiar and different (54.29.1–4). From the beginning, there is a new limiting element. Agrippa is called "the best of the men of that time" (ἄριστος τῶν καθ' ἑαυτὸν ἀνθρώπων); he is thus "excellent" (ἄριστος) only in comparison to his contemporaries (54.29.1). However, it is still high praise, because his generation includes Augustus himself, an issue that is openly acknowledged when Agrippa is shown to have "willingly" (ἐθελοντής) yielded to Augustus the first place that he himself deserved. Agrippa's "wisdom and courage" (σοφία καὶ ἀνδρεία) are also acknowledged as qualities he "handed over most profitably" (λυσιτελέστατα παρέχων) to Augustus (54.29.2). The whole assessment presents Agrippa as muting his own glory for the benefit of the *princeps* and good of the community. Finally, the equal care he took of both ensures that he neither became "obnoxious" (ἐπαχθής) to Augustus himself nor an "object of envy" (ἐπίφθονος) to anyone

---

85   Cass. Dio 51.15.4; Reinhold 1988, 137; Freyburger & Roddaz 2002, 141–2.
86   Martin Stone was my long-standing colleague and close collaborator whose many presentations on the cardinal virtues in late republican politics first inspired me to search for their presence in Dio's extant narrative. The text of his paper "Marcus Agrippa and the Platonic Virtues" (Sydney 2009) was one of those recovered after his death in 2015. Although it was not developed beyond a simple oral presentation, the kernel of the work is too important to omit here. Where it is necessary, I will quote his notes verbatim so that his contribution can be kept distinct from my own.

else.[87] Agrippa's excellence, founded on his service to the public interest, allows him to draw a middle way between the danger of showing up the *princeps* and inspiring the enmity of others. There is also reference to Agrippa's many benefactions to the city which have been treated fully earlier in the narrative.[88] Dio's constant use of the active voice makes very clear that this was all Agrippa's choice. Within the limits of his situation, Agrippa excels, even in using the changed political climate to create new opportunities for a display of virtue. The passage is closely aligned with concerns that Dio expresses throughout his history, the management of envy and the relationship between ruler and adviser being just two.[89]

Agrippa also presents himself as "eager" (ἐπιθυμητής) for "power" (δυναστεία) in his efforts to help Augustus establish sole rule, while at the same time "to the highest degree in favor of popular government" (δημοτικώτατος) "in the performance of good works" (εὐεργεσίαι). He wants to avoid becoming hateful to the boss and to avoid the envy of everyone else (54.29.3–4). He is a better man than the *princeps*, but he accepts his second place for the sake of political and social stability.

And yet, once again, one virtue that ought to be there is missing. There is no reference to deliberative justice. His beneficence looks rather lame in comparison.[90] This is not consistent with Dio's previous presentation of Agrippa where understanding of the role of deliberative justice is as manifest as his republicanism. For example, in Book 52, Dio's Agrippa specifically argues that "equality before the law" (ἰσονομία) represents the most just system (52.4.1). Justice lay in apportioning society's benefits equally to all those who contributed, with distinction made only on the basis of one's "excellence" (ἀρετή) (52.4.2); equality coupled with virtue being awarded its due of praise was the very thing that separated popular institutions from tyranny (52.5.1).[91]

---

87 Agrippa is thus the opposite of Cicero (38.12.7): "He was boorish and hateful (φορτικός τε καὶ ἐπαχθὴς ἦν), and as such was envied and despised (ἐφθονεῖτο καὶ ἐμισεῖτο) even by those he had once pleased"; Burden-Strevens 2015, 131–2.

88 Cass. Dio 49.42–3. For new readings of Agrippa's contribution to the urban landscape, Taylor *et al.* 2016, 40–1; Tan forthcoming.

89 Mallan 2016, 270; Jones 2016.

90 Stone: "Cicero considered *liberalitas* a slippery virtue along a demagogic slope to *largitio* (e.g. *Off*. 1.43). It must always be subordinated to true justice … Not only that. Cicero argues that all the other virtues are subordinate to basic justice, the fundamental social virtue (*Off*. 1.152–60). That is the one that is missing from Dio's list of Agrippa's virtues. Can the omission be inadvertent? Can the best man in his generation really lack the cardinal virtue of justice?" On Cicero's views of *liberalitas* see also Dyck 1996, 155–6.

91 Stone: "Dio is stuck. He sees monarchy as a necessity and his Agrippa assists in creating it (52.41.2). But in doing this he compromises his claim to justice, though Dio has presented

This sentiment stands in stark contrast both to Dio's own views about ἰσονομία (44.2.1) and to the overall assessment of Agrippa at the moment of his death. Leaving out deliberative justice in an overall assessment based on the cardinal virtues is, as we have seen, a "Ciceronian" way of saying that all other virtues are neutralized or negated.

Agrippa should not have been an enigma for Dio. He has great sympathy with Agrippa's choice, and he makes clear at other points of the narrative that he views Agrippa as a just as well as a generous contributor. For the Severan senator who believed that monarchy was the best form of government, but who still saw a role for himself as teacher and adviser to monarchs, the "right-hand man who was in fact better" offered a perfect model for his own role. If the scheme and the obituary were Dio's creation, deliberative justice should have been written into his virtues along with the other four. Its absence suggests that Dio, like Velleius, is working with an earlier construction. It suggests that whoever first composed the terms of reference of the obituary saw Agrippa as the great enabler. Some have raised the possibility that Aulus Cremutius Cordus might well have been a possible source.[92] As with Posidonius and the earlier books, certainty is impossible, but one of Agrippa's contemporaries is likely. In any case, this obituary, like that of Antonius, sits uncomfortably within the narrative and that alone suggests that, while Dio has highlighted elements that appealed to him greatly, he did not create its original terms.

7   Augustus and the Cardinal Virtues

The four virtues emerge to underpin the structure of the "speech" Dio assigns to the almost-Augustus when he attempts to relinquish control of the *res publica*. After a threatening opening, the civil war victor justifies his actions on the basis of *pietas*, both towards his father and the *res publica*. Then follow the virtues that he and Julius Caesar had displayed, including his "clemency and reasonableness" (ἐπιείκεια καὶ πρᾳότης: 53.6.1), his "sense of justice" (τὸ δίκαιον) in placing public affairs back in the hands of the Senate (53.6.2), his military courage, reinforced by the deeds of Julius Caesar (53.7) as well as moral courage, in that he is "greater in spirit" (μεγαλοψυχότερος) not only than his contemporaries but all the exemplary Romans of the past (53.8.1–4). Wisdom is specifically *not* claimed, for it belongs to the Senate and not to an individual

---

him as an eloquent lover of justice and proponent of Republicanism (52.2–13); Agrippa eulogizes justice at some places (e.g. 52.5.1, where justice [δικαιοσύνη] specifically distinguishes 'democracy' [δημοκρατία] from 'monarchy' [μοναρχία])".

92   Westall (2016) also proposes Cremutius Cordus as a source for Dio.

(53.8.5). Dio's Augustus claims the same virtues that appear on the Shield of Virtue, even though Dio himself does not mention this honor in his narrative.[93]

Tiberius' obituary for Augustus (56.35–41) closely echoes and amplifies the claims in Augustus' speech. Tiberius also extols Augustus' sense of justice in avenging his father Caesar against the odds, his courage in taking on powerful enemies. He is "more prudent and public spirited" (φρονιμώτατα καὶ δημωφιλέστατα) in negotiating the politics of 44–42. He demonstrates determination to spare his enemies as soon as he could do so (56.38.2), and his liberality was tempered by restraint (55.38.2–3). This fine sense of balance is informed by Augustus' "love of his fellow man" (φιλανθρωπία) (55.39.1) and leads eventually to undying fame (εὐκλεία).[94] Tiberius deliberately reminds his audience of Augustus' decision to step down and the wisdom of the senators in refusing to let him do so. Scholarship has regularly seen the overlap as a sign of Dio's free composition with a view to commenting on his own times.[95] Swan (2004, 325) notes its affinity with Antonius' speech for Caesar, but not the seminal speech of 27. Nor does he make reference to the role that the cardinal virtues play in its construction.

And yet they play a critical role. From as early as his account of Fabricius, Dio has chosen this criterion for assessing individual leaders. His reference to the four virtues at specific moments in his text reinforces their value in the political landscape of Rome as it moved from participatory government to the monarchical rule he preferred. Augustus himself had had to pass the test, and the results were written in gold on a monument that Dio would have noticed any time he attended a Senate meeting in the *curia*. Tiberius is made to summarize Augustus' report card and proclaim him the most perfect with respect to all four. All that is needed is to draw the right conclusion (56.41.9):

> Τοιγαροῦν διὰ ταῦτα εἰκότως καὶ προστάτην αὐτὸν καὶ πατέρα δημόσιον ἐποιήσασθε, καὶ ἄλλοις τε πολλοῖς καὶ ὑπατείαις πλείσταις ἐπεγαυρώσατε, καὶ τὸ τελευταῖον καὶ ἥρωα ἀπεδείξατε καὶ ἀθάνατον ἀπεφήνατε.

> It was for all this, therefore, that you, with good reason, made him your leader and a father of the people, that you honored him with many marks of esteem and with ever so many consulships, and that you finally made him a demigod and declared him to be immortal.

---

[93] Welch 2012, 307–12; forthcoming a. The four virtues are also present obliquely in Livia's plea for clemency for Cinna Magnus (55.16.3–5).
[94] For the same concept, see also 53.8.3, 56.41.2.
[95] Swan 2004, 325–6, with earlier references.

Tiberius' obituary mirrors and surpasses the virtues of the exemplary Romans of Dio's early books. Augustus' perfection in all four cardinal virtues thus specifically justifies his position as *princeps* and father of the Roman people.

8   Conclusion

There are three distinct modes in Dio's use of the four cardinal virtues. The first lapidary summaries reflect a Stoicizing tradition of assessing five Romans and three non-Romans against the Platonic-Stoic formulation of wisdom, justice, temperance, and courage. Lack of context makes it difficult to assess the exact role these passages played in the overall narrative, but proposing that these character references originate from an early first-century Stoicizing author is reasonable.

Next, the protagonists claim the virtues, but each fails the test in significant ways. Cicero has no courage and Agrippa lacks deliberative justice. Caesar claims the virtues, but Dio does not believe him. The influence of Cicero's *De officiis* on both his admirers and detractors is not hard to discern. The case of Marcus Antonius represents something else again. Within Dio's work alone, Antonius' story includes the virtues in four very different contexts. Dio is not the only author to do this. Plutarch also writes a biography of virtue lost rather than virtue never having existed, and in certain parts of his work Appian presents Antonius in ways that Dio's Calenus would recognize.[96] Even Cicero has to deny Antonius his virtues, and with increasing ferocity.[97] The consistency of this material, even allowing for difference of detail, suggests that it originated with Antonius' own self-promotion, although it must have been as quickly taken up by a friendly author. The war of words that preceded Actium could only argue that Antonius' virtues had dissipated, not that he never had them.

This background gives context to Augustus' speech of 27 and Tiberius' obituary. The claim to best-ness through a display of virtue (but with *pietas* replacing wisdom) is a product of a political discourse that had been current for over a decade. While there is no doubt that Dio will have adapted his material to suit his own narrative purposes, the presence of these specific qualities in the form that we find them is striking.

---

96   Welch forthcoming a.
97   Stone 2008, 227–38.

What room does this leave for Dio himself? The four virtues template as a means of assessing character is far too prevalent across his republican and Augustan books to be accidental. Dio must have also enjoyed criticizing Cicero for failing his own virtues test or showing up the inherent lies in material that praised Caesar's virtues when he did not believe in them. It is unthinkable that he did not develop the theme to demonstrate his familiarity with philosophical themes as well as rhetorical style. It is worth considering those Romans who have not been discussed with respect to the four virtues and who are assessed in different ways. No Camillus, no Pompeius, to name but two. Dio did not assess every individual against the same template, suggesting that the template itself was not of major importance to him, though the assessments were. Perhaps the fact that these criteria were so important in the self-justification of the first *princeps*, an individual for whom he had great admiration, made him sensitive to their appearance in other contexts. In any case, noting when and under what terms the Stoic scheme appears in his narrative allows us to observe an acute reader and commentator working hard to produce a history that reflected his own assessment of Roman virtues, as well as those of his predecessors.

Bibliography

Adler, E. (2011) *Valorizing the Barbarians: Enemy Speeches in Roman Historiography*, Austin.

Ahl, F. M. (1972) *Lucan: An Introduction*, London.

Atkins, E. M. (1990) "'*Domina et regina virtutum*': Justice and *societas* in *De Officiis*", *Phronesis* 35, 258–89.

Baronowski, D. W. (2011) *Polybius and Roman Imperialism*, London.

Barnes, J. & Griffin, M. (eds.) (1999) *Philosophia Togata II*, Oxford.

Beness, J. L. (2005) "Scipio Aemilianus and the Crisis of 129 B.C.", *Historia* 54, 37–48.

Burden-Strevens, C. (2015) *Cassius Dio's Speeches and the Collapse of the Roman Republic*, Dissertation: Glasgow.

Burden-Strevens, C. (2016) "Fictitious Speeches, Envy, and the Habituation to Authority: Writing the Collapse of the Roman Republic", in C. H. Lange & J. M. Madsen (eds.), *Cassius Dio: Greek Intellectual and Roman Politician* (Leiden & Boston): 193–216.

Burden-Strevens, C. (2018) "Reconstructing Republican Oratory in Cassius Dio's Roman History", in C. Gray *et al.* (eds.), *Reading Republican Oratory: Reconstructions, Contexts, Receptions* (Oxford): 111–34.

Burden-Strevens, C. & Lindholmer, M. (eds.) (2018) *Cassius Dio's Forgotten History of Early Rome: The 'Roman History' Books 1–21*, Leiden & Boston.

Capelle, W. (1932) "Griekische Ethik und römischer Imperialismus", *Klio* 25, 86–113.
Chrissanthos, S. G. (2001) "Caesar and the Mutiny of 47", *Journal of Roman Studies* 91, 63–75.
Coudry, M. (2018) "The 'Great Men' of the Middle Republic in Cassius Dio's *Roman History*", in C. Burden-Strevens & M. Lindholmer (eds.), *Cassius Dio's Forgotten History of Early Rome: The 'Roman History' Books 1–21* (Leiden & Boston): 126–64.
Dorandi, T. (2016) "Der 'gute König' bei Philodem und die Rede des Maecenas vor Octavian (Cassius Dio LII, 14–40)", *Klio* 67, 56–60.
Dyck, A. (1996) *A Commentary on Cicero's* de Officiis, Ann Arbor.
Erskine, A. (1990) *The Hellenistic Stoa: Political Thought and Action*, London.
Fantham, E. (1985) "Caesar and the Mutiny: Lucan's Reshaping of the Historical Tradition in *De bello civili* 5.237–373", *Classical Philology* 90, 119–31.
Fears, J. R. (1977) *Princeps a diis electus*, Rome.
Fears, J. R. (1981) "The Cult of Virtues and Roman Imperial Ideology", *Aufstieg und Niedergang der römischen Welt* 2.17.2, 827–948.
Ferriès, M.-C. (2012) "L'ombre de César dans la politique du consul Marc-Antoine", in O. Devillers & K. Sion-Jenkis (eds.), *César sous Auguste* (Paris): 55–72.
Fomin, A. (2016) "Speeches in Dio Cassius", in C. H. Lange & J. M. Madsen (eds.), *Cassius Dio: Greek Intellectual and Roman Politician* (Leiden & Boston): 217–37.
Freyburger, M.-L. & Roddaz, J.-M. (2002) *Dion Cassius: Histoire romaine, Livres 50 & 51*. Paris.
Frisch, H. (1946) *Cicero's Fight for the Republic*, Copenhagen.
Fromentin, V. (2018) "La fiabilité de Zonaras dans les deux premières décades de l'Histoire Romaine de Cassius Dion: le cas des discours", in C. Burden-Strevens & M. Lindholmer (eds.), *Cassius Dio's Forgotten History of Early Rome: The 'Roman History' Books 1–21* (Leiden & Boston): 27–52.
Fromentin, V. & Bertrand, E. (2008) *Dion Cassius: Histoire romaine, Livres 45 & 46*, Paris.
Gabba, E. (1979) "Per un' interpretazione politica del *de officiis*", *Rendiconti dell' Accademia dei Lincei* 34, 117–41.
Galinsky, G. K. (1996) *Augustan Culture: An Interpretive Introduction*, Princeton.
Gildenhard, I. (2007) *Paideia Romana: Cicero's Tusculan Disputations*, Cambridge.
Gómez Espelosín, F. J. (1993) "Appian's *Iberike*: Aims and Attitudes of a Greek Historian of Rome", *Aufstieg und Niedergang der römischen Welt* 2.34.1, 403–27.
Gowing, A. M. (1992) *The Triumviral Narratives of Appian and Cassius Dio*, Ann Arbor.
Griffin, M. T. & Atkins, E. M. (1991) *Cicero: On Duties*, Cambridge.
Griffin, M. & Barnes, J. (eds.) (1997) *Philosophia Togata I*, Oxford.
Halfmann, H. (2011) *Marcus Antonius*, Darmstadt.
Hölkeskamp, K.-J. (2013) "'Friends, Romans, Countrymen': Addressing the Roman People and the Rhetoric of Inclusion", in C. Steel & H. van der Blom (eds.), *Community and Communication: Oratory and Politics in Republican Rome* (Oxford): 11–28.

Holmes, T. R. (1923) *The Roman Republic and the Founder of the Empire*, Oxford.
Jones, B. (2016) "Cassius Dio – *Pepaideumenos* and Politician on Kingship", in C. H. Lange & J. M. Madsen (eds.), *Cassius Dio: Greek Intellectual and Roman Politician* (Leiden & Boston): 297–315.
Kemezis, A. (2014) *Greek Narratives of the Roman Empire under the Severans: Cassius Dio, Philostratus and Herodian*, Cambridge.
Kemezis, A. (2016) "Dio, Caesar and the Vesontio Mutineers (38.34–47): A Rhetoric of Lies", in C. H. Lange & J. M. Madsen (eds.), *Cassius Dio: Greek Intellectual and Roman Politician* (Leiden & Boston): 238–57.
Kennedy, G. A. (1968) "Antony's Speech at Caesar's Funeral", *Quarterly Journal of Speech* 54, 99–106.
Kidd, I. G. (1999) *Posidonius: The Translation of the Fragments*, Cambridge.
Kries, D. (2003) "On the Intention of Cicero's *De officiis*", *The Review of Politics* 65, 375–93.
Lange, C. H. (2018) "Cassius Dio on Violence, *Stasis*, and Civil War: The Early Years", in C. Burden-Strevens & M. Lindholmer (eds.), *Cassius Dio's Forgotten History of Early Rome: The 'Roman History' Books 1–21* (Leiden & Boston): 165–89.
Lange, C. H. & Madsen, J. M. (eds.) (2016) *Cassius Dio: Greek Intellectual and Roman Politician*, Leiden & Boston.
Langley, G. (2012) "Thucydides, Polybius, and Human Nature", in C. J. Smith & L. M. Yarrow (eds.), *Imperialism, Cultural Politics and Polybius* (Oxford): 68–83.
Lintott, A. W. (1997) "Cassius Dio and the History of the Late Roman Republic", *Aufstieg und Niedergang der römischen Welt* 2.34.3, 2497–523.
Long, A. A. (1995) "Cicero's Politics in *De officiis*", in A. Laks & M. Schofield (eds.), *Justice and Generosity: Studies in Hellenistic, Social and Political Philosophy* (Cambridge): 213–40.
Long, A. A. (1996) *Stoic Studies*, Cambridge.
Madsen, J. M. (2016) "Criticising the Benefactors: The Severans and the Return of Dynastic Rule", in C. H. Lange & J. M. Madsen, *Cassius Dio: Greek Intellectual and Roman Politician* (Leiden & Boston): 136–58.
Madsen, J. M. (2018) "From Nobles to Villains: The Story of the Republican Senate in Cassius Dio's *Roman History*", in C. Burden-Strevens & M. Lindholmer (eds.), *Cassius Dio's Forgotten History of Early Rome: The 'Roman History' Books 1–21* (Leiden & Boston): 99–125.
Mahy, T. (2013) "Antonius, Triumvir and Orator: Career, Style, and Effectiveness", in C. Steel & H. van der Blom (eds.), *Community and Communication: Oratory and Politics in Republican Rome* (Oxford): 329–44.
Mallan, C. (2016) "*Parrhêsia* in Cassius Dio", in C. H. Lange & J. M. Madsen (eds.), *Cassius Dio: Greek Intellectual and Roman Politician* (Leiden & Boston): 258–75.

Mallan, C. (2018) "The Regal Period in the *Excerpta Constantiniana* and in Some Early Byzantine Extracts from Dio's *Roman History*", in C. Burden-Strevens & M. Lindholmer (eds.), *Cassius Dio's Forgotten History of Early Rome: The 'Roman History' Books 1–21* (Leiden & Boston): 76–96.

Millar, F. (1961) "Some Speeches in Cassius Dio", *Museum Helveticum* 18, 11–22.

Millar, F. (1964) *A Study of Cassius Dio*, Oxford.

Moore, T. J. (2010) "Livy's Hannibal and the Roman Tradition", in W. Polleichtner (ed.), *Livy and Intertextuality* (Trier): 135–67.

Morrell, K. (2017) *Pompey, Cato, and the Governance of the Roman Empire*, Oxford.

Pelling, C. B. R. (1988) *Plutarch's Life of Antony*, Cambridge.

Pelling, C. B. R. (2006) "Judging Julius Caesar", in M. Wyke (ed.), *Julius Caesar in Western Culture* (Malden): 3–28.

Pelling, C. B. R. (2011a) "Velleius and Biography: The Case of Julius Caesar", in E. Cowan (ed.), *Velleius Paterculus: Making History* (Swansea): 157–76.

Pelling, C. B. R. (2011b) *Plutarch: Life of Caesar*, Oxford.

Ramsey, J. T. (2003) *Cicero*: Philippics I–II, Cambridge.

Ramsey, J. T. (2010) "Debate at a Distance: A Unique Rhetorical Strategy in Cicero's Thirteenth *Philippic*", in D. H. Berry & A. Erskine (eds.), *Form and Function in Roman Oratory* (Cambridge): 155–74.

Rees, W. (2011) *Cassius Dio, Human Nature, and the Late Roman Republic*, Dissertation: Oxford.

Reinhold, M. (1988) *From Republic to Principate: An Historical Commentary on Cassius Dio's Roman History Books 49–52 (36–29 B.C.)*, Atlanta.

Schofield, M. (2012) "The Fourth Virtue", in W. Nicgorski (ed.), *Cicero's Practical Philosophy* (Notre Dame): 43–57.

Schofield, M. (2013) "Cardinal Virtues: A Contested Socratic Inheritance", in A. A. Long (ed.), *Plato and the Stoics* (Cambridge): 11–28.

Setaioli, A. A. (2017) "Antony's Speech in Shakespeare's *Julius Caesar* and the Ancient Sources", *Prometheus* 43, 283–9.

Shackleton Bailey, D. R. (2002) *Cicero: Letters to Quintus and Brutus. Letter Fragments. Letter to Octavian. Invectives. Handbook of Electioneering*, Cambridge, MA.

Simons, B. (2009). *Cassius Dio und die Römische Republik. Untersuchungen zum Bild des römischen Gemeinwesens in den Büchern 3–35 der Romaika*, Berlin.

Steel, C. & van der Blom, H. (eds.) (2013) *Community and Communication: Oratory and Politics in Republican Rome*, Oxford.

Stone, A. M. (1999) "Tribute to a Statesman: Cicero and Sallust", *Antichthon* 33, 48–76.

Stone, A. M. (2008) "Greek Ethics and Roman Statesmen: *De officiis* and the *Philippics*", in T. Stevenson & M. Wilson (eds.), *Cicero's* Philippics: *History, Rhetoric and Ideology* (Auckland): 214–39.

Strasburger, H. (1965) "Poseidonios on the Problems of the Roman Empire", *Journal of Roman Studies* 55, 40–53.

Swan, P. M. (2004) *The Augustan Succession: An Historical Commentary on Cassius Dio's Roman History Books 55–56 (9 BC–AD 14)*, Oxford.

Syme, R. (1939). *The Roman Revolution*, Oxford.

Tan, J. (forthcoming) "How Do You Solve a Problem Like Marcus Agrippa?", in K. Morrell *et al.* (eds.) *The Alternative Augustan Age* (Oxford).

Taylor, R. *et al.* (2016) *Rome: An Urban History from Antiquity to the Present*, Cambridge.

Treggiari, S. (2002) *Roman Social History*, London.

Tweedie, F. (2015) "Appian's Characterisation of Scipio Aemilianus", in K. Welch (ed.), *Appian's Roman History* (Swansea): 169–84.

van der Blom, H. (2013) "Fragmentary Speeches: The Oratory and Political Career of Piso Caesoninus", in C. Steel & H. van der Blom (eds.), *Community and Communication: Oratory and Politics in Republican Rome* (Oxford): 299–314.

Vessey, D. W. T. (1982) "The Dupe of Destiny: Hannibal in Silius *Punica* III", *Classical Journal* 77, 320–35.

Wallace-Hadrill, A. (1981) "The Emperor and His Virtues", *Historia* 30, 298–323.

Walsh, P. G. (2000) *On Obligations*, Oxford.

Weinstock, S. (1971) *Divus Iulius*, Oxford.

Welch, K. (2009) "Alternative Memoirs: Tales from the 'Other Side' of the Civil War", in C. J. Smith & A. Powell (eds.), *The Lost Memoirs of Augustus* (Swansea): 195–223.

Welch, K. (2012) *Magnus Pius: Sextus Pompeius and the Transformation of the Roman Republic*, Swansea.

Welch, K. (2014) "The *lex Pedia* and Its Aftermath", in R. Westall (ed.), *A House Divided*. *Hermathena* 196/7, 137–62.

Welch, K. (ed.) (2015) *Appian's Roman History: Empire and Civil War*, Swansea.

Welch, K. (2019) "Selling Proscription to the Roman Public", in C. Rosillo-López (ed.), *Communicating Public Opinion in the Roman Republic.* (Stuttgart): 241–54.

Welch, K. (forthcoming a) "Shields of Virtue(s)", in K. Morrell, *et al.* (eds.) *The Alternative Augustan Age* (Oxford).

Welch, K. (forthcoming b) "History Wars: Who Avenged Caesar and Why Does It Matter?", in I. Gildenhard *et al.* (eds.), *Augustus and the Destruction of History: The Politics of the Past in Early Imperial Rome* (CJJ Supplements), Cambridge.

Welch, K. (forthcoming c) "The Virtuous Marcus Antonius."

Welwei, K-W. (1967) "Das Angebot des Diadems an Caesar und das Luperkalienproblem", *Historia* 16, 44–69.

Westall, R. (2016) "The Sources of Cassius Dio for the Roman Civil Wars of 49–30 BC", in J. M. Madsen & C. H. Lange (eds.), *Cassius Dio: Greek Intellectual and Roman Politician* (Leiden & Boston): 51–75.

Wright, A. I. (1997) *Cicero Reflected: The Image of a Statesman in the Century after His Death and Its Ideological Significance*, Dissertation: Sydney.

Yardley, J. & Barrett, A. A. (2011) *Velleius Paterculus: The Roman History: from Romulus and the Foundation of Rome to the Reign of the Emperor Tiberius*, Indianapolis.

PART 2

Characters, Institutions, and Episodes

CHAPTER 7

The Republican Dictatorship: an Imperial Perspective

Christopher Burden-Strevens

1   Introduction

The consular elections of 54 BCE were a chaotic affair even by late republican standards and represent a critical turning point in Roman constitutional history.[1] Arguably, genuine republican government had already ceased to function six years previously with the three-headed monster of Pompey, Caesar, and Crassus' alliance; but the actual collapse of republican institutions must be credited to the latter half of the 50s.[2] After many delays, by mid-October 54 all four candidates for the consulship of the following year had been charged with bribery.[3] One of the hopefuls, C. Memmius, confessed in the Senate that he and another candidate had formed a secret agreement with the incumbent consuls, Appius and Ahenobarbus: these were to support Memmius' candidacy in return for juicy consular provinces if he should be elected. Memmius' confession was (allegedly) instigated and encouraged by Pompey.[4] Attempts by the *interreges* to hold the *comitia* were checked by unfavorable omens and deliberate obstruction by tribunes.[5] Amid this crisis rumors were circulating of a plan to appoint Pompey as dictator, evidently with the support of the newly-elected tribune for 53, C. Lucilius Hirrus.[6] This did not come to pass. Plans for a dictatorship for Pompey fell through: some time earlier in 53 he declined the office, and Cn. Domitius Calvinus and M. Valerius Messalla Rufus finally

---

1   So Arena 2012, 1 n. 2.
2   Hence Cicero's grim allusion in April 54 to Pompey's supposed "list" of planned future consuls at *Att.* 4.8a.2. Steel 2013, 183 is right to treat this with a little scepticism, although compare App. *B Civ.* 2.19 on the events of the same year: "the consuls holding office yearly could not hope to lead armies or to command in war because they were shut out by the power of the triumvirate."
3   Cic. *Att.* 4.18.3. Previously only three were implicated: see *Att.* 4.17. For the candidates, see Gruen 1969.
4   Cic. *Att.* 4.17.2–3.
5   Cass. Dio 40.45.3.
6   Cic. *Q Fr.* 3.8.4–6, 3.9.3; Plut. *Pomp.* 54.2–3.

entered office in the summer of that year,[7] when the contest for the next year's appointments was already underway. That is not to say that Pompey emerged from the crisis of the preceding two years empty-handed, however: a compromise, seemingly orchestrated by the *interrex* Servius Sulpicius, had Pompey elected by the people (not "appointed" by the Senate, so it seems) to the sole consulship for 52 with senatorial consent.[8] He entered office on the 24th day of the intercalary month between February and March.

To this point our main surviving sources for this crisis – Appian, Asconius, Cassius Dio, Cicero, and Plutarch – are broadly in agreement. The real controversy emerges with Pompey's role in the episode and his motivations, especially regarding the dictatorship. According to Appian, Pompey was eager for the honor in 54–53 and indeed "deliberately oversaw events" so as to bring it about (πάνθ' ὑπερορῶντος ἐπίτηδες).[9] The desire to engineer a crisis would certainly explain Pompey's eagerness for Memmius to confess publicly his scandalous pact with Appius and Ahenobarbus. Appian alleges that Pompey deliberately postponed the *comitia* to exert the maximum damage, all the while publicly making a show of rejecting the dictatorship.[10] For Appian and also Plutarch,[11] Pompey's scheming was only scotched by Cato and Bibulus working together to oppose the "unadulterated tyranny of a dictatorship" (τῆς ἀκράτου καὶ τυραννικῆς ἐκείνης) and proposing the consulship *sine collega* as an innovative – but not unpalatably radical – compromise.[12] They maintain that Pompey's desire for the dictatorship was consistent throughout and his refusals a sham:[13] evidently he willed it in late 54, through 53, and even early in 52 (hence Cato and Bibulus' proposal). But in so doing they conflate the situation in late 54, when there were consuls in office, with 53 and 52, when there were not. In 54 an appointment to the dictatorship was possible in the regular way,

---

7   Cass. Dio 40.45.1 writes that Calvinus and Messalla were elected in the seventh month, but App. *B Civ.* 2.19 in the eighth.
8   See Ramsey 2016 for an excellent recent discussion of the circumstances surrounding Pompey's position as sole consul in 52. Our ancient sources suggest that the Senate arrogated to itself the authority to "appoint" Pompey as sole consul, so Liv. *Per.* 107, Val. Max. 8.15.8, Plut. *Caes.* 28.7, App. *B Civ.* 2.23, and Cass. Dio 40.50.4; modern historians have tended to follow this cue. Ramsey suggests (particularly from a reading of Asconius) that Pompey was in fact elected *per interregem*.
9   App. *B Civ.* 2.19.
10 App. *B Civ.* 2.20. This seems excessively cynical, but the *recusatio* is characteristic: see Vervaet 2010.
11 Plut. *Caes.* 28.7.
12 App. *B Civ.* 2.23; for the quote, Plut. *Pomp.* 54.3. See Ramsey 2016, 308–18 for discussion of the ways in which the proposal may have been made acceptable to conservatives.
13 So Meyer 1922, 210.

by the incumbent consuls *ex senatus consulto*. In 53, on the other hand, this was quite impossible; the only (understandably unattractive) option would be to revive the precedent of Sulla in an extraordinary appointment to the dictatorship by an *interrex*.[14]

Cassius Dio's take on the crisis is quite different. Dio's Pompey emerges as the savior of the electoral debacle of 54–53. Voluntarily declining the dictatorship in 53 upon returning to Rome, he takes pains to have Calvinus and Messalla Rufus elected, and in his sole consulship acted in accordance with the wishes of the Senate by eschewing the temptation to rouse an already excited *plebs*.[15] In a touch that is entirely Dio's invention, Pompey is even made to detest the prospect of a consulship *sine collega* (!): "he did not wish to hold office alone; for now that he had the glory that lay in the passing of such a vote, he wished to avoid the envy associated with it."[16] The desire to keep Caesar out of office emerges as a secondary motive on his part in Dio; this is unlikely to have been a real concern at this point in 52, since Caesar had a certain Vercingetorix to deal with. Dio's Pompey is, in other words, made to adopt (certainly) someone else's philosophical justification for a "republican" course of action he (probably) did not intend. Perhaps the historian's positive view of the general here may be inspired by Cicero. In a letter of November 54, Cicero is equivocal about Pompey's intentions, and writes that his public disavowal of a dictatorship, about which rumors had evidently been circulating at least since June, was inconsistent: when asked in private, he couldn't deny wanting it (*Pompeius plane se negat velle; antea mihi ipse non negabat*).[17] But here again we need to differentiate between the situation in late 54, when a dictatorship was possible in the regular fashion, and that of 53, when it was not. Dio's interpretation of Pompey's motivations is highly distinctive; very much unlike Appian and Plutarch, he believed that his refusal in 53 was genuine.

Our historian's view of Pompey's attitude to a sole consulship may not convince, but the interpretation of his hopes for a dictatorship in 53 (or rather lack thereof) merits serious consideration. The evidence discussed below

---

14 See Ramsey 2016, 309: "Pompey may well have found the dictatorship less appealing in 53 than he did in the latter half of 54, when his appointment could have been made in the time-honoured, non-Sullan manner by one of the consuls still in office." As Ramsey notes, Vervaet 2010, 155–9 treats the scenario in 54 as generally comparable to that of 53 and 52. But in 54, there were consuls in office; in 53 and 52, not so.

15 Cass. Dio 40.46, 40.50.

16 Cass. Dio 40.51.1. The contrast between the εὔκλεια of a voluntary grant of magnificent powers and the φθόνος attached to those powers is a paraphrase of Dio's speeches on the *lex Gabinia* (36.25.3–26.2), and the antithesis is made umpteen times elsewhere.

17 Cic. *Q Fr.* 3.8.5.

shows that it was evidently a discredited political solution, and anxieties about the office in general – and not only in connection with Pompey – appear to have been shared by a wider contingent than Cicero alone in 54–53. What we have here appears to be a deliberate choice on the historian's part to deviate from a quite uniform tradition regarding the general's ambitions for a dictatorship. It cannot be discounted that this emerges from his use of alternative sources, of course, but this will not bear fruit. For a start, the consistency of the extant accounts makes a deviant tradition guesswork: Appian, Cicero, and Plutarch all suggest that Pompey had a dictatorship in his sights. Moreover, Dio had access to these sources.[18] He seems to be forming a different interpretation on his own initiative.

Why make such a radical departure? This chapter proposes that Cassius Dio was especially preoccupied with the problematic nature of the republican dictatorship as an exercise of powers. Pompey's disavowal of that office and the honor he is paid as a result – which Dio frames uniquely as a genuine and more importantly *astute* political maneuver – is only one episode in a much wider exploration of the role played by the dictatorship in the fall of the Republic. Dio argues that by the first century BCE the dictatorship had become wholly unsuited to the needs of government: it was ineffective in practical terms as well as being politically toxic. Pompey's handling of the crisis of 54–53 showed his awareness of this fact, and so his political acumen; Caesar failed to observe this lesson, with fatal consequences. Yet at the same time, the historian firmly believed in the value of autocracy and the stabilizing power of sole rule in times of upheaval.[19] The statesmen of the *Roman History* are thus caught in a bizarre paradox, a different "crisis without alternative":[20] autocracy was needed to save the Republic, and yet could no longer operate within the traditional framework. The resolution to that paradox was Augustus.

The first part of this chapter sketches out Cassius Dio's view of the proper role of the Roman dictatorship, focusing on his commentary on its alleged foundation at the turn of the fifth century BCE. Unlike other historians, Dio

---

18   On Dio and Cicero, see Burden-Strevens 2018. For discussion of Dio and Appian, see Gowing 1992. Dio's relationship with Plutarch is less charted: Millar 1964 believes that references to Plutarch are Zonaras' interpolation.

19   At 44.2.1–5, Dio states gnomically that "if ever" there was a noble δημοκρατία, it only endured for a short time. For this thought see also fr. 110.2. At 53.19.1, he explicitly outlines his view that following the Augustan settlement, the Roman constitution was changed for the better; it was manifestly no longer possible to keep the people safe under a δημοκρατία. For this attitude see Tac. *Hist.* 1.1.1, 1.16.1; Sen. *Ben.* 2.20.2; App. *B Civ.* 4.133. See also Madsen 2016.

20   Famously, Meier 1966; see also Rilinger 2007, 132–50.

appears to have emphasized the positive potential of dictatorship as a temporary return to monarchy; his earlier books present numerous positive and successful examples of dictatorships in republican history. However, this was not to remain. The next part explores Dio's presentation of the dictatorship in a "second" phase, the period after Sulla, and shows that the historian problematized this office on both practical and moral grounds. He was not the first to do so; contemporary evidence from the 50s suggests the dictatorship as such was in disrepute, and not only in connection with Pompey. In that context, his view of Pompey's refusal as genuine (and astute) in 53 makes sense. Third and finally, this chapter briefly considers Dio's account of the earlier years of Augustus' principate in Books 52–4 and his own rejection of the dictatorship.

2 Phase One: the Ideal of Dictatorship

Let us start at the beginning. Blessed with hindsight, Dio seems to have viewed the inauguration of the first dictator Titus Lartius in 501 (or 498) as a moment of great importance.[21] Pausing his narrative of the Republic's early conflicts with the Sabines, Dio describes the institution of this office as a direct response to military and civic crisis: the indebted *plebs*, infuriated at their treatment by their patrician creditors, refused the draft when called upon to defend the Republic against the threat of the Latins, and demanded a cancellation of debts.[22] Dio then goes on to review the dictator's formal powers: the six-month tenure, immunity from *provocatio* and intercession by tribunes, and – a detail absent in our other historians – certain restrictions on his right to draw from the treasury and on riding mounted in the city. The surviving text is Zonaras' epitome, not Dio's: although no fragments of this material survive in the direct tradition, we can be reasonably confident of Zonaras' faithfulness, and can treat these as authentic in an albeit abridged format.[23]

One of the most striking aspects of Dio's account of Lartius' appointment as dictator is his view of its positive potential. Dio takes pains to stress the

---

21 Cassius Dio and Livy have "Lartius"; for "Larcius" see Cic. *Resp.* 2.32 and Dion. Hal. *Ant. Rom.* 5.73. "Largius" is also attested.
22 For the debate surrounding the historicity of the alleged "First" Latin War, see Cornell 1995 and Forsythe 2005. This does not concern us here: like all annalists Dio believed the tradition.
23 For Zonaras' faithfulness to Dio, see most recently Fromentin 2018, who shows the epitomator's method of preserving acts of speech and retaining points of transition between speech and narrative. Simons 2009, 25–32 outlines Zonaras' methods with the narrative proper. Further in Mallan 2018.

beneficial aspects of a temporary return to autocracy, especially during periods of instability:

> ... he possessed power equal in all respects to that of the kings. People hated the name of "king" on account of the Tarquins, but **desiring the benefit to be derived from sole leadership, which seemed to exert a potent influence amid conditions of war and revolution**, they chose it under another name.[24]

This is notably different from the accounts given in both Livy and Dionysius of Halicarnassus. In the former, Titus Lartius' appointment is treated as a cause for great apprehension: the terrified *plebs*, hard pressed with the sight of Lartius' *fasces*, had "no hope of help from another, nor right of appeal, nor any safety anywhere except in obedience."[25] The patricians' rationale for instituting the office is to inspire fear and quell the plebeian struggle temporarily to deal with the Sabines and Latins, objectives in which they succeeded. Dionysius' account is quite different. It is much more pessimistic and takes pains to associate dictatorship with monarchy in its degenerate form, tyranny. For Dionysius, the chief reason for a dictatorship was, above all (ὑπὲρ ἅπαντα), the supposed *lex Valeria de provocatione*: the Senate were seeking a specious mechanism "by which to deceive the poor and, without being detected, repeal the law that secured their liberty."[26] In that vein, the historian describes the dictatorship repeatedly as a form of tyranny as such. Dionysius asserts baldly that such a magistracy, being above the law, was a tyranny in fact if not by name:[27] it is compared directly to emergency powers in (for example) Thessaly and Sparta, where tyrannical powers ungoverned by law and custom were "concealed under more attractive titles" (ὀνόμασι περικαλύπτοντες αὐτὰς εὐπρεπεστέροις).[28] Viewing the events of 501/498 through the lens of the first century BCE, Dionysius and to a lesser extent Livy present the dictatorship as a problematic institution from its inception.

---

24 Zon. 7.13.
25 Liv. 2.18.8: *magnus plebem metus incessit, ut intentiores essent ad dicto parendum; neque enim ut in consulibus qui pari potestate essent, alterius auxilium neque prouocatio erat neque ullum usquam nisi in cura parendi auxilium.*
26 Dion. Hal. *Ant. Rom.* 5.70.4: καὶ γράφει προβούλευμα, δι' οὗ παρακρουσαμένη τοὺς πένητας καὶ τὸν βεβαιοῦντα τὴν ἐλευθερίαν αὐτοῖς νόμον ἀνελοῦσα ἔλαθεν.
27 Dion. Hal. *Ant. Rom.* 5.73.2: "the extent of the power which the dictator possesses is by no means indicated by the title; for the dictatorship is in reality an elective tyranny" (ἐπεὶ τό γε τῆς ἐξουσίας μέγεθος, ἧς ὁ δικτάτωρ ἔχει, ἥκιστα δηλοῦται ὑπὸ τοῦ ὀνόματος· ἔστι γὰρ αἱρετὴ τυραννὶς ἡ δικτατορία). See also 5.70.5.
28 Dion. Hal. *Ant. Rom.* 5.74.1–4.

Dio's view of the republican dictatorship is in fact far closer to Cicero's than to that of his fellow-historians. Leaving aside its routine or ritual functions (*clavi figendi causa*, for example, or holding games),[29] he evidently saw within the dictatorship the positive potential for a temporary resort to monarchy in times of crisis. Dio certainly did not wrongly believe (like Dionysius) that the *dictatura* was a form of tyranny by its nature. This is confirmed by his own commentary on the *lex Antonia* of 44 BCE, permanently abolishing that magistracy. He writes that the Romans took what they believed to be the best course for the future, *as if* the disgrace of men's deeds lay in their titles (ὥσπερ ἐν τοῖς ὀνόμασι τῆς τῶν ἔργων δεινότητος οὔσης), when in fact – he corrects the statesmen of April 44 on their mistake – the issue was not the dictatorship as such, but the combination of military command and a tyrannical character.[30] In other words, for our historian dictatorship was a legitimate mechanism for bringing stability to the state, with the temporary reality of monarchy but the necessary illusion of a civilian title. Whether this aspect of Dio's political thought was inspired by some intermediary is unclear, but its earliest (surviving) expression can be found in Cicero's *Republic*. Cicero's comment on the proper role of the dictatorship in the state is most clearly articulated in Book 2:

> ... and just as Tarquin subverted the whole fabric of royalty – not because he grasped a new sort of authority, but because he made a bad use of it – so let us oppose to him another: a good man, wise and expert in everything useful and dignified in civil life: a tutor and steward as it were of the commonwealth ... Tarquin being banished, **the royal title was as odious to the Roman people** as it had been regretted after the death or rather the disappearance of Romulus; **and as much as they wanted a king then, in like manner, after the expulsion of Tarquin, they could not endure the name of one** ... In these very times too, T. Larcius was appointed dictator, about ten years after the first consuls. **This was a new kind of authority, very much resembling, as we perceive, the royal power.**[31]

Now, the *Republic* is not without its difficulties. The text was written between around 54–51 BCE, when "democratic" institutions had effectively collapsed; it accordingly presents an ideal, not the reality, and this is evidently not a guide to Roman politics in practice. It is significant that Cicero may have been penning this book just when anxieties about a potential dictatorship for Pompey were

---

29 On which Lintott 1999, 109–13.
30 Cass. Dio 44.51.2–3.
31 Cic. *Resp.* 2.29–32.

at their height in late 54 and early 53.³² Furthermore, there are obvious inconsistencies in Cicero's attitude toward this magistracy if we look at his work in the round. Hence in a rare moment of praise for Antonius, the orator lauds his abolition of the dictatorship in the *lex Antonia*, "which by this time had come to possess kingly power, ripped out of the state by its roots."³³ Repeatedly he refers to the "universally catastrophic *dominatio* and *regnum* of Sulla in victory."³⁴ In private, he wrote to Cassius that with Caesar's assassination Rome had been liberated not only from a king (*non regno sed rege liberati videmur*) but from a *tyrannus*, whose injuries against the Republic had been avenged with his death (*ulta suas iniurias est per vos interitu tyranni*).³⁵ Naturally in that light we need not put too much faith in Cicero's praise of Caesar in the *Pro Deiotaro*, describing the dictator as "not only not a tyrant, but a most merciful man."³⁶ It was addressed directly to Caesar himself!

Nevertheless, all of these critiques are concerned with the reality of the dictatorship in the final decades of the *res publica* as exemplified in its two most controversial holders, Sulla and Caesar. What they do not do is simplistically criticize (as Dionysius) the dictatorship in and of itself as a tyrannical institution; for were that the case, why persist with it regularly for over three hundred years? In other words, these comments of Cicero are not a general view of the dictatorship, but a castigation of its corruption and usurpation by two specific holders. Hence for the conception of what this office *should* be and how it was intended to function under usual circumstances, we have the dialogue on the commonwealth. The *Republic* asserts the positive potential of the dictatorship in the mind of a contemporary observer, and in terms that are remarkably similar to Dio's later. Both our historian and Cicero note the odium for the name of kingship after the expulsion of Tarquin, but emphasize that the Romans of the late sixth century wanted a king all the same – hence, the dictator. Both also review the scope of the dictator's powers in positive terms, Dio highlighting the potential "benefit" of a sole ruler for the state in periods of instability and war, and Cicero focusing on the benefit to be derived from "a tutor and steward of the commonwealth." In that regard, the role of the ideal statesman, the *rector rei publicae*, can apparently be fulfilled by the dictator appointed in a time of crisis; Dio, as a theorist in his own right of republican institutions and

---

32   Cic. *Q Fr.* 2.12.1.
33   Cic. *Phil.* 1.2: *dictaturam, quae iam vim regiae potestatis obsederat, funditus ex re publica sustulit.*
34   Cic. *Har. Resp.*, esp. 54: *universus interitus aut victoris dominatus ac regnum.*
35   Cic. *Fam.* 12.1.1–2.
36   Cic. *Deiot.* 34.

their effect upon the practice of politics (see Coudry in this volume), was evidently receptive to this idea.³⁷

Thus from its first appearance in the *Roman History* Dio seems to have presented the Roman dictatorship in a radically different light from our two other main historians of early Rome, Dionysius and Livy. Dionysius in particular chose to view that office from its foundation through the lens of events in the first century BCE; this is plainly wrong and misleading. Our historian, in contrast, took a more measured approach. Like Cicero, he viewed the dictatorship as a temporary return to monarchical powers in the interests of the state, which was only corrupted by the individual ambitions of its most controversial holders – Sulla and Caesar. This, to reiterate, explains his commentary on the *lex Antonia*. The office itself was not the issue:³⁸

> But the consuls ... published a law that no one should ever again be dictator, invoking curses and proclaiming death as the penalty upon any man who should propose or support such a measure, besides openly setting a price upon the heads of any such. This provision they made for the future, **assuming that the shamefulness of men's deeds consists in the titles they bear, whereas these deeds really arise from their possession of armed forces and from the character of the individual incumbent** (ὥσπερ ἐν τοῖς ὀνόμασι τῆς τῶν ἔργων δεινότητος οὔσης, ἀλλ᾽ οὐκ ἐκ τῶν ὅπλων καὶ ἐκ τῶν ἑκάστου τρόπων καὶ γιγνομένων αὐτῶν), and they disgrace the titles of authority under which they chance to occur.

It is difficult to gauge how Dio's presentation of the dictatorship throughout most of its history related to his distinctively positive, "Ciceronian" take on the office at the time of its foundation. The text is lacunose, and even Zonaras' epitome preserves little detail except on the most famous of Rome's dictators. But the information that survives gives an almost consistently positive account. The presentation of Cincinnatus' dictatorship is conventional: the farmhand who valiantly crushed Spurius Maelius' *adfectatio regni*, and so forth.³⁹ Zonaras records that in 272 BCE the former dictator P. Cornelius Rufinus was removed from the Senate roll for transgressing sumptuary legislation, but this is hardly a reflection on the dictatorship as such.⁴⁰ Lucius Papirius Cursor (325 and 310?) and Aulus Cornelius Cossus Arvina (322?) are described positively

---

37 For discussion of Cicero's *rector rei publicae*, see Zarecki 2014.
38 Cass. Dio 44.51.2–3.
39 Cass. Dio fr. 23.2, fr. 20.
40 Zon. 8.6.

in connection with the Samnite wars.[41] The war with Hannibal is naturally a chance to display Roman valor. Fabius Cunctator emerges in particular favor: his strategy is described as wise and effective, and it is his impetuous master of horse Rufus, not the delaying dictator, who is made the subject of criticism.[42] The account of M. Junius Pera's efforts to rescue Rome as dictator in 216 is broadly approving, in particular his work to save the besieged people of Basilinae from hunger and his controversial last resort (not criticized by Dio-Zonaras) of conscripting even slaves and criminals to face the threat of Hannibal.[43] Finally, there is M. Furius Camillus. Although Dio records anger at his decision to ride on white horses in his triumphal procession,[44] the remaining detail of Camillus' several terms as dictator is laudatory: after being betrayed by his countrymen and going into exile, Camillus returns to quell the alleged conspiracy of Capitolinus and in a fifth dictatorship defeats the Gauls at the river Anio. Following his resignation in the proper term and his death, there was great public grief.[45]

These few episodes are all that remains of what must originally have been dozens of vignettes on the activities of Roman dictators between T. Lartius' inauguration and 202 BCE, when the office fell out of use. There is nothing here to support the conflation between dictatorship and tyranny – monarchy in its degenerate form – which we find in Dionysius. Instead, what we find in Dio's earlier history is a collection of examples consistent with his vision of the proper role of dictatorship in a functioning Republic: a legitimate and temporary return to monarchy in order to stabilize the state in times of desperate need.

3   Phase Two: the Dictatorship in Crisis

For Dio the final decades of the Republic represented the collapse of that vision. This is of course not surprising in view of the experiment with Sulla and Caesar; but the disappearance of the dictatorship as a viable exercise of powers in the first century BCE is in fact integral to his explanation of the crisis of the Republic and the emergence of Augustus' rule. This decline in the dictatorship from a genuine "stewardship of the commonwealth" in Cicero's words to

---

41   Zon. 7.26, Cass. Dio fr. 36.26.
42   Zon. 8.25–6.
43   Zon. 9.2.
44   Cass. Dio fr. 21.
45   Cass. Dio fr. 24.4.

an unworkable and discredited failure is already alluded to by Dio from its first appearance in the *Roman History*. To linger a moment longer on the inauguration of T. Lartius in Book 4:[46]

> The office of dictator extended for a period of not more than six months, in order that no such official by lingering on in the midst of so great power and unhampered authority should become haughty and be carried away by a passion for sole leadership. **This was what happened later to Julius Caesar, when, contrary to lawful precedent, he had been adjudged worthy of the dictatorship.**

This commentary – if genuinely Dio's – is significant. The historian appears to have used the earliest formation of the dictatorship as an opportunity to reflect on the development of the office over time and to foreshadow its transformation in the final decades of the Republic. There is every possibility that the *exemplum* of Julius Caesar here is a later interpolation of the epitomator. Narrative techniques such as allusion, prolepsis, and analepsis are common in Dio's history, but these are usually far more oblique than this explicit *exemplum*. Nevertheless, *exempla* are common to Dio's compositional technique – especially of course in the speeches – and the historian's particular interest in the role of the dictatorship within the Republic's permutations would certainly explain the choice to foreshadow Caesar's career at an early stage. The earlier portions of Dio's work present dictatorship in its proper form, adducing examples of the benefit provided to the state by a number of holders; the allusion to Caesar, on the other hand, points forward to the historian's argument about its degenerative role.

That argument at last arrives in explicit terms in Book 36 in the speech of Q. Lutatius Catulus. The ostensible rhetorical purpose of the speech is a long *dissuasio* against the *lex Gabinia* of 67 BCE, which proposed an extraordinary command of three years for an unspecified individual over the entire Mediterranean to combat the threat of piracy. Dio notes that, naturally, there was no need for Gabinius as *rogator* to name Pompey for him to immediately spring to mind as the ideal candidate for the piratical command. But in truth – and as Marianne Coudry has correctly shown – the piratical menace is of little importance in Dio's staging of the debate. The historian's actual purpose is to use this setting as the springboard for an extended discussion of republican politics, reflecting upon the corruption of political life and the

---

46   Zon. 7.13.

state of the constitution in the wake of Sulla.[47] It is in that context that we must place Catulus' comments on the dictatorship and can make sense of them. After his *exordium*, Dio's Catulus begins by criticizing extended periods of command as illegal and corrosive to the *res publica*: no individual can abide by ancestral customs, such as collegiality and healthy competition for status, if entrusted with repeated positions of power.[48] This, Dio argues, was precisely the problem with Marius and then Sulla: the latter became "what he was" as a result of successive periods of command, first of armies in the field and then as dictator and consul. Interestingly, Catulus then reviews other possibilities: why give an extraordinary and unconstitutional command to Pompey rather than relying on existing consuls and praetors? Alternatively, Catulus argues, the dictatorship might even be used to resolve the menace of Mediterranean piracy. The passage is revealing, and worth quoting in full:[49]

> But if it is indeed necessary to elect an official alongside the yearly magistrates, there is already an ancient precedent, that is, the dictator. However, our ancestors did not establish this office for every circumstance, nor for a period longer than six months. Therefore, if you do require such an official, it is possible for you to engage either Pompeius or any other man as dictator without transgressing the law nor failing to deliberate carefully for the common good – **on the condition that this be for no longer than the allotted time nor outside of Italy** (ἐφ' ᾧ μήτε πλείω τοῦ τεταγμένου χρόνον μήτε ἔξω τῆς Ἰταλίας ἄρξῃ). For you are not unaware, I think, that our ancestors zealously preserved this limitation, and that no dictator can be found who served abroad, aside from one who went to Sicily and achieved nothing. But if Italy requires no such person, and **if you cannot bear not only the function of a dictator but even the name – as is clear from your anger against Sulla** – (οὔτ' ἂν ὑμεῖς ὑπομείναιτε ἔτι οὐχ ὅτι τὸ ἔργον τοῦ δικτάτορος ἀλλ' οὐδὲ τὸ ὄνομα δῆλον δὲ ἐξ ὧν πρὸς τὸν Σύλλαν ἠγανακτήσατε) how could it be right to create a new position of authority over practically everything within Italy and outside it for three years? You all know what horrors come to states from such a course, and **how many have often disturbed our people because of their lust for extralegal powers** (ὅσοι διὰ τὰς παρανόμους φιλαρχίας τόν τε δῆμον ἡμῶν πολλάκις ἐτάραξαν) and have brought innumerable evils upon themselves.

---

47   Coudry 2016.
48   Cass. Dio 36.31.3–4.
49   Cass. Dio. 36.34.

At first glance these comments of Dio's speaker make little logical sense. Was the historian incompetent?[50] In order to combat the threat of piracy across the Mediterranean – a complex military operation over a wide geographical area – Catulus proposes a dictatorship which is by its nature restricted. The dictator must not leave Italy, and should resign within six months as have all dictators hitherto.[51] Moreover, these severe limitations are enumerated by the speaker himself. In other words, Catulus' suggestion is without worth in the context of 67.

But Dio is not using Catulus to propose a genuinely workable alternative to an extraordinary command for Pompey. Rather, this interjection from Catulus is used to illustrate clearly by example that in a world empire, Romans of the late Republic had little choice but to resort to dangerous extraordinary commands. Evidently – as Catulus shows – the dictatorship was wholly unsuitable as an emergency magistracy to address the exigencies of a large empire. The historian absolutely (and rightly) recognized that extended periods of command were corrosive to Republican traditions, engendering autocratic ambitions in those who received them; this is stated flatly by Catulus at the end of the excerpt.[52] Yet crises occurred within a republican empire just as in all empires: who could be tasked to address them if not the regular magistrates, limited by an impractical one-year term, or the dictator, limited by even more stringent restrictions? So far from dissuading the *Quirites* from choosing Pompey, Dio's Catulus merely reiterates that the existing framework furnished few other options. Dio clearly believed that "democratic" empires were immoderate and susceptible to *stasis*; he says himself that the scope of the empire required a capable autocrat to guide it.[53] Within the framework

---

50   Evidently not; the oblique reference to an unsuccessful dictator in Sicily is Aulus Calatinus (see Cass. Dio fr. 15), dictator in 249 BCE. Obviously Dio had done his research to insert this rather neat historical detail, and the recall suggests *hypomnemata* of particularly high quality.

51   Hinard 1999 suggests that this excerpt from the *dissuasio* of Catulus proves that Sulla resigned his dictatorship within the proper six-month term, possibly in time for the consular elections in July 81 for the following year.

52   This is the phenomenon termed by Suetonius *imperii consuetudo* or "habit of commanding": the psychological impact of extended periods of command, especially within the provinces, where poor communication and patchy senatorial oversight allowed the provincial governor essentially to rule alone in a far-flung corner of the empire. The best treatment of this is Eckstein 2004; for the thought of Dio on the destructive impact of *imperii consuetudo* in the Republic, see Burden-Strevens 2016.

53   Cass. Dio 44.2.4: "but for a city, not only so large in itself, but also ruling the finest and the greatest part of the known world ... for such a city, I say, to practice moderation under a democracy is impossible."

of traditional liberty, this individual was the dictator – "a ruler under another name," in Cicero's and later Dio's definition – yet this was no longer a practical option.

It may not have been a morally appealing one either. Dio uses this speech to make a clever inversion of his first comments on the foundation of the dictatorship: desiring the beneficial aspects of a monarchy, the Romans in the wake of Tarquin originally "chose it under another name." But in the aftermath of the Sullan experiment, it is the name of *dictatura*, not monarchy, that the Romans cannot stomach. Now, having Q. Lutatius Catulus (the younger) advance the view that the *Quirites* "cannot bear not only the function of a dictator but even the name" after Sulla is questionable. For a start, the speaker's own father had sided with Sulla, committing suicide rather than face Marius following the latter's occupation of Rome; and Catulus himself argued for the retention of the Sullan constitution during his consulship and an honorable burial upon his death.[54] He is not the most credible candidate to articulate these views of Dio. Melissa Barden Dowling has also suggested that there is no evidence that Sulla had yet entered political discourse as a negative *exemplum* by the time of this debate in 67 BCE, particularly in connection with cruelty or *crudelitas*; our earliest such citation seems to come in the late 60s at *In Catilinam* 3.10.[55] But in fact these themes seem to have been explored as early as 80 BCE in the *Pro Roscio*, albeit with only oblique reference to Sulla (for obvious reasons).[56] Cicero mentions the recent dictator in revealingly fawning terms – "that most gallant and illustrious man, whom I only name to honor" – and directs his criticism toward his client and freedman Chrysogonus.[57] But the disease of *crudelitas* is described in the peroration as endemic to the entire Republic and (significantly) as a recent phenomenon, "having taken clemency away from the hearts of even merciful men."[58] We are hard pressed not to think of Sulla, not least because his name is mentioned almost as much as Chrysogonus' – consistently either in extravagant rehearsal of the many reasons for which he could not *possibly* have been aware of his client's actions, or in the adulation which speaks of fear.[59]

---

54   Q. Lutatius Catulus Major, suicide: Cic. *Or.* 3.9, *Brut.* 307, *Tusc.* 5.56; Diod. 38.4.2–3; Vell. Pat. 2.22.3–4; Val. Max 9.12.4; Plut. *Mar.* 44.8; App. *B Civ.* 1.74. Q. Lutatius Catulus Minor, consulship: Sall. *Hist.* 1.47–8M; App. *B Civ.* 1.105.
55   Barden Dowling 2000.
56   I am indebted to Prof. Catherine Steel (Glasgow) for bringing this to my attention.
57   Cic. *Rosc.* 6.
58   Cic. *Rosc.* 154.
59   E.g. Cic. *Rosc.* 6, 21–2, 25–6, 110, 127, 130–1, 136, 143.

Dio thus problematizes the dictatorship in the late Republic on two bases in the *dissuasio* of Catulus. Firstly, there is a practical consideration: a "city which rules the world," in Dio's words, could not be governed democratically, and the demands of crisis within a wide empire necessarily required temporary returns to autocracy. Yet the conventional mechanism for such emergency measures – dictatorship – was not legally permissible within the existing framework, necessitating prolonged and corrosive periods of command. To my knowledge Dio is our only historian of this period to have given the dictatorship serious consideration in the failure of the Republic to manage its empire and as a practical justification for Augustus' rule. Secondly, there were moral concerns. If we give the words of Catulus any credence as a genuine attempt by the historian to portray *his* view of what people were thinking about dictatorship in the wake of Sulla – and allusions in the *Pro Roscio* might perhaps suggest an early origin for that kind of thought – then evidently Dio wished to argue that the dictatorship had come to be viewed as a toxic political solution. I have argued elsewhere that the set-piece orations, such as that of Catulus here, are the essential interpretative kernel of the *Roman History*.[60] The choice to explore these two problems with the dictatorship – practical and reputational – through a set-piece speech is entirely Dio's own. The office is unmentioned in his source for the main arguments of Catulus' oration,[61] and indeed in all parallel sources for the *lex Gabinia* of 67 BCE and the *lex Manilia* of the following year.[62] Unprompted by an intermediary, Cassius Dio wished to problematize the dictatorship at this point because he considered it historically important at this "turning-point" in the history of the late Republic.[63]

Did contemporary Romans share these anxieties? Gianpaolo Urso has argued that the "myth of Sulla" is in fact an imperial phenomenon: there is no reason to suppose that the dictatorship had seriously come under scrutiny at this point in the late Republic, especially if, with François Hinard, we accept that the dictator resigned appropriately within the six-month term.[64] But Dio suggests differently, and contemporary evidence may support his claim. Let us

---

60 Burden-Strevens 2015. It has at least long been recognized that the speeches are a window into Dio's thought, for which see Millar 1964, 79. Criticisms of Dio's tendency toward "moralizing" in the speeches (whose morals?) are often vague, e.g. Rodgers 2008.
61 Montecalvo 2014, 24–57 has shown that the historian drew the main arguments of Catulus' speech from the *De Lege Manilia*, where Cicero reports Catulus' and Hortensius' objections to Pompey's power. For further examples and a more assertive insistence that the historian was using the orator directly, see Burden-Strevens 2018.
62 E.g. App. *Mith.* 91–7; Plut. *Pomp.* 25.10; Sall. *Hist.* 5.20–4M; Val. Max. 8.15.9; Vell. Pat. 2.32.1–3.
63 So described by Coudry 2016.
64 Hinard 1999, rejected by Ramsey 2016, 310 n. 44; Urso 2016.

return to the electoral crisis of 54–53 BCE. Cicero's letters I have already mentioned briefly as a source for the main events, although their interest for us here lies in their value as a source for attitudes. The letters to Quintus and Atticus between June and December 54 BCE suggest a growing atmosphere of suspicion and concern about rumors of a dictatorship, and these anxieties appear to be shared by a wider group than the orator alone. On June 3 Cicero writes to Quintus of "some latent idea of a dictatorship" (*erat aliqua suspicio dictaturae*); but the rumors were unconfirmed, and in any case hopes for the resumption of proper *comitia* perhaps remained.[65] By late October this hope was withering and the possibility of an *interregnum* arose: in that context Cicero speaks to Atticus of "a whiff of dictatorship in the air, in fact a good deal of talk about it" (*est non nullus odor dictaturae, sermo quidem multus*).[66] In other letters from late October the tone is more panicked: Cicero puts Gabinius' acquittal in his trial for *maiestas* down to the "fear-inducing rumor of a dictatorship" (*dictaturae etiam rumor plenus timoris*).[67] Come November, Pompey seems to have been finally mentioned in explicit connection with such plans; it is only at this point at least that Cicero mentions his name. Cicero's claim that "the rumor of a dictatorship is not pleasing to *boni*" (*rumor dictatoris iniucundus bonis*) stresses questionable uniformity of opinion among a group to which he so often claimed to belong, although the difference in atmosphere is telling compared to June: "the proposal, as a whole, is looked upon with alarm, and grows unpopular ... there is nothing else being talked about in politics just now; at any rate, nothing else is being done" (*sed tota res et timetur et refrigescit ... aliud hoc tempore de re publica nihil loquebantur; agebatur quidem certe nihil*).[68] Finally, by December plans for a dictatorship for Pompey had definitely taken shape: "Appius is intriguing darkly; Hirrus is paving the way" (*Hirrus parat*). Although Cicero notes indifference on the part of the people, it is the *boni* who again are alarmed at the prospect (*populus non curat, principes nolunt*).[69]

One possible way of approaching this material is to consider it not as evidence of alarmed attitudes toward the dictatorship *as such* in the 50s, but rather as a reflection on Pompey. This is a false dichotomy – it seems to me concerned with both – and in any case does not explain the reaction to rumors of a dictatorship between the early and late summer 54 which do not seem to have been in connection with Pompey's name.[70] In Cicero's fulsome (and

---

65   Cic. *Q Fr.* 2.13.5.
66   Cic. *Att.* 4.18.3.
67   Cic. *Q Fr.* 3.4.1.
68   Cic. *Q Fr.* 3.8.4–6.
69   Cic. *Q Fr.* 3.9.3.
70   So Cic. *Att.* 4.18.3, *Q Fr.* 3.4.1.

negative) accounts of Pompey's political activities throughout the summer in his epistles to Quintus and Atticus, all manner of infractions are recorded.[71] Yet Pompey's name is nowhere in connection with a possible dictatorship until November; all Cicero records prior to that, possibly in June and certainly by October, is fearful rumors of a possible nomination. Given Cicero's distaste for *Magnus noster* in the letters of this period and the detail he provides on his activities, the absence of his name is surprising. I would (cautiously) suggest that Pompey was not at the center of rumors of a possible dictatorship until late in the year; Plutarch and Dio date this as late as C. Lucilius Hirrus' election to the tribunate in December, but this is too late.[72] The anxiety perhaps in June and certainly October is about a dictatorship as such, and not only Pompey.

Relying solely on Cicero for this picture is perilous, but can fortunately be supplemented. The evidence of coinage is controversial, but remarkably under-studied in connection with contemporary attitudes to the dictatorship, and never in conversation with Dio's history.[73] Like the letters, the numismatic material can be revealing of the opinions not only of their producer but also of messages he expected those who mattered to accept. If we wish to gauge the veracity of Dio's view that the dictatorship *per se* had become politically toxic in the late Republic then three *denarii* from the 50s are of special interest. The first we turn to is certainly the latest and easiest to date, minted shortly after the consuls for 53 finally entered office in the summer. The moneyer is M. Valerius Messalla,[74] son of the newly-elected consul Messalla Rufus. The obverse is perfectly conventional, hence the obverse legend (MESSAL·F) right and downwards of the helmeted head of Roma. But the reverse is extraordinary. Two curule chairs, flanked by S· C· (SENATV CONSVLTO) on either side, celebrate the successful resumption of republican magistracies and senatorial integrity: this message is reinforced with PATRE·COS above. Beneath there lies (probably) a horizontal scepter and certainly a diadem, a circular strip of fabric with a knot and two tails: the characteristic trapping of Hellenistic kingship.[75] The choice of images is deliberate and significant: the proper framework

---

71   Cic. *Att.* 4.15 (27 July), *Q Fr.* 3.1 (28 September), 3.2 (October), 3.3 (October), 3.4 (24 October).
72   Plut. *Pomp.* 54.2; Cass. Dio 40.45.5.
73   To my knowledge only one republican coin is ever discussed in connection with the *Roman History*: the famous silver *denarius* of Brutus of the EID MAR type, mentioned at Cass. Dio 47.25 (*RRC* 502/4). See Cahn 1988, 211–32 for a more recent die study of the issue.
74   On his post as *triumvir monetalis* in this year, see Syme 1986, 228.
75   On the diadem, see Carson 1957, 50–2 and Rawson 1975, 150. Scepticism that the reverse type portrays a diadem is peculiar: for roughly contemporary Roman types one need only compare with *RRC* 507/2, or for genuine Hellenistic examples the diademed heads of Philip V (e.g. *SNG* München 1124, *SNG* Alpha Bank 1049, *AMNG* 3.2).

FIGURE 7.1A AND B Republican *denarius*, 53 BCE (*RRC* 435/1)
©THE TRUSTEES OF THE BRITISH MUSEUM

of regular magistracies triumphs over tyrannical *regnum* – or, in a republican context, over recently thwarted plans for a dictatorship. In Crawford's words, the reverse type "portrays the subjection of the attributes of royalty to that of Republican legality; it reflects the (temporary) exclusion of Pompey from the possibility of achieving sole rule."[76] This was not the first time that Pompey was compared to a Hellenistic king: in 56 BCE the aedile Favonius quipped, upon seeing a white bandage attached to his leg, that it made little difference where on his body the diadem sat.[77] Although the trappings of the Hellenistic king are not categorically "tyrannical" – Classical tyranny is an ethical, not iconographical, phenomenon – republican political invective does not recognize that distinction. A Roman statesman who dresses and acts like a king is always a tyrant.

Here we should remember the disagreement between our literary sources. We have already seen that Appian, Plutarch, and Cicero all suggest that Pompey was maneuvering deliberately toward a dictatorship; his plans were only thwarted by Cato and Bibulus.[78] But Cassius Dio maintains that he voluntarily declined it and took pains to get consuls elected for 53 – "since in remembrance of Sulla's cruelty all hated that office."[79] Messalla's *denarius* does seem to sit ill with Dio's interpretation of Pompey's motivations – evidently

---

76 Crawford 1974, 457.
77 Val. Max. 6.2.7: *cui candida fascia crus alligatum habenti Fauonius 'non refert' inquit 'qua in parte sit corporis diadema.'*
78 App. *B Civ.* 2.23; Plut. *Pomp.* 54.3; Cic. *Q Fr.* 3.8.5.
79 Cass. Dio 40.46, 40.50.

a broader contingent than only Cicero were concerned about the general's plans. But at the same time, it supports his overall view about contemporary attitudes to the dictatorship, and so emphasizes Pompey's political acumen in refusing the office. We have to remember that controversial and (to many) alarming plans for a dictatorship have just been scotched. The choice of images – the scepter and diadem of a Hellenistic king, subordinated by the symbols of consular and senatorial authority – needs to be interpreted in that context. Andreas Kalyvas has argued that it is our Greek historians of the Republic, Dionysius and Appian, who first conceived of a relationship between the Roman dictatorship and Greek tyranny: they began a trend for critiquing the dictatorship using words and concepts borrowed from the Greek tradition.[80] This development in fact has earlier roots: this language is certainly identifiable in the events of 53 BCE, and it is Roman statesmen – not Greek historians – who were using that language.

The message of consular legitimacy in opposition to tyrannical rule appears in other numismatic evidence from the 50s. This may, or may not, be in connection with the electoral crisis and rumors of a dictatorship, depending on how we date the material. The coinage of M. Brutus furnishes some particularly well-known types. In the first, the obverse displays a personification of Libertas, right-facing with the legend downward and behind (LIBERTAS). The reverse features a procession of four individuals: the second and fourth in the quartet are evidently lictors carrying *fasces*, flanking a slightly larger figure on either side. The identification of this larger figure as L. Junius Brutus, the first Roman consul after the alleged expulsion of the Tarquins, is aided by the text in exergue: BRVTVS, identifying both the minter of the coin and the subject of the reverse type. The general themes and the interaction between those themes are quite clear: the eradication of tyranny from the state and its replacement by the republican magistracies, especially the consulship, standing as the guarantee of *libertas* (or at least an optimate interpretation of it).[81] These messages are replicated in a second well-known issue from the year of Brutus' moneyership: L. Junius Brutus returns again on the obverse, right-facing with the legend BRVTVS downward and behind; the reverse features a portrait of P. Servilius Ahala, who in republican mytho-history killed Sp. Maelius in 439 BCE to prevent his attempt to seize power.

---

80 Kalyvas 2007. Particularly important passages are App. *B Civ.* 1.99, 1.101 and Dion. Hal. *Ant. Rom.* 5.70, 5.73.
81 Arena 2012, 1–13.

FIGURE 7.2 Republican *denarius*, 54 BCE? (*RRC* 433/1)
© THE TRUSTEES OF THE BRITISH MUSEUM

FIGURE 7.3 Republican *denarius*, 54 BCE? (*RRC* 433/2)
© THE TRUSTEES OF THE BRITISH MUSEUM

The themes present in Brutus' coinage are of course especially relevant to 54–53, where the collapse of the consular elections left the way open for a dictatorship that many – not only Cicero – seem to have feared. The allusion to L. Junius Brutus, the expulsion of the Tarquins, and the institution of the consulship are telling in this context. However, the dating and interpretation of these coins is a subject of much debate. Michael Crawford suggests 54 BCE, viewing these issues as "part of a pattern of consistent opposition to Pompey's real or supposed intentions of achieving sole rule"; Matthew Rockman among others has retained this dating and interpretation on the basis of events in that year.⁸² But an alternative view is that Brutus' term as *triumvir monetalis* occurred a year earlier than previously thought and that these issues therefore date to 55 BCE, before the electoral and dictatorship debacle.⁸³ This argument is persuasive, although Cerutti goes too far in radically claiming that Brutus' *sole* intention in minting these coins was to advertise his family lineage and that they are silent on political events.⁸⁴ There is no room here to wade into this debate. But evidently these issues, which were produced some time in the 50s in or before 54 BCE, evince a distinct range of political concerns: anxieties about tyranny and *adfectatio regni*, concern for the proper functioning of republican magistracies, and arguments for the protection of traditional liberty.

The analysis that Dio offers, through Catulus, of the problem with the dictatorship in the final decades of the Republic is intriguing. He believed that the *Quirites* of this period had grown averse to the dictatorship as a toxic and discredited political institution. For a "living" articulation of that view in a specific context he used Catulus in Book 36 – though of course Dio makes clear in his own commentary on the *lex Antonia* that the office itself was not problematic, merely the perception of it. In Dio – and indeed, only in Dio – Pompey seems aware of these problems, and accounts for them in his decision to decline the honor. This interpretation merits our consideration for three reasons. Firstly, Dio was right. Contemporary evidence testifies to the atmosphere of anxiety in 54 surrounding plans for a dictatorship, and the earlier examples (such as Cicero's letters from June and October) may suggest that those anxieties were directed toward a dictatorship as such rather than merely toward Pompey. Secondly, Dio is to my knowledge unique in considering the practical limitations of the dictatorship as a causal factor in the proliferation of extraordinary commands that were corrosive to republican traditions. Why else insert this point in the debates surrounding the *lex Gabinia* of 67 BCE, which seems wholly irrelevant otherwise? In Dio's view at least, the *Quirites* had no other choice than Pompey for precisely the reasons his Catulus outlines. Third and finally, our historian's critique of the dictatorship is an important part of his explanation of and justification for Augustus' rule. And for that we must turn to some final comments.

---

82   Crawford 1974, 455; Rockman 1992, 14; also Hersh & Walker 1984 and DeRose Evans 1992, 146; the latter with a revised date of 59 BCE. The chronology of the coin hoards provided by Cerutti 1993, 71–2 shows that these issues must have been minted no later than 54 BCE.
83   Cerutti 1993 *passim*.
84   *Pace* Cerutti 1993, 80: "there is no evidence to support the claim that Brutus's two coin types were intended to allude to anything more than his ancestors' historical achievements."

4 The Final Phase: Finding a Replacement

In 22 BCE a period of pestilence and famine struck Rome, five years after the Augustan "Settlement" lavishly detailed in Books 52–3. According to Dio the starving *plebs* were convinced that the only answer to the crisis was to beg Augustus to assume the dictatorship and the *cura annonae*: both of these had been abolished as unconstitutional within a single year two decades previously. After shutting up the Senate in the *curia* and (allegedly) threatening to burn it down – a recurring formula in Dio's history[85] – the people presented their demands:[86]

> They took the twenty-four fasces and approached Augustus, begging him to consent to be made dictator as well as curator of the grain-supply, **just as Pompey had once done** (καθάπερ ποτὲ τὸν Πομπήιον). Under compulsion he accepted the latter of these, and ordered that two men be chosen each year from among those who had served as praetors at least five years previously, so as to see to the distribution of grain. **But he did not accept the dictatorship** (τὴν δὲ δικτατορίαν οὐ προσήκατο), and indeed rent his clothes when he could find no way of convincing the people otherwise, either by argument or begging. **For as he already had power and honor in excess of the dictators anyway, he rightly guarded against the envy and hatred that title would bring** (τήν τε γὰρ ἐξουσίαν καὶ τὴν τιμὴν καὶ ὑπὲρ τοὺς δικτάτορας ἔχων, ὀρθῶς τό τε ἐπίφθονον καὶ τὸ μισητὸν τῆς ἐπικλήσεως αὐτῶν ἐφυλάξατο).[87]

Dio's is the most detailed account that we have of this incident. Suetonius gives a short sentence stating the basic facts; Velleius Paterculus provides the same information in a fawning one-liner.[88] Augustus also briefly records the event himself: tellingly, he considered his public disavowal of a dictatorship one of his many proud distinctions.[89] But our historian is much fuller. He used this moment not only (like the *Res Gestae*) to emphasize Augustus' *civilitas* and refusal to aggrandize himself with further honors, but also to emphasize its constitutional significance. Dio's *princeps* had no need of a dictatorship,

---

[85] Libourel 1974.
[86] Cass. Dio 54.2.1–5 for the entire narrative of the episode.
[87] Note the similarity between this final idea and Pompey's attitude to the consulship *sine collega* at Cass. Dio 40.51.1, discussed above. Pompey, not Caesar, is the model for Augustus in the *Roman History*.
[88] Suet. *Aug.* 52; Vell. Pat. 2.89.5.
[89] Aug. *RGDA* 5.

since his power and honor surpassed it already; and he recognized – correctly (ὀρθῶς) – that the office would only serve to tarnish his reputation and bring him into suspicion. In other words, the historian *partly* interprets Augustus' success in managing his constitutional image through the lens of the dictatorship. We are reminded of the foreshadowing of Caesar in the historian's commentary on the earliest foundation of that office; Dio's Augustus does not repeat Caesar's mistake.

For Dio this mistake was not one of the reality of Caesar's power, but rather its presentation. The historian himself clearly did not believe that Caesar's rule was tyrannical. Far from it: he writes that those who plotted against him were motivated not by his faults, but from fear that his "goodness" (τὴν χρηστότητα αὐτοῦ) would not last.[90] His generosity and clemency put Sulla's cruelty to shame.[91] The dictator was, in Dio's presentation, a scheming vulture, pleonectic and wastrel at the same time, who absolutely aspired to kingship.[92] But he was no tyrant. Nevertheless, Dio's Caesar fails to understand the importance of appearances. He adopted the attire of the ancient kings of Alba, and a golden chair and crown set with jewels was to be carried into theaters, among other honors.[93] He allowed himself to grow conceited and puffed-up – and this, in Dio's view, is precisely what his enemies wanted: "the majority followed this course because they wished to make him envied and hated as quickly as possible, that he might the sooner perish."[94]

Augustus made no such error. His refusal of the dictatorship reiterates his political acumen: he is made to recognize the importance of the terms with which power is defined. Naturally that of "dictator" had become completely unpalatable. We have seen Dio's argument that it had in fact been so for many years, long before Caesar mistakenly adopted it; it was neither a practical nor attractive solution to the crisis surrounding the *lex Gabinia*, for example. Yet Dio believed that monarchy was absolutely essential for any stable state. When dictatorship failed, the *res publica* failed: Rome's recourse to a temporary monarchy had to be replaced. The answer lay in Octavian's rebirth as "Augustus" and *princeps*: a position of power greater than the dictator's which eschewed the "envy and hatred the title would bring" (τό τε ἐπίφθονον καὶ τὸ μισητὸν τῆς ἐπικλήσεως αὐτῶν).[95] In reinventing the role of monarchy within the state – a monarchy under a civil guise – and rejecting the discredited position of

---

90   Cass. Dio 42.27.4.
91   Cass. Dio 43.50.2.
92   Cass. Dio 44.11.1.
93   Cass. Dio 44.6.1–4.
94   Cass. Dio 44.7.3.
95   Cass. Dio 54.1.5.

dictator, Dio's Augustus is in fact following the advice of Maecenas in Book 52, which explains the historian's view in explicit terms:[96]

> If you really do desire the reality of monarchy but fear the name of it as an accursed thing, then decline the title of "king" and rule alone under the title of "Caesar." But if you come to require other epithets, then the people will give you the title of *imperator*, just as they gave it to your father; and they will revere you with another way of address (σεβιοῦσι δέ σε καὶ ἑτέρᾳ τινὶ προσρήσει), so that you may reap the crop of the reality of kingship without the odium which attaches to the name of "king."

On the one hand Maecenas' prediction that the Romans will "revere" Octavian with a new name (σεβιοῦσι δέ σε καὶ ἑτέρᾳ τινὶ προσρήσει) is a rather inventive *jeu d'esprit*; it is a verbal foreshadowing of the *princeps*' new title of Augustus, or σεβαστός.

But the rhetorical flair should not disguise the real force of this passage within Cassius Dio's argument about the transformation of dictatorship in the late Republic, its problems, and its replacement by the Augustan principate. From its earliest mention in the *Roman History* Dio sought to explore the dictatorship in a way distinctive within the historiography of the Republic. In keeping with his theoretical view of the weakness of democracy and the necessity of monarchy – particularly for a "city which rules the world" – Dio viewed dictatorship as a beneficial return to the best that monarchy had to offer. Describing it in terms reminiscent of Cicero's *Republic*, Dio resisted the temptation succumbed to by Dionysius, and to a lesser extent Livy, to view that office from its very inception through the prism of events in the first century BCE; less still to describe it simplistically as a form of tyranny. Rather, Dio (paradoxically) believed that a successful democracy required a viable resort to monarchy in times of crisis. In the late Republic that vision collapsed. When pressed with crisis in the Mediterranean in 67 BCE the *Quirites* could not call on their traditional offices for practical and moral reasons: Rome's emergency powers had not kept pace with the growth of empire, and in any case the dictatorship was a discredited solution. The disastrous alternative – Dio's Catulus warns – would be further extraordinary commands, and Pompey. Thirteen years later when republican institutions had entirely broken down, Dio records continuing aversion to the dictatorship, "since in remembrance of Sulla's

---

96   Cass. Dio 52.40.1–2.

cruelty all hated that office."⁹⁷ The again disastrous alternative was a sole consulship for Pompey in 52 BCE.

For Dio the failure of the dictatorship precipitated the failure of the Republic itself. We may find this outlandish. But concerns about a dictatorship in the electoral crisis of 54–53 BCE were evidently widespread, at least among the *boni*; these were articulated in the language of traditional liberty, privileging the dyarchy of consuls in conversation with the Senate and emphasizing the rejection of tyranny. Cassius Dio himself believed that such concerns were mistaken: the dictatorship itself was not the problem, merely the toxic combination of military force and an autocratic character. It is testament to his quality as an historian that he explains the actions of his historical characters, such as the Romans who voted for the *lex Antonia*, with rationales that he himself did not accept. Dio often resists the temptation to project his own views onto his actors. In Catulus in 67 or Cato and Bibulus in 53, we see individuals acting not as agents of Dio's hindsight, but as republican statesmen whose proximity to events blinds them to the nature of the problem, and who pose ineffective and ultimately catastrophic solutions for their predicament.

In the end, Dio's Augustus understood both the necessity of monarchy and the need to redefine it. To paraphrase the preface to Tacitus' *Annals*, he realized that he should be neither king nor dictator, but *princeps*.⁹⁸ His disavowal of the dictatorship in 22 BCE has its precedent in Pompey's refusal thirty years earlier; yet to Dio, Augustus' refusal – again like Pompey's – was not merely a show of *recusatio imperii*, much as it may have filled that additional purpose. Rather, it was an astute realization of the political reality, and a fulfillment of Maecenas' suggestion to cloak the fact of monarchy under new and acceptable titles. Here as so often in the *Roman History*, it pays to follow Maecenas' advice.

Bibliography

Arena, V. (2012) *Libertas and the Practice of Politics in the Late Roman Republic*, Cambridge.

Barden Dowling, M. (2000) "The Clemency of Sulla", *Historia* 49/3, 303–40.

Burden-Strevens, C. (2015) *Cassius Dio's Speeches and the Collapse of the Roman Republic*, Dissertation: Glasgow.

---

97   Cass. Dio 40.45.5.
98   Tac. *Ann.* 1.1.

Burden-Strevens, C. (2016) "Fictitious Speeches, Envy, and the Habituation to Authority: Writing the Collapse of the Roman Republic", in C. H. Lange & J. M. Madsen (eds.), *Cassius Dio: Greek Intellectual and Roman Politician* (Leiden & Boston): 193–216.

Burden-Strevens, C. (2018) "Reconstructing Republican Oratory in Cassius Dio's *Roman History*", in C. Gray *et al.* (eds.), *Reading Republican Oratory: Reconstructions, Contexts, Receptions* (Oxford): 111–34.

Cahn, H. (1988) "EIDibus MARtiis", *Numismatica e antichità classiche: Quaderni ticinesi* 18, 211–32.

Carson, R. (1957) "Caesar and the Monarchy", *Greece & Rome* 4/1, 46–53.

Cerutti, S. (1993) "Brutus, Cyprus, and the Coinage of 55 B.C.", *American Journal of Numismatics* 5/6, 69–87.

Cornell, T. J. (1995) *The Beginnings of Rome: Italy and Rome from the Bronze Age to the Punic Wars*, London.

Coudry, M. (2016) "Cassius Dio on Pompey's Extraordinary Commands", in C. H. Lange & J. M. Madsen (eds.), *Cassius Dio: Greek Intellectual and Roman Politician* (Leiden & Boston): 33–50.

Crawford, M. (1974) *The Roman Republican Coinage*, Cambridge.

DeRose Evans, J. (1992) *The Art of Persuasion: Political Propaganda from Aeneas to Brutus*, Ann Arbor.

Eckstein, A. (2004) "From the Historical Caesar to the Spectre of Caesarism: The Imperial Administrator as Internal Threat", in P. Baehr & M. Richter (eds.), *Dictatorship in History and Theory* (Cambridge): 279–98.

Forsythe, G. (2005) *A Critical History of Early Rome: From Prehistory to the First Punic War*, Berkeley.

Fromentin, V. (2018) "La fiabilité de Zonaras dans les deux premières décades de l'Histoire romaine de Cassius Dion: le cas des discours", in C. Burden-Strevens & M. Lindholmer (eds.), *Cassius Dio's Forgotten History of Early Rome: The 'Roman History' Books 1–21* (Leiden & Boston): 27–52.

Gowing, A. M. (1992) *The Triumviral Narratives of Appian and Cassius Dio*, Ann Arbor.

Gruen, E. (1969) "The Consular Elections for 53 B.C.", in J. Bibauw (ed.), *Hommages à Marcel Renard II* (Brussels): 311–21.

Hersh, C. & Walker, A. (1984) "The Messagne Hoard", *American Numismatic Society Museum Notes* 29, 103–34.

Hinard, F. (1999) "Dion Cassius et l'abdication de Sylla", *Revue des études anciennes* 101, 427–32.

Kalyvas, A. (2007) "The Tyranny of Dictatorship: When the Greek Tyrant Met the Roman Dictator", *Political Theory* 35/4, 412–42.

Libourel, J. (1974) "An Unusual Annalistic Source Used by Dio Cassius", *American Journal of Philology* 95/4, 383–93.

Lintott, A. (1999) *The Constitution of the Roman Republic*, Oxford.

Madsen, J. (2016) "Criticising the Benefactors: The Severans and the Return of Dynastic Rule", in C. H. Lange & J. M. Madsen (eds.), *Cassius Dio: Greek Intellectual and Roman Politician* (Leiden & Boston): 136–58.

Mallan, C. (2018) "The Regal Period in the *Excerpta Constantiniana* and in Some Early Byzantine Extracts from Dio's *Roman History*", in C. Burden-Strevens & M. Lindholmer (eds.), *Cassius Dio's Forgotten History of Early Rome: The 'Roman History' Books 1–21* (Leiden & Boston): 76–96.

Meier, C. (1966) *Res Publica Amissa. Eine Studie zu Verfassung und Geschichte der späten römischen Republik*, Wiesbaden.

Meyer, E. (1922) *Caesars Monarchie und das Principat des Pompejus. Innere Geschichte Roms von 66 bis 44 n. Chr.*, 3rd ed., Stuttgart & Berlin.

Millar, F. (1964) *A Study of Cassius Dio*, Oxford.

Montecalvo, M. S. (2014) *Cicerone in Cassio Dione*, Lecce.

Ramsey, J. T. (2016) "How and Why Was Pompey Made Sole Consul in 52 BC?", *Historia* 65/3, 298–324.

Rawson, E. (1975) "Caesar's Heritage: Hellenistic Kings and their Roman Equals", *Journal of Roman Studies* 65, 148–59.

Rilinger, R. (2007) "Die Interpretation des Niedergangs der römischen Republik durch 'Revolution' und 'Krise ohne Alternative'", in R. Rilinger (ed.), *Ordo und Dignitas. Beiträge zur römischen Verfassungs- und Sozialgeschichte* (Stuttgart): 123–50.

Rockman, M. (1992) "The Coins of the Roman Republic from 60 to 50 B.C.: Another Look at Chronology", *The Celator* 6/2, 8–14.

Rodgers, B. S. (2008) "Catulus' Speech in Cassius Dio 36.31–36", *Greek, Roman, and Byzantine Studies* 48, 295–318.

Simons, B. (2009). *Cassius Dio und die Römische Republik. Untersuchungen zum Bild des römischen Gemeinwesens in den Büchern 3–35 der Romaika*, Berlin.

Steel, C. (2013) *The End of the Roman Republic, 146 to 44 BC: Conquest and Crisis*, Edinburgh.

Syme, R. (1986) *The Augustan Aristocracy*, Oxford.

Urso, G. (2016) "Cassius Dio's Sulla: *Exemplum* of Cruelty and Republican Dictator", in C. H. Lange & J. M. Madsen (eds.), *Cassius Dio: Greek Intellectual and Roman Politician* (Leiden & Boston): 13–32.

Vervaet, F. J. (2010) "Abrogating Despotic Power through Deceit: The Pompeian Model for Augustan *dissimulatio*", in A. J. Turner, J. H. Kim On Chong-Gossard, & F. J. Vervaet (eds.), *Private and Public Lies: The Discourse of Despotism and Deceit in the Graeco-Roman World* (Leiden & Boston): 133–66.

Zarecki, J. (2014) *Cicero's Ideal Statesman in Theory and Practice*, London & New York.

CHAPTER 8

Spectacle Entertainments in the Late Republican Books of Cassius Dio's *Roman History*

Jesper Carlsen

Cassius Dio relates in Book 43 that, following his spectacular four triumphs in 46 BCE, C. Julius Caesar entertained the people with money, grain, and olive oil and entered his own forum. Then the Greek senatorial historian goes on to deal with the gladiatorial contests provided by the ten-year dictator in a wooden amphitheater built for this occasion (43.22.3–4):

> θέατρόν τι κυνηγετικὸν ἰκριώσας, ὃ καὶ ἀμφιθέατρον ἐκ τοῦ πέριξ πανταχόθεν ἕδρας ἄνευ σκηνῆς ἔχειν προσερρήθη. καὶ ἐπὶ τούτῳ καὶ ἐπὶ τῇ θυγατρὶ καὶ θηρίων σφαγὰς καὶ ἀνδρῶν ὁπλομαχίας ἐποίησεν, ὧν ἐάν τις τὸν ἀριθμὸν γράψαι ἐθελήσῃ, ὄχλον ἂν τῇ συγγραφῇ οὐδ᾽ ἀληθῆ ἴσως παράσχοι· πάντα γὰρ τὰ τοιαῦτα ἐπὶ τὸ μεῖζον ἀεὶ κομποῦται. τοῦτο μὲν οὖν καὶ ἐπὶ τῶν ἄλλων τῶν ὁμοίων τῶν ἔπειτα γενομένων ἐάσω, πλὴν εἰ μή τι πάνυ μοι δόξειεν ἀναγκαῖον εἰπεῖν εἶναι.

> He [Caesar] built a kind of hunting-theater of wood, which was called an amphitheater from the fact that it had seats all around without any stage. In honor of this and of his daughter he exhibited combats of wild beasts and gladiators; but anyone who cared to record their number would find his task a burden without being able, in all probability, to present the truth; for all such matters are regularly exaggerated in a spirit of boastfulness. I shall accordingly pass over this and other like events that took place later, except, of course, where it may seem to me quite essential to mention some particular point.[1]

It was the second time that Caesar honored a family member who had died several years before the gladiatorial contests provided by him. The first time Caesar organized gladiatorial shows was as curule aedile in 65 BCE in honor of his father, who had actually died thirty years earlier. Caesar not only assembled

---

1 Bernstein 1998, 332–5. Translations, unless otherwise stated, are taken from the Loeb Classical Library, but sometimes slightly revised.

so many gladiators that the Senate passed restrictions on the numbers of gladiators presented in a single show, but the event was also so magnificent that Caesar's aedilician colleague, M. Bibulus – as recorded both by Suetonius and Cassius Dio – remarked that he had suffered the same fate as one of the Dioscuri, Pollux: "for although this hero possessed a temple in common with his brother Castor, it was named after the latter only (τοῦ γάρ τοι ναοῦ κοινοῦ οἱ πρὸς τὸν ἀδελφὸν τὸν Κάστορα ὄντος, ἐπ' ἐκείνου μόνου ἡ ἐπωνυμία αὐτοῦ γίγνεται, 37.8.2)."[2]

The most important aspect of this highly rhetorical passage is not the gladiatorial performances put on by Caesar in honor of Julia, which he had already announced in 52 BCE. It is Cassius Dio's critical considerations of the unreliable sources of the numbers of gladiators and animals in the shows that is instructive for the understanding of his methods and approach. The Severan historian does not, however, himself, follow his own sound source criticism on these "trivial details" as he called them later in his narrative (Cass. Dio 73[72].18.3). As noted by R. F. Newbold (1975), the Greek historian frequently enumerates the figures of human participants, animals, and the duration of the spectacle entertainments. Newbold also observes that "at times one gets the impression Dio is incorporating a history of the games into his work. Perhaps too he wishes to use numerical standards by which to measure an individual's power and wealth, his ability to control and display resources."[3] An otherwise lost ancient history of Roman games may at first sight appear an attractive suggestion, but none of the numerous works on gladiatorial games published in the recent decades has discussed this proposal. And there are good reasons for this: there are no indications or hints in the ancient sources of the existence of such a narrative except the three lost volumes *On Games* by Suetonius.[4]

Cassius Dio is, in his own way, one of the most important literary sources on gladiatorial combats in Rome, but most modern scholars working on the topic have used him as a handy resource without examining the context. This is particularly evident from two fundamental and pioneering works on the so-called "spectacles of death." G. Ville's extremely detailed *La gladiature en Occident des origines à la mort de Domitien* (1981) refers to more than 150 different passages of Cassius Dio's *Roman History*.[5] Rather surprisingly, the Greek senatorial historian does not appear in the index of *Emperors and Gladiators*

---

2 Suet. *Iul.* 10.1; Cass. Dio 37.8. Ville 1981, 60 and 89–90; see also Poulsen 1992 for the name of the temple. On the restrictions see Suet. *Iul.* 10.2; Plut. *Caes.* 55; with Wiedemann 1992, 132 and Bernstein 1998, 301.
3 Newbold 1975, 591.
4 Wallace-Hadrill 1983, 46–8. One volume on Greek games was in Greek.
5 Ville 1981, 477.

(1992) by T. Wiedemann, but there are almost fifty notes with references to Cassius Dio, and again the Greek historian is used mainly as a quarry from which information is extracted in order to describe the development of the games and famous shows with innovations in the program. As this chapter will show, however, there are significant problems in doing so.

This paper has two aims. First, it will focus on the political role of gladiatorial contests and other public spectacle entertainments in the late republican books of Cassius Dio's *Roman History*. Second, the function and status of gladiators in the late Republic will be compared to Cassius Dio's hostile narratives concerning the two young emperors, Commodus and Caracalla, in order to analyze and discuss the Severan Greek senatorial historian's interpretation of events in the republican past and how much it was colored by his own experiences. It will be argued that the references to games in the late republican and Augustan books reflect Cassius Dio's own agenda and are part of a transition in the *Roman History*.

1 Gladiatorial Combats and Gladiators in the Late Republic

Cassius Dio mentions gladiators, gladiatorial contests, naval battles, and animal fights in no less than twenty-five passages in Books 36–52. Some are just brief observations such as the one that recalls Faustus Cornelius Sulla in 60 BCE, who "gave a gladiatorial contest in memory of his father and entertained the people brilliantly, furnishing them with baths and oil gratis" (ἀγῶνά τε μονομαχίας ἐπὶ τῷ πατρὶ ἐποίησε, καὶ τὸν δῆμον λαμπρῶς εἱστίασε, τά τε λουτρὰ καὶ <τὸ> ἔλαιον προῖκα αὐτοῖς παρέσχεν, 37.51.4).[6] Later Cassius Dio notes that Octavian – very unusually – celebrated the death of Sextus Pompeius in the East in 35 BCE by setting up a triumphal chariot in honor of his colleague M. Antonius in the Forum Romanum and by organizing games in the Circus Maximus, where prisoners of war and condemned criminals fought.[7] Earlier in his *Roman History* Cassius Dio recorded that Sextus Pompeius had staged a naval battle of captives in the Straits of Messina in 40 BCE and Caesar one in the Campus Martius in 46 BCE.[8] These brief references emphasize that the gladiatorial shows were an important political instrument used by all players

---

6 Ville 1981, 61.

7 Cass. Dio 49.18.6: Καῖσαρ ἱπποδρομίαν τε ἐποίησε καὶ τῷ Ἀντωνίῳ ἅρμα τε ἔμπροσθεν τοῦ βήματος καὶ εἰκόνας ἐν τῷ Ὁμονοείῳ ἔστησε ("Caesar held games in the Circus in honor of the event and set up for Antony a chariot in front of the rostra and statues in the temple of Concordia"). On such triumphal chariots see Lange 2015/2016.

8 Cass. Dio 48.19.1; Ville 1981, 229–30. Cass. Dio 43.23.3, 45.17.8.

in the civil wars to obtain support and popularity. It is also clear that *munera* and *venationes* were public events provided by public figures in their private capacity, but that the distinction between public and private spectacles in Rome gradually became blurred in the late Republic.[9]

The magnificent games with music, gymnastic contests, and chariot races that Cn. Pompeius Magnus held during his second consulship in 55 BCE, when he dedicated his theater, are the best example of the political aspects of the spectacle entertainments in the late Republic. According to Cassius Dio, many wild animals, including five hundred lions and eighteen elephants, were killed during these games. The appearance of elephants emphasized that Pompey was "the Great," and their killing, that Rome was in control of even the largest of land animals. These famous games, however, only achieved limited success. Cicero (*Fam.* 7.1) criticized them in a letter to his friend M. Marius in Pompeii and observed that the audience was greatly impressed by the elephants, but showed no enjoyment. According to Cassius Dio, the spectators even showed sympathy for the wounded elephants that "walked about with their trunks raised toward heaven."[10] As T. P. Wiseman (2009, 157) has pointed out, "the two occasions when a Roman politician was most literally a performer before an audience were the triumph and the games," and neither was a complete success for Pompey. Elephants in the Hellenistic world symbolized victory and were closely associated with Pompey's idealized model, Alexander the Great. In some kind of youthful confidence Pompey wanted to enter Rome in a chariot drawn by four elephants in his first triumph *ex Africa* (12 March 81 BCE), but the gateway was too narrow and he had to change over to horses.[11] Elephants once again ruined the public performance of Pompey in 55 BCE, although his theater was a magnificent building and still admired in the third century CE (Cass. Dio 39.38.1).

Inventions and novelties in the shows are themes to which Cassius Dio returns regularly in the late republican books. He relates that the audience at the end of the 60s went out during the show at lunch, and that "this practice, which began at that time, is continued even now, whenever the person in charge exhibits games" (καὶ τοῦτ' ἐκεῖθεν ἀρξάμενον καὶ νῦν, ὁσάκις ἂν ὁ τὸ κράτος

---

9 Wiedemann 1992, 6–7.
10 Cass. Dio 39.38.1–4; Wiedemann 1992, 60–3; Plass 1995, 28; Beacham 1999, 63–5; Fagan 2011, 249–52, with references to other sources on the elephants and the audience: Cic. *Fam.* 7.1.3; Pliny *HN* 8.20.
11 Pliny *HN* 8.4; Plut. *Pomp.* 14.3–4. See Bell 2004, 157–72, on Pompey and elephants, and Vervaet 2014, 132–6 on Pompey's first triumph with references, including the controversy on its date.

ἔχων ἀγωνοθετῇ, γίγνεται, 37.46.4).[12] In Book 36 he notices that the tribune of the plebs, L. Roscius Otho, passed a law that separated the seats in the theaters of the equestrians from others (36.42.1).[13] Later Cassius Dio says that a rhinoceros and a hippopotamus were seen for the first time in Rome during the games given by Octavian after his triple triumph in 29 BCE, and he briefly describes these two animals. This is, however, surely a mistake, as pointed out by M. Reinhold: according to Pliny the Elder, M. Aemilius Scaurus had been the very first to exhibit a hippopotamus together with four crocodiles in the magnificent games he gave when aedile in 58 BCE, while the games of Pompey the Great in 55 BCE mentioned above were the first to display a rhinoceros.[14] Cassius Dio also relates that Agrippa as aedile in 33 BCE set up seven bronze dolphins to indicate the number of laps completed in the chariot races in the Circus Maximus, and he attributed to Agrippa the eggs too, although they had already been introduced in 174 BCE;[15] perhaps Cassius Dio refers to new eggs of bronze provided by Agrippa, but the last two passages are a warning against taking all the information on spectacle entertainments in Cassius Dio's *Roman History* at face value. As quoted in the introduction, Cassius Dio stresses that his sources on games sometimes were tendentious, and if the third-century Greek historian had problems in presenting "the truth," a twenty-first-century historian is hardly better informed.

Gladiators were trained in fighting and killing, and several politicians used them as armed bodyguards in the violent conflicts in the last decades of the Republic and in the civil wars. This was especially true of the gangs of Clodius and Milo in the 50s BCE which included free men and slaves, as recorded by

---

12   Ville 1981, 392–3.
13   On the *lex Roscia theatralis* see Canobbio 2002, 11–41, with references to the other ancient sources on this law and modern scholarship.
14   Cass. Dio 51.22.5: καὶ θηρία καὶ βοτὰ ἄλλα τε παμπληθῆ καὶ ῥινόκερως ἵππος τε ποτάμιος, πρῶτον τότε ἐν τῇ Ῥώμῃ ὀφθέντα, ἐσφάγη. καὶ ὁ μὲν ἵππος ὁποῖός ἐστι, πολλοῖς τε εἴρηται καὶ πολὺ πλείοσιν ἑώραται· ὁ δὲ δὴ ῥινόκερως τὰ μὲν ἄλλα ἐλέφαντί πῃ προσέοικε, κέρας δέ τι κατ' αὐτὴν τὴν ῥῖνα προσέχει, καὶ διὰ τοῦτο οὕτω κέκληται. ("Wild beasts and tame animals were slain in vast numbers, among them a rhinoceros and a hippopotamus, beasts then seen for the first time in Rome. As regards the nature of the hippopotamus, it has been described by many and far more have seen it. The rhinoceros, on the other hand, is in general somewhat like an elephant, but it has also a horn on its very nose and has got its name because of this.") Reinhold 1988, 159, with references to Pliny *HN* 8.71 and 8.96, but note also Bell 2004, 242: "It was natural for Dio perhaps to identify the beginnings of a great new age of emperor-sponsored display with magnificently spectacular novelties."
15   Cass. Dio 49.43.1–2; Liv. 41.27.6; Reinhold 1988, 79–80; Bernstein 1998, 293. Cerutti 1993 argues unconvincingly that the eggs corresponded to the number of races on a single day, and the dropping of a dolphin signaled the start of a race. See also Lintott 1997, 2512–14, on Cassius Dio's "factual accuracy" in the late republican books.

Cassius Dio.[16] Later he mentions that the conspirators had stationed gladiators in the Theater of Pompey before the assassination of Caesar as a precaution.[17] Most interesting in this connection, however, is a strange story – worth quoting in full – that Cassius Dio relates about a group of gladiators that Marcus Antonius kept in Cyzicus in Bithynia for the triumphal games he expected to provide in order to celebrate his victory over Octavian. According to Cassius Dio, the gladiators, when they became aware of Antonius' and Cleopatra's defeat at Actium (51.7.2–7):

> ... ὥρμησαν ἐς τὴν Αἴγυπτον ὡς καὶ βοηθήσοντες αὐτοῖς, καὶ πολλὰ μὲν τὸν Ἀμύνταν ἐν τῇ Γαλατίᾳ πολλὰ δὲ καὶ τοὺς τοῦ Ταρκονδιμότου παῖδας ἐν τῇ Κιλικίᾳ, φίλους μέν σφισιν ἐς τὰ μάλιστα γενομένους, τότε δὲ πρὸς τὰ παρόντα μεταστάντας, πολλὰ δὲ καὶ τὸν Δίδιον κωλύοντά σφας τῆς διόδου ἔδρασαν. οὐ μέντοι καὶ διαπεσεῖν ἐς τὴν Αἴγυπτον ἠδυνήθησαν, ἀλλ᾽ ἐπειδὴ πανταχόθεν περιεστοιχίσθησαν, λόγον μὲν οὐδ᾽ ὡς οὐδένα, καίτοι τοῦ Διδίου συχνά σφισιν ὑπισχνουμένου, προσεδέξαντο, τὸν δὲ Ἀντώνιον μεταπέμψαντες ὡς καὶ ἐν τῇ Συρίᾳ ἄμεινον μετ᾽ αὐτοῦ πολεμήσοντες ἔπειτ᾽ ἐπειδὴ ἐκεῖνος μήτ᾽ αὐτὸς ἦλθε μήτ᾽ ἀγγελίαν τινὰ αὐτοῖς ἔπεμψεν, οὕτω δὴ νομίσαντες αὐτὸν ἀπολωλέναι καὶ ἄκοντες ὡμολόγησαν ἐπὶ τῷ μηδέποτε μονομαχῆσαι, καὶ τήν γε Δάφνην παρὰ τοῦ Διδίου, τὸ τῶν Ἀντιοχέων προάστειον, ἐνοικεῖν μέχρις ἂν τῷ Καίσαρι ταῦτα δηλωθῇ ἔλαβον καὶ οἱ μὲν ὑπὸ τοῦ Μεσσάλου ὕστερον ἀπατηθέντες ἐπέμφθησαν ἄλλος ἄλλοσε ὡς καὶ ἐς τὰ στρατόπεδα καταλεχθησόμενοι, καὶ ἐκ τρόπου δή τινος ἐπιτηδείου ἐφθάρησαν.

> ... set out for Egypt to bear aid to their rulers. Many were their exploits against Amyntas in Galatia and many against the sons of Tarcondimotus in Cilicia, who had been their strongest friends but now in view of the changed circumstances had gone over to the other side; many were also their exploits against Didius, who undertook to prevent their passing through Syria; nevertheless, they were unable to force their way through to Egypt. Yet even when they were surrounded on all sides, not even then would they accept any terms of surrender, though Didius made them many promises. Instead, they sent for Antony feeling that they would fight better even in Syria if he were with them; and then, when he neither came himself nor sent them any message, they at last decided that he had perished and reluctantly made terms, on condition that they were never

---

16   Cass. Dio 39.7.2, 39.8.1, 39.18.1. See Lintott 1999, 77–83.
17   Cass. Dio 44.16.2. These gladiators belonging to D. Brutus are also mentioned in other sources: Vell. Pat. 2.58.2; App. *B Civ.* 2.118–22.

to fight as gladiators. And they received from Didius Daphne, the suburb of Antioch, to dwell in until the matter should be brought to Caesar's attention. These men were later deceived by Messalla and sent to various places under the pretext that they were enlisted in the legions, and were then put out of the way in some convenient manner.[18]

According to Flavius Josephus, the Jewish king Herod also sent soldiers against the gladiators, so the account cannot be dismissed as purely fiction. Reinhold argues that the report seems to be a rhetorical topos and that the gladiators might have been Parthian prisoners of war who were trying to fight their way back home.[19] Perhaps there is more to this anecdote if the passage is seen in a broader perspective that includes Cassius Dio's own Bithynian background and the Severan context. He normally despised all gladiators, charioteers, and actors, but the gladiators of Marcus Antonius were stationed in Cyzicus in Bithynia, where one of the few amphitheaters in the Eastern Mediterranean is preserved. Unlike ordinary slaves, they showed courage and loyalty, before the agreement that they were never to fight as gladiators again and instead were enrolled in the army.[20]

Another recurrent theme in the late republican books of Cassius Dio's *Roman History* is the appearance of members of the elite, including women, in the arena and on the stage. During the gladiatorial contests and *naumachia* given by Caesar in 46 BCE not only condemned criminals and prisoners of war fought, but also equestrians and the son of a former praetor battled as gladiators, although the senator Fulvius Sepinus was prevented from doing so.[21] This practice continued after Caesar's death. In 41 BCE equestrians fought as *bestiarii* in the circus during the *Ludi Apollinares*, but when a former senator three years later desired to fight as gladiator, he was not allowed to do so. Laws were passed that prohibited senators from fighting in the arena and later also their sons and grandsons who were equestrians from appearing on the stage, but apparently without much success.[22] According to Cassius Dio,

---

18 Reinhold 1988, 132; Ville 1981, 294.
19 Joseph. *AJ* 15.195: "adding that Q. Didius had written that Herod had most zealously supported him in the matter of gladiators." Same in *BJ* 1.392: "for Q. Didius writes to me that you have sent a force to assist him against the gladiators."
20 See Groot 2008, 96, on Cassius Dio's contempt for actors, and Golvin 1988, 202–3 no. 176 (2nd cent. CE), for the amphitheater in Cyzicus.
21 Cass. Dio 43.23.4–5. He might be identical with the Furius Leptinus mentioned in Suet. *Iul.* 39. *RE* Fulvius (108) (Münzer); Syme 1979, 281–2. See also Ville 1981, 256; Levick 1983, 105.
22 Cass. Dio 48.33.4, 48.43.3, 54.2.5; Ville 1981, 256; Levick 1983, 106; Rawson 1991, 526.

the senator Q. Vitellius fought in the games given by Octavian after his triple triumph in 29 BCE. Reinhold identifies him with a brother of the Augustan procurator, P. Vitellius, who was the grandfather of the emperor Vitellius. Reinhold doubts that Octavian permitted the appearance and suggests that Cassius Dio is recording backstairs gossip about emperors and their ancestors.[23] There is, however, no reason to doubt the senatorial historian in this case. It seems that senators and equestrians sought opportunities to perform in the arena and on the stage, and the ban of equestrians fighting as gladiators was reinstituted by Tiberius after one was killed in games given by Drusus in 15 CE (Cass. Dio 57.14.3–4). Cassius Dio also records that the emperor Vitellius again forbade senators and equestrians from fighting as gladiators and performing in any spectacle in the theater, for which he was praised.[24]

Despite the Augustan prohibition, equestrians and noble women continued to appear on the stage without Augustus reacting, and an impoverished equestrian fought as a gladiator in 8 CE.[25] Only three years later *equites* were even given permission to fight as gladiators – a law which Cassius Dio admits "may cause surprise," and he tries to excuse Augustus by arguing that a ban did not help. The equestrian gladiators were apparently so exceptionally popular that even the emperor watched them in company with the praetors who, with a formal dispensation, provided these gladiatorial games.[26] The numerous

---

23 Cass. Dio 51.22.5; Reinhold 1988, 158–9.
24 Cass. Dio 65(64).6.3; Tac. *Hist.* 2.62.2. See also Murison 1999, 85, and Davenport 2014, 106–11. For restrictions of public performance by members of the elite 46 BCE–19 CE see Levick 1983, and in general Edmondson 1996, 106–8.
25 Cass. Dio 55.10.11, 55.33.4: λωφήσαντος δέ ποτε τοῦ λιμοῦ, ἐπί τε τῷ τοῦ Γερμανικοῦ ὀνόματι, ὃς ἦν τοῦ Δρούσου παῖς, καὶ ἐπὶ τῷ τοῦ ἀδελφοῦ αὐτοῦ, ἱπποδρομίας ἐποίησε, καὶ ἐν αὐταῖς ἐλέφας τε ῥινοκέρωτα κατεμαχέσατο καὶ ἀνὴρ ἱππεὺς πλούτῳ ποτὲ προενεγκὼν ἐμονομάχησε. ("When at last famine had abated, he conducted games in the Circus in the name of Germanicus, who was son of Drusus, and in that of Germanicus' brother. On this occasion an elephant overcame a rhinoceros and an equestrian who had once been distinguished for his wealth fought as a gladiator.") See Swan 2004, 217–18, for the textual problems in this section.
26 Cass. Dio 56.25.7–8: ἱππεῦσιν, ὃ καὶ θαυμάσειεν ἄν τις, μονομαχεῖν ἐπετράπη. αἴτιον δὲ ὅτι ἐν ὀλιγωρίᾳ τινὲς τὴν ἀτιμίαν τὴν ἐπ᾽ αὐτῷ ἐπικειμένην ἐποιοῦντο. ἐπεὶ γὰρ μήτ᾽ ὄφελός τι τῆς ἀπορρήσεως ἐγίγνετο καὶ τιμωρίας μείζονος ἄξιοι εἶναι ἐδόκουν, ἢ καὶ ἀποτραπήσεσθαι ἐνομίσθησαν, συνεχωρήθη σφίσι τοῦτο ποιεῖν. καὶ οὕτως ἀντὶ τῆς ἀτιμίας θάνατον ὠφλίσκανον· οὐδὲν γὰρ ἧττον ἐμονομάχουν, καὶ μάλισθ᾽ ὅτι δεινῶς οἱ ἀγῶνες αὐτῶν ἐσπουδάζοντο, ὥστε καὶ τὸν Αὔγουστον τοῖς στρατηγοῖς τοῖς ἀγωνοθετοῦσί σφας συνθεᾶσθαι. ("... And the equestrians – a fact which may cause surprise – were allowed to fight as gladiators. The reason was that some of them were making light of the loss of rights imposed as the penalty for such conduct. For inasmuch as there proved to be no use in forbidding it, and the guilty seemed to require a greater punishment, or else because it seemed possible that they might even be turned aside from this course, they were granted permission to take part in such contests. In this way they incurred death instead of loss of rights; for they

examples of senators, equestrians, and women fighting as gladiators or appearing on the stage raise the question whether, as suggested by several modern scholars, Augustus really was Cassius Dio's role model as Roman emperor.[27] Other instances of gladiators, charioteers, and actors of high status performing in public in Cassius Dio's *Roman History* appear in the narratives of the reigns of Gaius Caligula, Nero, Domitian, Commodus, and Caracalla.[28] Cassius Dio normally uses such appearances as part of the moral invective against notorious emperors, and two important differences between these emperors and Augustus must be stressed. First and foremost, Augustus never fought as a gladiator, appeared on a stage, or drove chariots in public; secondly, he did not force anyone else to do so. Nevertheless, Cassius Dio chose to include instances of high-status gladiators and actors in the books on Augustus and his reign, and this cannot solely be explained as a coincidence. The Greek senatorial historian was a deliberate writer; he certainly knew that his readers would connect such instances with Commodus and Caracalla, and in this way he avoided creating the impression of writing an Augustan panegyric. At the same time, the references in the *Roman History* to the voluntary appearances of members of the elite in the arena and on the stage under Caesar and Augustus are an allusion to later periods, where the same happened under some notorious emperors who even performed in public themselves as actors, charioteers, and gladiators. In this way Cassius Dio's account of public spectacle entertainments in the late Republic marks a transition in his work. Before comparing his hostile description of the two latter emperors I will briefly discuss the economic aspects of the spectacle entertainments that Cassius Dio also touches upon in his late republican books.

---

fought just as much as ever, especially since their contests were exceedingly popular, so that even Augustus used to watch them in company with the praetors who superintended the contests.") Ville 1981, 119–20; Levick 1983, 106–7; Swan 2004, 282–4; Groot 2008, 106–7 and 180.

27 Rich 1990, 13–18; Lange 2016, 105; see Reinhold & Swan 1990 in general for Cassius Dio's assessment of Augustus. Female gladiators appear during the reign of Nero (Cass. Dio 61.17.3, 62.3.1–2) and the Flavian dynasty (Cass. Dio 66.25.1 [Titus] and 67.8.4 [Domitian]). Cassius Dio also relates that Septimius Severus in 200 CE forbade women to fight in single combats (76[75].16.1). As noticed by Murison 1999, 198, Cassius Dio is perhaps the most important literary source on female gladiators, on which see Ville 1981, 263–4; Briquel 1992; Schäfer 2001; Carlsen 2014, 442–6.

28 Gaius Caligula: Cass. Dio 59.8.3; 59.10.1–5; Plass 1995, 48. Nero: Cass. Dio 61.9.1, 62.17.2–3. Domitian: Cass. Dio 67.14.3. For Commodus and Caracalla see below. Also: Newbold 1975, 591; Gowing 1997, 2569.

2   The Agrippa-Maecenas Debate and the Economics of Spectacle Entertainments

In 22 BCE Augustus limited the praetors to providing two annual gladiatorial shows in Rome with a maximum of sixty pairs of gladiators with grants from the treasury. Cassius Dio adds that the emperor also forbade "any of them to spend more than another from his own means on these festivals."[29] These restrictions ended the late republican rivalry between ambitious politicians and the drain on their resources of gladiatorial contests and other shows, but the new law made it possible for the emperor to provide his own, much more spectacular games. Outside Rome, the local elite still provided public entertainments without restrictions. Their costs could be heavy, even ruinous, and the public spectacles are one of many themes discussed in the famous dialogue between Agrippa and Maecenas on democracy versus monarchy in Book 52, in which chapters 28–30 of Maecenas' speech are dedicated to matters of economics.

In the long chapter 30, Cassius Dio has Maecenas suggest that the emperor should provide Rome with spectacles of every kind, but also that the economy of the provincial cities should be improved. A lengthy list of unproductive expenses that should be abolished is presented, and one of the many proposals is that the provincial cities should not (52.30.3–4):

> ... ἀγώνων πολλῶν καὶ παντοδαπῶν ἀναλώμασι δαπανάσθωσαν, ἵνα μήτε σπουδαῖς ματαίαις ἐκτρύχωνται μήτε φιλοτιμίαις ἀλόγοις πολεμῶνται. ἐχέτωσαν μὲν γὰρ καὶ πανηγύρεις καὶ θεωρίας τινάς, χωρὶς τῆς ἱπποδρομίας τῆς παρ' ἡμῖν ποιουμένης, μὴ μέντοι ὥστε καὶ τὸ δημόσιον ἢ καὶ τοὺς ἰδίους οἴκους λυμαίνεσθαι, ξένον τέ τινα ἀναγκάζεσθαι παρ' αὐτοῖς καὶ ὁτιοῦν ἀναλίσκειν ...

> ... waste their resources on expenditures for a large number and variety of public games, lest they exhaust themselves in futile exertions and be led by unreasonable rivalries to quarrel among themselves. They ought, indeed, to have their festivals and spectacles – to say nothing of the Circensian games held here in Rome – but not to such an extent that the public treasury or the estates of private citizens shall be ruined thereby, or that any stranger resident there shall be compelled to contribute to their expense.[30]

---

29   Cass. Dio 54.2.4. Ville 1981, 120–1; Wiedemann 1992, 8; Edmondson 1996, 79–81.
30   In general on these three chapters: Gabba 1962; Millar 1964, 108–11; France 2016; Carlsen forthcoming.

This is certainly not an Augustan problem, but reflects the economic problems of the provincial cities in Cassius Dio's own times. In the second century CE the provincial elite continually lamented the heavy costs of providing *munera* and other elements of euergetism. Hadrian released reluctant candidates for the priesthoods of the imperial cult in Aphrodisias in Caria from their obligations to provide gladiatorial shows at the town's annual festivals and allowed them to use the funds for the building of an aqueduct instead.[31] Later Marcus Aurelius introduced detailed restrictions on the permitted expenditures for the gladiatorial shows paid by the local chief priests of the imperial cult. With a *senatus consultum* in 177 CE, he reduced the expenses of the *munera* by dividing gladiators into five different categories according to their costs and by lowering the overall value of them.[32]

Maecenas' lengthy list of unproductive expenses that should be abolished in the provincial cities includes chariot races unconnected with athletic contests. They should be forbidden anywhere other than in Rome, and also maintenance of the winners of contests, unless in the Olympian and Pythian Games, should be abolished. This proposal is no evidence for legislation against chariot races in Italy outside Rome, as suggested by a few modern scholars; in his conclusions on public spectacles Maecenas summarizes that the expenses of public spectacle entertainments in the provincial cities should be modest in order to prevent rivalry inside the provincial elites and between cities.[33] Cassius Dio's concern thus is that the extravagant outlay on public spectacle entertainments sometimes drove ambitious men into debt. With such proposals he wanted to control the costly obligations of euergetism in order to protect the fortunes of the wealthy senatorial and provincial elites, who were the audience for his *Roman History* and also constitute the historian's own background as a well-born native of Nicaea in Bithynia.[34]

---

31   *SEG* 50 no. 1096 III = *AE* 2000, no. 1441; Reynolds 2000, 16–19; Coleman 2008.
32   *CIL* 2.6278 = *ILS* 5163; Wiedemann 1992, 134–7; Carter 2003.
33   Cass. Dio 52.30.8: τὰ δὲ δὴ λοιπὰ ἐμετρίασα, ἵν᾽ εὐδαπάνους τὰς ἀπολαύσεις καὶ τῶν θεωρημάτων καὶ τῶν ἀκουσμάτων ὡς ἕκαστοι ποιούμενοι καὶ σωφρονέστερον καὶ ἀστασιαστότερον διάγωσι. ("As to the other games, I have proposed to keep them within bounds, in order that each community by putting upon an inexpensive basis its entertainments for both eye and ear, may live with greater moderation and less factious strife.") See Humphrey 1986, 576–8, with references to previous scholarship, but note also Horsmann 1998, 18–19.
34   For the audience see Kemezis 2014, 22 and Carlsen 2016, 317, with further references. For Cassius Dio's life and career see Millar 1964, 5–24; Rich 1990, 1–4; and most recently Molin 2016.

3   Bad Emperors as Gladiators

Cassius Dio's criticism of the excessive expenses on gladiatorial contests and other spectacle entertainments is given particular expression in the narratives of emperors who appeared in the arena or on the stage, or drove chariots in public; in other parts of his *Roman History* Cassius Dio only points out that particular games given by senators in the late Republic or emperors and their relatives were very costly, but without offering any moral judgment.[35] There is, however, one important exception: Caesar's gladiatorial contests after his triumph in 46 BCE mentioned in the introduction to this chapter. According to Cassius Dio, Caesar was blamed for the many dead fighters and animals and because "he had expended countless sums" and "collected most of the funds unjustly" (43.24.1). These remarks on the high costs of the games and their wrongful funding allude to the later books of Dio's narrative. The most hostile description is that of Caracalla's extravagant use of money on soldiers and public games that the senatorial historian scorned and which the young emperor squeezed out of rich individuals. Sometimes he appointed wealthy freedmen to be directors of the games, and he demanded the construction of temporary buildings for entertainments during his journeys (78[77].9.7):

προσέτι καὶ θέατρα κυνηγετικὰ καὶ ἱπποδρόμους πανταχοῦ, ὅπουπερ καὶ ἐχείμασεν ἢ καὶ χειμάσειν ἤλπισε, κατεσκευάσαμεν, μηδὲν παρ' αὐτοῦ λαβόντες. καὶ αὐτίκα πάντα κατεσκάφη· οὕτω πως διὰ τοῦτο μόνον ἐγένετο, ἵν' ἡμεῖς ἐπιτριβῶμεν.

Moreover, we constructed amphitheaters and race-courses wherever he spent the winter or expected to spend it, all without receiving any contribution from him; and they were all promptly demolished, the sole reason for their being built in the first place being apparently, that we might become impoverished.

Caracalla took pleasure in seeing the blood of as many wild animals and gladiators as possible. He forced one gladiator to fight three times on the same day, and when the gladiator finally was killed, the emperor paid for the funeral.[36] Most damaging to the emperor's elevated position, Caracalla drove a chariot in public wearing the blue color and appeared in the arena himself, although the killing of 100 boars in one day must be an exaggeration to emphasize the

---

35   Newbold 1975, 592, with references to twelve passages.
36   Cass. Dio 78(77).6.2, 78(77).9.7–10.2. Horsmann 1998, 87.

extravagance of the emperor. According to Cassius Dio, the emperor also had the nickname, "Tarautas," from a gladiator "who was most insignificant and ugly in appearance and most reckless and bloodthirsty in spirit" (79[78].9.3).

In contrast to Caracalla, Marcus Aurelius disliked bloodshed so much that he let the gladiators fight with blunted weapons and refused to manumit the trainer of a man-eating lion despite the request of the populace.[37] Marcus Aurelius is one of the ideal emperors for Cassius Dio, and the monarchy turned into one of "iron and rust" (72[71].36.4) after his death.[38] The differences between "good" and "bad" emperors is especially manifest in the preserved excerpts on Marcus Aurelius' only son and successor, Commodus, who was obsessed with chariot-racing and gladiatorial combat. Book 73 of Cassius Dio's *Roman History* is filled with examples and details of a cruel emperor who appeared in the arena as a gladiator or *bestiarius*. The Greek senatorial historian records with contempt that the emperor fought as a left-handed *secutor* and received HS 1 million each day to appear as gladiator, while the other combatants only earned a very small sum of money. According to Cassius Dio's summary, Commodus killed many animals, including rhinoceroses, one giraffe, two elephants and five hippopotami.[39]

Cassius Dio himself was present in the Colosseum at the shows in 192 CE, when Commodus entered the arena as Mercury and shot one hundred bears in one day. Cassius Dio felt it necessary to explain to his readers at length why he describes the emperor's achievements in the arena (73[72].18.3–4):

> καὶ μή μέ τις κηλιδοῦν τὸν τῆς ἱστορίας ὄγκον, ὅτι καὶ τὰ τοιαῦτα συγγράφω, νομίσῃ. ἄλλως μὲν γὰρ οὐκ ἂν εἶπον αὐτά· ἐπειδὴ δὲ πρός τε τοῦ αὐτοκράτορος ἐγένετο καὶ παρὼν αὐτὸς ἐγὼ καὶ εἶδον ἕκαστα καὶ ἤκουσα καὶ ἐλάλησα, δίκαιον ἡγησάμην μηδὲν αὐτῶν ἀποκρύψασθαι, ἀλλὰ καὶ αὐτά, ὥσπερ τι ἄλλο τῶν μεγίστων καὶ ἀναγκαιοτάτων, τῇ μνήμῃ τῶν ἐσέπειτα ἐσομένων παραδοῦναι. καὶ μέντοι καὶ τἆλλα πάντα τὰ ἐπ' ἐμοῦ πραχθέντα καὶ λεπτουργήσω καὶ λεπτολογήσω μᾶλλον ἢ τὰ πρότερα, ὅτι τε συνεγενόμην αὐτοῖς, καὶ ὅτι μηδένα ἄλλον οἶδα τῶν τι δυναμένων ἐς συγγραφὴν ἀξίαν λόγου καταθέσθαι διηκριβωκότα αὐτὰ ὁμοίως ἐμοί.

---

37   Cass. Dio 72(71).29.3–4. Fagan 2011, 218–19.
38   For Marcus Aurelius as a model emperor: Kemezis 2014, 96, and Scott 2015, 160.
39   Cass. Dio 73(72).19.2–3. On Commodus the gladiator see Kyle 1998, 224–7; Fagan 2011, 139–40; Toner 2014. Torlone 2014, 416–17, warns against rumors and exaggerations in these accounts.

And let no one feel that I am sullying the dignity of history recording such occurrences. On most accounts, to be sure, I should not have mentioned this exhibition; but since it was given by the emperor himself, and since I was present myself and took part in everything seen, heard and spoken, I have thought proper to suppress none of the details, but to hand them down, trivial as they are, to the memory of those who shall live hereafter, just like any events of the greatest weight and importance. And, indeed, all the other events that took place in my lifetime I shall describe with more exactness and detail than earlier occurrences, for the reason that I was present when they happened and know no one else, among those who had any ability in writing a worthy record of events, who has so accurate a knowledge of them as I.[40]

The senators and equestrians attended with fear the shows of Commodus. According to Cassius Dio, who claims to have been present also on this occasion, the emperor, after killing an ostrich, cut off its head and advanced on the senators, holding the head in one hand and the bloody sword in the other in a threatening gesture.[41]

Cassius Dio stresses three times that he himself was an eye-witness of these spectacles where Commodus appeared as gladiator, but not all details in the narrative seem trustworthy. We may notice once again a young emperor who killed 100 wild animals in a single day, and many examples of Commodus' bloodthirstiness seem to be examples of manipulation and resemble the topos of a young, bad ruler appearing in the arena and as a charioteer, in contrast to his wise father.

The political importance of the public spectacle entertainments continued after the fall of the Republic. Theaters, circuses, and amphitheaters were recognized as places with communication between the audience and the emperors, and the excerpts of Cassius Dio's *Roman History* have preserved scattered remarks of popular demonstrations during public spectacles in Rome in the reigns of Gaius Caligula, Claudius, and Hadrian.[42] The most expressive episode took place in 190 CE and is described at length by both Cassius Dio and Herodian. Riots began during chariot races and resulted in the downfall of the powerful imperial freedman Cleander; this was not normal unrest over a food crisis, but a carefully organized disturbance planned by influential members

---

40 Edmondson 1996, 75–6.
41 Cass. Dio 73(72).20–1; Millar 1964, 132–3.
42 Cass. Dio 59.5.4, 61(60).29.3, 69.6.1–2. In general see Cameron 1976; Wiedemann 1992; Edmondson 1996.

of the senatorial elite, as demonstrated by C. R. Whittaker.[43] It was not an isolated case. The preserved excerpts of Cassius Dio's *Roman History* include thirteen instances of demonstrations during public spectacle entertainments in the years 180–217 CE, at which the Greek historian himself was sometimes present.[44] These episodes reflect the importance of popular protests and riots in Byzantium when Xiphilinus and Zonaras composed their epitomes; but they also reflect underlying views in Cassius Dio of the Roman people or mob as fickle and democracy as unstable.[45]

4   Epilogue

Spectacle entertainments play a crucial role in the narrative of Cassius Dio's *Roman History* in both the late republican and contemporary books. Dio is especially aware of their importance as a political instrument in the rivalry within the elite as the magnificent games provided by Pompey and Caesar illustrate. Dio also stresses the participation of gladiators in the violence and civil wars in the late Republic. He is, in several instances, our only written source on changes and developments in the gladiatorial contests, although he sometimes confuses times or persons as shown above. Newbold pointed out that the material presented by the Greek Severan senatorial historian "is dominated by two main concerns – status (with its cognate, property) and economics."[46] This paper has, however, demonstrated that Cassius Dio's narrative of the economic aspects of the public spectacle entertainments concentrates on certain emperors' extravagant outlay, and he recommends a reduction in the expenditure of the wealthy provincial elite on euergetism.

Cassius Dio is also extremely aware of the important political role such public spectacles played in Rome in the early empire, and he used the many anecdotes to characterize the reigns of the emperors. "Bad" rulers such as Gaius Caligula, Nero, Domitian, and especially Commodus and Caracalla appeared on the stage or in the arena themselves and forced members of the Roman elite and sometimes even women to do so.[47] This lack of respect for the senatorial order symbolized these emperors' depravity, while "good" emperors were expected to legislate against such public appearance by persons

---

43   Cass. Dio 73(72).13; Hdn. 1.12.3–13.6. Whittaker 1964, and more recently De Ranieri 1997.
44   Cass. Dio 76(75).4.2; Whittaker 1964, 360–2, with references.
45   Yavetz 1969, 5–6 and 141–6; Madsen 2016, 143–6.
46   Newbold 1975, 599.
47   For a comparison of Cassius Dio's portraits of Nero and Domitian see Schulz 2014, 427–30.

of high status. Augustus did this as well; there are also instances of high-status gladiators and actors during his principate, but these look like the exceptions that prove the rule. Augustus never fought as a gladiator or appeared on the stage, and he did not force any one to do so. The episodes in which members voluntarily appeared in the spectacle entertainments mark a transition in Cassius Dio's narrative colored by his own experiences during the reigns of Commodus and the Severans.

Bibliography

Beacham, R. C. (1999) *Spectacle Entertainments of Early Imperial Rome*, Yale.
Bell, A. (2004) *Spectacular Power in the Greek and Roman City*, Oxford.
Bernstein, F. (1998) *Ludi publici. Untersuchungen zur Entstehung und Entwicklung der öffentlichen Spiele im republikanischen Rom*, Stuttgart.
Briquel, D. (1992) "Les femmes gladiateurs: examen du dossier", *Ktema* 17, 47–53.
Cameron, A. (1976) *Circus Factions: Blues and Greens at Rome and Byzantium*, Oxford.
Canobbio, A. (2002) *La Lex Roscia Theatralis e Marziale: Il ciclo del libro V. Introduzione, edizione critica, traduzione e commento*, Como.
Carlsen, J. (2014) "Gladiators in Ancient Halikarnassos", in L. Karlsson *et al.* (eds.), *Labrys: Studies Presented to P. Hellström* (Uppsala): 441–50.
Carlsen, J. (2016) "Alexander the Great in Cassius Dio", in C. H. Lange & J. M. Madsen (eds.), *Cassius Dio: Greek Intellectual and Roman Politician* (Leiden & Boston): 316–31.
Carlsen, J. (forthcoming) "Cassius Dio's Roman Economic History", in C. H. Lange & J. M. Madsen (eds.), *Cassius Dio the Historian: Methods and Approaches* (Leiden & Boston).
Carter, M. (2003) "Gladiatorial Ranking and the *SC de Pretiis Gladiatorum Minuendis* (*CIL* II 6278 = *ILS* 5163)", *Phoenix* 57, 83–114.
Cerutti, S. (1993) "The Seven Eggs of the Circus Maximus", *Nikephoros* 6, 167–76.
Coleman, K. (2008) "Exchanging Gladiators for an Aqueduct at Aphrodisias (*SEG* 50.1096)", *Acta Classica* 51, 31–46.
Davenport, C. (2014) "The Conduct of Vitellius in Cassius Dio's *Roman History*", *Historia* 63, 96–116.
De Ranieri, C. (1997) "Retroscena politici e lotte dinastiche sullo sfondo della vicenda di Aurelio Cleandro", *Rivista storica della antichità* 27, 139–89.
Edmondson, J. C. (1996) "Dynamic Arenas: Gladiatorial Presentations in the City of Rome and the Construction of Roman Society during the Early Empire", in W. J. Slater (ed.), *Roman Theater and Society: E. Togo Salmon Papers I* (Ann Arbor): 69–112.

Fagan, G. G. (2011) *The Lure of the Arena: Social Psychology and the Crowd at the Roman Games*, Cambridge.

France, J. (2016) "Financer l'Empire: Agrippa, Mécène et Cassius Dion", in V. Fromentin *et al.* (eds.), *Cassius Dion: nouvelles lectures* (Bordeaux): 773–85.

Gabba, E. (1962) "Progetti di riforme economiche e fiscali in uno storico dell'età dei Severi", in *Studi in onore di A. Fanfani I* (Milano): 39–68.

Golvin, J.-C. (1988) *L'amphithéâtre romain. Essai sur la théorisation de sa forme et de ses fonctions*, Paris.

Gowing, A. M. (1997) "Cassius Dio on the Reign of Nero", *Aufstieg und Niedergang der römischen Welt* 2.34.3, 2558–90.

Groot, H. (2008) *Zur Bedeutung der öffentlichen Spiele bei Tacitus, Sueton und Cassius Dio. Überlegungen zur Selbstbeschreibung der römischen Gesellschaft*, Berlin.

Horsmann, G. (1998) *Die Wagenlenker der römischen Kaiserzeit. Untersuchungen zu ihrer sozialen Stellung*, Stuttgart.

Humphrey, J. H. (1986) *Roman Circuses: Arenas for Chariot Racing*, London.

Kemezis, A. (2014) *Greek Narratives of the Roman Empire under the Severans: Cassius Dio, Philostratus and Herodian*, Cambridge.

Kyle, D. G. (1998) *Spectacles of Death in Ancient Rome*, London.

Lange, C. H. (2015/2016) "Triumphal Chariots, Emperor Worship and Cassius Dio: Declined Triumphal Honours", *Analecta Romana Instituti Danici* 40/41, 21–33.

Lange, C. H. (2016) "Mock the Triumph: Cassius Dio, Triumph and Triumph-Like Celebrations", in C. H. Lange & J. M. Madsen (eds.), *Cassius Dio: Greek Intellectual and Roman Politician* (Leiden & Boston): 92–114.

Levick, B. (1983) "The *senatus consultum* from Larinum", *Journal of Roman Studies* 73, 97–115.

Lintott, A. W. (1997) "Cassius Dio and the History of the Late Roman Republic", *Aufstieg und Niedergang der römischen Welt* 2.34.3, 2497–523.

Lintott, A. W. (1999) *Violence in Republican Rome*, 2nd ed., Oxford.

Madsen, J. M. (2016) "Criticising the Benefactors: The Severans and the Return of Dynastic Rule", in C. H. Lange & J. M. Madsen (eds.), *Cassius Dio: Greek Intellectual and Roman Politician* (Leiden & Boston): 136–58.

Millar, F. (1964) *A Study of Cassius Dio*, Oxford.

Molin, M. (2016) "Biographie de l'historien Cassius Dion", in V. Fromentin *et al.* (eds.), *Cassius Dion: nouvelles lectures* (Bordeaux): 431–46.

Murison, C. L. (1999) *Rebellion and Reconstruction: Galba to Domitian: An Historical Commentary on Cassius Dio's* Roman History *Books 64–67 (A.D. 68–96)*, Atlanta.

Newbold, R. F. (1975) "Cassius Dio and the Games", *L'Antiquité Classique* 44, 589–604.

Plass, P. (1995) *The Game of Death in Ancient Rome: Arena Sport and Political Suicide*, Madison.

Poulsen, B. (1992) "The Written Sources", in I. Nielsen & B. Poulsen (eds.), *The Temple of Castor and Pollux I* (Rome): 54–60.

Rawson, E. (1991) *Roman Culture and Society. Collected Papers*, Oxford.

Reinhold, M. (1988) *From Republic to Principate: An Historical Commentary on Cassius Dio's Roman History Books 49–52 (36–29 B.C.)*, Atlanta.

Reinhold, M. & Swan, P. M. (1990) "Cassius Dio's Assessment of Augustus", in K. A. Raaflaub & M. Toher (eds.), *Between Republic and Empire. Interpretations of Augustus and His Principate* (Berkeley): 155–73.

Reynolds, J. M. (2000) "New Letters from Hadrian to Aphrodisias: Trials, Taxes, Gladiators and an Aqueduct", *Journal of Roman Archaeology* 13, 5–20.

Rich, J. W. (1990) *Cassius Dio: The Augustan Settlement (Roman History 53–55.9)*, Warminster.

Schäfer, D. (2001) "Frauen in der Arena", in H. Bellen & H. Heinen (eds.), *Fünfzig Jahre Forschungen zur antiken Sklaverei an der Mainzer Akademi 1950–2000. Miscellanea zum Jubiläum* (Stuttgart): 243–68.

Schulz, V. (2014) "Nero und Domitian bei Cassius Dio. Zwei Tyrannen aus der Sicht des 3. Jh. n. Chr.", in S. Bönisch-Meyer *et al.* (eds.), *Nero und Domitian. Mediale Diskurse der Herrscherrepräsentation im Vergleich* (Tübingen): 405–34.

Scott, A. G. (2015) "Cassius Dio, Caracalla, and the Senate", *Klio* 97, 157–75.

Swan, P. M. (2004) *The Augustan Succession: An Historical Commentary on Cassius Dio's Roman History Books 55–56 (9 BC–AD 14)*, Oxford.

Syme, R. (1979) *Roman Papers I*, Oxford.

Toner, J. (2014) *The Day Commodus killed a Rhino: Understanding the Roman Games*, Baltimore.

Torlone, Z. M. (2014) "Writing Arenas: Roman Authors and Their Games", in P. Christesen & D. G. Kyle (eds.), *A Companion to Sport and Spectacle in Greek and Roman Antiquity* (Oxford): 412–21.

Vervaet, F. J. (2014) "'*Si neque leges neque mores cogunt*': Beyond the Spectacle of Pompeius Magnus' Public Triumphs", in C. H. Lange & F. J. Vervaet (eds.), *The Roman Republican Triumph Beyond the Spectacle* (Rome): 131–48.

Ville, G. (1981) *La gladiature en Occident des origines à la mort de Domitien*, Paris.

Wallace-Hadrill, A. (1983) *Suetonius: The Scholar and His Caesars*, London.

Whittaker, C. R. (1964) "The Revolt of Papirius Dionysius A.D. 190", *Historia* 13, 348–69.

Wiedemann, T. E. J. (1992) *Emperors and Gladiators*, London & New York.

Wiseman, T. P. (2009) *Remembering the Roman People: Essays on Late-Republican Politics and Literature*, Oxford.

Yavetz, Z. (1969) *Plebs and Princeps*, Oxford.

CHAPTER 9

Cassius Dio's Catiline: "A Name Greater Than His Deeds Deserved"

Gianpaolo Urso

1

In 63, on the last day of the year (December 29th in the pre-Julian calendar), Cicero tried to address the people and remind them of his deeds against Catiline and the conspirators executed on December 5th.[1] But one of the tribunes, Q. Caecilius Metellus Nepos, supported by his colleague L. Calpurnius Bestia, interposed his veto and obliged Cicero to confine himself to the usual oath taken by consuls at the end of their term of office (*nihil contra leges fecisse*). Cicero reacted by substituting for the traditional oath a statement that by his actions alone the state had been preserved. The people responded by shouting their approval and swearing that he spoke the truth.

This, at any rate, is Cicero's version of the episode, which he mentions in a letter to Metellus Celer of January 62 (*Fam.* 5.2),[2] in the speech *Pro Sulla* (33–4), later in the same year,[3] and in the speech *In Pisonem* (6–7), of 55.[4]

---

1 I would like to thank Christopher Baron, Christopher Burden-Strevens, Josiah Osgood, Kathryn Welch, and Giuseppe Zecchini, who read an earlier draft of this text and gave many valuable suggestions. I am particularly grateful to John Ramsey, whose generous attention has helped me to improve my paper in several points. Texts and translations are taken from the Loeb Classical Library, except for a few small adaptations.
2 "And yet, on the last day of the year, as I am sure you have heard, he [Metellus Nepos] put upon me, consul and savior of the commonwealth, an insult which has never been put upon any holder of any magistracy, no matter how disloyal: he deprived me of the power to address an assembly before retiring from office. This affront, however, redounded greatly to my honor. In face of his refusal to let me do more than take the oath (*nam cum ille mihi nihil nisi ut iurarem permitteret*), I swore in loud tones the truest and finest oath that ever was, and the people likewise in loud tones swore that I had sworn the truth (*magna voce iuravi verissimum pulcherrimumque ius iurandum, quod populus idem magna voce me vere iurasse iuravit*)."
3 "I saved the lives of all the citizens, the peace of the world, this city, the home of us all, the citadel of foreign kings and nations, the light of mankind, the home of empire, by the punishment of five mad, abandoned men. Or did you think that I would not say in a court of law, when not on my oath, that which I had said on oath in a great public gathering (*in maxima contione*)?"
4 "At a public meeting, when upon laying down my office I was debarred by a tribune of the plebs from saying what I had intended, and when I was by him permitted to do no more than

Cicero's version seems to be confirmed by Plutarch (*Cic.* 23.1–2),[5] even though this is not significant since Plutarch's source is Cicero himself.[6] For the *Life of Cicero* Plutarch used (among other sources) the *commentarius* in Greek Περὶ τῆς ὑπατείας, written by Cicero in 60. So, it is not surprising that Plutarch's testimony corresponds to Cicero's version of this episode, at least in three key points: the contents of the oath, the support of *all* the people (*populus Romanus universus* = σύμπας ὁ δῆμος), and the oath taken by the people that Cicero spoke the truth.

The account given by Cicero (and Plutarch) is usually accepted by modern scholars.[7] There is however a rival version in Cassius Dio (37.38), which is generally and wrongly left out of account:

> Toward Caesar, accordingly, the masses were well disposed, for the reason given, but they were angry at Cicero for the death of the citizens, and displayed their enmity in many ways. Finally, when on the last day of his office he desired to present his account and defense of all that he had done in his consulship – for he certainly did take great pleasure not only in being praised by others but also in extolling himself – they made him keep silent and did not allow him to utter a word outside of his oath; in this they had Metellus Nepos, the tribune, to aid them. Nevertheless, Cicero, doing his best to resist them, added to his oath the statement that he had saved the city.

Dio's account is radically different from Cicero's. In Cicero, the people supported the consul; in Dio, it took a stand against him. In both versions there

---

take the usual oath (*cum is mihi tantum modo ut iurarem permitteret*), I swore without flinching that this commonwealth and this city had been saved by my sole efforts (*sine ulla dubitatione iuravi rem publicam atque hanc urbem mea unius opera esse salvam*). At that meeting the entire people of Rome (*populus Romanus universus*) accorded to me, not a vote of thanks which would pass with the day, but immortality, when, themselves upon oath, with one voice and one heart, they acclaimed an oath so proud and so memorable (*cum meum ius iurandum tale atque tantum iuratus ipse una voce et consensu approbavit*)."

5 "When these [Metellus and Bestia] assumed office, Cicero having still a few days of consular authority, they would not permit him to harangue the people, but placing their benches so as to command the rostra, would not suffer or allow him to speak; instead, they ordered him, if he wished, merely to pronounce the oath usual on giving up office, and then come down. Cicero accepted these terms and came forward to pronounce his oath; and when he had obtained silence, he pronounced, not the usual oath, but one of his own and a new one, swearing that in very truth he had saved his country and maintained her supremacy. And all the people confirmed his oath for him (ἐπώμνυε δὲ τὸν ὅρκον αὐτῷ σύμπας ὁ δῆμος)."

6 Ciaceri 1918, 131–2; Lendle 1967, 97; Marshall 1974, 807–8; Marshall 1976, 37; Moles 1982, 136–7; Forsythe 1992, 408–9; Drummond 1995, 12; Drummond 2013a, 1.373; Pelling 2002, 45–9.

7 Cf., e.g., Manni 1969, 136; Gelzer 2014, 96; Millar 1998, 113; Cape 2002, 153; Lintott 2008, 149.

is a figure who takes an unpopular stance: but in Cicero this figure is the tribune Metellus Nepos, whereas in Dio the consul finds himself the object of the people's displeasure. In Cicero, the consul substitutes a "new" oath for the traditional one; in Dio, he takes the usual oath, *adding to it* that he has saved the city.

Some further parallel evidence may help us to appreciate the value of Dio's testimony here.

(i) Attacks against Cicero had started in November 63. In the *Pro Murena* (81), Cicero hints at the invectives of a *tribunus designatus*.[8] This tribune can easily be identified with Bestia, who "complained about the conduct of Cicero, threw upon the most excellent consul the odium of a very grievous war" (Sall. *Cat.* 43.1), and accused him of being "a stirrer up of war" (App. *B Civ.* 2.3: πολεμοποιός), i.e., responsible for the *bellum Catilinae*. These attacks were renewed in December, after the execution of P. Cornelius Lentulus and his associates (Plut. *Cic.* 23.1).

(ii) On January 1st 62, Cicero delivered a speech in the Senate, claiming that "there were many (*permulti*) who regretted his saving of the commonwealth" (*Fam.* 5.2.1). *Permulti* cannot refer only to Metellus and Bestia, but must also include some others, apparently *many* others. These *permulti* do not appear in Cicero's version of the episode of the oath; in Dio's version, they are in the foreground.

(iii) A few days later, Metellus Nepos, supported by the praetor Caesar, presented a bill, proposing to recall Pompey to Italy to restore order. Two other tribunes interposed their veto (one of them was Cato). Furious riots took place in the Forum, between the supporters of Nepos and those of Cato (Plut. *Cic.* 23.2–3; *Cat. Min.* 26.2–29.1; Suet. *Iul.* 16.1; Cass. Dio 37.43).[9] So, Nepos did have his followers: they were the crowd that, according to Dio, "had made Cicero keep silent" on December 29th.

I do not mean to say that we must *prefer* Dio's version to Cicero's. But we can and must rectify Cicero's testimony through Dio's. It is true that Metellus and Bestia set themselves against Cicero; it is true that he claimed to have saved the Republic; it is true that *a part* of the crowd backed him: but on December 29th the two groups, which clashed some days later, were already confronting each other. Dio shows us the other side of the coin. His heterodox version fits perfectly with some of Cicero's vicissitudes in 62 and 61: the accusations of tyrannical attitude, by Torquatus *iunior*, at the trial against Sulla (Cic.

---

8 "For already in yesterday's assembly there thundered the dangerous voice of a tribune-elect, your colleague."

9 On these riots, cf. now David 2013, 24–5.

Sull. 21–22: *peregrinus rex*, 48; cf. *Cat.* 1.22, 2.14, 3.27–9, 4.9, 4.11);[10] the daily attacks on him (cf., e.g., *Arch.* 14); the first provocations by Clodius (Cic. *Att.* 1.16.10: *quo usque hunc regem feremus?*, on May 15th 61; 1.18.4, 1.18.8; *Sest.* 109);[11] Cicero's "apologetic" attitude between 61 and 59 (cf., e.g., *Att.* 1.16.1);[12] the celebrations on Catiline's grave in 59, after the conviction of C. Antonius Hybrida (*Flac.* 95);[13] and eventually with the vote of the *lex Clodia de exilio Ciceronis* in 58. Dio draws on a source which shares nothing with the "Ciceronian" tradition and which he considers authoritative, so much so that he chooses to follow its version, instead of that of Cicero, which Dio certainly knew.

Dio presents the episode of the oath as an example of Cicero's "lack of popularity" at the end of 63 and contrasts it with Caesar's "popularity." This is the topic of the previous chapter of Book 37. Here we find a famous chronological error, when Dio hints at Caesar's election as pontifex maximus (37.37.2): "Basing his hopes of it upon the multitude, especially because he had helped Labienus against Rabirius and had not voted for the death of Lentulus, he accomplished his purpose and was elected pontifex maximus."

The error is clear: Caesar had been elected pontifex maximus some months *before* the execution of Lentulus. Some scholars have supposed a sort of forgery on Dio's part, in order to develop a topic or to make his narration more vivid.[14] But the most important detail, in my opinion, is not the error: it is the statement that Caesar was popular *because he had voted against the execution of Lentulus*. This is more than a chronological error; this is a judgment. Now, this judgment is perfectly consistent with the heterodox version of the incident of December 29th, which Dio describes immediately after (37.38). Dio cannot have "invented" it: the comparison Caesar/Cicero was already in his source, and this source was neither Cicero nor Sallust.

---

10   Cf. Gruen 1973, 303; Ungern-Sternberg 1997, 98.
11   Cf. already *Att.* 1.14.5.
12   In 60, Cicero published the *Catilinarians* and other "consular" speeches (cf. Cic. *Att.* 2.1.3), reviewed and corrected where necessary, in the light of his new situation (Ciaceri 1918, 127–31; Syme 1964, 74; Lintott 2008, 136; Giovannini 2012, 182; *contra*, Cape 2002, 154). The hypothesis of an immediate publication (McDermott 1972; Price 1998, 108; Fezzi 1999, 291) disregards the fact that in June 60 Atticus still did not know these speeches (as the passage mentioned above clearly implies: Dyck 2008, 10; cf. also Spielvogel 1993, 38).
13   "When [Antonius] was condemned, the grave of Lucius Catiline was adorned with flowers and was the scene of a gathering of men most bold, the enemies of their country." Cf. Gruen 1973, 307; Rundell 1979, 306.
14   Drummond 1999, 151; Lachenaud & Coudry 2014, xxx.

2

In Dio's account there is no trace of the *Bellum Catilinae*. This has already been seen (Schwartz 1899, 1702), but it still deserves attention. Sallust was (and is) considered as one of the greatest historians of Rome: in theory, among the sources on Catiline, he should have been the first choice. The absence of Sallust in Dio's chapters on Catiline means that Dio has *decided* not to follow him: it is a deliberate choice on his part.

As for Cicero, I do not see any evidence of the *Catilinarians* in Dio either.[15] But scholars have detected similarities between Dio's chapters on Catiline and Plutarch's *Life of Cicero*. As argued in particular by Pelling (2002, 46, 59–60 nn. 5–6 and 8),[16] these similarities are ultimately due to the derivation from a common source, which could be identified with the main source of Plutarch, Cicero's Περὶ τῆς ὑπατείας. If this hypothesis is well-founded, behind Dio's testimony on the year 63 there should be Cicero *too*: not the *Catilinarians*, but the lost Περὶ τῆς ὑπατείας.

But in Dio we find some pieces of information which are not available anywhere else. Many of them present an anti-Ciceronian bias. This bias is characteristic of Cicero's portrayal in the *Roman History* and has already been studied,[17] but we must stress its importance for the reconstruction of the events of 63. Here are a few examples of significant details (of course, "significant" does not always mean "true"):

(i) The fictional[18] "first Catilinarian conspiracy" (Cass. Dio 36.44.3):

> Publius Paetus and Cornelius Sulla, a nephew of the great Sulla, who had been elected consuls and then convicted of bribery, had plotted to kill their accusers, Lucius Cotta and Lucius Torquatus, especially after the latter had also been elected consuls. Among others who had been suborned were Gnaeus Piso and also Lucius Catilina, a man of great audacity, who had sought the office himself and was angry on this account.

---

15 Urso 2016.
16 Cf. also Drummond 1995, 12–13; Drummond 1999, 148; Lachenaud & Coudry 2014, xxv.
17 Millar 1964, 46–55; Gowing 1992, 143–7; Lintott 1997, 2514–17; Lachenaud & Coudry 2011, xxxvi–xxxviii.
18 Frisch 1947; Seager 1964; Syme 1964, 87–102 (p. 101: "The whole edifice is ramshackle. It ought to have been demolished long ago"); Gruen 1969; Waters 1970, 196; Marshall 1974, 809–10; Marshall 1976, 68–72; Marshall 1985, 288; Phillips 1976, 441; Ramsey 1982, 125; Ramsey 2007, 231–2; Wiseman 1994, 342–3; Drummond 1999, 296; Lewis 2008, 292, 302.

In Dio's version, the instigators of the plot against the consuls of 65, L. Aurelius Cotta and L. Manlius Torquatus, are the two *consules designati* in 66, P. Autronius Paetus and P. Cornelius Sulla, whose election has been invalidated after their conviction for bribery: Autronius and Sulla try to kill those who have taken their place. This is likely to have been one of the charges brought against Sulla by L. Torquatus, son of the consul of 65, when he prosecuted Sulla under the *lex Plautia de vi* for being an associate of Catiline in 63 and earlier. By contrast, in Sallust's version, the plot is not organized by Autronius and Sulla, but by Catiline and Autronius (*Cat.* 18.5): "About the fifth of December, Catiline and Autronius shared their plan with [Cn. Piso] and prepared to murder the consuls L. Cotta and L. Torquatus on the Capitoline on the first of January." The name of Sulla is conspicuously absent from Sallust's account, which apparently fell under the influence of Cicero's defense of Sulla in 62. Cicero argued against any involvement by Sulla in the earlier conspiracy, elevating Catiline to a leading role with Autronius (*Sull.* 67–8).[19] After all, Catiline was dead and Autronius had already been convicted and sent into exile (*Sull.* 7, 10, 18, 71; *Att.* 3.2, 3.7.1), meaning that the two of them could hardly refute Cicero's reconstruction of the cast of characters in the early conspiracy. So, Dio's version has not fallen under the influence of Cicero's reconstruction of events.

(ii) The piece of information on the episode of October 63, concerning the anonymous letters that revealed an impending plot against the *optimates* (Cass. Dio 37.31):

(1) While they were making these preparations, information came to Cicero, first, of what was occurring in the city, through some letters which did not indicate the writer but were given to Crassus and certain others of the optimates; and upon their publication a decree was passed that a state of disorder existed (ταραχή) and that a search should be made for those responsible for it. (2) Next came the news from Etruria, whereupon they further voted to the consuls the custody of the city and of all its interests, as was their custom; for to this decree was added the command that they should take care that no harm came to the state. (3) When this had been done and garrisons had been stationed at many points, there was no further sign of revolution in the city, insomuch that Cicero was even falsely charged with blackmail; but the messages from the Etruscans confirmed the accusation, and led to the indictment of Catiline for violence.

---

19 Seager 1964, 342–3.

This episode is mentioned by Plutarch too (*Cic.* 15.1–3; *Crass.* 13.3),[20] but some interesting details can be found only in Dio. Two of them are remarkable. On the one hand, Dio alone talks about the proclamation of the state of emergency (ταραχή = *tumultus*: 37.31.1), distinct from the *senatus consultum ultimum* of October 21st (or 22nd) (37.31.2):[21] this detail cannot be invented and it is certainly trustworthy.[22] On the other hand, Dio alone says that the senatorial decree stated that "a search should be made for those responsible for it [the disorder]." This is very important for our interpretation of the facts, because it means that the conspirators, at this stage, were still unidentified. For Plutarch (who is following Cicero), the letters mentioned Catiline; this detail is implicitly denied by Dio (who is clearly following another source): *the anonymous letters only mentioned an impending plot.*[23] The senatorial decree was not explicitly promulgated *against Catiline*, as Cicero pretends in the *First Catilinarian* (Cic. *Cat.* 1.3: "We have, Catiline, a decree of the senate against you, potent and stern"); and the charge *de vi* against Catiline, which Dio mentions

---

20   Plut. *Cic.* 15.1–3: "Not long after this ... there came to the house of Cicero at midnight men who were the leading and most powerful Romans, Marcus Crassus, Marcus Marcellus, and Scipio Metellus; and knocking at the door and summoning the doorkeeper, they bade him wake Cicero and tell him they were there. Their business was what I shall now relate. After Crassus had dined, his doorkeeper handed him some letters which an unknown man had brought; they were addressed to different persons, and one, which had no signature, was for Crassus himself. Crassus read this letter only, and since its contents told him that there was to be much bloodshed caused by Catiline, and advised him to escape secretly from the city, he did not open the rest, but came to Cicero, terrified by the danger, and seeking to free himself somewhat from charges that had been made against him on account of his friendship for Catiline. Cicero, accordingly, after deliberation, convened the Senate at the break of day, and carrying the letters thither gave them to the persons to whom they had been sent, with orders to read them aloud. All the letters alike were found to tell of a plot"; *Crass.* 13.3: "In the treatise upon his consulship, Cicero says (ἐν δὲ τῷ Περὶ τῆς ὑπατείας ὁ Κικέρων ... φησί) that Crassus came to him by night with a letter which gave details of the affair of Catiline, and felt that he was at last establishing the fact of a conspiracy. And Crassus, accordingly, always hated Cicero for this, but was kept from doing him any open injury by his son."
21   For the date cf. Asc. 6C.
22   Hardy 1917, 189–90; Golden 2013, 128; Lachenaud & Coudry 2014, 164 n. 206.
23   According to Plutarch (*Crass.* 13.4), Crassus hated Cicero because he had treated the letters in his Περὶ τῆς ὑπατείας. But if we follow the *Life of Cicero*, it is difficult to understand the reasons of Crassus' hate, because, after all, Crassus himself had read in the Senate the message he had received. Remembering the episode, Cicero should not have aroused Crassus' indignation (Marshall 1974, 808), unless he had somehow "modified" the actual content of the letters. Perhaps this is exactly what happened in this case. Crassus had read an anonymous denunciation, which mentioned no name. According to Cicero's reconstruction (followed by Plutarch), Crassus had read a denunciation against Catiline, whose name he had mentioned. This could explain Crassus' feelings of hostility towards Cicero.

at 37.31.3, was not connected with the troubles in Rome, but with the rising, in Etruria, of Manlius and his veterans, who some weeks before had come to Rome supporting (without success) Catiline's candidacy at the consular elections. To be sure, Dio's piece of information is confused, in its details. In particular, Dio is clearly mistaking the circumstances that justified the declaration of the *tumultus* for those justifying the *senatus consultum ultimum*:[24] the latter was justified by the anonymous letters, the former by Manlius' rising in Etruria (which made necessary the enrollment of soldiers, the usual steps taken upon the declaration of a *tumultus*).[25] But Dio's account derives ultimately from a good source, and it is the best version of the episode (far better than that of Sallust).[26]

(iii) Dio's insistence on the incredulity of the Senate and of the people (37.29.3, 37.31.3), which fits with the over-cautious attitude of most senators at the meeting of November 8th (the occasion of the *First Catilinarian*), an attitude which is attested by Diodorus (40 fr. 5a): "Cicero put the question to the senators, whether it was their wish to banish Catiline from the city. The majority, abashed by the man's presence, remained silent."[27]

(iv) Dio's allusion to the use of intimidation with the informers. Dio says (37.33.1) that Cicero, "being a man of great influence, and one who gained many followers through his speeches, either by conciliation or by intimidation, had many men to report such occurrences to him." Cicero was accused of a "tyrannical attitude," as we have seen, and the intimidation is mentioned in the same way already by Diodorus (40 fr. 5: "Thus was the conspiracy brought to light, and the consul, by using now threats and terror, now kindly exhortations, learned from them full details of the plot"). So, Dio's words are not a rhetorical exaggeration, but the echo of an allegation against Cicero, reported by contemporary historiography.

---

24 Lintott 1999, 154.
25 Kunkel 1995, 228–9; Lintott 1999, 153–5; Urso 2001, 123–6; Golden 2013, 43–8.
26 Sallust makes here one of his biggest chronological mistakes (Schwartz 1897, 577; La Penna 1968, 86–8). In his account, the *senatus consultum ultimum* (*Cat.* 29.2) follows the rumors of Manlius' rising in Etruria (28.4–29.1), it precedes the start of the operations in Etruria, on October 27th (30.1; cf. Cic. *Cat.*, 1.7), but above all it follows the meeting of the *coniurationis principes* at M. Porcius Laeca's home, where the decision is made (for the umpteenth time ...) to kill the consul. Now, this meeting took place in the night of November 6/7 and was immediately followed by the *First Catilinarian*, on November 8 (Cic. *Cat.* 1.1). Describing the meeting of the conspirators before the *senatus consultus ultimum*, Sallust gives the (false) impression that the former has provoked the latter.
27 Cf. Bloch 1903; Reinach 1904; Münzer 1927, 2091; Pareti 1965 [1934], 357–8; Carcopino 1965, 81; Mazzarino 1966, 376; Gelzer 2014, 81; Ungern-Sternberg 1971; McGushin 1977, 184; Urso 2018.

(v) The attribution to Catiline of a "political platform" (Cass. Dio 37.30.2), which included relief from debt (χρεῶν ἀποκοπαί = *tabulae novae*) and the distribution of lands (this second point is not attested elsewhere and is probably untrue).[28] The only other source that hints at a "programme" is Sallust (*Cat.* 21.2), in the context of the (fictitious)[29] meeting of June 1 of 64, but the details are different (except for the mention of *tabulae novae*).

(vi) The concept of a "conspiracy of Lentulus." In the passage about the embassy of the Allobroges, which precedes the arrest of Lentulus and his associates, Dio writes (37.31.1):

Lentulus made preparations to burn down the city and commit murder with the aid of his fellow-conspirators (μετά τε τῶν ἄλλων συνομωμοκότων) and of the Allobroges, who while present on an embassy were persuaded to join *him* (ἀνέπεισε συμφρονῆσαί τε αὐτῷ).

I do not want to attribute to Dio more than what he actually says, but this passage seems to suggest that the leader of the conspiracy was not Catiline, but Lentulus, at least at that time (late November 63). Dio himself hints at the idea of a "conspiracy of Lentulus" in the speech of Philiscus to Cicero (38.25.4): "Surely you would not prefer to have *joined* with Catiline and *conspired* with Lentulus" (συνομόσας). The same goes for the "speech of Calenus," as we shall see. Most importantly, this concept is not Dio's "invention"! Appian uses it explicitly, describing the arrangements with the Allobroges (App. *B Civ.* 2.4):

Meanwhile ambassadors of the Allobroges, who were making complaint against their magistrates, were solicited to join *the conspiracy of Lentulus* in order to cause an uprising against the Romans in Gaul (Ἀλλοβρίγων πρέσβεις ... ἐς τὴν Λέντλου συνωμοσίαν ἐπήχθησαν ὡς ἀναστήσοντες ἐπὶ Ῥωμαίους τὴν Γαλατίαν).

---

28   Yavetz 1963, 492; Gruen 1974, 429; Drummond 1999, 153; Lachenaud & Coudry 2014, 163. *Contra*, Schietinger 2017, 174.

29   Schwartz 1897, 568–9; Gelzer 1923, 1699; Garzetti 1942, 33; Syme 1964, 75–7; Pareti 1965, 332–4; La Penna 1968, 101–2; Stockton 1971, 100–1; Gruen 1974, 417; Shatzman 1975, 221; Marshall 1976, 74; McGushin 1977, 155–6; Ramsey 2007, 117; Levick 2015, 50. This meeting seems to prefigure that of Catiline and his supporters before the elections' day of 63, described by Cicero in the *Pro Murena*.

The mention of the "conspiracy of Lentulus" both in Appian and in Dio cannot be a coincidence: it must originate from a common source. It is a kind of *lectio difficilior* and, perhaps, a more reliable definition of what took place in Rome between November and December 63.

(vii) The insistence on the ambiguous role of the consul C. Antonius Hybrida (Cass. Dio 37.30.3, 37.32.3, 37.33.3).[30] Sallust briefly mentions it, in connection with the year 64 and the first months of 63 (*Cat.* 26.1, 26.4); Dio repeatedly comes back to it in a more explicit way.[31]

(viii) Last and most important, Dio's eventual judgment on the episode (37.42.1): "Such was the career of Catiline and such his downfall; but he gained a greater name than his deeds deserved, owing to the reputation of Cicero and the speeches he delivered against him." This is Dio's own judgment, of course, but it is clearly based on the testimony of (at least) one source, which did not share the Ciceronian interpretation. And, what is more, Dio is perfectly right!

3

We cannot ignore the speech of Calenus (Cass. Dio 46.1–28). In the long debate which took place in early January 43, many "moderate" senators, trying to avoid a civil war, proposed to send ambassadors to Antonius in Cisalpine Gaul: Q. Fufius Calenus was one of them (Cic. *Phil.* 8.11–19). This speech is presented by Dio as the immediate answer to a speech by Cicero (45.18–47), and it is the *locus classicus* of the anti-Ciceronian tradition.[32] As Fromentin and Bertrand (2008, 151) have shown, Calenus becomes here "le porte-parole d'une tradition critique à l'égard des motivations de l'orateur."

Three passages of the speech of Calenus are interesting for us. The first one (46.2.3) is at the very beginning of the speech:

> Is he [Cicero] not the one who killed Clodius by the hand of Milo and slew Caesar by the hand of Brutus? The one who made Catiline hostile to us and put Lentulus to death without a trial? (ὁ τόν τε Κατιλίναν ἐκπολεμώσας ἡμῖν καὶ τὸν Λέντουλον ἄκριτον ἀπολέσας;)

---

30 Bertrand, Coudry, & Fromentin 2016, 307.

31 After the condemnation and exile in 59 of C. Antonius, whom he had defended, Cicero suggested that his former colleague had "sympathized" with the conspirators (cf., e.g., *Sest.* 8). But in 60 he should not have been so explicit. We must infer that these accusations were not included in the Περὶ τῆς ὑπατείας.

32 Alexander 2009, 372. Cf. Fromentin & Bertrand 2008, 21.

The second one (46.10.1) is less explicit (Catiline is not mentioned), but not less interesting:

> What public interest has been preserved or restored by you? Whom have you indicted that was really harming the city (τίνα δὲ ἀδικοῦντα ὄντως τὴν πόλιν), and whom have you brought to light that was in truth plotting against us (τίνα ἐπιβουλεύοντα ἀληθῶς)?

Then Catiline appears again in the third passage (46.20.2):

> Did you not basely destroy Catiline, who had merely canvassed for office but had otherwise done nothing dreadful (σπουδαρχήσαντα μόνον, ἄλλο δὲ μηδὲν δεινὸν ποιήσαντα)? Did you not pitilessly slay Lentulus and his followers, who were not only guilty of no wrong, but had neither been tried nor convicted, and that, too, though you are always and everywhere prating much about the laws and about the courts?

Everybody knows that Dio's version of this speech is not meant to be a trustworthy reconstruction of what Calenus actually said: the "speech of Calenus" and the preceding "speech of Cicero" are Dio's own compositions. But it is also widely acknowledged that the speech of Cicero is a re-elaboration of true Ciceronian material (in particular, of three *Philippics*: the second, the third, and the fifth) and provides a summary in Greek of many arguments employed by Cicero in late 44 and early 43.[33] As Fromentin (2016, 189) has recently shown, "ce qui fait l'originalité de Dion, c'est la synthèse de la matière des *Philippiques* ... et le transfert en grec de l'éloquence cicéronienne."

As for the speech of Calenus, opinions differ considerably. Some scholars consider it as a pure rhetorical exercise, with no real historical value;[34] others maintain that this speech presents, in a rhetorically revised way, some details of the anti-Ciceronian polemic of the late months of 44.[35] The arguments employed in favor of the first interpretation are sometimes feeble and tend to omit any discussion on the *historical* context of these speeches. If we consider the speech of Cicero as an original re-elaboration of the *Philippics*, i.e. of contemporary material, there is no reason to deny

---

33   Gabba 1957, 320; Millar 1961, 18; Millar 1964, 54; Gowing 1992, 237–8; Fromentin & Bertrand 2008, xxi; Fromentin 2016, 189.
34   Millar 1964, 53–4; Ferriès 2007, 405.
35   Syme 1939, 167 ("something at least" of the speech actually delivered by Calenus; *contra*: Gowing 1992, 238; Mallan 2016, 268); Gabba 1957, 322–3 (topics taken from the anti-Ciceronian polemic of 44–43).

a priori this status to the speech of Calenus and to consider it as a mere *pastiche*. The fact is, while the *Philippics* are still available to us, contemporary anti-Ciceronian texts are not, but they existed: Plutarch could still read the speeches of Antonius against Cicero.[36]

Now, let us consider the first of the three passages quoted above (46.2.3). It includes four accusations against Cicero. At least three of them were really made *before* January 43: Cicero had arranged the murder of Clodius, had inspired that of Caesar, and had put to death Lentulus without a trial. The first accusation, mentioned already in the *Pro Milone* (47), was certainly made immediately after Clodius' death (Asc. 37C): it was taken up again by Antonius in his speech to the Senate of September 19th in 44 (Cic. *Phil.* 2.21), in which he retraced in his own way the political career of his enemy. The second one was made by Antonius, as we know from Cicero's reply in the *Second Philippic* (25), taken up by Dio himself already in Book 45 (41.1). The third one had been made since December 63 and had led to the exile of Cicero five years after, as everybody knows.

So, three of the four accusations mentioned at 46.2.3 are certainly historical. With the fourth one – that is, "to have made Catiline hostile to Romans" – we are apparently in the same realm as that of the *Invectiva in Ciceronem* (2.3: "As if, indeed, your consulship were not the cause of that conspiracy ...").[37] But importantly, in Dio's Calenus we are again reading the attack made against Cicero *in late November 63*, led by the tribune L. Calpurnius Bestia (Cic. *Mur.* 81; Sall. *Cat.* 43.1; App. *B Civ.* 2.3).[38] Now, in January 43 Bestia was in Antonius' camp and he took part in the battle of Mutina (Cic. *Phil.* 11.11, 13.26).[39] So, here "Calenus" is mentioning an accusation that could be still evoked among the partisans of Antonius in the winter of 44/3. As we have seen, in narrating the episode of the oath of December 29th in 63 Dio employs one source according to which Caesar was popular "because he had not voted for the death of Lentulus" (37.32.2). In this passage we find the same vein, the same "flavor" of Calenus' allegations against Cicero.

It is worth remembering that in Appian's account of the debate of January 43, the role assigned by Dio to Calenus is performed by L. Calpurnius Piso. The two speeches are different in many respects: "they bear only superficial

---

36 Malcovati 1955, 475; Flacelière & Chambry 1977, 88–9; Scuderi 1984, 23; De Wet 1990, 84–5. *Contra*, Pelling 1988, 118. But the term φησί(ν), used in *Ant.* 2.2 and 10.2, and in *Cic.* 41.4, suggests that Plutarch could still read Antonius. Cf. also Ov. *Pont.* 1.1.23; Tac. *Ann.* 4.34.5; Suet. *Aug.* 7.3, 16.4, 63.4, 69.2–3.

37 Cf. Gabba 1957, 320; Fromentin & Bertrand 2008, xxix n. 34.

38 Cf. the discussion in Part 1 above.

39 Syme 1955, 134; Syme 1964, 71, 132; Broughton 1986, 46. *Contra*, Münzer 1897, 1367.

resemblances to each other."[40] But then it is all the more significant that also in the speech of Piso we find a hint, subtle but clear,[41] to the events of 63 (App. *B Civ.* 3.57): "Whom has Antonius put to death *in a tyrannical manner without trial* – he who is now in danger of being condemned himself without trial? Whom has he *banished from the city*?" So, it is certain: the conspiracy of 63 *was* mentioned in the debate of January 43, by the members of the "moderate" faction.

In the mid-40s, the recovery of the "Catilinarian" topic was not surprising.[42] Cato's death at Utica had evoked memories of 63, for his role in the debate of December 5th. For instance, Brutus mentioned it in his *Cato*. Shortly afterwards, Sallust made Cato and Caesar the real protagonists of his *Bellum Catilinae*. As for Cicero, he undertook the revision of his *De consiliis suis* (where he explicitly accused Crassus and Caesar of having been partisans of Catiline) and evoked once again Catiline (*Off.* 2.84), this time to attack the memory of Caesar. From 61 to 58, Cicero's consulship had been employed in the political debate as a *topos*, as a symbol of the *auctoritas senatus*,[43] both by Cicero and by his enemies. This happened once again in autumn 44. In his speeches of September 19th and October 2nd, Antonius attacked Cicero, recalling all his political career and in particular his consulship (Cic. *Phil.* 2.11–18). We have to bear in mind that in 63 the young Antonius lived in Lentulus' house: after the death of Antonius Creticus, father of Antonius, Julia, his mother, had married Lentulus. Antonius accused Cicero of not giving back Lentulus' corpse to his family (Cic. *Phil.* 2.17; Plut. *Ant.* 2.2). And the other consul of 63, C. Antonius Hybrida, was Antonius' uncle. So, for Antonius the conspiracy of 63 had been a family affair.

Now, according to the *Fourth Philippic* (6.15), in December 44 Antonius had claimed to be *like Catiline*: "He likes to boast of his resemblance to Catiline (*se similem esse Catilinae gloriari solet*), but though he is his equal in criminality, he is his inferior in energy." It is widely known that Cicero had compared Antonius to Catiline (*Phil.* 2.1, 2.118),[44] as he had always done with his enemies or adversaries, such as Clodius, Vatinius, Gabinius, or Piso.[45] This is probably

---

40   Mallan 2016, 264. Cf. Gowing 1992, 147–9.
41   Cf. Syme 1939, 168; Magnino 1984, 168.
42   Cf. Stone 1999, 50, 54 n. 23.
43   Tatum 1999, 77.
44   We find again this comparison in Bruttedius Niger (*FRHist* 72 fr. 1: "Certainly this benefit to the entire people was obvious: that that period of wretched slavery had been postponed from the time of Catiline to that of Antonius") and in Pliny the Elder (*HN* 7.117: "Your genius drove Catiline to flight; you proscribed M. Antonius").
45   Tatum 1999, 142–5.

why *Antonius'* pretension to be like Catiline has not received so far the attention it deserves. According to Boulanger and Wuilleumier (1959, 199), Antonius' pretension "semble due à l'imagination de Cicéron, désireux de rappeler ses propres exploits." But this explanation is not satisfying.⁴⁶ In the *Fourth Philippic*, Cicero is talking to the people and dealing with a topic that people certainly knew (Antonius had attacked Cicero not only in the Senate, but also *in contione*). In order to understand the true meaning of Cicero's words, we must ask ourselves if Antonius could simply *say*, in December 44, that he resembled Catiline. If we read the speech of Calenus without prejudices, the answer can only be affirmative. Antonius had left Rome on November 29th and threatened to attack Decimus Brutus, the outgoing governor of Cisalpine Gaul, who had announced his intention to resist the consul and not to give him the province. Faced with a growing opposition in the Caesarian milieu, Antonius could claim to have been forced to take up arms because of the hostility of his enemies, among whom there was Cicero. Antonius had already attacked his consulship, not only for political reasons, but also for personal family reasons; he had been compared to Catiline by Cicero himself; given the situation, he could polemically accept this comparison and turn it on Cicero. Antonius was not *boasting*, he was *complaining* that he was like Catiline. He was a victim of Cicero, as Catiline and Lentulus, Antonius' step-father, had been. In this context we can easily explain the fourth accusation by Calenus, according to which Cicero had made Catiline "hostile to us." This is not Dio's invention, nor the product of some Greek rhetor's imagination. At the end of December 44, Antonius and his partisans could evoke the memory of Catiline, suggesting that Cicero was trying to push him to war, *just as he had done with Catiline in 63*.⁴⁷

Antonius' charges against Cicero did not come from any old agitator, but from the man who had rallied almost all the Caesarians, who had been the promoter of the compromise with Brutus, and who remained the natural chief of the Caesarian "party." So, in late 44/early 43 it was still possible to propose alternative versions of Cicero's consulship without making a fool of oneself. "Catilinarian" allusions in Calenus' speech mirror a contemporary controversy

---

46 Cf. Seager 2007, 38: "Antony was allegedly accustomed to boast of the likeness."
47 According to Borgies (2016, 146), "l'on peut supposer que l'orateur retourne le nom de Catilina contre Marc Antoine, parce que ce dernier l'aurait aussi utilisé. Marc Antoine, dans ses édits, n'aurait donc pas seulement appelé Octavien Spartacus, mais aussi Catilina." This hypothesis (which Borgies attributes to Syme 1939, 127, but wrongly) is baseless: no source hints at such a statement by Antonius.

and cannot be dismissed as rhetorical fiction (even if, of course, they remain a great example of Dio's rhetorical skill).[48]

4

Contemporary traditions on the "conspiracy of Catiline" have now disappeared, but they certainly existed. They are clearly mirrored in the two last fragments of Diodorus' *Bibliotheca historica*.[49] Among the authors who dealt with the events of 63, we can mention:

- Atticus, who composed a Greek *commentarius* on Cicero's consulship (Cic. *Att.* 2.1.1);
- L. Lucceius, a senator who was Catiline's prosecutor at the trial *de sicariis* of 64 and certainly attended the meetings of late 63. In 55, Cicero asked Lucceius to expand his work on the social and civil war, and to add some chapters on Cicero's consulship, exploiting his Περὶ τῆς ὑπατείας (*Fam.* 5.12). We do not know Lucceius' answer;
- L. Scribonius Libo, whose work was published before May 45 (cf. Cic. *Att.* 13.30.3). The first two fragments concern the year 132 (*FRHist* 36 fr. 1 a–b), the third the year 47 (*FRHist* 36 fr. 2): he certainly dealt with Cicero's consulship too, but we do not know the size and the contents of this work;
- Brutus, who certainly dealt with the events of 63 in his *Cato*, where he called Cicero *optimus consul* (cf. Cic. *Att.* 12.21.1);
- Antonius, who in autumn 44 delivered several speeches against Cicero (cf. above), where he reconstructed in his own way Cicero's political career and, in particular, his consulship (cf. Cic. *Fam.* 12.2.1; *Phil.* 2.11–20, 5.19–20);
- Tanusius Geminus, whose work, written in the second half of the 40s, dealt with the years 66/5 (*FRHist* 44 fr. 2) and 55 (fr. 3). But we know almost nothing about him;
- Q. Aelius Tubero,[50] who fought at Pharsalus under Pompey and was the author of a Roman history *ab urbe condita* (*Historiae*). This work, written between 40 and 35, certainly dealt with contemporary history too (cf. *FRHist* 38 fr. 15 = Suet. *Iul.* 83.1). Some scholars ascribe to him certain "Catilinarian" allusions in Dionysius of Halicarnassus and Livy.[51] His father Lucius, a sen-

---

48 For the retention, in the speech of Calenus, of contemporary themes (and for their "Antonian" origin), cf. Meyer 1922, 621; Gabba 1957, 321–3; Lintott 1997, 2515–16; Stone 2008, 237; Welch in this volume.
49 Urso 2018.
50 Cf. Zecchini 1978, 193–200; Oakley 2013.
51 Rosenberg 1921, 138; Klotz 1940, 296; Wiseman 1994, 54–5; Richardson 2012, 110–11.

ator, *legatus* of Q. Cicero in Asia (Cic. *Q Fr.* 1.10), could provide him some original pieces of information, in particular on the Senate's meetings of autumn 63;

- C. Asinius Pollio, the best studied among all these authors,[52] whose *Histories* started from 60 (Hor. *Carm.* 2.1) but certainly opened with an *archaiologia*, as Sallust had done before him.[53] This *archaiologia* covered at least the years after 67 (where Sallust had arrived in his own *Histories* before his sudden death). Pollio's hostility towards Cicero is widely known. In the speech *Pro Lamia*, he included accusations against him that he "did not dare to include in his *Histories*" (Sen. *Suas.* 6.15). Among the sources mentioned here, Pollio was the one who is likely to have offered the less favorable version concerning Cicero's deeds of 63.

Some of these works, to be sure, are virtually unknown to us, and some of them were no longer available to Dio. Still, Dio claims to have read "everything or nearly so" that had been written on Roman history (fr. 1.2): it is evident that he knew at least one source, whose version of the Catilinarian conspiracy diverged in many respects from the version firmly established since the Augustan age: a source that mirrored a contemporary tradition, alternative both to Cicero and Sallust. This source stressed the controversies that followed Cicero's consulship already in 63 and afterwards; it shared with Diodorus some "heterodox" details, such as Cicero's use of intimidation; it conveyed important pieces of information, such as the distinction between the *tumultus* and the *senatus consultum ultimum* of October 63, and the fact that the "anonymous letters" delivered by Crassus to Cicero mentioned no name; it echoed some details of the "Antonian" version of the conspiracy of 63; and it led Dio to conclude with good reason that, after all, Catiline "gained a greater name than his deeds deserved."

One final remark. What is lacking in Dio's account on the conspiracy of 63 is a portrait of Catiline, while most of the extant sources, from Sallust (*Cat.*, 5.1–8, 15–16) onwards, consistently insist on his "devilish" nature.[54] Dio does not hesitate to offer his moral judgments on the great protagonists of those years, such as Lucullus (36.16), Pompey (36.24.5–6, 37.20.3–6), Cato (37.20), Caesar (37.37.3, 38.11.3–6), Cicero (37.38.2, 38.12.5–7), or Catulus (37.46.3). As for Catiline, Dio only says that he was θρασύτατος, "a man of great audacity"

---

52 André 1949; Gabba 1957; Zecchini 1982; Morgan 2000; Drummond 2013b (with additional bibliography).

53 Pollio started writing around 35, when Sallust died (Zecchini 1982, 1282; Morgan 2000, 61).

54 Val. Max. 4.8.3: *furor*; Plut. *Cic.* 10.2: "[Catiline] had once been accused of deflowering his own daughter and of killing his own brother"; App. *B Civ.* 2.2.4: ἔμπληκτος ἀνήρ, "a madman"; Flor. 2.12.1: *luxuria*.

(36.44.4): not much, for someone who had been depicted, in the "shield of Aeneas" (Verg. *Aen.* 8.666–70), as the prototype of the great Roman criminals.[55] Of course, we might argue that Dio did not want to repeat things already said by others before him. Most probably, he thought that an articulated portrait of Catiline was not worthwhile.

Bibliography

Alexander, M. C. (2009) "The *Commentariolum petitionis* as an Attack on Election Campaigns", *Athenaeum* 97/1–2, 31–57, 369–95.

André, J. (1949) *La vie et l'œuvre d'Asinius Pollion*, Paris.

Bertrand, E., Coudry, M., & Fromentin, V. (2016) "Temporalité historique et formes du récit. Les modalités de l'écriture dans les livres tardo-républicains", in V. Fromentin *et al.* (eds.), *Cassius Dion: nouvelles lectures* (Bordeaux): 303–16.

Bloch, G. (1903) "Note sur un passage de Diodore de Sicile, à propos de la première Catilinaire", in *Mélanges Boissier* (Paris): 65–70.

Borgies, L. (2016) *Le conflit propagandiste entre Octavien et Marc Antoine. De l'usage politique de la* vituperatio *entre 44 et 30 a.C.n.*, Bruxelles.

Boulanger, A. & Wuilleumier, P. (1959) *Cicéron. Discours, XIX: Philippiques 1 à 4*, Paris.

Broughton, T. R. S. (1986) *The Magistrates of the Roman Republic*, Vol. 3, Atlanta.

Cape, R. W. (2002) "Cicero's Consular Speeches", in J. M. May (ed.), *Brill's Companion to Cicero: Oratory and Rhetoric* (Leiden, Boston, & Köln): 113–58.

Carcopino, J. (1965) *Jules César*, 2nd ed., Paris.

Ciaceri, E. (1918) *Processi politici e relazioni internazionali. Studi sulla storia politica e sulla tradizione letteraria della repubblica e dell'impero*, Rome.

David, J.-M. (2013) "Les règles de la violence dans les assemblées populaires de la République romaine", *Politica antica* 3, 11–29.

De Wet, B. X. (1990) "Contemporary Sources in Plutarch's *Life of Antonius*", *Hermes* 118/1, 80–90.

Drummond, A. (1995) *Law, Politics, and Power: Sallust and the Execution of the Catilinarian Conspirators*, Stuttgart.

Drummond, A. (1999) "Tribunes and Tribunician Programmes in 63 B.C.", *Athenaeum* 87/1, 121–67.

Drummond, A. (2013a) "M. Tullius Cicero", in *FRHist*, Vol. 1, 368–79; Vol. 2, 760–73; Vol. 3, 476–82.

Drummond, A. (2013b) "C. Asinius Pollio", in *FRHist*, Vol. 1, 430–45; Vol. 2, 854–67; Vol. 3, 521–30.

---

55   Savage 1940–1941, 226; Paratore 1981, 297; McKay 1998, 217; Muse 2007, 592.

Dyck, A. R. (2008) *Cicero: Catilinarians*, Cambridge.

Ferriès, M.-C. (2007) *Les partisans d'Antoine (des orphelins de César aux complices de Cléopâtre)*, Paris.

Fezzi, L. (1999) "La legislazione tribunizia di Publio Clodio Pulcro (58 a.C.) e la ricerca del consenso a Roma", *Studi classici e orientali* 47/1, 245–341.

Flacelière, R. & Chambry, É. (1977) *Plutarque. Vies*, Vol. 13, Paris.

Forsythe, G. (1992) "The Municipal *origo* of T. Volturcius", *American Journal of Philology* 113/3, 407–12.

Frisch, H. (1947) "The First Catilinarian Conspiracy: A Study in Historical Conjecture", *Classica et Mediaevalia* 9/1, 10–36.

Fromentin, V. (2016) "Denys d'Halicarnasse, source et modèle de Cassius Dion?", in V. Fromentin *et al.* (eds.), *Cassius Dion: nouvelles lectures* (Bordeaux): 179–89.

Fromentin, V. & Bertrand, E. (2008) *Dion Cassius: Histoire romaine, Livres 45 & 46*, Paris.

Gabba, E. (1957) "Note sulla polemica anticiceroniana di Asinio Pollione", *Rivista storica italiana* 69/3, 317–39.

Garzetti, A. (1942) "M. Licinio Crasso. III", *Athenaeum* 30, 12–40.

Gelzer, M. (1923) "Sergius (23)", in A. Pauly, G. Wissowa, & W. Kroll (eds.), *Realencyclopädie der classischen Altertumswissenschaft* (Stuttgart): IIA/2, 1693–711.

Gelzer, M. (2014) *Cicero. Ein biographischer Versuch*, 2nd ed., Stuttgart.

Giovannini, A. (2012) "Le *senatus consultum ultimum*. Les mensonges de Cicéron", *Athenaeum* 100/1–2, 181–96.

Golden, G. K. (2013) *Crisis Management during the Roman Republic: The Role of Political Institutions in Emergencies*, Cambridge.

Gowing, A. M. (1992) *The Triumviral Narratives of Appian and Cassius Dio*, Ann Arbor.

Gruen, E. S. (1969) "Notes on the 'First Catilinarian Conspiracy'", *Classical Philology* 64/1, 20–4.

Gruen, E. S. (1973) "The Trial of C. Antonius", *Latomus* 32/2, 301–10.

Gruen, E. S. (1974) *The Last Generation of the Roman Republic*, Berkeley.

Hardy, E. G. (1917) "The Catilinarian Conspiracy: A Re-study of the Evidence", *Journal of Roman Studies* 7, 153–228.

Klotz, A. (1940) *Livius und seine Vorgänger*, Leipzig.

Kunkel, W. (1995) *Staatsordnung und Staatspraxis der römischen Republik*, Vol. 2, Munich.

Lachenaud, G. & Coudry, M. (2011) *Dion Cassius: Histoire romaine, Livres 38, 39 & 40*, Paris.

Lachenaud, G. & Coudry, M. (2014) *Dion Cassius: Histoire romaine, Livres 36 & 37*, Paris.

La Penna, A. (1968) *Sallustio e la "rivoluzione" romana*, Milan.

Lendle, O. (1967) "Ciceros Ὑπόμνημα περὶ τῆς ὑπατείας", *Hermes* 95/1, 90–109.

Levick, B. (2015) *Catiline*, London & New York.

Lewis, R. G. (2008) *Asconius: Commentaries on Speeches of Cicero*, Oxford.

Lintott, A. W. (1997) "Cassius Dio and the History of the Late Roman Republic", in *Aufstieg und Niedergang der römischen Welt*, 2.34.3, 2497–523.
Lintott, A. W. (1999) *Violence in Republican Rome*, 2nd ed., Oxford.
Lintott, A. W. (2008) *Cicero as Evidence: A Historian's Companion*, Oxford.
Magnino, D. (1984) *Appiani bellorum civilium liber tertius*, Florence.
Malcovati, E. (1955) *Oratorum Romanorum fragmenta liberae rei publicae*, 2nd ed., Turin.
Mallan, C. (2016) "*Parrhêsia* in Cassius Dio", in C. H. Lange & J. M. Madsen (eds.), *Cassius Dio: Greek Intellectual and Roman Politician* (Leiden & Boston): 258–75.
Manni, E. (1969) *Lucio Sergio Catilina*, 2nd ed., Palermo.
Marshall, B. A. (1974) "Cicero and Sallust on Crassus and Catiline", *Latomus* 33/4, 804–13.
Marshall, B. A. (1976) *Crassus: A Political Biography*, Amsterdam.
Marshall, B. A. (1985) *A Historical Commentary on Asconius*, Columbia.
Mazzarino, S. (1966) *Il pensiero storico classico*, Vol. 2.1, Bari.
McDermott, W. C. (1972) "Cicero's Publication of his Consular Orations", *Philologus* 116/2, 277–84.
McGushin, P. (1977) *Bellum Catilinae: A Commentary*, Leiden & Boston.
McKay, A. G. (1998) "*Non enarrabile textum*? The Shield of Aeneas and the Triple Triumph in 29 BC (*Aen.* 8.630–728)", in H.-P. Stahl (ed.), *Vergil's* Aeneid: *Augustan Epic and Political Context* (London): 199–221.
Meyer, E. (1922) *Caesars Monarchie und das Principat des Pompejus. Innere Geschichte Roms von 66 bis 44 n. Chr.*, 3rd ed., Stuttgart & Berlin.
Millar, F. (1961) "Some Speeches in Cassius Dio", *Museum Helveticum* 18/1, 11–22.
Millar, F. (1964) *A Study of Cassius Dio*, Oxford.
Millar, F. (1998) *The Crowd in Rome in the Late Republic*, Ann Arbor.
Moles, J. (1982) "Plutarch, *Crassus* 13, 4–5, and Cicero's *de consiliis suis*", *Liverpool Classical Monthly* 7/9, 136–7.
Morgan, L. (2000) "The Autopsy of C. Asinius Pollio", *Journal of Roman Studies* 90, 51–69.
Münzer, F. (1897) "Calpurnius (25)", in A. Pauly, G. Wissowa, & W. Kroll (eds.), *Realencyclopädie der classischen Altertumswissenschaft* (Stuttgart): III/1, 1367.
Münzer, F. (1927) "Lutatius (8)", in A. Pauly, G. Wissowa, & W. Kroll (eds.), *Realencyclopädie der classischen Altertumswissenschaft* (Stuttgart): XIII/2, 2082–94.
Muse, K. (2007) "Sergestus and Tarchon in the *Aeneid*", *Classical Quarterly* 57/2, 596–605.
Oakley, S. P. (2013) "L. and Q. Aelius Tubero", in *FRHist*, Vol. 1, 360–7; Vol. 2, 746–59; Vol. 3, 469–75.
Paratore, E. (1981) *Virgilio. Eneide*, IV, Milan.
Pareti, L. (1965) "Catilina", in Id., *Studi minori di storia antica*, Vol. 3 (Rome): 291–444 [= Id., *La congiura di Catilina*, Catania, 1934].

Pelling, C. B. R. (1988) *Plutarch: Life of Antony*, Cambridge.
Pelling, C. B. R. (2002) *Plutarch and History: Eighteen Studies*, Swansea.
Phillips, E. J. (1976) "Catiline's Conspiracy", *Historia* 25/4, 441–8.
Price, J. J. (1998), "The Failure of Cicero's *First Catilinarian*", in C. Deroux (ed.), *Studies in Latin Literature and Roman History* 9 (Bruxelles): 106–28.
Ramsey, J. T. (1982) "Cicero, *Pro Sulla* 68 and Catiline's Candidacy in 66 BC", *Harvard Studies in Classical Philology* 86, 121–31.
Ramsey, J. T. (2007) *Sallust's* Bellum Catilinae, 2nd ed., Oxford.
Reinach, T. (1904) "Catulus ou Catilina?", *Revue des études grecques* 17, 5–11.
Richardson, J. S. (2012) *The Fabii and the Gauls: Studies in Historical Thought and Historiography in Republican Rome*, Stuttgart.
Rosenberg, A. (1921) *Einleitung und Quellenkunde zur römischen Geschichte*, Berlin.
Rundell, W. M. F. (1979) "Cicero and Clodius: the Question of Credibility", *Historia* 28/3, 301–28.
Savage, J. J. (1940–1941), "Catiline in Vergil and in Cicero", *Classical Journal* 36/4, 225–6.
Schietinger, G.-P. (2017) "Lucius Sergius Catilina. Karriereperspektiven und Karriere eines *homo paene novus* in der späten Römischen Republik", *Klio* 99/1, 149–91.
Schwartz, E. (1897) "Die Berichte über die Catilinarische Verschwörung", *Hermes* 32, 554–608.
Schwartz, E. (1899) "Cassius (40)", in A. Pauly, G. Wissowa, & W. Kroll (eds.), *Realencyclopädie der classischen Altertumswissenschaft* (Stuttgart): III/2, 1684–722.
Scuderi, R. (1984) *Commento a Plutarco, "Vita di Antonio"*, Florence.
Seager, R. (1964) "The First Catilinarian Conspiracy", *Historia* 13, 338–47.
Seager, R. (2007) "Ciceronian Invective: Themes and Variations", in J. Booth (ed.), *Cicero in the Attack: Invective and Subversion in the Orations and Beyond* (Swansea): 25–46.
Shatzman, I. (1975) *Senatorial Wealth and Roman Politics*, Bruxelles.
Spielvogel, J. (1993) Amicitia *und res publica. Ciceros Maxime während der innenpolitischen Auseinandersetzungen der Jahre 59–50 v.Chr.*, Stuttgart.
Stockton, D. (1971) *Cicero: A Political Biography*, Oxford.
Stone, M. (1999) "Tribute to a Statesman: Cicero and Sallust", *Antichthon* 33, 48–76.
Stone, M. (2008) "Greek Ethics and Roman Statesmen: *De officiis* and the *Philippics*", in T. Stevenson & M. Wilson (eds.), *Cicero's Philippics: History, Rhetoric and Ideology* (Auckland): 214–39.
Syme, R. (1939) *The Roman Revolution*, Oxford.
Syme, R. (1955) Review of T. R. S. Broughton, *The Magistrates of the Roman Republic*, *Classical Philology* 50/2, 127–38.
Syme, R. (1964) *Sallust*, Berkeley & Los Angeles.
Tatum, W. J. (1999) *The Patrician Tribune: Publius Clodius Pulcher*, Chapel Hill & London.
Ungern-Sternberg, J. von (1971) "Ciceros erste Catilinarische Rede und Diodor XL 5a", *Gymnasium* 78/1–2, 47–54.

Ungern-Sternberg, J. von (1997) "Das Verfahren gegen die Catilinarier, oder: Der vermiedene Prozeß", in J. von Ungern-Sternberg (ed.), *Große Prozesse der römischen Antike* (Munich): 85–99, 204–6.

Urso, G. (2001) "*Tumultus* e guerra civile nel I secolo a.C.", in M. Sordi (ed.), *Il pensiero sulla guerra nel mondo antico* (Milan): 123–39.

Urso, G. (2016) "La nuova *Budé* di Cassio Dione XXXVI–XXXVII", *Histos* 10, i–viii. (https://research.ncl.ac.uk/histos/documents/2016RD01UrsoonLachenaudandCoudry.pdf).

Urso, G. (2018) "Catilina 'avant Salluste'. Remarques sur deux fragments de Diodore de Sicile", in O. Devillers & B. B. Sebastiani (eds.), *Sources et modèles des historiens anciens* (Bordeaux): 153–66.

Waters, K. H. (1970) "Cicero, Sallust and Catiline", *Historia* 19/2, 195–215.

Wiseman, T. P. (1994) "The Senate and the *populares*, 69–60 B.C.", in *The Cambridge Ancient History* (2nd ed.): Vol. 9, 327–67.

Yavetz, Z. (1963) "The Failure of Catiline's Conspiracy", *Historia* 12/4, 485–99.

Zecchini, G. (1978) *Cassio Dione e la guerra gallica di Cesare*, Milan.

Zecchini, G. (1982) "C. Asinio Pollione: dall'attività politica alla riflessione storiografica", in *Aufstieg und Niedergang der römischen Welt*, 2.30.2, 1265–96.

CHAPTER 10

Dio and the Voice of the Sibyl

Josiah Osgood

οἱ μὲν οὖν ἄνθρωποι τοιαῦτα ὑπὸ τῶν χρημάτων ἐποίουν, τὸ δὲ δὴ θεῖον κεραυνῷ κατ' ἀρχὰς εὐθὺς τοῦ ἐχομένου ἔτους τὸ ἄγαλμα τοῦ Διὸς τοῦ ἐν τῷ Ἀλβανῷ ἱδρυμένου βαλὸν τὴν κάθοδον τοῦ Πτολεμαίου χρόνον τινὰ ἐπέσχε.[1] (2) τοῖς γὰρ Σιβυλλείοις ἔπεσιν ἐντυχόντες εὗρον ἐν αὐτοῖς ἐγγεγραμμένον αὐτὸ τοῦτο "ἂν ὁ τῆς Αἰγύπτου βασιλεὺς βοηθείας τινὸς δεόμενος ἔλθῃ, τὴν μὲν φιλίαν οἱ μὴ ἀπαρνήσασθαι, μὴ μέντοι καὶ πλήθει τινὶ ἐπικουρήσητε· εἰ δὲ μή, καὶ πόνους καὶ κινδύνους ἕξετε."

CASS. DIO 39.15.1–2

While mortals were acting this way under the influence of money, Heaven, at the start of the next year, struck with a thunderbolt the statue of Jupiter set up on the Alban Mount and so held back Ptolemy's return for some time. For consulting the Sibylline verses, they discovered written there the following: "If the king of Egypt comes requesting aid, do not refuse him friendship, but do not help him with a multitude; otherwise you shall know both toils and dangers."[2]

∴

With these words Cassius Dio introduces the Sibylline oracle first made public at the start of 56 BCE that was to roil Roman politics for years to come. By the historian's own account (39.12–15), King Ptolemy had arrived in Rome the prior year, seeking refuge from his subjects. They were irate over the money he was squeezing out of them to pay for the bribes he had extended to the Romans in exchange for confirmation of his rule. Claiming that he had been

---

[1] For useful comments on various drafts of this paper I am indebted to Christopher Baron, Kit Morrell, Celia Schultz, and John Ramsey. Kit Morrell also generously shared her own work in progress. Thanks go, too, to the full audience at the Fiesole conference for helpful feedback.
[2] Translations of Cassius Dio throughout this paper are based on those in the Loeb Classical Library edition. I also consulted with great profit the text, translation, and commentary for Book 39 in Lachenaud & Coudry 2011.

driven from his kingdom, and helped by Lentulus Spinther, the consul of 57 who was set to leave for Cilicia, Ptolemy succeeded in getting the Romans to agree to restore him. The outraged Alexandrians then sent 100 ambassadors to counter Ptolemy's charges. But before the ambassadors could make it to Rome, Ptolemy unleashed men of his own to ambush and murder them. Of those who escaped, some were later murdered in Rome, others were bribed to stay silent, and Ptolemy offered more bribes to Romans too. Such was the power of the royal bribes, the head of the embassy did not dare to appear before the Senate when summoned and the Senate was unwilling to debate the sacrilegious murders of the ambassadors until after Ptolemy left Rome. But then the words of the Sibyl, with their uncharacteristic clarity, pierced through all the deception.

As Dio goes on to relate (39.16.1–2, 39.55–63), after the oracle's dissemination made use of an army impossible, Ptolemy's plans for regaining his throne were delayed, with Spinther never even trying. Eventually, Gabinius, the governor of Syria, on the instructions of his old crony Pompey, restored the king. Gabinius and Pompey, Dio insists (39.55.3, 39.56.4), did so in defiance of the Sibylline oracle. This new round of impiety and greed further enraged the Romans, still angry about the scandalous events of 57. When a terrible flood inundated Rome in 54, the people were convinced that the gods were angry and demanded that Gabinius be put to death.

Cassius Dio's account of the oracle, and indeed of the whole checkered tale of Ptolemy's restoration, is by far the fullest to survive from antiquity and is, along with the evidence of Cicero's speeches and letters, essential to the many modern reconstructions of the episode.[3] But little attention has been paid to the major role that the oracle plays within Dio's history. In this paper, I first explore Dio's other mentions of Sibylline oracles, in which he often foregrounds questions of authenticity or applicability – exactly what he does *not* do in his account of 56. Comparison of his version of events with the Ciceronian evidence shows that Dio has good information at his disposal, and actually offers an account more balanced than many modern ones. It is only when he discusses the restoration of Ptolemy by Gabinius, and Gabinius' subsequent trial in Rome, that he loses balance, swallowing almost whole a partisan tradition.

Dio's specific choices, along with the use he makes of the oracle more generally, buttress his overall interpretation of Roman politics in the last days of the Republic. By taking the oracle seriously, he foreshadows the menace he believes hung over Rome in the mid-50s. He also underscores a sense of divine

---

[3] These include: Shatzman 1971; Wiseman 1994, 391–2, 397, 399–400, 401–2; Tatum 1999, 194–204, Siani-Davies 2001, 1–38; Santangelo 2013, 145–6.

displeasure with the Romans and the willingness of all-powerful politicians, awash in money, to neglect the wishes of Senate and People to the detriment of ordinary citizens. Dio's use of the oracle highlights a nightmarish blurring of an increasingly turbulent Rome with violence-ridden Alexandria. By paying clear attention to Dio's unique account, we gain new knowledge of Rome in the 50s BCE as well as the historian's own powerful vision of how the Republic came to an end.

1 Dio and Sibylline Oracles

To understand Dio's treatment of the oracle of 56 it is useful first to consider Sibylline oracles more generally, and Dio's references to them.[4] Sibylline oracles were, typically, prophecies written in Greek verse, difficult to interpret but potentially of great significance in maintaining relations between mortals and gods. According to tradition, Tarquin the Proud bought three books of these prophecies from the Sibyl herself.[5] This particular set of books was then deposited in the Temple of Jupiter on the Capitoline and it could only be consulted by the priestly college of the quindecimviri, and only then on the order of the Senate, with which by tradition ultimate religious authority lay.[6] When the collection was destroyed with the burning of the Capitol in 83 BCE, the Senate arranged for a commission to travel to at least one of the Sibyl's traditional homes (Erythrae, in Asia Minor) to obtain a new set of oracles.[7] The quindecimviri, sifting through the verses gathered, had final say on what was included in this new collection. Despite all the care taken, it should be noted, the Senate's actions did not stop other Sibylline oracles from circulating. A famous example was the claim made by the praetor of 63 BCE, P. Cornelius Lentulus Sura, that, according to the Sibylline Books, he would be the third Cornelius to rule Rome.[8]

---

[4] For fuller accounts of Sibylline oracles (on which I have drawn here) see Parke 1988, 1–22, 136–51, 190–215; Potter 1994, 71–87, 147–58; Orlin 1997, 76–97; Santangelo 2013, 128–48.
[5] The Cumaean Sibyl, specifically, at least according to later versions. Note that one version (Lactant. *Div. inst.* 1.6.10–11) identifies the Tarquin in question as Tarquinius Priscus, the fifth king of Rome, rather than Tarquinius Superbus, the seventh.
[6] The number of members in the priestly college rose over time, from two to ten and then (perhaps with Sulla) to fifteen; for convenience I use "quindecimviri" throughout.
[7] Dion. Hal. *Ant. Rom.* 4.62.6; Tac. *Ann.* 6.12.3; Fenestella *FRHist* 70 fr. 19.
[8] See Cic. *Cat.* 3.9; Sall. *Cat.* 47.2; Plut. *Cic.* 17.5; App. *B Civ.* 2.4, with, e.g., Ramsey 2007, 181–2; Santangelo 2013, 143–5.

While large parts of Dio's history fail to survive, to judge by the epitome of Zonaras, the historian covered Tarquin's purchase of the books, and he certainly referred to a consultation of them on at least one occasion after 56.[9] In 38 BCE, following a series of portentous events, "the Sibylline verses were consulted" (ἀνεγνώσθη ... τὰ Σιβύλλεια ἔπη, 48.43.5). They confirmed what several mortals, inspired by the Mother of the Gods, had already declared: that that goddess was angry with the Romans. The books also prescribed that a statue of Virtus should be taken to the sea and bathed. Without a doubt, the books were consulted at other points of time that fall within Dio's extant books, but the historian need not always include mention of these consultations.

In Dio's other references to Sibylline oracles, it is less clear that the source was the books in the keeping of the quindecimviri. For example, in the great Gallic rising of the 220s BCE, "the Romans were frightened by an oracle of the Sibyl which told them they must beware of the Gauls when a thunderbolt should fall on the Capitol near the Temple of Apollo" (χρησμός τις τῆς Σιβύλλης τοὺς Ῥωμαίους ἐδειμάτου, φυλάξασθαι τοὺς Γαλάτας δεῖν κελεύων ὅταν κεραυνὸς ἐς τὸ Καπιτώλιον πλησίον Ἀπολλωνίου κατασκήψῃ, fr. 50.1). Was this oracle actually found in the books kept by the quindecimviri? Perhaps. Or perhaps it was one of those that circulated informally. What about the oracle of 42 BCE that required shifting the day of Caesar's birthday feast so that it not overlap with the Ludi Apollinares (47.18.6)? Sometimes Dio specifically raises the possibility that inauthentic Sibylline oracles, or reports of them, could circulate. He suggests that in 44 BCE, "a report spread, whether true or false – such reports are to some degree usually fabricated – that the priests known as the quindecimviri were spreading the report that the Sibyl had said the Parthians would never be conquered in any other way than by a king" (λόγου γάρ τινος, εἴτ᾽ οὖν ἀληθοῦς εἴτε καὶ ψευδοῦς, οἷά που φιλεῖ λογοποιεῖσθαι, διελθόντος ὡς τῶν ἱερέων τῶν πεντεκαίδεκα καλουμένων διαθροούντων ὅτι ἡ Σίβυλλα εἰρηκυῖα εἴη μήποτ᾽ ἂν τοὺς Πάρθους ἄλλως πως πλὴν ὑπὸ βασιλέως ἁλῶναι, 44.15.3).[10] Given how strictly the Senate limited access to the Sibylline Books – recall that even the quindecimviri were not supposed to consult the books unless instructed to – it makes sense that rumors would spread of their contents, and such rumors of course might contain distortions.

---

9 Tarquin: Zonaras 7.11.1–5. Routine consultation of 38 BCE: Cass. Dio 48.43.4–5.

10 According to Suetonius (*Iul.* 79.3), before Caesar's death a report spread that one of the quidecimviri was going to announce at "the next Senate meeting" that according to the *libri fatales* Parthia could only be conquered by a king; App. *B Civ.* 2.110 reports a story circulating that there was a Sibylline prophecy that Parthia would never submit to Rome unless a king marched against them. Cic. *Div.* 2.110–12 also refers to a similar rumor, saying that it proved to be false.

A particularly revealing passage for how Dio understood Sibylline oracles occurs at the start of his narrative of the year 19 CE (57.18.3–5). Among various alarming signs Dio notes an oracle, "reputed to be an utterance of the Sibyl" (λόγιόν ... τι ὡς καὶ Σιβύλλειον) and he actually quotes from it: "When thrice three hundred revolving years have run their course, / Civil strife upon Rome destruction shall bring, and the folly, too, / of Sybaris ..." (τρὶς δὲ τριηκοσίων περιτελλομένων ἐνιαυτῶν / Ῥωμαίους ἔμφυλος ὀλεῖ στάσις, καὶ ἁ Συβαρῖτις / ἀφροσύνα). He notes that the oracle did not actually apply – the chronology was wrong – but still it was taken so seriously that Tiberius denounced the verses as spurious and launched an investigation of all prophetic books.[11] Shortly after the Great Fire under Nero, Dio recounts later in his history (62.18.3–4), the populace of Rome recalled the verses, and then when Nero dismissed them as inauthentic, the crowd started to chant another oracle, which they claimed was a genuine Sibylline prophecy: "Last of the sons of Aeneas, a mother-slayer shall govern" (ἔσχατος Αἰνεαδῶν μητροκτόνος ἡγεμονεύσει). "And so it proved," Dio notes, Nero turning out to be the last of the Julii. Thus for Dio the prophecy was authentic – but it was hard to know if it had been truly spoken beforehand by the Sibyl or if the crowd was suddenly inspired.[12]

To generalize, Dio acknowledges the possibility of genuine, divinely inspired prophecy, but he also recognizes the difficulty in discerning true Sibylline oracles from spurious ones and the possibility of using oracles that were inauthentic, or inaccurately applied, to try to sway public opinion. It makes sense, then, that he often shows oracles implicated in politics. Not only did Tiberius try to suppress prophetic books; as Dio notes (54.17.2), in 18 BCE Augustus "ordered that the Sibylline Books, which had become faded through lapse of time, should be copied by the priests, with their own hands, in order that no one else might read them" (τὰ ἔπη τὰ Σιβύλλεια ἐξίτηλα ὑπὸ τοῦ χρόνου γεγονότα τοὺς ἱερέας αὐτοχειρίᾳ ἐκγράψασθαι ἐκέλευσεν, ἵνα μηδεὶς ἕτερος αὐτὰ ἀναλέξηται).[13]

We are now ready to turn to the oracle of 56. In many of his accounts of oracles, as we have seen, Dio raises issues of authenticity and applicability of the material and also access to it. It is odd, then, that in the narrative of 56,

---

11   For a full discussion of this oracle, along with other signs of unrest at this time – including a Senate decree concerning Jewish and Isiac rites – see Newbold 1974.
12   In fact, Dio has probably inaccurately assigned the "Last of the sons of Aeneas" prophecy, as I discuss briefly in the conclusion.
13   Augustus' measure was evidently in preparation for the Ludi Saeculares; separately, in 12 BCE, according to Suetonius (*Aug.* 31.1), Augustus made a collection of prophetic books and burned most of them, only keeping a selection of those judged to have been written by the Sibyl.

while access is a key issue, authenticity and applicability are not – especially because these *were* issues for at least some contemporaries. Is there an explanation for this?

2 The Oracle as History

According to Dio, the oracle of 56 was uncovered in a standard way but its publication was utterly novel. After the thunderbolt struck the statue of Jupiter, the books were consulted – and as Dio points out, the coincidence between their contents and the ongoing saga of Ptolemy's restoration was amazing. According to the historian, "the meaning of the oracle, as usually happens, was spread about" (ὁ νοῦς τῶν ἐπῶν διεθρυλήθη, ὥσπερ εἴωθε γίγνεσθαι, 39.15.4). This accords with Dio's other accounts of the circulation of Sibylline verses, for example in 44 BCE. But in 56, the tribune Gaius Cato "grew afraid that it would be kept secret, and he led the priests in front of the crowd and forced them to divulge the oracle on the spot before the Senate could take any action whatsoever on the matter" (ἔδεισε μὴ συγκρυφθείη, καὶ ἔς τε τὸν ὅμιλον τοὺς ἱερέας ἐσήγαγε, κἀνταῦθα, πρὶν ὁτιοῦν τὴν γερουσίαν ἐπ' αὐτοῖς χρηματίσαι, ἐξεβιάσατό σφας ἐκλαλῆσαι τὸ λόγιον, 39.15.4). The oracle was then translated into Latin and distributed in an edict. Dio does not say, but as we shall see, almost certainly this was a prose translation – and Dio's own direct quotation is in prose too. This translation and the publication of it by Gaius Cato were utterly novel: as Dio suggests (39.15.3), by tradition it was up to the Senate to decide how much of an oracle to release.

In his account of the oracle's dissemination, Dio suggests that there was no ambiguity in its content and that its effect on politics was decisive. After quoting the oracle, he immediately writes: "amazed by the coincidence between these words and the events that had happened at that time, they rescinded everything they had decided on this subject, persuaded by the tribune Gaius Cato" (κἀκ τούτου τὴν συντυχίαν τῶν ἐπῶν πρὸς τὰ τότε γενόμενα θαυμάσαντες ἀπεψηφίσαντο πάντα τὰ περὶ αὐτοῦ ἐγνωσμένα, Γαΐῳ Κάτωνι πεισθέντες δημάρχῳ, 39.15.3). The subject of the sentence is left unspecified, but to judge by what he later writes (39.16.1–2) as well as the evidence of Cicero (on which more in a moment), Dio is probably referring to a decree passed by the Senate. His vagueness, though, combined with the prominence he attaches to Gaius Cato and Cato's publicizing of the oracle, gives the impression that it was the people of Rome who insisted that Ptolemy must not be restored by Spinther, despite the Senate's earlier decree. At several points later in Book 39, Dio highlights how the decision about Ptolemy in 56 reflected the views of the larger community. Note in particular 39.55.1 ("although the Romans had voted not to help [Ptolemy]," καίτοι τῶν Ῥωμαίων τήν τε ἐπικουρίαν ἀπεψηφισμένων) and 39.56.4 ("despite the people and Sibyl declaring that the man should not be restored," ἀπειρηκότος δὲ καὶ τοῦ δήμου τῆς τε Σιβύλλης μὴ καταχθῆναι τὸν ἄνδρα). These latter references may be slightly abbreviated: what the Senate actually voted in 56 was not to restore Ptolemy with a "multitude" – that is to say, with an army. After all, the Sibyl did say not to refuse the king friendship altogether.

It was only after Gaius Cato's actions, Dio emphasizes (39.16), that the Senate took up debate on what to do in response to the oracle. Lentulus Spinther, the consul of 57 who was then to govern Cilicia, had already been entrusted with the task of restoring Ptolemy. Now, at the start of 56, some in the Senate argued that he should still carry out that task, but without an army. Others urged that Pompey with two lictors should escort Ptolemy home – and this was the plan Ptolemy now favored. The tribune A. Plautius read out at a *contio* a letter from Ptolemy to this effect. But fearing that Pompey would obtain yet more power, the senators opposed it – and, according to Dio, the Senate did nothing more. The people of Rome, led by Gaius Cato, had settled the matter.

A great deal of evidence survives in the Ciceronian correspondence as well as Cicero's oratory that allows us to assess Dio's account. While Dio in many respects offers far less detail, it can be said at once that overall he is well-informed. The oracle was indeed disseminated in Latin, as Cicero quotes from it a couple of times, including the words *sine multitudine*.[14] This phrase shows that the Latin version was not in hexameters, as one would expect for Sibylline verses, but was in prose. The Ciceronian evidence also confirms that there was a proposal in the Senate for Lentulus Spinther to carry out Ptolemy's restoration without an army.[15] Apparently it did not pass. There also was, as Dio correctly writes, a counter-proposal concerning Pompey, which certainly did not pass.[16] Its contents remain vague in the Ciceronian materials, but we do learn, separately, that L. Caninius Gallus, who entered the tribunate in late 57, promulgated a bill that Pompey should escort the king "without an army but with two lictors."[17] This bill was not passed, and if proposed in the Senate, it failed

---

14   Cic. *Fam.* 1.7.4 (SB 18), *Q Fr.* 2.2.3 (SB 6); note also *Rab. Post.* 4, citing a part of the oracle not quoted by Dio.
15   See esp. Cic. *Fam.* 1.1.1–3 (SB 12); also *Fam.* 1.2.1–2 (SB 13), 1.4.1–2 (SB 14); *Q Fr.* 2.2.3 (SB 6).
16   Cic. *Fam.* 1.1.3 (SB 12), 1.2.1 (SB 13); *Q Fr.* 2.2.3 (SB 6).
17   Plut. *Pomp.* 49.6; cf. Cic. *Q Fr.* 2.2.3 (SB 6); *Fam.* 1.7.3 (SB 18), 1.4.1 (*Caninius et Cato negarunt se legem ullam ante comitia esse laturos*, SB 14). Commenting on the last passage, Shackleton Bailey (1977, 1.299) argues that Caninius had to have proposed the law by the end of December (since the *comitia* referred to were scheduled for January 20th), but if we assume Plutarch reports the law correctly, then it surely had to have been proposed

there too. Ultimately, according to the Ciceronian evidence, while the Senate did early on decree that nobody should restore the king with "a multitude," for to do this would be dangerous to the *res publica*, it did not block restoration altogether, leaving open the possibility that Lentulus could attempt to do so, but with caution.[18] Dio's account, therefore, appears to be fundamentally sound.

But there is a big difference between it and Cicero. Writing to Lentulus Spinther himself, Cicero repeatedly hints that he thinks the oracle – which so amazingly coincided with a hot political issue – was fake.[19] At one point, Cicero even wrote that the people did not really believe the oracle, but felt that it was a "sham religious scruple introduced by your enemies and detractors" (*a tuis invidis atque obtrectatoribus nomen inductum fictae religionis*, *Fam.* 1.4.2 [SB 14]). While at points Cicero hints there was significant popular interest in the issue, overall his writings, in sharp contrast to Dio, assign little role to the people of Rome in driving the politics of Ptolemy's restoration.[20]

Modern scholars have tended to favor Cicero's idea of a trumped-up oracle in their reconstructions, and even take it a step further. They are inclined to see the oracle as part of a complicated plot to prevent Pompey from getting the command to restore Ptolemy, perhaps masterminded by Crassus, with help from the tribune Gaius Cato and Clodius.[21] While a full discussion is neither possible nor essential here, it should be pointed out that, even according to the Ciceronian evidence, Pompey never openly expressed interest in the job and always publicly supported Lentulus; Pompey factored into the debate only *after* the oracle created an unanticipated problem.[22] Moreover, there is little reason to believe that the people would not take the oracle seriously, especially after the sacrilegious treatment of the Alexandrian ambassadors.[23] According to a fragment of the historian Fenestella, Gaius Cato, immediately after entering

---

after the discovery of the oracle. For a full discussion of the problem, see Morrell 2019, suggesting that the oracle was actually discovered in December. Another possibility is that Plutarch refers to a later proposal than Cicero at *Fam.* 1.4.1.

18 See esp. Cic. *Fam.* 1.1.1 (SB 12), 1.2.1 (SB 13), 1.5b.1 (SB 16); *Q Fr.* 2.2.3 (*periculosum rei publicae*, SB 6); and (for Cicero's cunning suggestions on how Lentulus should proceed, *sine multitudine*) 1.7.4 (SB 18). In this last passage we learn that the Senate did attempt to block restoration altogether, but the decree was vetoed.
19 Cic. *Fam.* 1.1.1 (SB 12), 1.4.2 (SB 14), 1.7.4–6 (SB 18).
20 Hints of popular interest: e.g., Cic. *Fam.* 1.2.4 (SB 13), 1.4.2 (SB 14).
21 E.g., Taylor 1949, 85–6; Tatum 1999, 200. But see, e.g., Wiseman 1994, 391–2; Morrell 2017, 126–7; Morrell 2019.
22 This would not necessarily rule out Cicero's claim in letters of January 56 (*Fam.* 1.1.8 [SB 12], 1.2.3 [SB 13]) that agents of Ptolemy *secretly* plotted for Pompey to be entrusted with the king's reassignment.
23 A point noted by Morrell 2017, 126–7 and developed fully in Morrell 2019.

his tribunate in 57, was already arousing hostility against Ptolemy and Lentulus Spinther at *contiones*.[24] I would suggest that Dio's account, which treats the oracle as authentic and something Romans did take seriously, actually is more balanced than the standard one in modern histories. But the more important point, for this paper, is that even if Dio did not know the Ciceronian correspondence, his own overall view of oracles might have predisposed him at least to raise a question about the oracle. But instead, like the people, he had conviction in the prophecy.

Dio returns to it repeatedly in his account of Ptolemy's restoration by Gabinius later in Book 39, to which we now turn. As Dio puts it, "although the Romans had voted not to help [Ptolemy] and were still very angry about the bribery he had engaged in," Pompey and Gabinius carried out the restoration (καίτοι τῶν Ῥωμαίων τήν τε ἐπικουρίαν ἀπεψηφισμένων καὶ πρὸς τὰς δωροδοκίας τὰς ὑπ' αὐτοῦ γενομένας δεινῶς ἔτι καὶ τότε διακειμένων, 39.55.1–2). Dio elaborates in a long sentence (39.55.2–3):

> τοσοῦτον γὰρ αἵ τε δυναστεῖαι καὶ αἱ τῶν χρημάτων περιουσίαι καὶ παρὰ τὰ ψηφίσματα τά τε τοῦ δήμου καὶ τὰ τῆς βουλῆς ἴσχυσαν, ὥστε ἐπιστείλας μὲν ὁ Πομπήιος τῷ Γαβινίῳ τῆς Συρίας τότε ἄρχοντι, στρατεύσας δὲ ἐκεῖνος, ὁ μὲν τῇ χάριτι ὁ δὲ τῇ δωροληψίᾳ καὶ ἄκοντος αὐτὸν τοῦ κοινοῦ κατήγαγον, μηδὲν μήτε ἐκείνου μήτε τῶν τῆς Σιβύλλης χρησμῶν φροντίσαντες.

> The dominance of a few powerful men (*dynasteiai*) and the surfeit of wealth had such power against the votes of the People and the Senate that after Pompey sent orders to Gabinius, who was then governing Syria, and after Gabinius carried out a campaign – the one acting out of a sense of gratitude, the other out of a bribe received – they restored the king, contrary to the wish of the state, paying no attention either to it or to the oracles of the Sibyl.

While Dio also asserts that Gabinius' withdrawal from his own province of Syria into Egypt violated law, the defiance of the Sibyl is even more prominent in the subsequent narration. The only restraint that the oracle imposed on Gabinius was to raise the bribe he demanded of the king (39.56.5). In Rome, citizens were furious, and Cicero stoked their anger, while also hectoring the Senate to consult the Sibylline Books again, expecting that they included a punishment for anyone who violated the oracle's injunctions.[25] Pompey and

---

24   *FRHist* 70 fr. 2.
25   For this and what follows, I am paraphrasing Cass. Dio 39.59–63.

Crassus, as consuls of 55, refused to bring Cicero's proposal to a vote, but the next year's consuls did arrange for the books to be consulted. Nothing pertinent was found, but then once again the gods intervened: the Tiber river suddenly rose so high that it inundated huge portions of Rome, destroying large swathes of housing and claiming the lives of many Romans too. According to Dio, who describes the flood in a magnificent paragraph (39.61), the Romans were more furious than ever and demanded Gabinius be put to death before worse disasters followed. The Senate passed a decree urging that Gabinius be treated harshly. Upon his return to Rome, Gabinius was put on trial for the restoration but, despite his palpable guilt, managed an acquittal thanks to massive bribery as well as arguments by friends of Pompey and Caesar that "another time and another king was spoken of by the Sibyl" (ἄλλον τέ τινα καιρὸν καὶ ἄλλον βασιλέα πρὸς τῆς Σιβύλλης εἰρῆσθαι, 39.62.3). This is Dio's sole hint of doubt about the applicability of the oracle, and clearly Dio introduces it only to dismiss it; as for authenticity, there is no doubt. When Gabinius was put on trial a second time, on charges of extortion, he was found guilty, primarily because he failed to bribe the jurors sufficiently, Dio claims.

Once again, comparison with contemporary evidence illuminates key features of Dio's account, including a partisanship lacking from earlier in Book 39.[26] Cicero's letters to his brother Quintus do suggest there was real popular anger directed at Gabinius, at least after his secretive return to Rome on September 27th: "when he had to appear to answer a charge of *maiestas* on C. Alfius' order, he was almost knocked down by a huge, hate-filled assembly of the whole people" (*cum edicto C. Alfi de maiestate eum adesse oporteret, concursu magno et odio universi populi paene adflictus est, Q Fr. 3.1.24* [SB 21]). But with a major grudge against Gabinius because of his role in exiling Cicero, Cicero may be exaggerating. After all, he savors the thought of adding an episode into the second book of his epic *Vicissitudes*, in which Apollo will appear in an assembly of the gods to foretell of Gabinius' ignominious return.[27] Cicero had been publicly denouncing Gabinius long before the secretive return to Rome ("Catiline's pet dancer"; "glutton"; "enemy of the Senate"; "hireling of the king of Alexandria"); in general Dio accepts this Ciceronian portrait, whether he read it directly in Cicero's speeches, or in a later tradition indebted to the speeches, or both.[28]

---

26 I have drawn here on discussions of Gabinius' trials, including Gruen 1974, 322–7; Fantham 1975; Williams 1985; Morrell 2017, 165–71.
27 Cic. *Q Fr.* 3.1.24 (SB 21).
28 Cicero's denunciations: e.g., *Prov. Cons.* 9–12, *Pis.* 48–50, *Planc.* 86–7. Sanford 1939 was a pioneering discussion of the influence of the orator's hostile portrait on the later tradition.

From Cicero's letters and oratory, despite his bitterness toward Gabinius, we actually can reconstruct a more balanced account of the initial *maiestas* trial than Dio's. Fearful of alienating Pompey, Cicero did not attack Gabinius with all his ferocity, as Dio asserts, but with remarkable mildness.[29] The actual prosecutor, according to Cicero, was simply incompetent.[30] Moreover, though Dio gives no indication of it, there was a fairly robust defense of Gabinius. Perhaps not all would have placed much credit in testimony from Pompey that Ptolemy Auletes had written to him stating that he had given no money to Gabinius, except for military purposes.[31] But Gabinius also made a plea that the interests of Roman security required him to go to Egypt to deal with Archelaus, the son of Mithridates the Great's star general of the same name.[32] Claiming actually to be the son of Mithridates and accepting Queen Berenice's invitation to share the throne of Egypt, Archelaus could be seen by jurors as a serious threat. Siani-Davies (2001, 32) suggests that Gabinius did not have Ptolemy return to Alexandria until after the defeat of Archelaus and the pacification of Egypt – thereby allowing Gabinius to claim that he had not actually restored Ptolemy with an army. At the same time, some might have recognized what Cicero and Dio would not, that the complaints the Syrian *publicani* made in the Senate about Gabinius very possibly stemmed from his own efforts to rein them in – although this was more pertinent in the *repetundae* trial.[33] And while Cicero in his private correspondence bemoaned Gabinius' acquittal – "the Republic is no more" – even Cicero does not suggest that the verdict was achieved by bribery.[34]

A more casual detail that emerges from one of Cicero's letters shows an even bigger distortion in Dio. A letter from late October or early November of 54 to Quintus describes the massive flooding that Rome was experiencing (*Q Fr.* 3.5.8 [SB 25]). This was *after* Gabinius' acquittal for *maiestas*, and indeed Cicero says that Homeric verses about Zeus raining in anger at men who render crooked judgments were circulating. While Dio also dates the flood to 54,

---

Williams 1985 discusses problems with Dio's account of Gabinius' governorship of Syria in depth.

29 Cic. *Q Fr.* 3.4.1–3 (SB 24), 3.5.5 (SB 25).
30 Cic. *Q Fr.* 3.3.3 (SB 23), 3.4.1 (SB 24); *Att.* 4.18.1 (SB 92).
31 Cic. *Rab. Post.* 34.
32 See esp. Cic. *Rab. Post.* 20.
33 Complaints of *publicani*: Cic. *Q Fr.* 2.12.2 (SB 16), 3.2.2 (SB 22). See further Morrell 2017, 81–2.
34 Cic. *Q Fr.* 3.4.1 (SB 24). He does speak of *Pompei mira contentio, iudicium sordes* (*Att.* 4.18.1 [SB 92]).

he unmistakably assigns it to *before* Gabinius' return to Rome, and so can argue it reflected divine anger at the restoration of Ptolemy.[35]

This potentially creates a problem in our understanding of Dio. While for events of early 56, I have argued, he offers an accurate and rather balanced account, for Gabinius' return and trial he clearly does not. Should the latter conclusion force us to revise the view we take of the earlier part of Book 39? And to ask a more specific question: why in the earlier part of the book does he fail to implicate Pompey in any of the plotting, while later he portrays Ptolemy's restoration on Pompey's orders in the worst light possible? The answers, I shall now show, have much to do with Dio's larger historiographic choices.

3   The Oracle as Historiography

We should begin by observing that, while Dio's account of Gabinius' Syrian governorship and his subsequent trials may reflect a hostile tradition – and more positive accounts were available – it makes sense within Dio's larger narrative.[36] Gabinius' very introduction in the *Roman History*, as the tribune who proposed the extraordinary command against the pirates that would go to Pompey, should make us only expect the worst of him (36.23–36). Although Dio is not sure whether Gabinius was put up to making the proposal by Pompey or was hoping to ingratiate himself, "certainly he did not act out of any goodwill for the state, for he was a most wicked man" (οὐ γάρ που καὶ ὑπ' εὐνοίας αὐτὸ τῆς τοῦ κοινοῦ ἐποίησε· κάκιστος γὰρ ἀνὴρ ἦν, 36.23.4). To help the law pass, Gabinius gives a thoroughly dishonest speech (36.27–9), telling the people they must pass the law because it was beneficial to the common welfare – exactly what he does not care about!

The account of Gabinius' governorship and trials reinforces not only his own disregard of the public interest but illustrates a larger pattern. Just as early in Book 39 Ptolemy subverts Roman institutions through his bribes, so does Gabinius. And the rules of the game dictate that, like most of the senators in Rome in 57 who took those bribes, Gabinius must prioritize making money.[37] This is why the chance to restore Ptolemy is irresistible to him. This is why he

---

35   Shackleton Bailey 1980, 220, commenting on *Q. Fr.* 3.5.8, notes the error in Dio's chronology.
36   More positive accounts: Jos. *AJ* 14.82–104 (note esp. 104); *BJ* 1.160–78. Modern discussions (with various opinions) include Sanford 1939, 78–88; Nisbet 1961, 188–92; Badian 1972, 109–10; Morrell 2017, 81–2. On Dio's Gabinius, see also Lindholmer in this volume.
37   For Dio's original emphasis on the problem of electoral bribery, in particular, see the paper of Coudry in this volume; and for the relationship between imperialism and politics, Bertrand in this volume.

harassed Syria, inflicting more damage than pirates – who were then flourishing, Dio notes with exquisite irony (39.56.1). And this is why he was at one time planning to campaign against "the Parthians and their wealth" (39.56.2). It was no matter to Gabinius that his province suffered – from pirates! – when he abandoned it for Egypt (39.59.2).

Now to turn back to the oracle: if Dio dismissed it as a fake, or even hinted at that possibility by making it a move in a game of political plotting, it would have made the overall narrative of Book 39 and his account of the late Republic as a whole less compelling. The oracle, like the portent that precedes its discovery, charges his history with a sense of dread, bringing in warnings from the gods that are alarming in their own right while also suggesting worse to come. Desecration, portents and prophecies, and predictions of impending horrors were, indeed, a real part of the discourse of Roman politics in the 50s: Cicero's speech *De Haruspicum Responso* shows this well.[38] Dio is reflecting this, but since he wrote from hindsight, he also can show us the all too real "toils and dangers" that (he believes) the Romans later endured as a result of Gabinius' actions. It was not Gabinius who was punished, but countless numbers of Romans who lost their houses, even their lives, in the flood. The danger persisted for many days, in fact, as houses weakened by the water later collapsed. The devastation was "by the contrivance of some divinity," people surmised, and Dio agrees (ἐκ παρασκευῆς δαιμονίου τινός, 39.61.1). His readers might think back to the horrific events that immediately followed the pact between Caesar, Pompey, and Crassus and their schemes to give each other whatever they wanted, at the expense of the people.[39] With a sudden storm that ripped up trees by the roots, shattered houses, and sank Tiber boats, Heaven – *to daimonion* – signaled not just dissatisfaction with the triumvirs but also the disasters in store for the people in the years of unrest that lay ahead. For readers, the storm is a signal too, of the dark turn history is taking. Divine signs, including the Sibylline oracle, are one of Dio's narrative devices.

The oracle also has a more specific historiographic function. It helps to underscore the growing violence, corruption, and bribery in Rome, and also the growing neglect of SPQR by powerful individuals (*dynasteiai*) – all subjects of increased importance in Book 39.[40] While the book opens with an account of Caesar's war against the Belgae, as soon as we get to *res internae* we are

---

38 Beard 2012 offers a stimulating discussion of the speech.
39 See esp. Cass. Dio 37.58.
40 For a good discussion of the major themes of Book 39 and surrounding books as well as the way Dio shapes his material to support his program, see Lachenaud & Coudry 2011, xiii–xxv, lxxii–lxxx. On *dynasteiai* see Kemezis 2014, 104–20 and also the paper of Lindholmer in this volume.

plunged into the violence of the campaign to restore Cicero. As Dio writes, "there was bloodshed throughout practically the whole city" (σφαγαὶ κατὰ πᾶσαν ὡς εἰπεῖν τὴν πόλιν ἐγίγνοντο, 39.8.2). And then "on account of King Ptolemy there was further upheaval" (Πτολεμαίου τοῦ βασιλέως ἕνεκα αὖθις ἐκινήθησαν, 39.12.1). More violence ensued, and also massive bribery of Romans by Ptolemy. And then comes the thunderbolt that leads to consultation of the Sibylline Books (39.15.1). So even before the oracle is revealed, Dio has established the interrelationship between increasingly atrocious behavior by the Romans and divine displeasure.[41] The voice of the Sibyl confirms it, asserting that Roman misdeeds will have disastrous consequences. The oracle validates the historian's own themes.

The crucial question for Dio, after the oracle is revealed, is who would disregard it, and how could one get away with doing so when it was patently against the wishes and best interests of the people. Attentive readers can already guess the answer: at the end of Book 37, Dio established that the triumvirs would manage public affairs among themselves, doing whatever they wished, disregarding the public interest.[42] Their followers, too, would do what they wished, with impunity. Only Cato and a few others protested, writes Dio, and it was in vain. A key sentence in Book 39 comes when Dio begins his account of Ptolemy's restoration by Pompey and his follower Gabinius; they could get away with it because "the dominance of a few powerful men and the surfeit of money had such power against the votes of the People and the Senate" (39.55.2). This, we should note, comes after Dio's scathing account of Pompey and Crassus' bid for the consulship and the way they laid hold of everything they wanted once in office in 55. Cato's opposition, once again, was in vain, and it was countered with violence.

As much as the actions of his governorship, Gabinius' acquittal for his flouting of the oracle thus is in keeping with Dio's understanding of the politics of the period and *dynasteiai* more generally. Gabinius' bribes – only a fraction of those he himself had received – easily bought him immunity, and by Dio's account it was really only his cheapness in the second trial that led to a conviction. The seething anger of the people was a secondary factor. To be sure, Gabinius' conviction did seem to show the limits of Pompey's grip – but as Dio cannot help noting (39.63.5), Gabinius would later be restored by Caesar, thus affirming the dominance of the *dynasteiai*.

---

41 This was a contemporary concern, as is well brought out by Morrell 2019.
42 For this and what follows: Cass. Dio 37.57–58.1.

A final point about the oracle is that it helps Dio to highlight a dangerous nexus between Roman and Egyptian politics. To get his way in Rome, King Ptolemy must bribe Romans – and to cover the bribes he treats his own Egyptians with force. In Rome itself, he carries out murders and hands out more bribes to hush everything up and get the Romans put on trial mostly acquitted. Ptolemy is a mirror for Gabinius. To get *his* way in Rome, Gabinius must bribe Romans in advance of his return – and to fund himself he treats provincials with force. Back in Rome, he tries to hush things up and buy juries. As Dio writes (39.55.4), Gabinius, like others of his day, was teaching the lesson that immunity from punishment for violent crimes could be bought. But the arch-teacher was Ptolemy. While Gabinius himself relies in Rome on bribery, rather than violence, Pompey and Crassus and their henchman Trebonius use plenty of Ptolemy-style violence (39.33–6), again showing that if the Egyptian king is not their teacher, he is at least their mirror too.

A notable feature of Book 39 is Dio's inclusion of several violence-filled scenes in Alexandria, along with a reflection on the Alexandrian disposition to violence.[43] As he writes: "in seditions, which with them are abundant and on a big scale, they are constantly engaged in murders and they consider life as nothing in comparison to the immediate rivalry, but pursue destruction in such rivalries as if it were one of the best or most essential things" (ἐν ταῖς στάσεσι, πλείσταις δὴ καὶ μεγίσταις παρ' αὐτοῖς γιγνομέναις, διὰ φόνων τε ἀεὶ χωροῦντες καὶ τὸ ζῆν παρ' οὐδὲν πρὸς τὴν αὐτίκα φιλονεικίαν τιθέμενοι, ἀλλὰ καὶ ὥσπερ τι τῶν ἀρίστων ἀναγκαιότατον τὸν ἐν αὐταῖς ὄλεθρον διώκοντες, 39.58.2). While in many ways, the people of Rome are presented as victims in Book 39 of Dio, they also at moments turn into a dangerous mob – ruthless contestants in a violent struggle for power. They threaten to burn down the Senate and the senators within it because of a grain shortage.[44] And politicians like Clodius, Milo, and Trebonius have supporters as zealous as any Alexandrian.[45] The Clodians rush to their champion's aid with fire and threaten to burn his opponents down; Trebonius' attendants drive Cato's supporters away from a voting assembly, even killing some. The intrigues of these politicians are as murderous as those of Alexandrians.

The oracle relates to this not just because it specifically links Rome with Egypt but also because it reveals impiety, even sacrilege, at the heart of the crisis of the Republic. Increasing impiety, as Dio sees it, would culminate in the horror of civil war, a crime and punishment in one. The historian subtly

---

43 Cass. Dio 39.12.1–2, 39.57–8.
44 Cass. Dio 39.9.2.
45 See especially Cass. Dio 39.7–8, 39.18–19, 39.31–6.

but unmistakably foreshadows this at the end of Book 39 (39.64–5). After the death of Julia, supporters of Pompey and Caesar buried her on the Campus Martius – ignoring the opposition of the consul Domitius Ahenobarbus, who insisted it was a violation of religious law to do this without a Senate decree. And then, to insure that Pomptinus gets a Gallic triumph, an illegal voting assembly was held, and then the tribunes in retaliation decided to cause him some trouble in his procession – "so that there was bloodshed" (ὥστε καὶ σφαγὰς συμβῆναι). With these awful words the book ends, but Dio's readers know the "toils and dangers" are hardly over yet.

4 Epilogue and Conclusion

I have argued here that while Dio allows us to hear the authentic words of a Sibylline prophecy made public in 56 BCE, he also uses the prophecy as a historiographic device. Some confirmation for his interest in using oracles to make larger points is provided by the way he brings into his account of the Great Fire under Nero the two prophecies mentioned earlier, the one beginning "When thrice three hundred revolving years ..." and the other "Last of the sons of Aeneas ..." (62.18.3–4). As Champlin (2003, 184–5) has argued, both of these oracles seem misplaced: the lines "Whence thrice three hundred revolving years ...," first associated with the year 19 CE, have nothing to do with the Fire, while the line chanted by the *plebs*, "Last of the sons of Aeneas, a motherslayer shall govern," was less pertinent to the concerns of the people in 64 CE. As Champlin puts it, the *plebs urbana* surely could have done better than just dredging up the old news of Agrippina's murder. What is more, as Champlin also observes, neither Tacitus nor Suetonius suggests that the people blamed Nero in any way for the fire. Dio has reassigned material here to contribute to his own portrait of Nero the arsonist, victimizing a powerless *plebs urbana* – and to foreshadow the awful civil war that would break out in 68.

None of what I have argued should make us conclude that Dio did not believe in prophecies. He did, just as others Romans did, although they were comfortable with the idea that fakes might circulate: this was, in part, why the Senate and, later, the emperors, showed such interest in the matter. If an oracle was authentic, it was destined to come true; the only question then was when. As Dio himself asks: "What does prophesying mean, if a thing is going to occur in any case, and if there can be no averting it either by human skill or by divine providence?" (τί γάρ που καὶ βούλεται <τὸ> προσημαίνειν, εἴ γε πάντως τέ τι ἔσται καὶ μηδεμία ἂν αὐτοῦ ἀποτροπὴ μήτ' ἀνθρωπίνῃ περιτεχνήσει μήτ' αὖ θείᾳ προνοίᾳ γένοιτο;, fr. 57.22). Of course, in 56 BCE, as Dio saw it, the Romans still had their destiny in their own hands, at least barely. The oracles associated with the Great Fire partake of a more fatalistic view, in which events seem to be beyond an individual Roman's control.[46] Dio's account of the Sibylline oracle of 56 reveals to readers Dio's belief in divinely-inspired oracles, but is also at the heart of his project of charting where power lay among mortals.

Bibliography

Badian, E. (1972) *Publicans and Sinners: Private Enterprise in the Service of the Roman Republic*, Ithaca, NY.

Beard, M. (2012) "Cicero's 'Response of the *haruspices*' and the Voice of the Gods", *Journal of Roman Studies* 102, 20–39.

Champlin, E. (2003) *Nero*, Cambridge, MA.

Fantham, E. (1975) "The Trials of Gabinius in 54 BC", *Historia* 24/3, 425–43.

Gowing, A. M. (1992) *The Triumviral Narratives of Appian and Cassius Dio*, Ann Arbor.

Gruen, E. S. (1974) *The Last Generation of the Roman Republic*, Berkeley.

Kemezis, A. (2014) *Greek Narratives of the Roman Empire under the Severans: Cassius Dio, Philostratus and Herodian*, Cambridge.

Lachenaud, G. & Coudry, M. (2011) *Dion Cassius: Histoire romaine, Livres 38, 39, & 40*, Paris.

Millar, F. (1964) *A Study of Cassius Dio*, Oxford.

Morrell, K. (2017) *Pompey, Cato, and the Governance of the Roman Empire*, Oxford.

Morrell, K. (2019), "'Who Wants to Go to Alexandria?': Pompey, Ptolemy, and Public Opinion, 57–56 BC", in C. Rosillo López (ed.), *Communicating Public Opinion in the Roman Republic* (Stuttgart): 151–74.

Newbold, R. F. (1974) "Social Tension at Rome in the Early Years of Tiberius' Reign", *Athenaeum* 52, 110–43.

Nisbet, R. G. M. (1961) *Cicero: In L. Calpurnium Pisonem Oratio*, Oxford.

Orlin, E. M. (1997) *Temples, Religion, and Politics in the Roman Republic*, Leiden & New York.

Parke, H. W. (1988) *Sibyls and Sibylline Prophecy in Classical Antiquity*, London.

Potter, D. S. (1994) *Prophets and Emperors: Human and Divine Authority from Augustus to Theodosius*, Cambridge, MA.

Ramsey, J. T. (2007) *Sallust's* Bellum Catilinae, 2nd ed. Oxford.

Sanford, E. M. (1939) "The Career of Aulus Gabinius", *Transactions and Proceedings of the American Philological Association* 70, 64–92.

---

46 Dio's attitude to divinely inspired prophecy and fatalism more generally: Millar 1964, 179–81; Gowing 1992, 29–31; Potter 1994, 164.

Santangelo, F. (2013) *Divination, Prediction and the End of the Roman Republic*, Cambridge.
Shackleton Bailey, D. R. (1977) *Cicero*: Epistulae ad familiares, Cambridge.
Shackleton Bailey, D. R. (1980) *Cicero*: Epistulae ad Quintum fratrem et M. Brutum, Cambridge.
Shatzman, I. (1971) "The Egyptian Question in Roman Politics (59–54 BC)", *Latomus* 30/2, 363–9.
Siani-Davies, M. (2001) *Cicero's Speech* Pro Rabirio Postumo, Oxford.
Tatum, W. J. (1999) *The Patrician Tribune: Publius Clodius Pulcher*, Chapel Hill & London.
Taylor, L. R. (1949) *Party Politics in the Age of Caesar*, Berkeley.
Williams, R. S. (1985) "*Rei publicae causa*: Gabinius' Defense of His Restoration of Ptolemy Auletes", *Classical Journal* 81/1, 25–38.
Wiseman, T. P. (1994) "Caesar, Pompey and Rome, 59–50 B.C.", in *The Cambridge Ancient History* (2nd ed.): Vol. 9, 368–423.

PART 3

Civil War and the Victory of Augustus

CHAPTER 11

Responding to Civil War: M. Claudius Marcellus Aeserninus and M. Caelius Rufus in Cassius Dio, Book 42

Andrew G. Scott

Cassius Dio's account of the final conflict between Caesar and Pompey in 48 BCE, culminating in the battle of Pharsalus and Pompey's eventual death in Egypt, dominates Books 41 and 42 of the *Roman History*. Dio's narrative of these events is highly impressionistic and aims to stress the strains and frustrations of civil war.[1] In addition to the reactions of the military and people of Rome that he depicts in these sections, Dio includes two episodes that highlight varying responses to civil war. The first is the conflict in Spain, instigated by the praetor Quintus Cassius Longinus. My particular concern here is the figure of Marcus Claudius Marcellus Aeserninus. Despite his being a more minor figure in this story, Dio depicts Marcellus as a character caught between the two sides of civil war. After turning his attention to the affairs of Rome of 48 BCE, Dio gives significant attention to the upheaval attempted by Marcus Caelius Rufus. Caelius, as *praetor peregrinus*, incited the plebs by proposing debt relief, in an attempt to expand his own political power. Having failed in this endeavor and stripped of his office, Caelius fled Rome and attempted rebellion with Milo, and eventually was killed doing so. In Dio's version, Caelius' deeds are presented in such a way as to suggest that Caelius acted in the uncertainty that surrounded the outcome at Pharsalus, and that his break with Caesar was one of opportunity, though ultimately ill-considered.

In this paper I will examine how and why Dio told these two stories within the larger context of the civil war between Caesar and Pompey. Dio's version of these events differs from the surviving sources in the order of their telling, the motivations of the characters involved, and the emphases of the individual authors. While it is true that Dio might have been drawing on source material that no longer survives, it seems equally, if not more, likely that Dio manipulated these stories according to his own concerns and preoccupations, specifically

---

1 For this thematic focus over these two books, see Freyburger-Galland, Hinard, & Cordier 2002, xxvii. For Dio's text throughout this paper, I have used Boissevain's edition. All translations of Dio are from Cary's Loeb edition; other translations are my own.

the behavior of individuals during times of unrest and uncertainty. I propose first to make a comparison of the sources, then to explore other instances in the history where Dio shows similar concerns, especially in the contemporary portion of his work.

Lurking behind this investigation is the question of Dio's use of source material. The search for Cassius Dio's sources, especially in the surviving books, has been one of the main methods of inquiry into Dio's text, and it has also been one of the most frustrating. At times scholars have been certain of particular sources employed by Dio, whereas others, most notably Millar, have denied the usefulness of source criticism.[2] As Dio's reputation as an historian has gradually improved, and as the field in general has been more receptive to authorial manipulations of source material, Dio's commentators have been more willing to give him credit for fashioning, or refashioning, certain parts of his history.[3] Indeed, in what follows, I will argue that Dio selected and arranged his material in a way that reflects the concerns of his own times and that likely does not mirror what he found in his source material.[4]

1   Cassius Dio on 48 BCE

As noted above, Dio's account of the year 48 BCE runs between two books, 41 and 42.[5] At the beginning of his narration, Dio establishes that the year will be defined by the conflict between Caesar and Pompey, who, in his words, were really in charge of everything (41.43.4–5). Dio then proceeds to follow

---

2   For Dio's sources for Books 41–2, primarily Livy, see Schwartz 1899, 1702–3; De Franchis (2016, 191–4), however, has recently provided a critique of this view. Judeich (1885, 199) sees Dio as dependent on Livy for his material on the affairs of 48 BCE in Spain discussed below (though see also p. 50, which includes a stemma showing Dio's use of both Livy and the *Bellum Alexandrinum*), whereas Grohs (1884, 75) thinks that Dio used the account in the *Bellum Alexandrinum*. See also Manuwald (1979, 251–4) for Dio's use of Livy and other sources for Books 45–54. Berti (1988, 7–28), however, argues against the tendency to see Dio as a "Livian" historian and provides a helpful overview of the diverging viewpoints on Dio's sources for Books 41–2. Westall (2016) has recently advanced the thesis that Dio used Cremutius Cordus for 49–30 BCE. In general, Millar (1964, 34–8) is more circumspect about our ability to detect Dio's use of individual sources.

3   See, e.g., Pelling 1982 and Berti 1988, 21–8.

4   One might compare, e.g., the view of Miles (1995, 99) regarding Livy's construction of his first five books: "... the interpretation of Roman history in Livy's first pentad ... represents a particular synthesis of recent ideas, a synthesis that did not exist in the literary tradition before Livy."

5   On what follows in this paragraph, see also Freyburger-Galland, Hinard, & Cordier 2002, xxvi–xlvi and Kemezis 2014, 117–19.

this conflict until its logical end, namely the death of Pompey in Egypt. Dio highlights the struggle between the two sides in various ways.[6] For example, he provides a dramatic introduction to the final showdown between Caesar and Pompey, including a discussion of the comparable means by which Pompey and Caesar communicated their competing claims for power (41.57). There follows a description of the similarities of their two forces and the difficulty of inducing men to fight in civil war (41.58). Dio's ensuing description of the fighting between the two sides is equally impressionistic, highlighting the contradictions and paradoxes of the skirmish (41.60). Finally, Dio discusses Pompey's flight, an action that contradicts Pompey's previous care in taking proper precautions (42.1.2). Pompey's death scene is followed by a short obituary, which discusses the man's life of contradiction (42.5). Dio then proceeds to wrap up events in Egypt. It is from here that Dio turns his attention to the affairs in Spain. These sections serve a thematic purpose in Dio's account, highlighting the vicissitudes of civil war and the contradictory action caused by such conflicts. In the episode from Spain that follows, we are presented with a sort of test case by which Dio can explore the effects of civil war beyond its immediate actors.

2 M. Claudius Marcellus Aeserninus in Spain

Dio devotes two chapters to the conflict in Spain (42.15–16), a significant amount considering that his narrative of the civil war rarely strays from the characters of Caesar, Pompey, and Cato.[7] Among the extant sources, the story is told in its longest form in the *Bellum Alexandrinum*. To judge by the *periocha* of Book III, it seems that Livy also recorded a version of the story. Dio's use of source material for these episodes has been conjectural and inconclusive, and arguments have been made for his use of both the *Bellum Alexandrinum* and Livy. It is not my intention to try to settle this debate. Rather, I will briefly look at the account in the *Bellum Alexandrinum* and then examine the significance of the differences among the accounts.

In the *Bellum Alexandrinum*, the author moves to the events in Spain by prefacing his remarks with the notice that Spanish events were occurring within the same period that Caesar was fighting Pompey at Dyrrhachium and faring well at Pharsalus, and was also involved in the affairs at Alexandria. Caesar

---

6 For Dio's dramatization of this action, see Berti 1988, 22–5. Freyburger-Galland, Hinard, & Cordier (2002, xli–xlvi) analyze this section of the history in tragic terms.

7 On this focus, see Freyburger-Galland, Hinard, & Cordier 2002, xxxiv–xli.

had left Quintus Cassius Longinus as governor in Spain, a decision that led to discord, as Cassius was hated there. Although Cassius attempted to curry favor with his men by granting them several donatives, the move only served to diminish the force's discipline. Cassius further darkened his reputation by extracting as much money as possible from the provincials (*B Alex.* 48–9). The provincials thus planned his assassination, and were strengthened in their resolve by Cassius' levying of a fifth legion.

When Caesar summoned Cassius and his men to Africa, in order to counteract the reinforcements that Juba had sent to Pompey, Cassius brought his men down to Corduba, where he became a victim of a failed assassination attempt.[8] Believing that Cassius was dead, the soldiers declared L. Laterensis praetor in his place. When news of Cassius' survival made its rounds, the majority of legions remained loyal to Cassius, and Cassius ordered the arrest of the alleged conspirators. Meanwhile, news came to Cassius of Caesar's defeat of Pompey. Cassius then raised money and carried out a conscription of knights (*B Alex.* 56). These actions caused the provincials to hate Cassius even more. There followed an insurrection of some troops near Obucula, who elected T. Thorius as their leader (*B Alex.* 57). In response, Cassius sent his quaestor M. Claudius Marcellus Aeserninus to Corduba, though word soon came that Corduba had revolted, and that Marcellus had joined them. The author of the *Bellum Alexandrinum* confesses that there were various reports, and it was uncertain whether Marcellus had gone to their side willingly or by force.[9]

Thorius proceeded to march to Corduba, claiming that he wished to retake the province in the name of Pompey (*B Alex.* 58). The author suggests that this was done primarily to keep the fight going against Cassius, who was gathering troops in the name of Caesar. The author then opines that Thorius might have taken this action out of love for Pompey and hatred of Caesar, but insists that whatever Thorius' thought process at the time, he was reporting the common conjecture (*sed id qua mente, communis erat coniectura*). The soldiers were in agreement and thus had Pompey's name inscribed upon their shields. The citizens of Corduba, however, met the soldiers, begging that they not be asked to act against Caesar and that they might find common cause in their hatred of Cassius. So affected by this display, the soldiers saw that they had no need for Pompey's name. They thus erased his name from their shields and said that the revolt would be directed against Cassius. They then chose Marcellus as their leader. They joined together with the Cordubans and camped nearby. After Cassius destroyed the area around Corduba, the legions begged Marcellus to

---

8 This event and the following can be found in *B Alex.* 51–5.
9 For other references to various reports in this section, see Gaertner & Hausburg 2013, 90 n. 61.

lead them in battle against Cassius and his troops.[10] Marcellus reluctantly led the men out, since he knew that whichever side was victorious, harm would be done to Caesar.

Marcellus' reluctance to fight continues in the following chapter (*B Alex.* 61). Although pursuing Cassius and trying to hold him at bay, Marcellus wished to refrain from fighting, which the author believes was impossible, given the enthusiasm of his men. He eventually was forced to engage, when Bogud came with troops in support of Cassius. Marcellus and his men, however, could not be moved from their positions (*B Alex.* 62). Soon thereafter Lepidus came to settle the dispute, and found Marcellus immediately amenable (*B Alex.* 63). Cassius, however, resisted and tried to flee the province. On his journey, he perished when his boat sank in a storm upon the Ebro (*B Alex.* 64).

This story in the *Bellum Alexandrinum* has been described as focusing on emotions and expectations and having a strong counterfactual element.[11] It also contains elements of uncertainty of action, primarily with the characters of Thorius and Marcellus. Indeed, the author of the *Bellum Alexandrinum* admits that it is impossible to know what motivated each actor at various points. These points of uncertainty are important, for it allows others working in the same tradition to imbue their characters with motivations as they see fit, and it is exactly at these places that we find differences in the account of the *Bellum Alexandrinum* and Dio, as we will see.

Dio's description of these events is much shorter, and naturally much less detailed. In his telling, Dio reduces the number of characters to two, Quintus Cassius Longinus and Marcus Claudius Marcellus Aeserninus, with particular attention on the latter. As in the *Bellum Alexandrinum*, Dio's story is ostensibly about the rebellion in Spain against Q. Cassius Longinus. When a few soldiers tried to kill Longinus but failed, men from Corduba, along with some of Pompey's former soldiers, made M. Claudius Marcellus Aeserninus their leader (42.15.2–3). In his initial description of Marcellus, Dio states that he was not fully committed to the endeavor, but recognized the instability of the situation and the chance that they might turn out either way. Thus, he played both sides, speaking and acting entirely from the middle and waiting to see whether Caesar or Pompey might win out.[12]

---

10 *B Alex.* 60.1, a description that Gaertner & Hausburg (2013, 110) see as a demonstration of Cassius' poor leadership, in contrast to Caesar's elsewhere; they also adduce a number of other passages that are critical of Cassius.
11 Gaertner & Hausburg 2013, 121.
12 Cass. Dio 42.15.3: οὐ μὴν καὶ ὅλῃ τῇ γνώμῃ αὐτοὺς προσεδέξατο, ἀλλὰ τό τε ἀστάθμητον τῶν πραγμάτων ὁρῶν καὶ τὴν ἔκβασίν σφων ἐφ' ἑκάτερα προσδεχόμενος ἐπημφοτέριζε καὶ διὰ μέσου πάντα καὶ ἔλεγε καὶ ἔπραττεν, ὥστε, ἄν τε ὁ Καῖσαρ ἄν τε καὶ ὁ Πομπήιος κρατήσῃ, ἀμφοτέροις

From there Marcellus' actions matched his thoughts, and he actively began to play both sides. To show Pompey favor, he took to himself Pompey's former soldiers and opposed Cassius, an ally of Caesar. To demonstrate his allegiance to Caesar, he claimed he was maintaining peace among men who wished to revolt against Cassius. Dio accentuates this contraposition by placing it in an extended μέν … δέ construction (42.15.4):

> Πομπηίῳ μὲν γάρ, ὅτι τούς τε μεταστάντας πρὸς αὐτὸν ἐδέξατο καὶ τῷ Λογγίνῳ τὰ τοῦ Καίσαρος πράττειν λέγοντι ἀντεπολέμησεν, ἐχαρίσατο, Καίσαρι δὲ ὅτι καὶ τοὺς στρατιώτας, ὡς καὶ τοῦ Λογγίνου νεωτερίζοντός τι, παραλαβὼν τούτους τε αὐτῷ ἐτήρησε καὶ ἐκεῖνον οὐκ εἴασε πολεμωθῆναι.

> He favored Pompey, on the one hand, by receiving those who had transferred their allegiance to him and by fighting against Longinus, who declared he was on Caesar's side; on the other hand, he did a kindness to Caesar in taking charge of the soldiers when, as he would say, Longinus was beginning a rebellion, and in keeping these men for him and not allowing their commander to become hostile.

Dio then includes two deviations from the story as it is recounted in the *Bellum Alexandrinum*. Dio writes that Marcellus himself erased Pompey's name that the soldiers had written on their shields so that he might stay in the middle of affairs (42.15.5). This detail differs from the *Bellum Alexandrinum*, which states that the soldiers did the erasing. Dio also goes so far as to claim that Marcellus could have defeated Cassius but refused, instead making it so that he could not be blamed by either man (42.16.1). In the *Bellum Alexandrinum*, on the other hand, Marcellus merely wished to refrain from fighting, and there is no indication that his victory was guaranteed. Dio concludes the story with the notice that Marcellus held out until Caesar defeated Pompey (42.16.2). While this turn of events made Marcellus prey to Caesar's anger and led to his exile, later he was restored and honored. Cassius, on the other hand, lost his office and died on the Ebro.

σφίσι συνηγωνίσθαι δόξαι. ("The latter, however, did not accept their appointment with his whole heart, but seeing the uncertainty of events and looking for them to turn out either way, he played a double game, taking a neutral attitude in all that he said and did, so that whether Caesar or Pompey should prevail he might seem to have fought for the victor in either case.")

Although the overall story is largely similar in both texts, Dio's version of events shows important differences. As noted earlier, Dio's story focuses on just two individuals, a pairing that seems to highlight the recklessness of Cassius and the hesitancy of Marcellus. This aspect is enhanced by Marcellus' increased agency in Dio's version, such as in his erasing of the name of Pompey from his soldiers' shields and his active delaying of conflict. Finally, the timing of events seems important. In the *Bellum Alexandrinum*, the activities at Corduba seem to occur after Pompey's defeat at Pharsalus, with the author noting that Cassius was apprised of the defeat prior to the conflict between the two factions (*B Alex.* 56). In Dio, on the other hand, Marcellus takes actions that place him in a neutral position between Caesar and Pompey, so that he might seem to have fought on both sides and thus benefit from whichever of the two was victorious (42.15.3).

The differing depictions of Marcellus in these two accounts have led scholars to suggest the use of different source material. Some have posited that the negative portrayal of Cassius and the positive one of Marcellus in the *Bellum Alexandrinum* reflect the account of someone who took part in the events in Spain, and even without going this far would suggest the work of a partisan of Caesar.[13] On the other hand, the supposedly negative depiction of Marcellus in Dio can be traced to Dio's source, Livy.[14] Yet Dio's Marcellus need not be read negatively, but rather as an *exemplum* of pragmatic and calculated response to the uncertainty of civil war. Although the identity of this M. Claudius Marcellus Aeserninus is not completely certain, it seems to be the case that he is the same consul of 22 BCE who is mentioned by Dio (54.1.1) and named as a *quindecimvir sacris faciundis* at the time of the *ludi saeculares* in 17 BCE.[15] It is perhaps this aspect of Marcellus' career, namely his ability to survive and later thrive, that attracted Dio. Yet the question of Dio's source or sources lurks in the background, as Dio may have transmitted the story as it appeared in Livy or

---

13 The views are collected by Gaertner & Hausburg 2013, 90 n. 63.
14 It seems that implicit in this view is the belief that Livy was sympathetic to Pompey, thus Judeich 1885, 199, cited by Gaertner & Hausburg 2013, 90 n. 63. Thus Livy would have been responsible for the negative portrayal of Marcellus, a partisan of Caesar. Yet on a more basic level, one would expect, on this view, to find a positive portrayal of Pompey in Dio, if Dio were following Livy. For Livy's Pompeian leanings, see, e.g., Syme 1959, 58–60 and Hayne 1990. Dio's depiction of Pompey, however, is mixed at best, as can be seen in Dio's death notice for Pompey, cited above, in which Dio uses the figure of Pompey as an example of the fickleness of human fortune; cf. Millar 1964, 47 and Kemezis 2014, 112–15.
15 *CIL* 6.32323, ll. 151, 168; *PIR²* C 926.

elsewhere. Unfortunately, the notice in the *periocha* to Livy 111 is sparse.[16] Yet even if Dio did use a source other than the *Bellum Alexandrinum*, this would constitute an authorial preference for one version of events over another. Indeed, the fact that Dio included this story at all in a one-thousand-year history of Rome is an important authorial decision and suggests that he felt that the episode was thematically important. This choice, either to select among the traditions or to manipulate his source material, might also be inferred from a later episode in Book 42. Indeed, there are reasons to believe that Dio has made a sort of pairing of the characters of Marcellus and M. Caelius Rufus in this book, and it is to this topic that I now turn.

3 The Demise of M. Caelius Rufus

The events at Corduba conclude Dio's section on the foreign affairs of 48 BCE, and from there he moves to the affairs of Rome (42.17.1). Dio's narrative continues to stress the uncertainty of civil war. Dio writes that as long as matters between Caesar and Pompey were unsettled (ἔν τε ἀμφιλόγῳ καὶ ἐν μετεώρῳ), the people "ostensibly" (ἐκ μὲν τοῦ προφανοῦς) showed favor to Caesar (42.17.1). He goes on to report, however, that those who hated Caesar and preferred Pompey did so in private, which was the opposite of what they said and did publicly (42.17.3). Various reports also induced some to fear, while others became bold (42.17.3). Even when the outcome of the battle of Pharsalus was announced it was not considered trustworthy (42.18.1). While some took down statues of Pompey, others feared he would re-engage the conflict (42.18.2). Indeed, many did not believe that Pompey had died until they saw his signet ring (42.18.3). Only at that point was Caesar praised as victor and Pompey was reviled (42.19.1). The people also displayed all sorts of sycophancy, which they thought would win them Caesar's favor. In this section, Dio twice notes the counterfactual nature of their fawning: they acted as if Caesar were present and watching them, and they acted as if to gratify Caesar, rather than out of necessity (42.19.2). The following section details the honors and privileges that were then voted to Caesar (42.20).

It is in this context that we should understand the story of M. Caelius Rufus, which follows. The transition to this story is a bit abrupt, but its opening

---

16 *Propter Q. Cassii praetoris avaritiam crudelitatemque Cordubenses in Hispania cum duabus Varronianis legionibus a partibus Caesaris desciverunt.* ("Because of the cruelty and greed of praetor Quintus Cassius, the people of Corduba in Spain and two of Varro's legions deserted Caesar's cause.")

sentence shows connections to the Marcellus narrative discussed above, including the use of a counterfactual phrase (42.22.1):

ὁ δὲ δὴ Καίλιος ὁ Μᾶρκος καὶ ἀπώλετο τολμήσας τὰ περὶ τῶν δανεισμάτων ὑπὸ τοῦ Καίσαρος ὁρισθέντα, καθάπερ ἡττημένου τε αὐτοῦ καὶ ἐφθαρμένου, λῦσαι, καὶ διὰ τοῦτο καὶ τὴν Ῥώμην καὶ τὴν Καμπανίαν ἐκταράξας.

Marcus Caelius actually lost his life because he dared to set aside the laws established by Caesar regarding loans, assuming that their author had been defeated and had perished, and because as a result he stirred up Rome and Campania.

We can begin to see Caelius as the counterpoint to Marcellus. Whereas Marcellus was acutely aware of playing both sides, Caelius fell victim to emotion. Likewise, while Marcellus kept a rebellion from fomenting and thus preserved his life (and eventually advanced his career), Caelius began a rebellion and lost his life.

In Dio's version of events, Caelius was a partisan of Caesar and owed his promotion to the praetorship to this allegiance.[17] Dio notes that because Caelius failed to receive a promotion to urban praetor, he turned against both his colleague Trebonius and against Caesar's laws. This move eventually led Caelius to dole out free rent and forgive all debts (42.22.3–4). Dio's account stresses both Caelius' ambition and the breakdown of normal elections, as he states that Caesar chose Trebonius to be urban praetor, rather than have the office chosen by lot, as was customary (ὥσπερ εἴθιστο). In this way Dio highlights the factionalism of the period, which was part and parcel of his characterization of the period as ruled by "dynasts" rather than according to proper constitutional law.[18]

In order to counteract Caelius' actions, the consul P. Servilius Isauricus convened the Senate under the protection of soldiers. Despite opposition by the tribunes, he managed to have the tablets proclaiming Caelius' actions removed (42.23.1). Caelius, however, chased away the tribunes and got into an

---

17   Cass. Dio 42.22.2. This detail is an interesting tidbit, especially in light of a letter from Caelius to Cicero, which seems to have been written in January of 48 BCE (*Fam.* 8.17; for the date, see Gelzer 1968, 228 n. 1). This letter details Caelius' hesitation to join Caesar's side, as well as the fact that the people of Rome were more sympathetic to Pompey. Thus, Dio's account might accurately reflect both Caelius' uncertainty and general ambivalence about siding with either Caesar or Pompey. For Caelius' move to Caesar's side, see Clauss 1990, 536, and for his career in general, Sumner 1971, 247–8; 1973, 146–7.

18   For the power of dynasts in the late Republic, see Lange in this volume, and below.

argument with Isauricus. This prompted the Senate to meet again under guard, and they resolved to keep Caelius from acting as praetor in any capacity. They even pulled him from the rostra while he was speaking and smashed his chair (42.23.3).

Caelius, now with no powers or prospects at Rome, departed for Campania, intending to meet up with Milo, who was planning a rebellion (42.24.1).[19] Dio again stresses Caelius' anger, which he seems to associate with Caelius' poor decision-making. Dio also makes note of Caelius' desire to join Milo in order that he might do as much harm as possible to Caesar (42.24.3). By feigning a desire to go to Caesar, Caelius gained the right to depart from the consul, despite the consul's suspicion of his intentions. Caelius made his way to Campania, only to find that Milo had been killed in Apulia and that war had been declared against him by the consul (42.25.1–2). Caelius then made his way to Bruttium, where he was murdered by partisans of Caesar (42.25.3).

The story of Caelius' demise is described in several different sources.[20] The primary method of reconstruction of the episode has been to assimilate the sources and iron out the differing details.[21] In what follows, however, I will focus on the differences as possible insights into how each author dealt with the story in the context of his own work. In the *Bellum Civile*, Caesar presents the conflict as one of personal difference between Caelius and Trebonius, and by extension Caesar himself. At the beginning of the year, Caesar passed a decree to manage the large amount of unpaid debt (*B Civ.* 3.1.2–3).[22] In a later passage, Caesar fuses together the decree itself, which he calls equitable, and the character of Trebonius, who Caesar says possessed humaneness, and who acted with clemency and moderation.[23] Caelius, on the other hand, is described as "rather harsh" (*durior*) and his efforts a "disgraceful undertaking" (*turpem causam*, *B Civ.* 3.20.4–5). Once his attempts, both legal and violent, failed, Caelius, motivated by "dishonor and resentment" (*ignominia et dolore*, *B Civ.* 3.21.4), pretended to set out to Caesar, though secretly he communicated

---

19   On the connection between Caelius and Milo, see Lintott 1974, 70 and Rosivach 1980–1981, 205. For Caelius' earlier defense of Milo, see Gruen 1995, 340–4.
20   In addition to the sources surveyed here, the event is mentioned briefly by Orosius (6.15.10) and Jerome (*ad Eus.* 2.137.2). A full listing of sources can be found in Cordier 1994, 574–7; see also Volponi 1970, 266 n. 7.
21   See, e.g., Volponi 1970, 265–76 and Cordier 1994.
22   On this measure and other possible inclusions, see Carter 1993, 140–1.
23   *B Civ.* 3.20.2: *sed fiebat aequitate decreti et humanitate Treboni, qui his temporibus clementer et moderate ius dicendum existimabat.* ("But this occurred because of the fairness of the decree and the decency of Trebonius, who thought that in these circumstances the law should be carried out with clemency and moderation.")

with Milo and met up with him in Italy.[24] Milo and Caelius, however, soon perished separately, and Caesar notes that this beginning of serious matters turned out to have a quick and simple outcome.[25]

The Livian *periocha* lacks any indication of Caelius' personal motivations, though the brevity of the notice must of course be taken into account. Velleius Paterculus, on the other hand, probes these motivations more deeply. For Velleius, Caelius was driven by his own debt, which Velleius connects generally to revolution.[26] As noted above, Dio thought that Caelius acted against Caesar's laws out of anger for being passed over as *praetor urbanus*.[27] Dio's claim that Caelius was motivated by resentment reflects Caesar's account of the affair, though his use of anger as an explanatory mechanism has a bit of stock sense to it.[28] It may be the case that Dio was drawing on the account of Caesar and reflecting the political snub at the root of Caelius' activities, and this reason perhaps might have been found in Livy as well. Yet Velleius' interpretation is also valuable, though perhaps less for its actual claim than for its existence as proof of ancient authors' tendency to attribute motivations to characters.

Another consideration is the section of Dio's history in which this story falls, which Kemezis has recently called the *dynasteiai*-mode. In this mode, the few men striving for influence do little other than advance their own claims for power, and nothing is done in the interest of the people. Kemezis also observes that dynasts act entirely in the pursuit of power, or to thwart the ambitions of their competitors.[29] It is interesting to place Caelius in this light. His actions on behalf of the debtors are put in terms of his own ambition, and when he is curbed by his colleague, he attempts to harm Caesar and gain power for himself through revolution. We can therefore observe Dio's efforts to assimilate

---

24 As Clauss (1990, 537–8) notes, Caesar suppresses the fact that he was the reason for Caelius' displeasure and prefers to stress Caelius' removal from office and other related measures against him. Yet Caesar's claim that Caelius was motivated by *ignominia et dolor* is oddly similar to Caelius' own words in a letter to Cicero, in which he states that he is acting *doloris atque indignitatis causa*, seemingly with reference to his activities as praetor in 48 (*Fam.* 8.17.2).

25 *B Civ.* 3.22.4: *ita magnarum initia rerum, quae occupatione magistratum et temporum sollicitam Italiam habebant, celerem et facilem exitum habuerunt.* ("Thus the beginnings of serious matters, which caused Italy to be disturbed by a concern for the magistracies and the circumstances of the moment, had a swift and simple conclusion.")

26 Woodman 1983, 273. See also Clauss 1990, 538 n. 31 for scholars who follow this line of thinking.

27 Volponi (1970, 265–6), e.g., considers Caelius to have been motivated more by political concerns than economic ones. This also seems to be the stance of Wiseman (1971, 174).

28 Dio attributes such motivation elsewhere; cf., e.g., Julius Martialis' anger toward Caracalla for lack of promotion, 79(78).5.3.

29 Kemezis 2014, 110–11; see also Cordier 2003, 233–4.

Caelius' behavior to other powerful individuals in this period. The effect of this assimilation is to demonstrate that Caelius was not on par with the others, that he was a secondary character both in Dio's narrative and in the political realities of the period.

The chronological placement within each narrative also seems to be important for a proper understanding of Caelius' motivation in each account.[30] In Caesar's narrative, the introduction to this entire episode, *eisdem temporibus*, provides an important dating mechanism. Chapters 7–19 of Book 3 of the *Bellum Civile* detail Caesar's activities on the Adriatic coast, and the notice that the Caelius episode occurred at about the same time indicates that the conflict in Rome and subsequent uprising ought to be placed in the opening months of 48 BCE. The timing is further stressed by Caesar's use of *initio magistratus*, which indicates that Caelius began his work on behalf of the debtors from the very beginning of the year. The *periocha* of Livy's Book 111 lists Caelius' actions as the first of that book, also indicating that it occurred early in 48, if the listing of events in the *periocha* can be trusted to transmit the order of affairs in Livy.[31] Velleius Paterculus, however, places Caelius' actions contemporaneous with Caesar's fighting at Pharsalus in August of 48, thus seemingly indicating that Caelius was attempting to take advantage of Caesar's absence from Rome (2.68.1–2).[32]

This alternative tradition, if we can call it that, seems to have informed Dio's version of events. While Dio does not provide a strong chronological marker for the events, the Caelius episode seems to appear in his history either during or after the conflict at Pharsalus, a period that in Rome was full of uncertainty, in Dio's telling.[33] At 42.17.1, Dio transitions to the urban affairs of 48, describing popular reaction to the unsettled conflict between Caesar and Pompey. At 42.18.1, Dio notes that news of the outcome of the battle of Pharsalus made its way to Rome, which caused further consternation among the people. He then spends two chapters detailing the honors that Caesar received (42.20–21), before beginning his story of Caelius' demise. This timeline suggests that Dio has placed this event from early 48 at about the same time or after the battle of Pharsalus in that year. Indeed, it seems that the uncertainty of affairs, which Dio had been stressing throughout Books 41–2, informed Caelius' decision to

---

[30] On the differing dates and timelines of the available sources, see also Volponi 1970, 273–6.
[31] For this issue, see Syme 1959, 29; Bingham 1978, 474.
[32] Despite Woodman's (1983, 157) objection that Velleius' use of *dum* in this passage should not be taken literally, it is hard to think that the reader (ancient or modern) would not associate these events chronologically.
[33] At 42.18.1, Dio writes that when news of Pharsalus reached Rome, the people were hesitant (ὀκνήσας) and that the outcome was improbable (ὁ παράλογος).

rebel. This view is further strengthened by Dio's notice that Caelius went from being among the most devoted to Caesar to stirring up rebellion. Cary's translation of καθάπερ ἡττημένου τε αὐτοῦ καὶ ἐφθαρμένου (42.22.1) as "assuming that their author had been defeated and had perished" is too forceful and should likely read, "just as if he [Caesar] had been defeated and perished," yet it still correctly transmits the sense that Caelius was motivated to act in the uncertainty during or after the battle of Pharsalus.

Aside from its chronological accounting, Velleius' passage on Caelius seems important for other reasons. This episode, paired with the stories of the tribunes Caesetius Flavus and Epidius Marullus of 43 BCE, forms a digression in Velleius' narrative and returns to events passed over in their proper chronological place.[34] This grouping suggests that by the early empire Caelius' story had become a sort of literary *exemplum*. Woodman (1983, 156) has suggested that Velleius was intrigued by Caelius' *persona*, and that his story was a cautionary tale of the political violence that men of Velleius' generation detested. As noted above, we can also observe Dio's interest in Caelius' *persona*, specifically his motivations for action. While the annalistic tradition, as seen in Book III of Livy's history, suggested inclusion of the Caelius episode in a narration of the year 48, Dio might also have been interested in Caelius for other reasons, as his structuring of Book 42 suggests.

These comments of course raise the questions of Dio's use of Livy and Dio's annalistic form. On the latter question, despite earlier analyses to the contrary, it has recently been argued that Dio's use of an annalistic structure for the late Republic is loose, and that he manipulated it for his own interpretative purposes.[35] Indeed, Dio is willing to break his annalistic structure in order to complete his narration of certain events.[36] It has also been remarked, with specific reference to Books 41–2, that Dio's structure is more thematic than chronological, organized geographically and also dramatically.[37] If we assume that Dio understood the proper chronological order of the urban affairs of 48, then we would expect Caelius' story to begin his account of events at Rome, which he clearly marks off at 42.17.1. Yet his preference, as we have seen, is

---

34   For similar groupings of malcontents, see Lobur 2011, 213–14.
35   Lindholmer forthcoming: "Thus the assertion of previous scholarship that Dio follows the annalistic model in a relatively simplistic way is problematic as Dio is only accorded an occasional flexibility with the annalistic method, which is attributed to mere narrative convenience. Rather, Dio's extant Late Republic is not primarily governed by an annalistic structure but instead by Dio's own interpretative aims, while the annalistic conventions are a tool in the support and presentation of this interpretation."
36   As, for example, in his account of Caesar's Gallic campaign, 40.32–44.
37   Freyburger-Galland, Hinard, & Cordier 2002, xxvi.

to detail the uncertainty at Rome surrounding the conflict between Caesar and Pompey and to describe public and private reactions to the outcome at Pharsalus. This introduction effectively sets up the Caelius episode as an example of someone attempting to gain power for himself in the midst of the uncertainty of civil war. Caelius can therefore be seen as a counterpoint to Marcellus earlier. Whereas Marcellus understood that vacillation and remaining in the middle helped to insure his own safety during this unpredictable time, Caelius attempted to exploit the uncertainty of civil war, though he misjudged the outcome and ultimately died as a result.

4   Thematic Connections

Thus far I have been suggesting that Dio saw in the figures of M. Claudius Marcellus Aeserninus and M. Caelius Rufus two examples, loosely paired, that present varying responses to civil war. As a writer of the entirety of Roman history from the beginnings of the city to his own day, Dio both read of and experienced civil war on multiple occasions. In what follows, I will try to connect these two episodes thematically to Dio's overall history, in order to further strengthen the case made above and to highlight some of Dio's chief concerns throughout his history. I will make particular use of scenes and characters from Dio's contemporary history, as I believe his own experiences greatly informed his view of the rest of Roman history.[38]

As discussed above, Dio frames the individual responses of Marcellus and Caelius with more general and popular reactions to the civil wars. Several similar examples can be found in the history of Dio's own day. Just as popular reaction to news of Pharsalus was mixed and trust in this notice varied, so Dio mentions popular reaction to news of the death of Commodus, an event that ushered in a period of civil war.[39] Dio writes that people thought news of Commodus' death was a test of their loyalty to him, and although they hoped it was true, they feared wishing for his death more than favoring Pertinax (74[73].2.5–6[*Exc. Val.*]). Dio describes the situation just a few years later in similar terms. He states that everyone pretended to favor Septimius Severus, though they had trouble disguising their true feelings, and those that

---

38   For this view, see, e.g., Bleicken 1962, 446. For interest during the principate in the civil wars of the late Republic, see the survey in Jal 1963, 257–359.

39   Dio's literary career began in the aftermath of these civil wars, with smaller works on dreams and signs that foretold Severus' rise to power and on the civil wars themselves, the latter of which Dio incorporated into his larger history of the Romans (73[72].23.1–3[Xiph.]).

pretended too much ended up being discovered (76[75].8.5[*Exc. Vat.*]). A similar scene occurs in the conflict between Macrinus and Elagabalus in 218 CE, and in this instance Dio notably states that such behavior is typical of civil war (79[78].35.2):

μέχρι μὲν δὴ οὖν ἐν ἀμφιβόλῳ τὰ πράγματα ἦν, μετέωροι καὶ αὐτοὶ καὶ οἱ στρατιῶται οἵ τε ἰδιῶται ἦσαν, οἱ μέν τινες αὐτῶν ταῦτα οἱ δὲ ἐκεῖνα κατὰ <τὸ> στασιωτικὸν καὶ βουλόμενοι καὶ εὐχόμενοι καὶ διαθρυλοῦντες.

Up to now everything hung in the balance, both they and the soldiers, and the citizens as well, in suspense, with different people wishing and praying and spreading by rumor different things, as is the way with factional strife.

The constancy of human behavior in this instance indicates the universality of the theme in Dio's text, and comparable sentiments regarding the civil wars of the late Republic can be found elsewhere in Dio's history.[40]

Dio also shows an interest in those who are able to survive the changes of emperor in his own times. Of particular interest are those who engineer conspiracies against the emperor and manage to live on. Dio, for example, is sure to note the length of survival of those who plotted against Commodus, namely Laetus, Eclectus, and Marcia. We find out, for example, that Eclectus remained close to the emperor Pertinax, Commodus' successor, and even died with him, an act that roused Dio's admiration (74[73].10.2[Xiph.]). Furthermore, Dio reports that Laetus and Marcia were put to death by Didius Julianus, whereas Narcissus, Commodus' strangler, managed to survive into the reign of Septimius Severus.[41] P. Valerius Comazon is another such example. This man aided Elagabalus' uprising against Macrinus (79[78].39.4), and later became praetorian prefect, consul, and city prefect under Elagabalus (80[79].4.1–2, 80[79].21.2[Xiph.]), and Dio appears to name him as the sole survivor of Elagabalus' reign (80[79].21.3[Xiph.]).

Still, these survivors are few, which likely reflects the difficulty of outliving rebellion, as seen in the case of Caelius. A more practical tool for survival was vacillation, as Dio and his fellow senators show on multiple occasions throughout Dio's contemporary history. In a scene similar to the equivocation of the people mentioned above, Dio describes the senatorial response to the civil war

---

40 Cf., e.g., Cass. Dio 41.7.6, 43.37.3, and 47.6.2. See also Lange in this volume.
41 Cass. Dio 74(73).16.5(Xiph.). Dio also discusses Laetus' duplicity as a means for survival; see 74(73).6.1–3(Xiph./*Exc. Val.*) and 74(73).8.1–10.3.

between Septimius Severus and Clodius Albinus (76[75].4.1–2[Xiph.]). Despite the entire world being stirred up by these affairs, Dio and his fellow senators kept quiet, not favoring one side or the other.

An individual example of this behavior can be found in the figure of Aemilianus, discussed in the context of Severus' war against Pescennius Niger. This Aemilianus was a lieutenant (ὑποστρατήγῳ) of Niger, and in Dio's view by staying in the middle and watching the events play out (τε μεσεύων καὶ ἐφεδρεύων), he showed himself to be superior to all of the senators in both understanding and experience (75[74].6.2[Xiph./Exc. Val.]).[42] Likewise, Dio himself can be counted among those who stayed in the middle during civil war. Dio appears to have been like the majority of the senators, who preferred to keep quiet and preserve their lives. Dio provides various examples of his own vacillation and silence, which appears to have been rewarded. Not only did Dio survive this perilous period, he also thrived in his political career, holding the offices of praetor in 194 CE and consul, likely sometime during the reign of Septimius Severus. He was also a member of the *consilium* of both Severus and Caracalla, curator of Pergamum and Smyrna under Elagabalus, and he held various governorships and finally a second consulship, jointly with the emperor Alexander Severus.[43]

5 Conclusion

Books 41 and 42 of Cassius Dio's *Roman History* present a highly dramatized and thematic approach to the events of 48 BCE. Dio emphasizes, through impressionistic descriptions, the perils and uncertainty of civil war, leading up to the battle of Pharsalus and the death of Pompey. He also highlights the emergence of autocratic rule under Julius Caesar in his description of the honors and privileges that became Caesar's after Pharsalus. Dio's treatment of these years contains two anecdotal tales, which focus on the figures of M. Claudius Marcellus Aeserninus and M. Caelius Rufus, respectively. Dio's attention to these characters in particular seems to show the author's preoccupation with responses to civil war, specifically vacillation and confrontation. In the story of Marcellus, we observe the value of vacillation, as his playing both sides in the

---

42 For his career, see *PIR*² A 1211. Aemilianus' ability to stay in the middle of affairs (μεσεύων) mirrors Aeserninus' behavior (διὰ μέσου, 42.15.3). See also 41.46.1 for such behavior, in Dio's eyes, as characteristic of times of civil war.

43 An overview of Dio's career, with references and citations, can be found in Swan 2004, 1–2.

conflict of Caesar and Pompey allowed him to survive, and eventually thrive in his political career. Caelius, on the other hand, demonstrates the futility of resistance or opposition. Motivated by his anger of being passed over for a desired office, Caelius attempted to expand his political power, and, once thwarted, he fomented rebellion and lost his life. The themes contained in these stories can also be seen elsewhere in Dio's history, particularly the contemporary portion. Dio stresses the safety that lay in not choosing sides and attempting to remain neutral, and he also suggests that this was the more common path for senators, a point that can especially be seen in his own career.

It is likely that Dio's own personal experiences informed his view of the Roman past, and it was perhaps this point of view that influenced his decision to present the stories of Marcellus and Caelius in such a way. When reading Dio's version of these events against the surviving sources, it appears that Dio intentionally selected these stories because of their resonating themes and also shaped them to complement his view of history. It seems that we can therefore observe, however obliquely, some of Dio's authorial choices, his possible manipulation of his source material, his seeming re-ordering of the sequence of events, and his attribution of motivations to certain characters in the year 48 BCE. These observations suggest that Dio was a meticulous reader of his sources and a careful selector of material, and that he was attentive to highlighting themes that ran throughout the entirety of his work.

Bibliography

Berti, N. (1988) *La guerra di Cesare contro Pompeo: commento storico a Cassio Dione, libri XLI–XLII*, Milan.

Bingham, W. J. (1978) *A Study of the Livian "Periochae" and Their Relation to Livy's "Ab Urbe Condita"*, Dissertation: University of Illinois at Urbana-Champaign.

Bleicken, J. (1962) "Der politische Standpunkt Dios gegenüber der Monarchie: die Rede des Maecenas Buch 52, 14–40", *Hermes* 90, 444–67.

Carter, J. M. (1993) *Julius Caesar: The Civil War Book III*, Warminster.

Clauss, J. (1990) "The Ignoble Consistency of M. Caelius Rufus", *Athenaeum* 78, 531–40.

Cordier, P. (1994) "M. Caelius Rufus, le préteur récalcitrant", *Mélanges de l'école française de Rome* 106, 533–77.

Cordier, P. (2003) "Dion Cassius et la nature de la 'monarchie' Césarienne", in G. Lachenaud & D. Longrée (eds.), *Grecs et Romains aux prises avec l'histoire: représentations, récits et idéologie* (Rennes): 231–46.

De Franchis, M. (2016) "Tite-Live modele de Cassius Dion, ou contre modele?", in V. Fromentin *et al.* (eds.), *Cassius Dion: nouvelles lectures* (Bordeaux): 191–204.

Freyburger-Galland, M., Hinard, F., & Cordier, P. (2002) *Dion Cassius: Histoire romaine, Livres 41 & 42*, Paris.

Gaertner, J. F. & Hausburg, B. C. (2013) *Caesar and the Bellum Alexandrinum: An Analysis of Style, Narrative Technique, and the Reception of Greek Historiography*, Göttingen.

Gelzer, M. (1968) *Caesar: Politician and Statesman*, translated by P. Needham, Cambridge, MA.

Grohs, H. (1884) *Der Wert des Geschichtswerkes des Cassius Dio als Quelle für die Geschichte der Jahre 49–44 v. Chr.*, Leipzig.

Gruen, E. S. (1995) *The Last Generation of the Roman Republic* (with new introduction), Berkeley.

Hayne, L. (1990) "Livy and Pompey", *Latomus* 49, 435–42.

Heimbach, W. (1878) *Quaeritur quid et quantum Cassius Dio in historia conscribenda inde a L. XL. usque ad L. XLVII. e Livio desumpserit*, Bonn.

Jal, P. (1963) *La guerre civile à Rome: étude littéraire et morale*, Paris.

Judeich, W. (1885) *Caesar im Orient. Kritische Übersicht der Ereignisse vom 9. August 48 bis October 47*, Leipzig.

Kemezis, A. (2014) *Greek Narratives of the Roman Empire under the Severans: Cassius Dio, Philostratus and Herodian*, Cambridge.

Lindholmer, M. (forthcoming) "Exploiting Conventions: Dio's Late Republic and the Annalistic Tradition", in C. H. Lange & J. M. Madsen (eds.), *Cassius Dio the Historian: Methods and Approaches* (Leiden & Boston).

Lintott, A. W. (1974) "Cicero and Milo", *Journal of Roman Studies* 64, 62–78.

Lobur, J. A. (2011) "Resuscitating a Text: Velleius' History as Cultural Evidence", in E. Cowan (ed.), *Velleius Paterculus: Making History* (Swansea): 203–18.

Manuwald, B. (1979) *Cassius Dio und Augustus: philologische Untersuchungen zu den Büchern 45–56 des dionischen Geschichtswerkes*, Wiesbaden.

Miles, G. B. (1995) *Livy: Reconstructing Early Rome*, Ithaca, NY.

Millar, F. (1964) *A Study of Cassius Dio*, Oxford.

Pelling, C. B. R. (1982) Review of G. Zecchini, *Cassio Dione e la guerra gallica di Cesare*, *Classical Review* 32, 146–8.

Rosivach, V. J. (1980–1981) "Caelius' Adherence to the Caesarian Cause", *Classical World* 74, 201–12.

Schwartz, E. (1899) "Cassius (40)", in A. Pauly, G. Wissowa, & W. Kroll (eds.), *Realencyclopädie der classischen Altertumswissenschaft* (Stuttgart): III/2, 1684–722.

Sumner, G. V. (1971) "The *lex annalis* under Caesar", *Phoenix* 25, 246–71.

Sumner, G. V. (1973) *The Orators in Cicero's Brutus: Prosopography and Chronology*, Toronto.

Swan, P. M. (2004) *The Augustan Succession: An Historical Commentary on Cassius Dio's Roman History Books 55–56 (9 B.C.–A.D. 14)*, Oxford.

Syme, R. (1959) "Livy and Augustus", *Harvard Studies in Classical Philology* 64, 27–87.

Volponi, M. (1970) "M. Celio Rufo, ingeniose nequam," *Memorie dell'Istituto Lombardo* 3: 197–280.

Westall, R. (2016) "The Sources of Cassius Dio for the Roman Civil Wars of 49–30 BC", in J. M. Madsen & C. H. Lange (eds.), *Cassius Dio: Greek Intellectual and Roman Politician* (Leiden & Boston): 51–75.

Wiseman, T. P. (1971) *New Men in the Roman Senate, 139 B.C.–A.D. 14*, Oxford.

Woodman, A. J. (1983) *Velleius Paterculus: The Caesarian and Augustan Narrative (2.42–93)*, Cambridge.

CHAPTER 12

Cassius Dio on Sextus Pompeius and Late Republican Civil War

Carsten Hjort Lange

Recent years have seen a revival of interest in the civil war period from the death of Caesar onwards, with notable contributions such as Osgood (2006) and Welch (2012). In contrast to the classic treatment by Syme – who in a Tacitean vein saw all the protagonists as opportunists and their ideological claims as mere "political catchwords" (1939, 149–61) – recent contributions have given more weight to ideological claims and their justifications. However, as this article will suggest, although these factors played their part, opportunistic self-interest must have remained a key determinant. This is evident in Cassius Dio. Dio emulates Thucydides and his model of *stasis* (Thuc. 3.81.4–5; cf. 3.70–85), including Thucydides' views on human nature, and expresses a somewhat bleak, or alternatively, "realist" take on the late Republic. One typical issue during the civil war was the changing of sides: that is, to stop supporting one person or group and start supporting another. But how do we, as historians, approach these defections? Börm considers three different approaches to civil war and *stasis* itself (2018, 56–7): firstly, *stasis* or civil war as a by-product of interstate war; secondly, class struggle as represented in economic inequality and social tensions; and finally, civil war as a product of power struggles among the elite. This latter possibility is especially important for my purposes: any analysis of defections and the shifting allegiances of elite protagonists must approach the Roman civil wars through the lens of elite power-struggles.[1]

But when we approach Roman civil war in relation to these different ancient and modern conceptual approaches, there are issues: not least the fact that there is a burgeoning tendency in current scholarship to critique concepts such as *optimates* and *populares*,[2] and the need for a new approach to factional politics, as advocated by Steel.[3] I fully endorse this critique. According to Seager

---

[1] We should not forget the soldiers in this matter, seeking booty and so forth (but also acting as "a" political force in its own right), in the traditional manner experienced in foreign wars.
[2] Robb 2010; *contra* Wiseman 2009, 5–32.
[3] Steel 2013, esp. 236: "The simple binary model of *optimates* (best men) and *populares* is clearly inadequate to explain the position of Pompeius, Crassus and Caesar in 59 and again in 55, or the motives of those men attacking them"; cf. Beard 2015, 342: "It is often hard to make

(1972, 56) the term *factio* is not often used in republican politics to describe political interactions between Romans.[4] Similarly, the notion of "republicans" versus "non-republicans" seems highly problematic, as does "opposition."[5] There are numerous alternative concepts and approaches to signify alliances and factions within Roman society, some out of favor with scholars, some with potential: *partes*; *factio* or factions; networks of *clientelae*; alliance formations; warring groups; and warlords and alternative states as Rich and Crawford have recently suggested, respectively (Rich 2018; Crawford 2008). The most famous examples of alliance formations in Roman politics during the late Republic are undoubtedly the so-called First and Second Triumvirates, in principle the joining of dynasts, including their supporters, and with corresponding changes in the "parties" to which each was opposed.

Whatever approach we prefer, the concept of "dynasts," as used by Dio, seems in many ways a good starting point, as it is central to the description of the period by one of our main sources (cf. App. *B Civ*. 2.17, 19 on Caesar, Pompeius, and Crassus). According to Dio, Roman politics during the late Republic was centered on dynasts and their supporters. The connection between dynasts and their supporters, as indeed the connections amongst the dynasts themselves, was often and unsurprisingly loosely defined (and thus an individual-based approach seems the best way forward). Significantly, whatever "concept" was used to describe these changes in sides, this was a story of power and, according to Dio as well as Thucydides, such behavior in times

---

much coherent sense of the shifting coalitions and changing aims of the various players in the different rounds of this conflict." She goes on to suggest that self-interest was one factor, together with indecision and political realignment.

4 A reference to the domination of a faction had clear civil war connotations, and in late republican Rome a *factio* was associated with oligarchy: see *RGDA* 1.1; Sall. *Iug*. 31.15, *Cat*. 32.2; Caes. *B Civ*. 1.22.5, *B Gal*. 6.11.2; Cic. *Brut*. 164, *Att*. 7.9.4, *Rep*. 1.44, 1.68–9, 3.44; Vell. Pat. 2.18.6; Val. Max. 3.2.17; Tac. *Hist*. 1.13; Flor. 2.4.6, 2.9.8. For more examples, see Seager 1972; he accepts that factional politics existed, but also that this is not closer to the truth than "parties" (58). This seems a rather odd conclusion, mainly due to the many central descriptions of factions. Related to this, whatever we call the changing of sides (from what to what), this clearly happened often and as a result needed and needs to be described.

5 The concept does not necessarily mean "united opposition" – it might refer to "divided opposition" – but the question remains of how we define such an alleged opposition, with no common ground apart from perhaps opposition to the triumvirs. It can hardly just mean those defending the *res publica*, as all warring parties claimed to do. It is a generally ill-defined term. Even if we, for the sake of argument, accept the presence of such an opposition, this group was never homogeneous: see now also Berdowski 2015 (an English version is planned of this important work); *contra* Welch 2012, 31, talking about Sextus as "an important leader of the post-Philippi opposition," the issue being what kind of opposition we are talking about, including allegedly common goals. An individual-based approach seems preferable.

of civil war was a typical part of human nature. But, notwithstanding the vicissitudes of chance and indecision, I propose that the concept of the "balance of power" may enable us to get closer to how these changes in sides worked. This concept is returning to the forefront of international politics, partly due to new civil wars.[6] Approaching the phenomenon of civil war in Rome through the lens of the "balance of power" may help us to understand how alliances (for example groups of dynasts) and group fragmentation materialized, and how such factions formed and re-formed during periods of ancient civil war (Levy & Thompson 2010, 38–43). There is much added value to be gained in thinking about Dio as a (historical) theorist of factions, *stasis*, and civil war. In his telling of the story of young Caesar and Sextus Pompeius we are offered a showcase of the impact of civil war, and the historian's approach to it through narrative, as a "realist" and as a distinct historiographer of *stasis* and civil war.[7] As in Thucydides, violence, *stasis*, and civil war are coeval with political life and an integrated part of human nature and the practice of politics.[8]

Dio offers one perspective as part of his description of the triumvirs' war against Sextus Pompeius, vividly describing human nature in times of civil war (48.29.3):

> τοσοῦτος μὲν δὴ καὶ τῶν στάσεων καὶ τῶν πολέμων παράλογός ἐστι, δίκῃ μὲν οὐδὲν τῶν τὰ πράγματα ἐχόντων νομιζόντων, πρὸς δὲ δὴ τάς τε ἀεὶ χρείας καὶ τὰ συμφέροντά σφων τό τε φίλιον καὶ τὸ πολέμιον ἐξεταζόντων, καὶ διὰ τοῦτο τοὺς αὐτοὺς τοτὲ μὲν ἐχθροὺς τοτὲ δὲ ἐπιτηδείους σφίσι πρὸς τὸν καιρὸν ἡγουμένων.

---

6   Christia (2012) draws on *Realist International Relations Theory* and the *Balance of Power* concept (usually used in the analysis of interstate conflicts), to present a compelling new approach to the question of the formation and disintegration of alliances amongst warring groups in modern civil war conflicts (2012, esp. 32–54 on theory). Indeed, hers is the first detailed study of the ways in which civil war factions choose allies. She has convincingly shown that relative power considerations, not shared identity considerations, determine alliance formations. Similar considerations operate within the warring groups, however homogeneous they may appear. Internal group fractionalization, therefore, is always a potential problem. And adding to the issue of group formation, group identity needs to be handled with caution: "collective actors in violent conflict cannot be treated as if they were unitary, bounded entities" (Demmers 2017, 13).

7   For a rather different reading of Dio and his views on young Caesar, see Markov in this volume.

8   Palmer 2017, 409.

So great, indeed, is the perversity that reigns in factional strife and war; for men in power take no account of justice, but determine on friend and foe according as their own interests and advantage at the time dictate, and accordingly they regard the same men, now as their enemies, now as their friends, according to the occasion.[9]

In other words, self-interest is vital in civil war. To carry this idea further, in principle all individuals and warring groups naturally aimed to emerge on the winning side (Christia 2012, 3).[10] Changing sides at the opportune moment could mean survival, especially if there was no credible guarantee that the victor would not strip them of power following victory.[11]

The question remains of how Sextus fits into this highly dynamic political landscape. New trends have undoubtedly warned against underplaying the role of Sextus and his relative position during the period, but issues remain:[12] how was Sextus portrayed and understood in the ancient evidence, in historiographical terms, as part of a larger narrative? This article will consequently focus on Dio's views and approaches to Sextus within his late republican narrative. To begin, it examines the phenomenon of defection and side-switching in Dio's civil war narratives, especially the 44–43 BCE period. Afterward, I wish to turn to the Treaty of Misenum in 39 BCE in more detail as a case-study.

1   Cassius Dio: Historiography, Sextus Pompeius, and Changing Sides

In Book 52 Dio emphasizes that in 29 BCE the Romans reverted to monarchical government (52.1.1): "Such were the achievements of the Romans and such their suffering under the kingship (*basileia*), under the *demokratia* [Republic], and under the dominion of a few (*dynasteiai*), during a period of seven hundred and twenty-five years." Civil war is a catalyst; and in this case it ended up bringing about monarchy.[13] In fact, and perhaps surprisingly, Sextus is

---

9   Cf. Cass. Dio 44.51.2–3: misdeeds arise from possession of armed forces and character.
10   Emphasized by Cicero's friend Caelius in 50 BCE: "I don't suppose that it escapes you that in a domestic quarrel, men ought to take the more respectable side so long as the struggle is political and fought without weapons; but when it comes to actual fighting, they should choose the stronger, and regard the safer course the better" ([Cic.] *Fam.* 8.14.3 [SB 97]).
11   Adding to that, the sides themselves could change, e.g., in 44–43 BCE, or – if you were a supporter of Sextus Pompeius – in 39 BCE.
12   Powell & Welch 2002; Welch 2012; Gerrish 2015.
13   On Dio's (positive) account on Augustus and monarchy, see Madsen in this volume.

not singled out for criticism for his changing of sides during the civil war period.[14] This suggests that Dio regarded Sextus as one of the dynasts of the late Republic (cf. 56.37.1–7, including a "list" of dynasts). This was about the balance of power, whereas individuals – that is, individual actors, distinct from dynasts with their networks of support – were not always so lucky when they switched sides. Menas, the freedman of Sextus, is a prime example. The now-fragmentary testimony of M. Valerius Messalla Corvinus on the war against Sextus focuses partly on Menas (*FRHist.* 2.896–9); but the most telling piece of evidence from Messalla about the nature of side-switching and defection in civil war comes much later, preserved in Seneca: Messalla calls Q. Dellius "the horse-jumping acrobat of the civil wars" (*Suas.* 1.7 = *FRHist.* 2.899 [fr. 6]: *desultorem bellorum civilium*). This would have been a fitting description of Menas, but also for many other participants during the civil war period. Dio in the last sentence of chapter 54 sums up his views on Menas (48.54.7):

ὁ δὲ δὴ Μηνᾶς ἄπιστός τε φύσει ὢν καὶ τὰ τοῦ κρείττονος ἀεὶ θεραπεύων, καὶ προσέτι καὶ ἀγανακτήσας ὅτι μηδεμίαν ἀρχὴν εἶχεν ἀλλὰ τῷ Σαβίνῳ ὑπετέτακτο, πρὸς τὸν Σέξτον αὖθις ηὐτομόλησεν.

But Menas, who was naturally untrustworthy and always cultivated the stronger side, and was furthermore vexed because he held no command but had been made subordinate to Sabinus, deserted again to Sextus.

The dynasts allegedly were different, but Menas did what they often did, cultivating the stronger side, and trying to survive. Dio concludes that Menas was untrustworthy, and was ultimately slain (49.37.6). Sextus, as well as all other faction leaders or dynasts, were actors in their own right and with their own interests. *They*, unlike Menas, played the great game of power.[15]

Epstein's study on *inimicitia* (1987) provides us with ample proof that Roman politics functioned along similar lines to modern political decision-making

---

14 For a critique of the changing of sides, see Xenophon (*Hell.* 2.3.32): "It is true, of course, that all sorts of changes in government are attended by loss of life, but you, thanks to your changing sides so easily, share the responsibility, not merely for the slaughter of a large number of oligarchs by the commons, but also for the slaughter of a large number of democrats by the aristocracy." (καὶ εἰσὶ μὲν δήπου πᾶσαι μεταβολαὶ πολιτειῶν θανατηφόροι, σὺ δὲ διὰ τὸ εὐμετάβολος εἶναι πλείστοις μὲν μεταίτιος εἶ ἐξ ὀλιγαρχίας ὑπὸ τοῦ δήμου ἀπολωλέναι, πλείστοις δ' ἐκ δημοκρατίας ὑπὸ τῶν βελτιόνων.)

15 Hadas 1930, 82: "But it seemed plain that Sextus's war was a war in his personal interest only."

during times of civil war. *Inimicitia* was one of many elements contributing to a person's motivation (64), clearly so in times of civil war. Three examples will suffice: Appian, at *Bella Civilia* 1.107, talks of the potential for civil war to result from personal differences. Sallust at *Catiline* 10.5 suggests that friendship and enmity was not about merits, but convenience. He also suggests, in chapter 41 of the *Jugurtha*, that:

> The institution of parties and factions (*partes et factiones*), with all their attendant evils (*ac deinde omnes malae artes*), originated at Rome ... as the result of peace and of an abundance of everything that mortals prize most highly. (2) For before the destruction of Carthage the people and Senate of Rome together governed the *res publica* peacefully and with moderation. There was no strife among the citizens either for glory or for power (*neque gloriae neque dominationis certamen*); fear of the enemy preserved the good morals of the state (*metus hostilis ... civitatem retinebat*). (3) But when the minds of the people were relieved of that dread, wantonness and arrogance naturally arose (*lascivia atque superbia*), vices which are fostered by prosperity. (4) Thus the peace for which they had longed in time of adversity, after they had gained it, proved to be more cruel and bitter than adversity itself. (5) For the nobles began to abuse their position and the people their liberty, and every man for himself robbed, pillaged, and plundered (*sibi quisque ducere trahere rapere*). Thus the community was split into two parties (*in duas partes*), and between these the state was torn to pieces.[16]

Thus Sallust contrasts the great foreign wars of Rome with periods of civil strife and civil war. Epstein concludes that factions were about personal bonds rather than ideology (1987, 80).[17] Granted, we cannot and should not eliminate ideology from the Roman civil wars entirely: a famous and problematic example is Cicero and young Caesar as strange allies at Mutina, but ideological alignments were rapidly restored. However, we should not forget the multiple descriptions of human nature in civil war in the ancient evidence, including the role of un-ideological or extra-ideological motivations for individuals joining a particular side. The impossibility of neutrality, as well as good fortune or indeed bad luck, naturally played an important role in such decisions. We might conclude that in Dio's case the issue is his bleak view of human nature;

---

16 On Sallust's use of Thucydides, see Canfora 2006, 735-40.
17 This is similar to Kalyvas (2006) and Christia (2012), focusing on personal animosities (prior to conflict).

but again, Epstein as well as modern theory, together with parallel ancient evidence, shows us that Dio's views on the actions of individuals and dynasts during civil war should not be taken lightly.

If we are to understand Dio's view of the phenomenon of *stasis* and civil war, then several passages are indispensable; they are therefore worth quoting in full. Firstly, Dio acknowledges the role of self-interest: he writes at 37.39.3 on the Catiline conspiracy that "… most men form both friendships and enmities with reference to others' influence and their own advantage" (πρός τε γὰρ τὰς δυνάμεις τινῶν καὶ πρὸς τὰ ἑαυτῶν συμφέροντα καὶ τὰς ἔχθρας τάς τε φιλίας οἱ πολλοὶ ποιοῦνται). In a similar vein, Dio writes later in Book 37 (55.2–3) that:

> For, on the one hand, it seemed to him [Caesar; 60 BCE] that all men work more zealously against their enemies than they cooperate with their friends (πάντες ἄνθρωποι τοῖς ἐχθροῖς ἀντιπράττειν ἢ συναγωνίζεσθαι τοῖς ἐπιτηδείοις), not merely on the principle that anger and hatred impel more earnest endeavors than any friendship (ἥ τε ὀργὴ καὶ τὸ μῖσος σφοδροτέρας τὰς σπουδὰς πάσης φιλίας ποιεῖ), but also because, when one man is working for himself, and a second for another, success does not involve the same degree of pleasure, or failure of pain, in the two cases. (3) On the other hand, he reflected that it was easier to stand in people's way and prevent their reaching any prominence than to be willing to lead them to great power …

So according to Dio, hatred was always more important than friendship; and self-interest played its part. The historian adduces similar ideas later, at 45.8.3–4, in his account of the rapprochement of young Caesar and Antonius after a period of alienation. He writes:

> For when men become reconciled after some great enmity, they are suspicious of many acts that have no significance and of many chance occurrences; in brief, they regard everything, in the light of their former hostility, as done on purpose and for an evil end (πᾶν γὰρ ἑνὶ λόγῳ ὡς καὶ ἐξεπίτηδες καὶ ἐπὶ κακῷ τινι γιγνόμενον πρὸς τὸ προϋπάρξαν ἔχθος λαμβάνουσι). And in the meantime those who are neutral (οἱ διὰ μέσου ὄντες) aggravate the trouble between them by bearing reports back and forth under the pretence of good-will and thus exasperating them still further (προσποιήσει εὐνοίας ἐπιπαροξύνουσιν αὐτούς). (4) For there is a very large element which is anxious to see all those who have power at variance with one another, an element which consequently takes delight

in their enmity and joins in plots against them. And the one who has previously suffered from calumny is very easy to deceive with words adapted to the purpose by friends whose attachment is free from suspicion. Thus it was that these men, who even before this had not trusted each other, became now more estranged than ever.

We may conclude that in Dio, as well as in Thucydides (3.82.8), neutrality was impossible. Atticus was, it would seem, the odd one out (Nepos *Att.* 11.5). However, in Thucydides neutrality is impossible because neither faction will trust the neutral party (thus an external compulsion); but in this passage of Dio, at least, the compulsion seems to be internal.

If we consider Sextus Pompeius from the time when he was in Spain (46 BCE) to the battle of Naulochus (36 BCE), an interesting picture of his "civil-war" career emerges, which can be summarized in seven points: (1) Spain and the battle at Munda against Caesar, followed by insurgency; (2) agreement with Lepidus and the *res publica*; (3) election to the *praefectura classis* and assuming control over Sicily in his capacity (as he no doubt will have claimed) as *praefectus classis et orae maritimae ex senatus consulto*;[18] (4) the proscriptions, in which he loses his assignment and is, according to Dio, declared a *hostis* despite (allegedly) having had nothing to do with the killing of Caesar (46.48.4); (5) Brundisium, where he is declared the enemy of the triumvirs due to problems with the grain supply and raids on Italy; (6) the Pact of Misenum, in which Sextus becomes the *de facto* fourth triumvir; and, finally, (7), when in 38 BCE the relationship collapses, war is "declared," and in 36 Sextus is defeated

---

18   RRC 511/1: *PRAEF·CLAS·ET·ORAE·MARIT·EX·SC*. He received this assignment early in 43 BCE (Vell. Pat. 2.73.2; App. *B Civ.* 3.4, 4.84). Dio provides the context (46.40.3): "In a word, all that had been done for Caesar to thwart Antonius was now voted to others to thwart Caesar himself. And to the end that, no matter how much he might wish it, he should not be able to do any harm, they arrayed all his personal enemies against him. Thus to Sextus Pompey they entrusted the fleet, to Marcus Brutus Macedonia, and to Cassius Syria together with the war against Dolabella." (τό τε σύμπαν ὡς εἰπεῖν, ὅσα τῷ Καίσαρι ἐπὶ τὸν Ἀντώνιον ἐγεγόνει, ταῦτα ἐπ᾽ αὐτὸν ἐκεῖνον ἄλλοις ἐψηφίσθη. καὶ ὅπως γε ἂν μηδ᾽ ἂν τὰ μάλιστα βουληθῇ τι κακὸν δρᾶσαι καὶ δυνηθῇ, πάντας αὐτῷ τοὺς ἐχθροὺς ἐπήσκησαν· τῷ τε γὰρ Πομπηίῳ τῷ Σέξτῳ τὸ ναυτικὸν καὶ τῷ Βρούτῳ τῷ Μάρκῳ τὴν Μακεδονίαν τῷ τε Κασσίῳ τήν τε Συρίαν καὶ τὸν πόλεμον τὸν πρὸς τὸν Δολοβέλλαν ἐνεχείρισαν.) This is all looked at from young Caesar's perspective (see also Welch 2012, esp. 185–6). Sextus lost the assignment when he was proscribed (Cass. Dio 47.12.2, 48.17.1). Of course, the Senate was in Rome, not at Sicily. The actor-and-self-interest-approach appears pertinent. Sextus, as did Antonius later, may have claimed that he was legitimate and that the triumvirs were indeed the illegitimate party.

at Naulochus. In effect, this is rather similar to young Caesar's behavior, as well as others during the civil war period.[19]

To add a further dimension to the story, Caesar's final triumph, following his defeat of Pompeius' sons at Munda in 45 BCE, was over civil opponents only.[20] After Gnaeus' defeat, Sextus established a base in eastern Spain, recruiting an army from survivors of the Pompeian forces and the local communities and using guerrilla tactics in his fight against the *res publica* (as famously Sertorius before him). He inflicted several defeats on Caesarian commanders – including gaining a legion after putting Asinius Pollio to flight[21] – and established control over much of Spain by 44 BCE (for Sextus' activity in Spain see Lowe 2002). After being appointed governor of Narbonese Gaul and Nearer Spain in 44, Lepidus opened negotiations with Sextus, who agreed to withdraw from Spain. In the agreement Sextus was promised a way back from exile to Rome and the opportunity to buy back his family property there; we will return to this in a moment.[22] Cicero (*Phil.* 5.40–1) mentions a proposal he made to honor Lepidus because he had avoided civil war with Sextus Pompeius. This is similar to the joint ovation of 40 between Antonius and young Caesar (Degrassi 1947, 86–7, 568; cf. 342–3, Fasti Barb.). The Fasti Triumphales and the Fasti Barberiniani both suggest that Lepidus had won a triumph *ex Hispania* (Degrassi 1947, 86–7, 567; 342–3 Fasti Barb.). In both cases, this was peace through diplomatic concord, as opposed to civil war. The fact that Sextus Pompeius did not receive a triumph, jointly with Lepidus, may mean that most likely he was still in principle perceived as the tolerated (former) enemy, as I have suggested at greater length elsewhere (Lange 2016, 83–6). Syme (2016, 199) rightly concludes that Sextus was ready to lay down arms and come to terms with the government of Rome; this was a serious blow to the liberators, as Cicero's exhortation to Sextus, "*Sextum scutum abicere nolebam*," suggests (Cic. *Att.* 15.27.1, 16.1.4, 15.29.1: "I did not want Sextus to throw away the shield"). Dio's take on the story is as follows (45.10.6):

καὶ οὕτως ὁ Σέξτος νικήσας πάντα ὀλίγου τὰ ταύτῃ κατέσχε. δυνατοῦ δὲ ἤδη αὐτοῦ ὄντος ὁ Λέπιδος τῆς τε ὁμόρου Ἰβηρίας ἄρξων ἀφίκετο, καὶ ἔπεισεν αὐτὸν ἐς ὁμολογίαν ἐλθεῖν ἐπὶ τῷ τὰ πατρῷα κομίσασθαι. καὶ οὕτω καὶ ὁ Ἀντώνιος

---

19 Remembering Mutina it is needless to say that Augustus did not mention in *RGDA* 1 that he had collaborated with the assassins of Caesar.
20 Liv. *Per.* 116; Vell Pat. 2.56; Suet. *Iul.* 37; Plin. *HN* 14.97; Quint. *Inst.* 6.3.61; Plut. *Caes.* 56.7; Cass. Dio 43.42; Flor. 2.13.88–9.
21 A deal was necessary after his victory over Asinius Pollio in 43. See Hadas 1930, 54–5; Berdowski 2011, 40.
22 Vell. Pat. 2.63.1; App. *B Civ.* 2.107, 3.46; Cass. Dio 43.51.8, 45.10.6.

διά τε τὴν τοῦ Λεπίδου φιλίαν καὶ διὰ τὴν τοῦ Καίσαρος ἔχθραν ψηφισθῆναι ἐποίησεν.

In this way Sextus conquered and gained possession of nearly the whole region. When he had thus become powerful, Lepidus arrived to govern the adjoining portion of Spain, and persuaded him to enter into an agreement on the condition of recovering his father's estate. And Antonius, influenced by his friendship for Lepidus and by his hostility toward Caesar, caused such a decree to be passed.

There is however more to the story (Cass. Dio 45.9.4): Sextus had been pardoned by Caesar, and this was now confirmed. He was to receive back the money gained by the selling of his ancestral estate, but Antonius retained the lands. This seems to have been part of Antonius' policy to win over people in the fight against young Caesar (45.9). Lepidus then arrives and a deal is struck between the two, with Sextus recovering his father's estate (as above). The maximizing of one's own interests, so typical for a period of civil war, is visible in this development. Antonius was later again going to act according to his own best interests, or so he thought, after the Treaty of Misenum, again with Sextus as the loser – to which I will return momentarily. Antonius should be given due credit for outmaneuvering Sextus politically during this great game of the dynasts.

However we look at this – dynasts or not – Sextus changed sides from that of the rebellion and that of his father Pompeius Magnus, to that of the consul Antonius. This may have been the reason why Dio found it necessary to emphasize that the brothers both bore the name of Pompeius (42.5.7). He thus (or so we can almost claim!) defected to a Caesarian: a significant volte-face, even though we must bear in mind that this Caesarian had, in fairness, called an amnesty on 17 March 44 BCE to prevent further bloodshed. Acceptance of an amnesty had effectively meant sparing the surviving assassins of Caesar. Antonius hoped to make an alliance with the slayers of the tyrant, who themselves were trying to survive. However, after the burial of Caesar the assassins were certainly not safe. Later at Mutina the alliances, as pointed out above, become even stranger. The balance of power is evident: Caesar's assassins and Caesar's heir were on the same side, this time opposing Antonius, with Caesar's veterans fighting on opposing sides. The focus had shifted towards a mutual enemy, an alliance against the strongest faction: Antonius (cf. Cass. Dio 45.14.1–3).

In April 43 BCE, after the Mutina war, the Senate appointed Sextus *praefectus classis*. Dio (later in his narrative, 40 BCE) sums up the problems facing the triumvirs after the proscription of Sextus in detail (48.17): when he was proscribed he naturally resumed preparations for war, or perhaps more precisely, tried to maximize his position in a civil war period. He started building ships (*triremes*), receiving deserters, and winning the support of pirates, through whom he hoped to become master of the sea off Italy. This would enable him to harass harbors and engage in pillaging raids. In the end he took Sicily. In effect this was the doing of the triumvirs' having proscribed Sextus.[23]

The inherent problems in the Roman system of the late Republic have been masterfully described by Crawford as one of "alternative states." These "alternative states," mostly in the provinces, such as Sertorius in Spain in the 70s, Pompeius in the east in the 60s, and Caesar in Gaul in the 50s, included alternative career structures and a local manpower resource, due to the Roman and Italian settlement overseas (2008, 636; of course non-Roman allies were key too). Men who had served an "alternative state" often showed little interest in returning to the Roman state. They are, according to Crawford, an integrated part of the period. The dynasts of the late Republic, on this model, behave like (alternative) states, even negotiating with other states (2008, 637). But the true importance of this model is that it turns Rome into something of a *failed* state, lacking control over the military and indeed the dynasts.[24] The *consilia* of these dynasts are like those of the rulers of states (637–8). This all

---

23 The question remains as to whether this marks Sextus Pompeius as a "republican," on which see recently Harris (2016, 99): "… but if Sextus ever, after Philippi, imagined that the republican political system could be restored (and there is no evidence to that effect) he would have been dreaming." The coinage is the only direct evidence for Sextus Pompeius' "ideology," and Welch wants us to believe that it was co-ordinated with that of Brutus and Cassius (2012, 182–95). The chief theme of Sextus Pompeius' coinage is his family – his father and brother – and the ties of *pietas* between them, and linked motifs like the Neptune cult (*RRC* 511; see also Rich 2018, 285). The coinage of Sextus makes no reference to *libertas* or related themes, in marked contrast to the coinage of Brutus and Cassius, with all its explicit references to the Ides of March and related issues. Looking at Sextus' operations in 42–40 BCE, were he a dedicated "republican," we might have expected positive action in support first of Brutus and Cassius, and later of L. Antonius. In fact his failure to take the offensive, at the time of the Perusine War and later, is Appian's central criticism of him (*B Civ*. 5.25, 143; cf. Powell 2002, 104–5; Welch 2012, 226). Sextus' role as a "republican" rests on Cicero's letters (*Att*. 14.13 for example). This raises many issues, not least the incorrect assumption that an individual's sympathies and particular circumstances never change. This presents a static picture of alliance formation. And we may add: was Cicero right in the first place?

24 See Strachan 2013, 42. To my mind, however, there remain some problems in supporting the idea that Rome imploded or failed in any modern sense of the concept *as a state* in the late Republic, mainly because the different factions of the civil war fought *for the supremacy of* the state, not in order to dissolve it, even if this partly occurred with the victory of Augustus. For a more developed argument, see Lange 2016, 20–4. Having said that,

greatly weakened the central government in Rome itself. Many players during the late republican civil war were not, however, Crawford's "alternative states." Rather, they were dynasts/factions. Furthermore, Caesar, Pompeius, and their elite associates always wanted to use what they had acquired in their "alternative states" to advance their careers on their return to Rome. The civil war broke out in 49 BCE not because Caesar did not want to leave Gaul but over the terms on which he would return to Rome. Sextus, however, was an "alternative state" – and behaved, Dio says, like a head of state (47.12.3) – or, to use similarly interesting language, a warlord, another concept currently in vogue; that is, an individual controlling a small slice of territory, usually in defiance of genuine state authority and through a combination of patronage and force (see Marten 2011, 303). Undoubtedly, the dominant warlord in the later phase of the civil wars during the late Republic was Sextus.[25] However, after Philippi and Perusia, there was surely no realistic prospect of overthrowing both Antonius and young Caesar. The best that Sextus and other survivors could realistically hope for would be to join with either one or both of the chief triumvirs. His preference was perhaps throughout for combining with Antonius against young Caesar, but failing that he was prepared to combine with them both, as at Misenum. His maneuvering before the agreement is best interpreted just as seeking to gain the best deal.[26]

2   The Pact of Misenum

Sextus Pompeius became part of the inner circle of the Triumvirate after the meeting at Misenum in 39 BCE due to his "alternative Sicilian state": he had the potential to be a sufficiently dangerous opponent due to this competitive state building.[27] Sextus in effect became another Lepidus, the fourth man in

---

the lack of control of the dynasts, the legions, as well as the fact there was continuous civil war, do indeed support the idea that Rome was a failed state.

25   Rich (2018, 284): "With Sicily (and for a time also Sardinia) as his base, Sextus was able to build up a substantial fleet and use it to raid shipping and the Italian coast to such effect that in 39 Antony and Octavian were constrained to come to terms with him at Misenum. However, this settlement soon broke down, and the ensuing war ended in 36 with decisive victory for Octavian ...". Rich later concludes (285): "Sextus was never able to challenge for the control of the central government, and from the perspective of those holding that government he was in rebellion except for brief periods in 44–43 and 39–38."

26   Cf. App. *B Civ.* 5.70: Menodorus argued for keeping up the war in the hope of better terms; 5.71: Sextus was hoping to take Lepidus' place.

27   On the Treaty of Misenum, see now mainly Berdowski 2011. On competitive state building, see Kalyvas 2006, 218. Dio (47.36.4, 47.38.1) suggests that Sextus was making an attempt

a constellation dominated by Antonius and young Caesar. The triumvirs had little choice but to accommodate him,[28] even if they viewed him as a renegade. This story is best told not as a piece of historiography, but rather in more traditional terms as a piece of narrative history, including mainly Appian, in order to establish what really happened and – as far as we can tell – to better establish Dio's role in the telling of the story.[29]

Arrangements made at the time of the Pact of Misenum in 39 BCE imply that the Triumvirate would be extended for a second term. Consuls were designated up to 31, with young Caesar and Antonius due to hold the consulship, each for the third time, in that year (cf. App. *B Civ.* 5.73; Cass. Dio 50.10.1). According to Dio (48.35.1) the triumvirs appointed the consul-designates for eight consecutive years. Vervaet (2010, esp. 84–6) rightly emphasizes that the Misenum Treaty would have involved adjustment, as Dio (48.36.4–5) subsequently indicates that Sextus Pompeius secured magistracies for himself and his associates, acting in this regard as a typical dynast (Appian suggests that the deal was done at Misenum). Appian (*B Civ.* 5.73) states that Antonius and young Caesar hoped in their third consulships to restore the *politeia*.[30] The anticipated second triumviral term, it was thus suggested, would be the last, as they envisaged that by this point they would have accomplished the triumviral assignment and could restore their powers to the Senate and People.[31]

According to Appian, Sextus Pompeius wanted to take the place of Lepidus in the Triumvirate, who was not present at Misenum, and share power with

---

on Italy in 42 BCE (the triumvirs were not masters of the sea: see Cass. Dio 47.37.6, 48.7.4, 48.19.2, 48.38.1).

28 De Souza 1999, 190, talks of the recognition of the strength of Sextus.
29 The different factions changed sides during conflict, and this forced them to rethink their justification. The triumvirs had their "pirates and slaves narrative" (Lange 2016, 115–21). This is supported by two letters written by young Caesar which accuse Sextus Pompeius of encouraging piracy (App. *B Civ.* 5.77, 80). This may derive from the autobiography of Augustus (Smith forthcoming; alternatively, Asinius Pollio or Seneca; for Appian's use of the autobiography, see his citation of the speeches by L. Antonius and young Caesar before Perusia [App. *B Civ.* 5.42–5, *Ill.* 14]), and importantly, the letters can be dated to 36 BCE (neither 5.77 nor 5.80 are mentioned in the index of quoted passages of Welch 2012; Welch 2015). The piracy narrative was not developed late (as it was necessary for the triumph; Lange, as above). As for Sextus, he had a different narrative: he was a *de facto* head of state and acted as such. One issue in particular has had an enormous effect on the recent scholarship concerning Sextus, namely the question as to whether he was a pirate or not, or perhaps more precisely, whether he used piratical methods (so for example raids, a standard way of fighting in ancient times): see Hadas 1930, 70; Syme 1939, 228; De Souza 1999, 185–95; Powell & Welch 2002; Welch 2012; Osgood 2006, 203; Lange 2009, 33–8.
30 "To restore the government to the people" (ἀποδώσειν τῷ δήμῳ τὴν πολιτείαν).
31 Lange 2009, 30–1; Welch 2012, 230–51.

Antonius and young Caesar.[32] Even if we differentiate between changing of sides (supporting a particular dynast) and making a treaty with fellow dynasts, the fact remains that our evidence claims that Sextus wanted to join the Triumvirate. This is a question of balance of power. Appian's view is supported by parallel evidence, but not Dio, or perhaps better, only indirectly as the logical consequence of the deal. This of course does not suggest that Sextus agreed with whatever politics the triumvirs had – this is about alliances. A deal was proposed: Sextus was to withdraw from Italy and stop giving sanctuary to slaves. Furthermore, he was to end his naval blockade (hindering the grain ships arriving in Rome). As part of the deal Sextus would gain authority over Sicily, Sardinia, and Corsica, and be elected consul *in absentia*.[33] Dio (48.36.3) adds that all exiles apart from the assassins of Caesar could return, thus echoing the policy of restoration visible at Sulla's Mithridatic triumph in 81. Furthermore, Sextus was to be consul and augur, and to receive money from his father's estate, and to govern Sicily, Sardinia, and Achaia for five years.[34] He should also not receive deserters; he should acquire no more ships, and he should have no bases in Italy.

The terms of the Misenum Treaty are intriguing.[35] The evidence clearly suggests that Antonius did not want to hand over the Peloponnese to Sextus.[36] Welch suggests that the surrender of land was the result of an earlier deal between Sextus and Antonius,[37] but what is important is that Sextus and Antonius clearly also had differences and competing interests. The triumvirs, certainly young Caesar, had realized that Sextus' fleet was a problem as they had no fleet to counter his; there was consequently a paragraph on shipbuilding. Dio (48.36.1–2) adroitly describes the problem facing the triumvirs, suggesting that, where young Caesar and Antonius brought their armies to the conference, Sextus brought along his fleet.

Returning to the idea that the factions wanted to use what they had acquired in their "alternative states" to advance their careers on their return

---

32 App. *B Civ.* 5.71–2; cf. Vell. Pat. 2.77; Liv. *Per.* 127; Plut. *Ant.* 32.1.

33 In 35 BCE (consulship in absence: App. *B Civ* 5.72; Vervaet 2010, 86–7).

34 On Sulla's triumph, see Lange 2016, 101–5. For the assignments in a timeframe equal to those of the triumvirs, see Lange 2009, esp. 19; for a different view see Eckert 2016, esp. 80 (cf. 201), who underestimates the impact of civil war and the necessity to turn something negative into something more positive (for one example, Sulla ended the civil war and as a result the *restitutio* in connection with Praeneste was portrayed as something positive). Sextus' titles of augur and consul designate were cancelled by young Caesar and Antonius in their Tarentum agreement in 37 BCE (Dio 48.54.6).

35 App. *B Civ.* 5.71–2; Cass. Dio 48.36.3–6 (48.35–6 for the treaty); Berdowski 2011.

36 App. *B Civ.* 5.77; Cass. Dio 48.46.1.

37 Welch 2012, esp. 230–8.

to the metropolis, Sextus interestingly marks a key contrast here: even under the Misenum Treaty his return to the metropolis was not envisaged – he was to hold the consulship in absence. This, however, was not necessarily because he did not want to return to Rome, but (also) because the triumvirs would not allow this. Without going into much detail on military matters, it is clear that Sextus could hardly have hoped to win the war, certainly not against the combined efforts of the triumvirs. Importantly, the treaty terms in effect acknowledged that Sextus had engaged in raiding, as I mentioned earlier.[38] The reason for such raids is almost always the same, namely the inability, due to military weakness, to employ conventional methods of fighting (Boot 2013, xxiii). Sextus' tactics thus emerged entirely from the necessities of the composition of his forces: one of the reasons for which he was so dangerous, even if he could not win (at least on his own), was the opportunity for asymmetrical tactics offered by his fleet, his main military asset.

After the collapse of the Misenum Treaty, young Caesar started to make ready for war by building a fleet (Hadas 1930, 118–19, with evidence). As during the First Punic War, a victory in Sicily was only possible with a fleet. Having said that, a victory on land was also part of the equation. The ending of the war would always include a land battle, or the surrender of one party; Sextus never had a chance in this numbers game:[39] the invasion force is one matter, the total number of troops available to young Caesar something rather different. From the outset Sextus sought a political victory. His strategy therefore clearly had elements of attrition, that is to say raiding and starving Rome. The reasons behind this are obvious, if we accept that he was an actor in his own right and with his own interests: Sextus wanted to become the fourth triumvir.[40]

---

38 As for the operational mode of Sextus, the (guerrilla) raids were irregular, based on ambush, harassment, and attrition, but at the same time an extremely effective form of warfare: Vell. Pat. 2.73.3; Flor. 2.18.1–2; Plut. *Ant.* 32.1; App. *B Civ.* 5.77, 80; Cass. Dio 48.46.4–5. On the hunger in Rome see Cass. Dio 48.18.1; App. *B Civ.* 5.43; and Oros. 6.18.19. According to Powell 2002, 103: "Seizing Sicily, he used the island – along with Sardinia and Corsica – not to launch a full-scale invasion of Italy but to mount a naval blockade of Rome's seaborne imports, and most importantly of her grain supply." This may be so, but blockading was an act of war. This is thus equal to the famous "Starvation Blockade" of World War I, with the British Navy successfully blockading Germany in a war of attrition (see Halpern 2006). Berdowski (2011, 44–5) rightly stresses that a regular land invasion would have been impossible (without support – that is, without Antonius). Sextus in fact tried to implement his father's "Themistoclean" strategy (see Cic. *Att.* 10.8.4). Cicero found the idea of blockading Italy into starvation absolutely horrendous.

39 Brunt 1971, esp. 498–500; 507–8 on the fleet.

40 Simpson (2012) has recently advocated a promising new theory of war that takes into account the transformation of modern warfare. He redefines the traditional paradigm of war and outlines two types: (1) those fought to establish military conditions for a political

Where does all this leave us? It is time to look in further detail at Sextus as an actor in his own right and with his own interests.[41] I am not denying that Appian in Book 5 (*B Civ.* 5.54) suggests an early deal between Antonius and Sextus. Appian (*B Civ.* 5.61–2) even went as far as to suggest that the triumvirs disagreed on what to do with the enemy, probably because young Caesar was unhappy that Antonius had intervened in Italy, where he presided.[42] This all occurred as relationships between the triumvirs declined: young Caesar took over Gaul when the governor Calenus died, and then there was the civil war at Perusia (App. *B Civ.* 5.51; Dio 48.20.3). There is no denying that after the Perusine War Antonius arrived at Brundisium in 40 BCE and Rome was on the verge of another conflict, this time between the two triumvirs. Their soldiers, however, refused to fight. Berdowski (2011, 33–4; App. *B Civ.* 5.56–7) rightly suggests that in this environment young Caesar was not afraid of Sextus' military potential, but of a potential cooperation between Sextus and Antonius. He also suggests that Sextus helped Antonius, perhaps unrequested, during this period just before Brundisium, conquering Sardinia and attacking coastal regions in southern Italy. This may however be a story invented to discredit Antonius. In his account of the developments after Philippi, Dio (48.2.1–2) emphasizes that Sicily and Sardinia were the property of all triumvirs: they were occupied by Sextus, but this was clearly only a temporary setback. Young Caesar was to make war on Sextus if he made a hostile move (48.2.2). Consequently, even if the story of Sextus and Antonius is right – which it most likely is, as another potential deal between dynasts – it soon changed afterward, as Antonius decided to continue his arrangements with young Caesar. If anything, Antonius was using Sextus in his own struggle. In the end the settlement of Brundisium extended the triumvirs' assignment: the new task given to young Caesar, as I mentioned earlier, was to deal with Sextus and thus to conclude the civil war.[43] Under these extreme circumstances Antonius, logically, was ready to make a deal with Sextus should it be necessary (Osgood 2006, 187). Dio (48.20.1) sums it up as follows:

---

solution – a military outcome sets conditions for a political solution; and (2) those that directly seek political, as opposed to military, outcomes, which lies beyond the scope of the traditional paradigm.

41 Correspondingly, Welch's section entitled *The Antonian-Republican alliance of 40 and the pact of Brundisium* does invite a rather different conclusion (2012, 230–8).
42 Suet. *Aug.* 13.3; Lange 2009, 26–33.
43 App. *B Civ.* 5.65; Cass. Dio 48.28.4; Lange 2009, esp. 29–33.

> διά τε οὖν ταῦτα καὶ διὰ τὸ τοὺς φεύγοντας αὐτὸν ὑποδέχεσθαι τήν τε τοῦ Ἀντωνίου φιλίαν πράττειν καὶ τῆς Ἰταλίας πολλὰ πορθεῖν, καταλλαγῆναί οἱ ὁ Καῖσαρ ἐπεθύμησε· διαμαρτὼν δὲ τούτου ἐκείνῳ μὲν Μᾶρκον Οὐιψάνιον Ἀγρίππαν πολεμῆσαι ἐκέλευσεν.

> For these reasons, and because Sextus was harboring the exiles, cultivating the friendship of Antonius, and plundering a great portion of Italy, Caesar desired to become reconciled with him; but when he failed of that, he ordered Marcus Vipsanius Agrippa to wage war against him.

Even if Dio refers to a potential deal between Antonius and Sextus, as also mentioned by Appian, both statements certainly point towards a balance of power game between the leading dynasts (see below, Dio 48.29.1).[44]

Appian (*B Civ.* 5.65) refers to the task of eliminating Sextus: "[Young] Caesar was to make war against Pompeius unless they should come to some arrangement, and Antonius was to make war against the Parthians to avenge their treachery toward Crassus" (πολεμεῖν δὲ Πομπηίῳ μὲν Καίσαρα, εἰ μή τι συμβαίνοι, Παρθυαίοις δὲ Ἀντώνιον, ἀμυνόμενον τῆς ἐς Κράσσον παρασπονδήσεως). In the end Sextus took the bait and made a deal with the triumvirs. This was also the setting for the joint ovation of Antonius and young Caesar in 40 BCE. All combatants during this period were clearly keeping their options open. The triumvirs simply had no choice but to accommodate Sextus, and there was always pressure for peace and for potential alliances.[45]

If we turn to subsequent developments, the Brundisium Treaty later suggests that Antonius had come around and accepted Sextus as a problem, or alternatively, had decided that the alliance with young Caesar was more important than that with Sextus. Dio writes in Book 48 (29.1), "They accordingly divided the empire anew in this way and undertook in common the war against Sextus, although Antonius through messengers had taken oaths by which he had bound himself to Sextus against Caesar" (τὴν μὲν οὖν ἀρχὴν οὕτως αὖθις διεδάσαντο, τὸν δὲ δὴ πόλεμον τὸν πρὸς τὸν Σέξτον ἐκοινώσαντο, καίτοι τοῦ Ἀντωνίου ὅρκους πρὸς αὐτὸν δι᾽ ἀγγέλων ἐπὶ τῷ Καίσαρι πεποιημένου). This sentence more than anything shows Dio's views on the matter, but at the same time it most likely reflects the reality of the historical situation: the three men were dynasts, and this was about the balance of power. Earlier deal or not, Antonius decided

---

44 It needs of course to be acknowledged that there were others who really did not want more civil war, e.g., the veterans and the *plebs urbana* among others.
45 App. *B Civ.* 5.68–9; Cass. Dio 48.16.3.

to stick to young Caesar, but at the same time hoped for a deal with Sextus, as Appian suggests. Brundisium turned Sextus into the enemy.

Dio's account supplements the picture further. At 48.30.4 he again mentions an agreement between Sextus and Antonius to make war on young Caesar; but then realizing that it was not meant to be, Sextus ordered Menas to raid Italy. The result comes in chapter 31 (48.31.4): the enemy again reverted to a "friend," as the triumvirs were forced to make a deal with Sextus. This again clearly singles him out as a dynast, as an important player of the period. Appian (*B Civ.* 5.52) suggests that Sextus attempted to make an alliance with Antonius against young Caesar, and that Antonius was flexible in his response. If young Caesar was his ally, he would try to make peace between Sextus and young Caesar; if young Caesar was his enemy, Sextus would be his ally. In Appian (*B Civ.* 5.63) there is a reply from young Caesar: he wants Antonius to send Sextus home to Sicily. The context now is a possible agreement between the two triumvirs. It does not conclusively show that an agreement was ever reached between Antonius and Sextus. This is about interests and about actors positioning themselves in a growing crisis, seeking to identify the likely victor, while at the same time trying to maximize personal gain. We might suggest that young Caesar always wanted war with Sextus, but Sextus certainly knew this, as did Antonius.[46]

As I have already mentioned, the Misenum agreement nevertheless collapsed soon after. Appian (*B Civ.* 5.77) summarizes the problems: it is the accord between Sextus and young Caesar which broke down, and logically this explanation focuses on these two, since it was they who faced each other in Italy. Adding to that, another reason for the collapse of the agreement was the taxes owed to Antonius from the Peloponnese, and thus to Antonius by Sextus. Furthermore, Sextus was accused of building more ships and raiding the seas, possibly true.[47] Nobody could blame him. Sextus knew his fleet was his only chance, as his army was smaller. These details are part of the equation. Referring to the Misenum Treaty, Dio, as mentioned earlier, clearly states that Sextus was not allowed to build more ships; he should not accept deserters and not keep any bases on the mainland of Italy. This was never going to be an agreement between friends: this is about politics and containment. This is

---

[46] Welch 2002, 53: "My own view is that Sextus would never willingly have negotiated with Octavian and that the Treaty of Misenum, which in many respects does him so much credit, was the best of a bad bargain and a compromise he was forced to make."

[47] See Welch 2012, 261–5, who attempts to blame young Caesar for the collapse, and dismisses accusations of piracy.

about mistrust. This is truly about the balance of power. Appian (*B Civ.* 5.77) in the end may be right in suggesting that they all disregarded the treaty.

There can be no doubt that in 39 BCE, Sextus for his part was ready to make a deal with the triumvirs. This, or so I believe, had nothing to do with republican sentiments, but with power and survival.[48] Welch is right to suggest a necessary compromise (2012, 53); this was, I hope to have shown, essential for all the dynasts of the period. Her conclusion (2012, 235), however, that Antonius wanted to change to the "republican" side is unsubstantiated by the ancient evidence. Antonius, later accompanied by young Caesar, simply knew Sextus had to be stopped, but at the same time, he, Antonius, and the other dynasts, kept their options open. The main difference was that young Caesar, it seems, preferred war, while Antonius sought an arrangement. As for Sextus: he knew there was no realistic prospect of overthrowing both Antonius and young Caesar. In Dio, these are related to the balance of power between the dynasts and *unrelated* to personal sentiments concerning that which is or is not "republican."

In the end Sextus was used in the political game between Antonius and young Caesar, even if he actively tried to end up on the winning side: he realized that he had been excluded and as a result he ordered raids on Etruria and other places (Cass. Dio 48.30.4–5). His options were limited. Scholars have been baffled by Antonius' decision to desert the "alliance" with Sextus.[49] All participants, however, were opportunistic. The Misenum Treaty was cynical in as much as it was a necessary deal for all parties (*contra* Welch 2012, 238). Sextus required a political solution; young Caesar sought to neutralize Sextus; and Antonius hoped to maximize his own share of power. The same is true of Lepidus, although he tends to be overlooked. That Sextus was ambivalent toward the Misenum agreement is hardly a surprise (App. *B Civ.* 5.70–2), but the other participants viewed it in much the same way. Dio should be given the final word (48.36.2–3). Summing up, Dio opines that "… it was perfectly evident to all from this very circumstance that it was from fear of each other's military strength and from necessity that they were making peace, the two because of the people and Sextus because of his adherents" (καὶ ἀπ'

---

48 Levy & Thompson 2010, 39: the primary aim of states is survival.
49 See Welch 2012, 236 and n. 95 with list of scholars, including Gabba 1971, 156: "It is more difficult to understand why, at the meeting of Tarentum in 37 BC, Antony had helped him. I do not think it was only because of the promise of veterans from Italy for his campaign against the Parthians, in exchange for ships given to his brother-in-law: as is known, this promise was never kept. More probably his fidelity to the Caesarian cause induced him to help his colleague."

αὐτοῦ τούτου δῆλον πᾶσι γενέσθαι ὅτι ἔκ τε τοῦ φόβου τῆς παρασκευῆς σφων καὶ ἐξ ἀνάγκης, οἱ μὲν διὰ τὸν δῆμον ὁ δὲ διὰ τοὺς συνόντας οἱ, ἐσπείσαντο). The treaty was all about the balance of power, certainly so in Dio. This new perspective of the balance of power not only helps us to conceptualize the treaty in a different way; it additionally explains why in the end it did not work. For now at least it was important for Antonius and young Caesar to remain in alliance, unsurprisingly, and as a result Sextus lost the "battle" and in 36 BCE the war.

As a postscript if might be added that even Lepidus had made contact with Sextus according to Dio (49.8.3–4), seeking a possible ally in a potential struggle against young Caesar around the time of the battles in 36 BCE. The whole struggle between the triumvirs and Sextus is portrayed as one between *four* dynasts, contemplating different alliances in order to succeed. To recapitulate Dio's adroit maxim on the rapprochement between Antonius and young Caesar in Book 37 seems a fitting way to conclude: "most men form both friendships and enmities with reference to others' influence and their own advantage" (37.39.3).

3   Summing Up: Dio on Sextus Pompeius

When looking at Dio's views on human nature and the struggle during the late republican civil war, the beginning of Book 47 is a telling source of evidence: the alliance of the Triumvirate was not about the equal sharing of power, but ultimately about gaining full power for each of the dynasts (47.1.1). Chapter 5 of this book then emphasizes how the general populace fitted this fight between the dynasts (47.5.3–4):

> ἄλλως μὲν γὰρ ἤ τις ἢ οὐδεὶς ἐς ἔχθραν ἀπ' ἰδίας τινὸς αἰτίας τοῖς ἀνδράσιν ἐκείνοις, ὡς καὶ σφαγῆναι πρὸς αὐτῶν, ἐληλύθει· τὰ δὲ δὴ κοινὰ πράγματα καὶ αἱ τῶν δυναστειῶν διαλλαγαὶ καὶ τὰς φιλίας τάς τε ἔχθρας τὰς σφοδρὰς αὐτοῖς ἐπεποιήκεσαν. (4) πάντας γὰρ τοὺς τῷ πέλας συναραμένους τέ τι καὶ συμπράξαντας ἐν πολεμίου μοίρᾳ οἱ ἕτεροι ἐτίθεντο.

> For in general, almost nobody had incurred the enmity of those men for any mere private cause, to such an extent as to be murdered by them; but it was their public relations and their changing of their allegiance from one political leader to another that had created for the Romans not only their friendships, but also their violent enemies. For everyone who had made common cause or cooperated with his neighbor in anything was regarded by all the rest in the light of an enemy.

Dio's bleak view is even more pronounced later, at 47.6.2: civil war and its attendant self-interest could bring one into conflict even with relatives.

The question then remains of where to place Sextus within this discussion. Dio viewed him as one of the dynasts of the period; simply put, all Sextus really wanted was to be an equal partner in the little cabal of dynasts and get his father's estate back in the process. Even so, focusing on Dio's narrative, we see, unsurprisingly, Sextus as mainly interesting in relation to young Caesar and the main struggle between Antonius and young Caesar. But having said that, Sextus played his part; the "realist" Dio is interested in the balance of power. This also means that the shifting alliances within the group were not (always) criticized: this was part of the game.

Dio (48.16.3) perhaps somewhat surprisingly suggests that in 40 BCE young Caesar decided to seek friendship with Sextus because he was "more trustworthy or even stronger" than Antonius (ὡς καὶ πιστότερον ἢ καὶ ἰσχυρότερον τοῦ Ἀντωνίου). The story speaks volumes about Dio's take on the period: all dynasts or warring parties (Antonius, Lepidus, Sextus Pompeius, and young Caesar) needed to look at politics in the light of the balance of power. The death of Sextus in many ways sums up the unfortunate dynast (49.17–18): Sextus still tried to play his game and ended up angering Antonius, who decided that he should be killed, only to reverse the decision all too late. After the war against Sextus ended, hostilities between the two remaining triumvirs resumed, as usual in Dio's account. This was a struggle between the dynasts, a struggle in which the smaller dynast Sextus ended up losing his life, as so many others. As for Dio, he viewed all this through his specific lens: this was about civil war between warring dynasts, but importantly, the positive end result, or so at least in Dio, was the coming of the monarchy of Augustus.

Bibliography

Beard, M. (2015) SPQR: *A History of Rome*, London.

Berdowski, P. (2011) "The Treaty of Misenum (39 B.C.) and the 'Fourth Tyrant'", in S. K. Rucinski, K. Balbuza, & K. Królczyk (eds.), *Studia Lesco Mrozewicz ab amicis et discipulic dedicate* (Poznań): 31–46.

Berdowski, P. (2015) Res gestae Neptuni filii. *Sextus Pompeius i rzymskie wojny domowe*, Rzeszów.

Boot, M. (2013) *Invisible Armies: An Epic History of Guerrilla Warfare from Ancient Times to the Present*, New York.

Börm, H. (2018) "*Stasis* in Post-Classical Greece: The Discourse of Civil Strife in the Hellenistic World", in H. Börm & N. Luraghi (eds.), *The Polis in the Hellenistic World* (Stuttgart): 53–83.

Brunt, P. A. (1971) *Italian Manpower 225 B.C.–A.D. 14*, Oxford.

Canfora, L. (2006) "Thucydides in Rome and Late Antiquity", in A. Rengakos & A. Tsakmakis (eds.), *Brill's Companion to Thucydides* (Leiden & Boston): 721–53.

Christia, F. (2012) *Alliance Formation in Civil Wars*, Cambridge.

Cornell, T. J. (ed.), (2013) *The Fragments of the Roman Historians*, Vol. 1–3, Oxford = FRHist.

Crawford, M. H. (2008) "States Waiting in the Wings: Population Distribution and the End of the Roman Republic", in L. De Ligt and S. Northwood (eds.), *People, Land, and Politics: Demographic Developments and the Transformation of Roman Italy 300 BC–AD 14* (Leiden & Boston): 631–43.

Degrassi, A. (1947) *Inscriptiones Italiae* Vol. 13/1, *Fasti Consulares et Triumphales*, Rome.

Demmers, J. (2017) *Theories of Violent Conflict: An Introduction*, London & New York.

De Souza, P. (1999) *Piracy in the Graeco-Roman World*, Cambridge.

Eckert, A. (2016) *Lucius Cornelius Sulla in der Antiken Errinnerung*, Berlin & Boston.

Epstein, D. F. (1987) *Personal Enmity in Roman Politics 218–43 BC*, Oxford & New York.

Gabba, E. (1971) "The Perusine War and Triumviral Italy", *Harvard Studies in Classical Philology* 75, 139–60.

Gerrish, J. (2015) "*Monstruosa Species*: Scylla, Spartacus, Sextus Pompeius and Civil War in Sallust's *Histories*", *The Classical Journal* 111/2, 193–217.

Hadas, M. (1930) *Sextus Pompey*, New York.

Halpern, P. G. (2006) "World War I: The Blockade", in B. A. Elleman & S. C. M. Paine (eds.), *Naval Blockades and Seapower. Strategies and Counter-Strategies, 1805–2005* (London & New York): 91–103.

Harris, W. V. (2016) *Roman Power. A Thousand Years of Empire*, Cambridge.

Kalyvas, S. N. (2006) *The Logic of Violence in Civil War*, Cambridge.

Lange, C. H. (2009) Res Publica Constituta*: Actium, Apollo and the Accomplishment of the Triumviral Assignment*, Leiden & Boston.

Lange, C. H. (2016) *Triumphs in the Age of Civil War: the Late Republic and the Adaptability of Triumphal Tradition*, London.

Levy, J. S. & Thompson, W. R. (2010) *Causes of War*, Oxford.

Lowe, B. J. (2002) "Sextus Pompeius and Spain: 46–44 BC", in A. Powell & K. Welch (eds.), *Sextus Pompeius* (London): 65–102.

Marten, K. Z. (2011) "Warlords", in H. Strachan & S. Scheipers (eds.), *The Changing Character of War* (Oxford): 302–15.

Osgood, J. (2006) *Caesar's Legacy: Civil War and the Emergence of the Roman Empire*, Cambridge.

Palmer, M. (2017) "*Stasis* in the War Narrative", in R. K. Balot *et al.* (eds.), *The Oxford Handbook of Thucydides* (Oxford): 409–25.

Powell, A. (2002) "'An Island amid the Flame': The Strategy and Imagery of Sextus Pompeius, 43–36 BC", in A. Powell & K. Welch (eds.), *Sextus Pompeius* (London): 103–33.

Powell, A. & Welch, K. (eds.) (2002) *Sextus Pompeius*, London.

Rich, J. (2018) "Warlords and the Roman Republic", in T. Ñaco del Hoyo & F. Lopez Sánchez (eds.), *War, Warlords and Interstate Relations in the Ancient Mediterranean* (Leiden & Boston): 266–94.

Robb, M. A. (2010) *Beyond Populares and Optimates: Political Language in the Late Republic*, Stuttgart.

Seager, R. (1972) "*Factio*: Some Observations", *Journal of Roman Studies* 62, 53–8.

Simpson, E. (2012) *War from the Ground Up: Twenty-First-Century Combat as Politics*, New York.

Smith, C. (forthcoming) "The Lives of Augustus", in Y. Lehmann (ed.), *Festschrift for Martine Chassignet*.

Steel, C. (2013) *The End of the Roman Republic 146 to 44 BC: Conquest and Crisis*, Edinburgh.

Strachan, H. (2013) *The Direction of War: Contemporary Strategy in Historical Perspective*, Cambridge.

Syme, R. (1939) *The Roman Revolution*, Oxford.

Syme, R. (2016) *Approaching the Roman Revolution: Papers on Republican History* (ed. F. Santangelo), Oxford.

Vervaet, F. J. (2010) "The Secret History: The Official Position of Imperator Caesar Divi filius from 31 to 27", *Ancient Society* 40, 79–152.

Welch, K. (2002) "Sextus Pompeius and the Res Publica", in A. Powell & K. Welch (eds.), *Sextus Pompeius* (London): 31–63.

Welch, K. (2012) *Magnus Pius: Sextus Pompeius and the Transformation of the Roman Republic*, Swansea.

Welch, K. (ed.) (2015) *Appian's Roman History: Empire and Civil War*, Swansea.

Wiseman, T. P. (2009) *Remembering the Roman People: Essays on Late-Republican Politics and Literature*, Oxford.

CHAPTER 13

Like Father Like Son: the Differences in How Dio Tells the Story of Julius Caesar and His More Successful Son

Jesper Majbom Madsen

This chapter focuses on how Dio writes the history of Gaius Julius Caesar and Octavian. Although these men followed similar ways of becoming sole ruler and had what seems to have been the same appetite for power, Dio offers two very different narratives on the role they played in Roman politics. He also presents them with different personalities: where Caesar is described as overly ambitious, hungry for unlimited power and what Dio sees as essentially hollow honorary decrees, Octavian comes across as a selfless savior figure who introduced or reintroduced monarchical rule to ensure peace and stability after what had been turbulent times in Roman politics.

The question here to be addressed is why Dio offers profoundly different accounts of two men whose routes to supreme power follow what appear to be similar paths. Dio's favorable attitude to Octavian and of the reign of Augustus are often explained as the result of how the historian saw monarchical rule as the most stable form of constitution – and thus, as far superior to the free competition and unlimited quest for power that had characterized Roman politics in the republican period. Because Augustus established a lasting version of a monarchical government, he was the natural hero in Dio's narrative.[1] It is therefore only to be expected that Dio would celebrate Augustus and the changes he made both to the constitution and to political culture. But as will be argued in the following, Dio's account of the two men did more than celebrate Augustus for providing a more stable form of government: what Dio also hoped to achieve, so it seems, was to offer more general thoughts about what constituted the ideal form of constitution and how monarchical rule should be organized.

---

1 Bleicken 1962, 447, 454; Millar 1964; 112; Reinhold 1988, 165; Aalders 1986, 295; De Blois 1998, 3406; see Reinhold & Swan 1990, 169; Gowing 1992, 25–6, 35; Swan 2004, 14–17; Kemezis 2014, 131–4; Madsen 2016a, 146–9. Note that all translations of Dio are from Earnest Cary's Loeb Classical Library edition.

To reach that end, Dio shapes his own personal version of Augustus by offering a narrative that supports his own view of the optimal form of monarchy against which later emperors were measured. Therefore, Dio is not simply offering what was essentially the version of Augustus as it would have come across in the emperor's autobiography or a view he obtained from reading the pro-Augustan tradition; and, at the same time, he was able to offer more than an account of the challenges that dominated political life in his contemporary Rome.[2] There is little doubt that Dio's view of history and of Augustus was heavily influenced by his often first-hand experience of Roman politics and the emperors of his day. Yet, in what follows, it is emphasized that Dio wrote his *Roman History* with the intention of offering what he believed to be an accurate account of the history of Rome and its people. But when reading the entire work it is also apparent that one of several objectives is to convince the reader that free competition for unlimited power (*demokratia*) was a disastrous way forward for the Romans and that it had to be replaced by a more stable form of monarchy.

In the following discussion, I will try to show to what extent Dio was ready to go to convey that message; and I will also show that Dio expected his readers to assume that monarchic rule was already an established and acknowledged form of government when Caesar was voted the dictatorship for life. There are elements to suggest that Dio aims to convey the message that what he describes as Caesar's monarchy was hereditary and could be passed on to his nephew in his will and that Octavian therefore had a legal right to succeed Caesar as the next supreme ruler of Rome. Interestingly, this allows Dio the opportunity to present Octavian as a legitimate heir to the power he so vigorously fought for and to present him in a more positive way. Another point to be made is that Augustus performed better than Caesar because he had new ideas and because he came into Roman politics as a sort of outsider, who was not compromised by the selfish and overly ambitious political elite which had characterized Rome's political culture throughout the republican period.

According to Dio, Caesar's rise to supreme power was a step in the right direction. When Caesar assumed the role as dictator, the problem of uncontrolled ambitions was not, however, something of the past: as Dio demonstrates in the account of how Caesar was killed, members of the Senate envied his powers and regretted that he was now the new sole ruler of Rome (44.1.1). As Burden-Strevens argues elsewhere in this volume, Dio sees the dictatorship as a reasonable but temporary resort in times of crises but has, as noted by

---

2 On how Dio's work on non-contemporary eras is seen as a reflection of his own time, see Reinhold & Swan 1990, 168–73; Swan 2004, 14.

Burden-Strevens, reservations against an office that in the late Republic seems to have outlived itself. Not surprisingly, then, Augustus refrained from using it as he settled affairs after the civil war.

A dictatorship for life was the closest one would come to monarchical rule in late republican Rome without having to be *rex*, and the characterization of Caesar's reign as a golden monarchy suggests that Dio saw Caesar's few years as sole ruler as something different than the traditional dictatorship (47.15.4).[3] What troubled Dio was not so much the label on Caesar's powers but his personality: his vanity and the continuous quest for glory, which brought him to a point where by accepting the many extravagant honors from the People and the Senate he lifted himself above his peers and so effectively became their master rather than a legitimate sole ruler. To Dio it was the unstoppable urge for pomp and honors that elevated him into a sphere between the mortal and the divine, above the laws and detached from any constitutional regulation.

Now, Octavian was seemingly no less ambitious or less drawn towards supreme power than his great-uncle before him. To be sure, he too applied every means available to him to attain his objectives, including civil war, a march on Rome, and politically motivated killings.[4] Just like Caesar, Octavian received a series of honors that were previously unheard of such as the admission of his name to the Salian hymn and libations at both private and public dinners in Rome, honors that had clear divine connotations.[5] But one could argue together with Dio that, unlike Caesar, Octavian was not part of the political class in Rome that had dominated Roman politics for centuries and that he, therefore, was not part of the political class that had brought Rome to the brink of dissolution, or at least not in the same way as Caesar, Pompey, or men like Sulla and Marius.[6]

Therefore, in Dio's version, Octavian represents a new beginning to Roman politics. The young heir is seen as a man with different values than those of his great-uncle and his generation of politicians. Octavian was not, Dio assures us over and over again, naturally cruel or driven by personal ambition or an urge

---

3   On how Dio believes monarchy to be the ideal form of constitution see Aalders 1986, 295; Reinhold 1988, 165; Bleicken 1962, 447; De Blois 1998, 3406; Kemezis 2014, 131–4. On Caesar's golden monarchy see Gowing 1992, 35.

4   On the coup that Octavian was behind see Syme 1939, 1–9. On the proscriptions see Syme 1939, 190–1; Gowing 1992, 254–63. On how Octavian led his army towards Rome and inserted himself as consul see Osgood 2006, 58–60. On the ambitions of Octavian see Levick 2010, 28–31.

5   Lange 2009, 129–30.

6   That Octavian is characterized as a political outsider is apparent from the claim that he was young and too briefly involved in Roman politics to have made enemies (Cass. Dio 47.7.1–3). See also Gowing 1992, 256.

for glory and power as had been Caesar and most of the other protagonists in late republican Rome.⁷ As pointed out by Markov elsewhere in this volume, Dio still draws our attention to Octavian's many apparent flaws: his brutality, arrogance, and hypocrisy that were an unavoidable part of human nature and therefore also part of Octavian's personality. Nevertheless, it was he who put an end to civil wars and offered the Romans peace and a more stable form of government, not because he wanted power, but because he was called upon to do so by both the People and the Senate.⁸

As we shall see in what follows, this was an ideal that would only be possible if Octavian were prepared to follow in the footsteps of his great-uncle and restore monarchy. Ancient commentators widely agree with Dio that civil war was a sign that the state was falling apart.⁹ But as we will return to below, Dio explicitly describes the wars following the death of Caesar, which he says were more brutal than any of the previous wars fought between Romans, as a necessity to re-establish monarchy.

The implications are worth paying attention to. Dio is one of the key sources for the lives of the two men and for late republican Rome because his narrative offers a detailed account of the political instability in the period. In Dio, we get accounts of episodes where violence is used to solve political disputes; we also find an analysis of motives and strategies that we can hold up against Appian's narrative on the civil war. The way in which Dio tells the story of the two Caesars has considerable impact on our understanding of the period and our knowledge of the political climate and of the different roles played by the protagonists. When we use Dio as a source for the history of Caesar, Octavian, and the reign of Augustus, it is therefore essential to acknowledge the clear-cut agenda to always promote monarchical rule and consequently see almost every politician in late republican Rome as irresponsible, selfish, overly ambitious, indifferent to people's needs, or ignorant of what was in the best interests of the state. Also, it is important to acknowledge that the two portraits of Caesar and his successor are interconnected. As I will argue in the following, Caesar's flaws are emphasized while Octavian's role in the civil war is explained and justified. The angle Dio chooses for his narrative makes the seemingly more brutal great-nephew come across as the

---

7 On how Octavian comes across as the example of a more conscious dynast see Kemezis 2014, 120–6.
8 The clearest example of how Dio portrays Augustus as the legitimate monarch is found in Book 53, where Dio describes how he was voted absolute powers when he offered to lay down his powers after having punished his great-uncle's murderers and restored the state (53.11–12). On how Octavian ended the civil war see also 56.44.2 with Swan 2004, 14.
9 Armitage 2017, 68–74; Lange 2017; Lange forthcoming; Madsen forthcoming.

devoted savior who did what was needed to reinstate the monarchical form of government that his great-uncle had managed to introduce in his few years as sole ruler.

1 Julius Caesar: a Passion for Power

For Dio, the problem with democracy was that it encouraged a competition among members of the political elite, as they were forced to act in a system where they had to outbid each other in order to be elected to magistracies or to win commands against prestigious enemies, which again were essential to ensure further advancement. In his account of the political climate in late republican Rome, Dio describes a zero-sum game, where one man's political and military success meant that others were necessarily losing ground. Success was met with jealousy and attempts to slow down the reform-minded and victorious magistrates and generals in the fear that their achievements would earn support among the plebs.[10] An example from the *Roman History* that testifies to how Dio did not see envy and competition for prestigious posts as a problem only in late republican Rome is when Marcus Furius Camillus was prosecuted for paying Apollo a tenth of the spoils from Veii as promised should he win the war (Zon. 7.21.1).[11] Dio describes how Camillus' friends turned against him and asserts that envy within the elite was the real reason why the successful general was forced to leave the city (Cass. Dio fr. 24.4–6).[12] Yet, the differences between the two periods, as Dio sees it, was not the political jealousy, personal ambitions, or incidence of violence that he believed was an integral part of democratic rule; rather, killing one's political opponents became an intrinsic part of Roman politics from Tiberius Gracchus onwards.[13]

To Dio, the first of the Gracchi brothers represents an example of how politically dysfunctional republican Rome was. Dio indicates how Gracchus' attempt to allocate land to veterans and Rome's poor was driven more by ambition to rule than to solve the complications of land distribution. It is also symptomatic of Dio's view of the late Republic that he focuses on the way in

---

10   On how Dio constructs a narrative where the senatorial elite was trying to win the favor of the people see Madsen 2016a, 142–6. See also Madsen 2018 on how envy, hatred, and unlimited personal ambitions were already part of early Roman politics.
11   For the account by Livy see 5.21–8. On Camillus' triumph after Veii see also Lange 2016, 94–7.
12   See also Madsen 2018, 109–10.
13   On the shift in Roman politics and how political disagreement evolved into civil war see Cass. Dio fr. 83.

which Tiberius sought re-election as tribune, something that portrays him as a man prepared to undermine the constitution and push the state towards serious political strife. As someone who had no warm feelings for the republican constitution, Dio could have chosen an angle where he acknowledged the attempt to bring forward a model to solve one of Rome's key social challenges. In fact, Dio's Tiberius chooses a way forward where formality and what the historian deems as poor intentions override what could have been an attempt to follow a different path.[14]

A third example is the episode in which the Senate, led by a vindictive Lucullus and an incompetent Afranius as consul, refused to ratify Pompey's acts from the eastern campaign (37.49.4). Dio did not admire Rome's new champion of the East and the manner in which he acquired the command against Mithridates and Tigranes; he had no sympathy for the way the general used his popular support to push Lucullus out of the way in what was in Dio's eyes a war that was already won. What Dio outlines here is a political climate along the lines of what Meier (1966, 201–5) characterizes as a crisis without alternative, defined as a political reality in which the Senate repeatedly depended on the acts of strong individuals who were then, in their turn, discredited in the attempt to take some of the air out of their sails.

When seen in this light, Caesar's victory in the civil war against Pompey and the form of government he introduced on his return to Rome were a much needed improvement; in Dio's opinion it was the only way forward if Rome was to break the political deadlock that had characterized the late Republic.[15] Dio offers his readers a narrative where, after the civil war, Caesar was finally able to take control of Rome's legions and enforce discipline among the soldiers – traits he later holds as key elements for what constitutes the ideal ruler. When victorious, Caesar took the ideals of *clementia* to a whole new level, forgiving those who had fought against him and inviting several of his former enemies back into the inner circle of the decision-making process. The decision not to prosecute his enemies among the senators at Ilerda in 49 BCE is another trait of the ruler that Dio normally sees as mark of good government (41.23.1):

---

14   See Dio fr. 83.3–6 on how Tiberius Gracchus chose to use popular support to win back his position in Roman politics. Dio is here frank in his claim that Tiberius used land as a tool to win popularity, even if the historian acknowledges that Tiberius saw a need to redistribute the land. See also Lintott 1994, 65; Flower 2010, 80–6; Steel 2013, 15–20. On how Plutarch follows the same tradition in which Tiberius is seen as determined to bypass the Senate see Plut. *Ti. Gracch.* 16.1.

15   Dio's view is expressed most clearly in the beginning of Book 44, where Caesar's murderers are accused of having overturned the first stable form of government Rome had had for a long time.

καὶ αὐτοῖς ἀκριβῶς ἑκάτερον ὁ Καῖσαρ ἐφύλαξεν· οὔτε γὰρ ἀπέκτεινε τὸ
παράπαν τῶν ἐν τούτῳ τῷ πολέμῳ ἁλόντων οὐδένα, καίτοι ἐκείνων ποτὲ ἐν
ἀνοχῇ τινι ἀφυλάκτως τινὰς τῶν ἑαυτοῦ ἔχοντας φθειράντων.

Caesar kept each of his promises to them scrupulously. He did not put to death a single man captured in this war, in spite of the fact that his foes had once, during a truce, destroyed some of his own men who were caught off their guard.

Caesar is also praised for having solved a threatening financial crisis that emerged when, in the light of a new round of civil war, creditors called back their loans (41.37.1). It is critical to note that Caesar is celebrated for having included both the leaders of the Senate and at times the whole body in the decisions he made (43.27.1):

Καὶ ταῦτα μέντοι, τά τε ἄλλα ὅσα ὑπὲρ τοῦ κοινοῦ ἐβουλεύετο, οὔτ' ἰδιογνωμονῶν
οὔτ' ἰδιοβουλῶν ἔπραττεν, ἀλλὰ πάντα δὴ πάντως τοῖς πρώτοις τῆς βουλῆς,
ἔστι δ' ὅτε καὶ πάσῃ αὐτῇ ἐπεκοίνου.

All these and the other undertakings which he was planning for the common weal he accomplished not on his own authority nor by his own counsel, but communicated everything in every instance to the leaders of the Senate, and sometimes even to that entire body.

In this part of the narrative of Caesar's reign, the dictator comes across, if not as a savior figure in the same sense as Augustus, then at least a kind of politician who introduces a form of monarchy where he took the responsibility for government upon himself but included the political elite in decision-making by listening to advice from the members of the Senate. In effect, this is the kind of solution Dio has Maecenas recommend to Augustus – and is the form of government he praises Augustus for having introduced.

With such positive description, Dio pushes the reign of Caesar into another category of monarchical government that surpasses the aspect of a temporary emergency that tied it to the dictatorship. This allows the author to describe Caesar's reign not only as a step in the right direction but also as the introduction of monarchical rule that Octavian would later reinsert and stabilize.[16] Dio acknowledges Caesar as Rome's dictator and comments briefly on the moment

---

16   On the ideal form of government see Cassius Dio 52.19–21. See Reinhold, 1988, 188–92. See also Burden-Strevens in this volume.

when he was made dictator for life, but refers to Caesar's rule as monarchy in the same way as he describes the later reign of Augustus. One example is when, nearing the death of Caesar, Dio compares democracy with monarchy, making it clear to his readers that Caesar's years as supreme ruler would fall into the latter category (44.2.1–3).[17]

Now, despite Dio's acknowledgment of Caesar's ideas about how to govern Rome, the dictator was never one of his favorites. In his account of late republican Rome, Caesar is presented as overly ambitious and manipulative – a man whose lack of modesty brought his early fall. The account Dio offers of Caesar's leadership is the story of a populist whose ambition it was to be first of all Romans at any cost. In a direct comparison with Pompey, we learn that Pompey wanted to be second to no man, honored and loved by what Dio describes as a willing people, while Caesar wanted to rule and command everyone, even those who hated him, and was happy to bestow honors on himself (41.54.1). Dio's Caesar had little eye for what was in the best interests of the state, which, in effect, made him no different from most other members of the political elite in republican Rome.

The land reform that Caesar when consul pushed through the assembly in 59 is an example of how Dio presents him as a populist whose primary aim was to win the favor of the people. We are offered a long description of the way in which the senators had been included every step of the way in the preparation of the law, and Dio underlines how the former landowners would be given compensation when giving up their land and how most senators were unable to find any real faults with the proposal (38.2). But what seems to be a well-planned piece of legislation on the part of the new consul appears as a clever way of maneuvering the Senate into a position where the members had little choice but to support the bill – something, Dio says, that would improve Caesar's popularity considerably.

The scene captures Dio's view of republican Rome. Caesar advances what Dio acknowledges is a much-needed reform to redistribute the land and, perhaps more importantly, to allow Pompey to live up to the promises he made to the soldiers who fought with him in the East. It would, Dio tells us, solve a pressing social problem, increase the surplus from the land (the new lots would be worked more intensively), and would prevent the question of distribution of land to Pompey's veterans from becoming a dangerous situation.

---

17   See also Dio 45.1.2 on how Caesar hoped to pass his monarchy on to Octavian along with his name and authority. For further discussion see below.

It is symptomatic of Dio's account of late republican Rome that Caesar is not allowed the role of a politician who, including the Senate in the process, made a meaningful attempt to solve one of the problems that had troubled Roman politics for most of the first century BCE. Instead, he appears to be part of the problem. Dio states in the first sentence of Book 38 that Caesar proposed the land reform in order to strengthen his own reputation with the people.[18]

Despite the way Dio openly acknowledges that Caesar was on the right track, the portrait he offers is shaped in such a way that it fits the overarching idea of a political elite out of touch with what was in the best interests of the people. The first time that the reader hears of Caesar is when he supports the *lex Manilia* that ordered Lucullus to hand over his command to Pompey (36.43). Caesar's support of Pompey is described as a move by someone who hoped that, by backing the law, he one day would benefit from having supported Pompey, a true champion of the people. That Lucullus was losing ground in central Anatolia is not ignored but appears to be beside the point, and there is no effort to suggest that Lucullus was other than in full control of the situation. With this approach, Dio ignores the trouble Lucullus had in the East when he struggled to end the war, and the historian does not take into consideration the setback Lucullus had when his legates, without him present, moved out against Mithridates and lost. With Mithridates in control of Pontus and Tigranes back in Cappadocia, Lucullus was losing, despite the promising start. Consequently, the decision to recall Lucullus and replace him with Pompey was a sensible one both from a political and military point of view (36.16–17).

In Dio's version, it is in the unstoppable urge for power and glory that Caesar falls short as both man and monarch. Caesar may have offered *clementia* and so kept large parts of the Senate in the decision-making process, but he demonstrated no sign of modesty in the powers he required or in the extraordinary honors that he so willingly accepted from the People and the Senate. The Senate is blamed for deliberately exploiting Caesar's vanity by using extravagant honors to maneuver Caesar into a position where he would be exposed to envy and hatred, which in turn shaped the rationale that the dictator was a tyrant whom it would be honorable to kill (44.3.1–2):

> Ἔσχε δὲ ὧδε, καὶ αἰτίαν τήνδε ὁ θάνατος αὐτοῦ ἔλαβεν· οὐ γὰρ δὴ καὶ ἀναίτιον πάντῃ τὸ ἐπίφθονον ἐκτήσατο, πλὴν καθ' ὅσον αὐτοὶ οἱ βουλευταὶ ταῖς τε καινότησι καὶ ταῖς ὑπερβολαῖς τῶν τιμῶν ἐξάραντές τε αὐτὸν καὶ φυσήσαντες

---

[18] On how Dio thought the law had the potential to solve social problems and ensure a more effective use of the lands see 38.1.3.

ἔπειτα ἐπ' αὐταῖς ἐκείναις καὶ ἐμέμφοντο καὶ διέβαλλον ὡς ἡδέως τέ σφας λαμβάνοντα καὶ ὀγκηρότερον ἀπ' αὐτῶν ζῶντα. ἔστι μὲν γὰρ ὅτε καὶ ὁ Καῖσαρ ἥμαρτε, δεξάμενός τέ τινα τῶν ψηφισθέντων οἳ καὶ πιστεύσας ὄντως αὐτῶν ἀξιοῦσθαι, πλεῖστον δὲ ὅμως ἐκεῖνοι, οἵτινες ἀρξάμενοι τιμᾶν αὐτὸν ὡς καὶ ἄξιον, προήγαγον ἐς αἰτίαν οἷς ἐψηφίζοντο.

It happened as follows, and his death was due to the cause now to be given. He had aroused dislike that was not altogether unjustified, except in so far as it was the senators themselves who had by their novel and excessive honors encouraged him and puffed him up, only to find fault with him on this very account and to spread slanderous reports how glad he was to accept them and how he behaved more haughtily as a result of them. It is true that Caesar did now and then err by accepting some of the honors voted him and believing that he really deserved them; yet those were most blameworthy who, after beginning to honor him as he deserved, led him on and brought blame upon him for the measures they had passed.

The Senate is left with most of the blame for how Caesar's authority was gradually but deliberately undermined, but the dictator is criticized for believing that the honors were somehow justified and for sending mixed signals about his attitude towards kingship.[19] The unresolved question of Caesar's regal aspirations – including the cult that made him some sort of super-human – forced him into a position where he lifted himself above his peers, out of the context of politics, and so made him the tyrant it would be honorable to slay. Murdering him was wrong, unlawful, and reckless, as it threw Rome into a new period of civil war. But in Dio's version, Caesar carried much of the responsibility for his own death because of the powers and meaningless honorific titles he assumed.

---

19   Dio describes how Caesar treated the Senate arrogantly when he did not rise to greet the senators as they came to meet him in front of the temple to Venus. The incident caused much criticism and Dio describes how attempts were made to explain how Caesar remained seated because of stomach issues, not convincing many (44.8). In his account of why Caesar was murdered, Suetonius goes a long way to explain how Caesar's untamable quest for glory and prestige was what, justifiably perhaps, led to his death. Apart from the extravagant honors, both Suetonius and Plutarch point at how Caesar's elevated status made him act superior towards members of the Senate, as if he were king or in one way or other their master (Suet. *Iul.* 75–9; Plut. *Caes.* 60–1).

2 Augustus: the Legitimate Monarch

Turning to the way in which Dio lays out the narrative of the first year after Octavian's arrival at Rome, one gets the impression that Caesar's dictatorship was a hereditary monarchy that could be transferred to an heir. After the victory over Pompey, Dio describes how the title *imperator* (*autokrator*) was added to Caesar's name. The title was no longer offered to victorious generals, and Dio also mentions that Caesar's children and grandchildren were given the right to call themselves *imperatores*. In that sense, *imperator* was no longer an honorific title tied closely to military victory but a mark of the elevated position of Caesar and his family in Roman society (43.44.2–4):[20]

> τό τε τοῦ αὐτοκράτορος ὄνομα οὐ κατὰ τὸ ἀρχαῖον ἔτι μόνον, ὥσπερ ἄλλοι τε καὶ ἐκεῖνος πολλάκις ἐκ τῶν πολέμων ἐπεκλήθησαν, οὐδ᾽ ὡς οἵ τινα αὐτοτελῆ ἡγεμονίαν ἢ καὶ ἄλλην τινὰ ἐξουσίαν λαβόντες ὠνομάζοντο, ἀλλὰ καθάπαξ τοῦτο δὴ τὸ καὶ νῦν τοῖς τὸ κράτος ἀεὶ ἔχουσι διδόμενον ἐκείνῳ τότε πρώτῳ τε καὶ πρῶτον, ὥσπερ τι κύριον, προσέθεσαν. καὶ τοσαύτῃ τε ὑπερβολῇ κολακείας ἐχρήσαντο ὥστε καὶ τοὺς παῖδας τούς τε ἐγγόνους αὐτοῦ οὕτω καλεῖσθαι ψηφίσασθαι, μήτε τέκνον τι αὐτοῦ ἔχοντος καὶ γέροντος ἤδη ὄντος. ὅθενπερ καὶ ἐπὶ πάντας τοὺς μετὰ ταῦτα αὐτοκράτορας ἡ ἐπίκλησις αὕτη, ὥσπερ τις ἰδία τῆς ἀρχῆς αὐτῶν οὖσα καθάπερ καὶ ἡ τοῦ Καίσαρος, ἀφίκετο. οὐ μέντοι καὶ τὸ ἀρχαῖον ἐκ τούτου κατελύθη, ἀλλ᾽ ἔστιν ἑκάτερον·

> Moreover, they now applied to him first and for the first time, as a kind of proper name, the title of imperator, no longer merely following the ancient custom by which others as well as Caesar had often been saluted as a result of their wars, nor even as those who received some independent command or other authority were called by this name, but giving him once for all the same title that is now granted to those who hold successively the supreme power. And such excessive flattery did they employ as even to vote that his sons and grandsons should be given the same title, though he had no child and was already an old man. From him this title has come down to all subsequent emperors, as one peculiar to their office, just like the title "Caesar." The ancient custom has not, however, been thereby overthrown, but both usages exist side by side.

---

20 See also Urso forthcoming. In his comment on the titles offered to Caesar, Plutarch does not mention that the title *imperator* was added to Caesar's first name (*Caes.* 57.1–5). Suetonius mentions the honor as part of the extraordinary honorific decrees that in his mind ended up costing Caesar his life (Suet. *Caes.* 76.1).

That Caesar's monarchy was something that he could pass onto an heir is further underlined in the first passage in Book 45, where Dio describes how it was Caesar's hope that his great-nephew would succeed him as the next ruler of Rome (45.1.2):

ἄπαις τε γὰρ ἐκεῖνος ὢν καὶ μεγάλας ἐπ᾽ αὐτῷ ἐλπίδας ἔχων ἠγάπα τε καὶ περιεῖπεν αὐτόν, ὡς καὶ τοῦ ὀνόματος καὶ τῆς ἐξουσίας τῆς τε μοναρχίας διάδοχον καταλείψων ...

For Caesar, being childless and basing great hopes upon him [Octavian], loved and cherished him, intending to leave him as successor to his name, authority, and sovereignty ...

The idea of hereditary monarchy is Dio's own. First, as the Romans were uneasy about the entire concept of monarchy, it would have been premature for Caesar to see himself as a kind of Greek monarch who could keep his position as the supreme ruler in his family. When Octavian arrived at Rome, none of the ancient commentators, including Dio, have him raise the claim that he was to be given Caesar's powers. Octavian acknowledged Antony's status as consul and asked for the funds he was owed (Cass. Dio 45.5.1–4). Also, there would have been nothing in Caesar's will to suggest that he was passing his political power on to his grand-nephew. When Octavian made his first attempt to enter Roman politics after Antony dismissed his claim to his heritage, he did so seeking election as tribune (45.5.3). Instead, the idea of hereditary monarchy seems to have been Dio's way to set up a continuity between Caesar's dictatorship, which he elsewhere refers to as a golden monarchy, and the reign of Augustus. By giving Octavian the hereditary right to succeed Caesar as Rome's supreme ruler, he not only justifies the role Octavian played in the civil war but also gives it a gloss of legitimacy.

After having established how Octavian had a right to avenge his great-uncle and follow in his footsteps, Dio moves on to describe the determination with which the young heir set out to pursue Caesar's murderers and how he made plans to acquire what was rightfully his – a move that even the gods endorsed (45.4.2–3):

καὶ ἐκεῖνος σφαλερῶς μὲν καὶ ἐπικινδύνως ἐποίησεν ὅτι τήν τε ἡλικίαν τὴν ἄρτι ἐκ παίδων ἄγων (ὀκτωκαιδεκέτης γὰρ ἦν) καὶ τὴν διαδοχὴν καὶ τοῦ κλήρου καὶ τοῦ γένους καὶ ἐπίφθονον καὶ ἐπαίτιον ὁρῶν οὖσαν, ἔπειτ᾽ ἐπὶ τοιαῦτα ὥρμησεν ἐφ᾽ οἷς ὅ τε Καῖσαρ ἐπεφόνευτο καὶ τιμωρία οὐδεμία αὐτοῦ ἐγίγνετο, καὶ οὔτε

LIKE FATHER LIKE SON

τοὺς σφαγέας οὔτε τὸν Λέπιδον τόν τε Ἀντώνιον ἔδεισεν· οὐ μέντοι καὶ κακῶς βεβουλεῦσθαι ἔδοξεν, ὅτι καὶ κατώρθωσε. τὸ μέντοι δαιμόνιον πᾶσαν οὐχ ἀσαφῶς τὴν αὐτόθεν μέλλουσάν σφισι ταραχὴν ἔσεσθαι προεσήμηνεν· ἐς γὰρ τὴν Ῥώμην ἐσιόντος αὐτοῦ ἶρις πάντα τὸν ἥλιον πολλὴ καὶ ποικίλη περιέσχεν.

He, too, acted in a precarious and hazardous fashion; for he was only just past boyhood, being eighteen years of age, and saw that his succession to the inheritance and the family was sure to provoke jealousy and censure; yet he set out in pursuit of objects such as had led to Caesar's murder, which had not been avenged, and he feared neither the assassins nor Lepidus and Antony. Nevertheless, he was not thought to have planned badly, because he proved to be successful. Heaven, however, indicated in no obscure manner all the confusion that would result to the Romans from it; for as he was entering Rome a great halo with the colors of the rainbow surrounded the whole sun.

The account of the year between Octavian's arrival at Rome and the moment he agreed on the alliance with Antony and Lepidus can be divided into three stages: the arrival and the balanced but failed attempt to acquire his inheritance; the conflict with Antony and the war of Mutina; and finally the march against Rome and the formation of the Triumvirate.

As for the arrival at Rome, Dio sketches a portrait of a young man who immediately sets out to acquire his great-uncle's funds so that he can fulfill the promises made in the will. At first he is horrified by the news of Caesar's violent death but also reluctant to act until he ascertains that he had been chosen as Caesar's heir (43.3.1). But from the moment that the adoption was confirmed, he threw himself into the midst of Roman politics setting all his financial means, his soldiers, and his great-uncle's clients in motion to avenge the murder and re-establish the monarchy (43.3.2).

Octavian is presented as following a justified strategy when he entered the city as a private citizen. He is praised for not having made random allegations, and it is seen as a mature step that he paid court to Antony, acknowledging his status as consul. That Antony returns the gesture with arrogance allows Dio to paint the picture of an uncivilized man who had acquired funds that were not rightfully his; the reader is reminded once more that fear and envy often stood in the way of necessary decision. In this case, Antony is said to have been concerned that the young heir would be able to use the name Caesar and the dictator's veterans and clients to become the next ruler of Rome (45.5.3–4). A few paragraphs later, Dio reaches the conclusion that Octavian made the right decision when he entered the political scene to take hold of public affairs, even if it was thought to be a risk, and that, by doing so, he proved to be one of the most vigorous and able leaders of all time (45.5.1–2):[21]

> Οὕτως ὁ πρότερον μὲν Ὀκτάουιος, τότε δὲ ἤδη Καῖσαρ, μετὰ δὲ τοῦτο Αὔγουστος ἐπικληθεὶς ἥψατο τῶν πραγμάτων, καὶ αὐτὰ καὶ κατέπραξε καὶ κατειργάσατο παντὸς μὲν ἀνδρὸς νεανικώτερον, παντὸς δὲ πρεσβύτου φρονιμώτερον. πρῶτον μὲν γάρ, ὡς καὶ ἐπὶ μόνῃ τῇ τοῦ κλήρου διαδοχῇ, καὶ ἰδιωτικῶς καὶ μετ' ὀλίγων, ἄνευ ὄγκου τινός, ἐς τὴν πόλιν ἐσῆλθεν·

> In this way he who was formerly called Octavius, but already by this time Caesar, and subsequently Augustus, took a hand in public affairs; and he managed and dealt with them more vigorously than any man in his prime, more prudently than any graybeard. In the first place, he entered the city as if for the sole purpose of succeeding to the inheritance, coming as a private citizen with only a few attendants, without any display.

There is an issue about who was to blame for how the situation evolved from verbal abuse to war between two of Caesar's supporters. Octavian, who we are told had the right to succeed his great-uncle, comes across as respectful when he asked to have his inheritance handed over to his household. That the argument between the consul and Caesar's heir turned into the war at Mutina is laid out as entirely Antony's fault. When he chose to humiliate Caesar's lawful heir by sending him away without the funds he needed to fulfill the promises in his great-uncle's will, he left the young heir with no choice other than to call upon Caesar's veterans and have them help him take what was legally his, and in addition see to it that Caesar's murderers were brought to justice – something, Dio repeats, Antony never tried to do.

The alliance between Octavian and the Senate against Antony is another example of the lengths Octavian was prepared to go to in order to prevent Antony from becoming too powerful (46.29.1–2). Dio acknowledges that the choice of ally was controversial but moves on to explain how Octavian knew that he was in no position to fight Antony and his father's murderers at the same time; he deemed Antony more dangerous than the Senate (45.14). Dio then turns the problematic alliance into an example of how politically skillful Octavian was. The move is then made to resonate with how he is said to have played the game of public affairs better and more vigorously than any of the other parties involved. Octavian is not envious of Antony's potential power but

---

21 On this passage see also Markov in this volume.

careful not to let his enemy become too powerful. One should remember that Dio allows his young favorite to stand out as someone who had justice on his side but also as one who was surrounded by enemies and therefore had to act unscrupulously in order to avenge his great-uncle and follow in his footsteps.

After the battle at Mutina, where the coalition managed to free Decimus Brutus and force Antony to flee further into Gaul, Dio considers the delicate question of how the Romans were to commemorate their young general. Dio feels Octavian was entitled to become consul and describes how both the Senate and the People entered dangerous territory when they failed to acknowledge the role he had played in the victory against Antony. It was they who brought the threat of a new sack of Rome upon themselves. Predictably, given that Dio tells the story of late republican Rome, the Senate failed to meet the expectations of the young general or to realize that the next step was going to be another war if they continued the strategy. Instead of gaining the expected honors, Octavian was held responsible for the death of the two consuls and was ordered to hand his troops over to Decimus (46.40.1). If that was not enough, the Senate and the People tried to contain Octavian's political influence by voting him honors less significant than the ones he expected, such as the right to cast his vote with the ex-consuls or the opportunity to seek election as praetor and run for consul earlier than normal.

When, as a consequence of the insults, Octavian turned on Rome and had his soldiers threaten the Senate, in Dio's eyes it was a necessary next step to ensure that he was not to be eliminated or left on the sidelines, and Dio immediately turns to the formation of the Triumvirate and ensuing proscription to show the connection between the Senate's inability to work with Octavian and the Triumvirate. According to the historian, Octavian made the alliance with Antony and Lepidus because it was the only way to match the strength of Caesar's murderers in the wealthy East, particularly when the Senate remained on their side, and therefore the only way he could carry out his plans (46.52). The change of alliance is, once again, held to be part of what had to be done if Octavian was to avenge his great-uncle and reinstate the monarchy.

It is altogether a brutal arrangement Dio unveils in the following chapters, when he offers a vivid description of how the list of proscribed Romans was put together. From what he writes, it is clear to the reader that many innocent Romans died brutal and unjustified deaths because their funds were needed in the coming war or because they disagreed or had disagreed with one or more of the triumvirs. We learn how the triumvirs were ready to sacrifice even their close friends to get the names of their enemies on the list, which, in Dio's eyes, proved that this round of political murders was more brutal than the one Sulla called for forty years earlier (47.5). In Dio's version, the Triumvirate comes across as nothing short of a military regime with little legitimacy. Killing senators in considerable numbers and running the state without leaning on the Senate are elements that Dio usually criticizes heavily.[22] Yet, he goes a long way to keep the reputation of Octavian as unsoiled as possible, as he assures readers that the young man was not the most brutal of the three (47.7.1–4).

> Ταῦτα δὲ ἐπράττετο μὲν ὑπό τε τοῦ Λεπίδου καὶ ὑπὸ τοῦ Ἀντωνίου μάλιστα (πρός τε γὰρ τοῦ Καίσαρος τοῦ προτέρου ἐπὶ μακρότατον τιμηθέντες, καὶ ἐν ταῖς ἀρχαῖς ταῖς τε ἡγεμονίαις ἐπὶ πλεῖστον γενόμενοι, πολλοὺς ἐχθροὺς εἶχον), ἐδόκει δὲ καὶ ὑπὸ τοῦ Καίσαρος κατὰ τὴν τῆς δυναστείας κοινωνίαν γίγνεσθαι, ἐπεὶ αὐτός γε οὐδέν τι συχνοὺς ἀποκτεῖναι ἐδεήθη· τῇ τε γὰρ φύσει οὐκ ὠμὸς ἦν, καὶ ἐν τοῖς τοῦ πατρὸς ἤθεσιν ἐνετέθραπτο. πρὸς δ' ἔτι νέος τε ὢν καὶ ἄρτι ἐς τὰ πράγματα παριὼν οὔτ' ἄλλως ἀνάγκην πολλοὺς σφοδρῶς μισεῖν εἶχε καὶ φιλεῖσθαι ἤθελε. σημεῖον δὲ ὅτι, ἀφ' οὗ τῆς τε πρὸς ἐκείνους συναρχίας ἀπηλλάγη καὶ τὸ κράτος μόνος ἔσχεν, οὐδὲν ἔτι τοιοῦτον ἔπραξεν. καὶ τότε δὲ οὐχ ὅσον πολλοὺς οὐκ ἔφθειρεν, ἀλλὰ καὶ ἔσωσε πλείστους, τοῖς τε προδοῦσι τοὺς δεσπότας ἢ τοὺς φίλους χαλεπώτατα καὶ τοῖς συναραμένοις τισὶν ἐπιεικέστατα ἐχρήσατο.

These acts were committed chiefly by Lepidus and Antony; for they had been honored by the former Caesar for many years, and as they had been holding offices and governorships for a long time they had many enemies. But Caesar seems to have taken part in the business merely because of his sharing the authority, since he himself had no need at all to kill a large number; for he was not naturally cruel and had been brought up in his father's ways. Moreover, as he was still a young man and had just entered politics, he was under no necessity in any case of hating many persons violently, and, besides, he wished to be loved. A proof of this is that from the time he broke off his joint rulership with his colleagues and held the power alone he no longer did anything of the sort. And even at this time he not only refrained from destroying many but actually saved a very large number; and he treated with great severity those who betrayed their masters or friends and very leniently those who helped others.

---

22 The Triumvirate is described in negative terms as an oligarchy (48.34.1), as a dynasty (46.34.4), and as an enslavement of the Roman people (50.1.2). Also, the alliance is said to have been of three men who hated each other desiring power for themselves (46.54–55.4). See also Gowing 1992, 35.

That the young triumvir's acts were reasonable, justifiable, and excusable is underlined several times. One instance is when, before the war at Actium, Dio has the two generals address their soldiers. In his speech Antony assures his army that they will be victorious as they are superior in numbers and better equipment, while Octavian in his address is allowed to say that he would prevail because justice was on his side.[23] Another example is from Book 56, where Dio draws some concluding remarks on the reign of Augustus. In the overall assessment of the importance of Augustus' reign, Dio says that by combining monarchy and democracy, Augustus ensured stability and freed the Romans from tyranny and the unlimited ambitions that were the main reason why members of the political elite had fought each other over the right to rule the Romans or to command their armies. He then goes on to say (56.44.1):

Εἰ γάρ τινες καὶ τῶν προτέρων τῶν ἐν τοῖς ἐμφυλίοις πολέμοις γενομένων ἐμνημόνευον, ἐκεῖνα μὲν τῇ τῶν πραγμάτων ἀνάγκῃ ἀνετίθεσαν, τὴν δὲ δὴ γνώμην αὐτοῦ ἐξ οὗ τὸ κράτος ἀναμφίλογον ἔσχεν ἐξετάζειν ἠξίουν· πλεῖστον γὰρ δὴ τὸ διάφορον ὡς ἀληθῶς παρέχετο. καὶ τοῦτο μὲν καθ᾽ ἕκαστον ἄν τις τῶν πραχθέντων ἐπεξιὼν ἀκριβώσειε· κεφάλαιον δὲ ἐφ᾽ ἅπασιν αὐτοῖς γράφω ὅτι τό τε στασιάζον πᾶν ἔπαυσε καὶ τὸ πολίτευμα πρός τε τὸ κράτιστον μετεκόσμησε καὶ ἰσχυρῶς ἐκράτυνεν, ὥστε εἰ καὶ βιαιότερόν τι, οἷα ἐν τοῖς παραλόγοις φιλεῖ συμβαίνειν, ἐπράχθη, δικαιότερον ἄν τινα αὐτὰ τὰ πράγματα ἢ ἐκεῖνον αἰτιάσασθαι.

If any of them [men who lived during the civil wars] remembered his former deeds in the course of the civil wars, they attributed them to the pressure of circumstances, and they thought it fair to seek for his real disposition in what he did after he was in undisputed possession of the supreme power; for this afforded in truth a mighty contrast. Anybody who examines his acts in detail can establish this fact; but summing them all up briefly, I may state that he put an end to all the factional discord, transferred the government in a way to give it the greatest power, and vastly strengthened it. Therefore, even if an occasional deed of violence did occur, as is apt to happen in extraordinary situations, one might more justly blame the circumstances themselves than him.

---

23 On Antony's speech to his soldiers see Cass. Dio 50.16. On Octavian's focus on moral values see Cass. Dio 50.24–6.

The story of Octavian has all the elements that Dio would normally despise. A young ambitious man outside his station and with his own private army forces the Senate to support his claim to become consul long before the usual legal age and without having followed the traditional *cursus honorum*. He is what Dio elsewhere would depict as one of the dynasts, or private warlords, who used the powers of privately recruited armies to threaten his way into the center of Roman politics.[24] In order to assume and retain full control over the Roman state and in order to rule by himself, he engages in the most brutal war ever fought between Romans in which all parts of the empire and every social group suffered considerably.[25]

Inspired by Thucydides' thoughts on civil strife and political violence, Dio explains Octavian's acts in the civil war period as the result of human nature but justifies the untraditional political choices by blaming them on democracy. In order to stay ahead in the struggle to punish those behind the murder of Caesar and to reinsert the monarchy, Octavian had no other choice but to gather his father's soldiers, wage war on Antony at Mutina, march on Rome to secure the consulship, and form the Triumvirate to take on Brutus and Cassius in the East.[26]

As part of the attempt to explain Octavian's political moves, Dio downplays the demand for the consulship by describing how the soldiers acted on their own account, and the reader is led to believe that Octavian gave orders that weapons were not to be brought to the meeting (46.43.5). While the remark about how the soldiers acted on their own initiative when they threatened the senators to support the claim serves to improve the image of the young general, Dio still justifies Octavian's frustration when he moves on to criticize how Sextus Pompeius, a pirate in his eyes, was given control over Rome's fleet or how Brutus and Cassius were offered commands in the East instead of being punished for the murder of Caesar (46.40.3).

With the account of how it was Decimus Brutus who was celebrated for having won the battle at Mutina, Dio completes the picture of the way in which the Senate did everything in its power to outmaneuver Caesar's heir and prevent him from entering the political scene. This brings us to the conclusion that if Caesar's murderers were to be punished and the monarchy re-established, war

---

24   On how Octavian fits Dio's description of a dynast see Kemezis 2014, 124–5. The parallel to Pompey is obvious but Dio ignores it.

25   Osgood 2006, 67. On the social consequences of the proscription see App. *B Civ.* 4.13; Gowing 1992, 92. On the resistance against the veteran settlement in Italy see Osgood 2006, 164; Syme 1939, 208.

26   See the papers of Lange and Markov in this this volume. See also Lange 2017; Lange forthcoming; Madsen forthcoming.

was the only option. With the legitimate right to follow Caesar and with the right and obligation to punish those behind the coup against his great-uncle and the state, Octavian could only act as he did. As Dio underlines in the conclusion of Book 56 quoted above, circumstances required war and violence in order to prevail.

3   Monarchy Returns

By comparing the ways in which Dio writes about Caesar and in the end his more successful great-nephew, we learn more about the way he works as a historian and about the agenda he followed throughout the *Roman History*. One question that Dio's narrative raises is why the portraits and the historical verdicts of the two Caesars turn out so differently. Part of the answer relates to the fact that Caesar did not secure a more lasting solution to the chaos and instability of late republican Rome because, tempted by pomp and hollow honorific decrees, he lost all sense of modesty when he won the war against Pompey. As is pointed out by Gowing, Dio's Stoic approach to nature leads him to the conclusion that character is formed in the early years of life and therefore is not subject to fundamental change later in life.[27] Caesar's appetite for glory followed him into his years as dictator, which made it difficult for him to win and maintain support from his peers. He did include the Senate and his former enemies in the decisions he made, but could not help elevating himself above the rest of the political elite, which, in the end, made him come across as their master more than a legitimate supreme ruler.

In the account of the reign of Augustus, Dio describes how he introduced a form of monarchy that won the necessary support among his peers because he had a more developed sense of modesty and was determined to have his political powers renewed. By not holding any of his powers for life he was not a tyrant but an elected and legitimate monarch who ruled on a mandate from Rome's political institutions. It is in the way he kept his powers temporary that Dio sees Augustus' reign as a combination of monarchy and democracy (56.43.4).

Dio draws a distinction between the two when he describes that Octavian did not accept every honorific decree that was offered to him, and he points to how Augustus was never worshipped as a god in Rome and Italy (51.20.6–8). That Dio is wrong or willfully misleading simply adds to the impression

---

27   Gowing 1992, 91.

of a historian who adapts his portrait of Augustus to fit his own ideal of what constitutes a modest and legitimate ruler.[28]

Augustus was not a god or a king but a citizen with the authority from Rome's political institutions to take the responsibility for government upon himself (53.14.2). Because of the respect he had for Rome's political institutions, he did not cross the line of tyranny but served as supreme ruler whom the Roman People and the Senate repeatedly asked to continue when he offered to give his powers back after he had returned from Egypt (53.11–12). Dio's account of how Octavian offered to lay down his power may well be a product of Dio's intention to write a historic account as accurately as possible but contradicts his view of how it was Octavian's right and intention all along to succeed his great-uncle. To solve the problem, the historian describes how Caesar wanted prestige and power for its own sake, while Augustus took the responsibility for rule upon himself, reluctantly, and carried on because he was asked to do so.[29]

Another reason why Dio offers a description of Octavian's route to power and of the reign of Augustus that is different from the way he treats Caesar is probably to be seen in the need to keep his ideal ruler as free of blame as possible. Yet, it is important to underline that Dio is not writing panegyric. He does not try to keep Octavian spotless, as pointed out by Markov in this volume. The story of how he became Rome's absolute ruler contains criticism, such as in the case of Perusia. It is true that the sacrifice of Roman knights and senators is described as second-hand information, but Dio does not question the story or try to justify the atrocity. Instead, the battle and the killings are left hanging in the air as an example of the kind of things civil war made the best kind of people do.[30] Some of the acts Octavian carried out during the war were no doubt despicable, even in Dio's eyes, but just as the lack of modesty was a part of Caesar's personality, so was Octavian a fair and reasonable man, which then meant that the horrible acts of violence did not define who he was.

Later, when the narrative moves into the imperial period, Dio dedicates much of his account to how Augustus made every effort to include the Senate in the decision-making process. The new first citizen tried to bring the Senate back into the political process in the role of his valued advisers. Unsurprisingly, Augustus follows the path that Dio sets out in the Agrippa-Maecenas dialogue. We hear how Augustus tried to get the senators involved by requiring that they

---

28   Madsen 2016b, 295–7.
29   On the renewal of Augustus' powers see Cass. Dio 54.12.4–5, 55.6.1, 55.12.3.
30   Lange forthcoming.

participate in the Senate meeting, how he gave them the opportunity to learn in advance about the laws that were being discussed, and how he allowed them to speak freely both in the Senate and on the meetings of the *consilium principis*.[31]

When seen as a whole, Dio is not simply offering Augustus' official version of the war or an account of how he led Rome towards a better future. There is no reason to assume that Dio did not know or use Augustus' autobiography and other pro-Augustan sources, but there is a larger moral behind the narrative than the attempt to write the history of the civil war period or the early empire with whatever sources Dio had at his disposal. As has already been pointed out, Dio treats republican history, including the civil war period, as steps towards a more stable form of monarchical rule but also a period in its own right that played its own decisive role in the history of Rome.[32]

As has already been pointed out by Rich, it was Dio's ambition to write about the challenges Augustus faced as he became Rome's next ruler, and it would be wrong to see the books on the civil wars and Augustus' reign as merely an attempt to draw attention to the political reality of his own time or, for that matter, simply as a step on the way to the imperial period, allegedly Dio's real interests.[33] What Dio does is to shape his narrative in such a way that monarchical rule in the form he sketches was not only the best form of government for any state but a form of constitution that had already been put in place by Caesar before his wrongful death.

Dio's thoughts on how Octavian had the right to succeed Caesar collide with his pronounced scepticism towards dynastic succession and the view that political and military qualifications would exceed family relations and social background.[34] But what makes the situation different in 44 BCE was how Octavian offered new thoughts about how to introduce a more stable form of monarchy than the one Caesar would have been able to provide. In that sense, Octavian did not continue where his great-uncle had left off but came from outside the political establishment with new ideas and the determination to change the nature of Roman politics.

---

31 Madsen 2016a, 146–9.
32 See Gowing 1992, 93.
33 On how Dio was more interested in the imperial period than in the previous years of Rome's history see Gowing 1992, 35; Rich 1990, 14.
34 Madsen 2016a, 149–54; Rantala 2016, 164–5; Osgood 2016, 180–3, 189. On Nerva's adoption of Trajan see Cass. Dio 68.4.1–2.

Bibliography

Aalders, G. J. D. (1986) "Cassius Dio and the Greek World", *Mnemosyne* 39/3–4, 282–304.

Armitage, D. (2017) *Civil Wars: A History of Ideas*, New York.

Bleicken, J. (1962) "Der politische Standpunkt Dios gegenüber der Monarchie: die Rede des Maecenas Buch 52, 14–40", *Hermes* 90/4, 444–67.

De Blois, L. (1998) "Emperor and Empire in the Works of Greek-speaking Authors of the Third Century AD", in *Aufstieg und Niedergang der römischen Welt* 2.34.4, 3391–443.

Flower, H. I. (2010) *Roman Republics*, Oxford.

Gowing, A. M. (1992) *The Triumviral Narratives of Appian and Cassius Dio*, Ann Arbor.

Kemezis, A. (2014) *Greek Narratives of the Roman Empire under the Severans: Cassius Dio, Philostratus and Herodian*, Cambridge.

Lange, C. H. (2009). *Res Publica Constituta: Actium, Apollo and the Accomplishment of the Triumviral Assignment*, Leiden & Boston.

Lange, C. H. (2016) "Mock the Triumph: Cassius Dio, Triumph and Triumph-Like Celebrations", in C. H. Lange & J. M. Madsen (eds.), *Cassius Dio: Greek Intellectual and Roman Politician* (Leiden & Boston): 92–114.

Lange, C. H. (2017) "Stasis and Bellum Civile: A Difference in Scale", *Critical Analysis of Law* 4/2, 129–30.

Lange, C. H. (forthcoming) "Cassius Dio on Perusia: A Study in Human Nature during Civil War", in J. M. Madsen & C. H. Lange (eds.), *Cassius Dio the Historian: Methods and Approaches* (Leiden & Boston).

Levick, B. (2010) *Augustus. Image and Substance*, Harlow & London.

Lintott, A. (1994) "Political History, 146–95 BC", in *The Cambridge Ancient History* (2nd ed.): Vol. 9, 40–103.

Madsen, J. M. (2016a) "Criticising the Benefactors: The Severans and the Return of Dynastic Rule", in C. H. Lange & J. M. Madsen (eds.), *Cassius Dio: Greek Intellectual and Roman Politician* (Leiden & Boston): 136–58.

Madsen, J. M. (2016b) "Cassius Dio and the Cult of Iulius and Roma at Ephesus and Nicaea (51.20.6–8)", *Classical Quarterly* 66/1, 286–97.

Madsen, J. M. (2018) "From Nobles to Villains: The Story of the Republican Senate in Cassius Dio's *Roman History*", in C. Burden-Strevens & M. Lindholmer (eds.), *Cassius Dio's Forgotten History of Early Rome: The 'Roman History' Books 1–21* (Leiden & Boston): 99–125.

Madsen, J. M. (forthcoming) "In the Shadow of Civil War: Cassius Dio and his Roman History", in C. H. Lange & F. J. Vervaet (eds.), *The Historiography of Late Republican Civil War* (Leiden & Boston).

Meier, C. (1966) *Res Publica Amissa: eine Studie zur Verfassung und Geschichte der Späten römischen Republik*, Wiesbaden.

Millar, F. (1964) *A Study of Cassius Dio*, Oxford.
Osgood, J. (2006) *Caesar's Legacy: Civil War and the Emergence of the Roman Empire*, Cambridge.
Osgood, J. (2016) "Cassius Dio's Secret History of Elagabalus", in C. H. Lange & J. M. Madsen (eds.), *Cassius Dio: Greek Intellectual and Roman Politician* (Leiden & Boston): 177–90.
Rantala, J. (2016) "Dio the Dissident: The Portrait of Severus in the Roman History", in C. H. Lange & J. M. Madsen (eds.), *Cassius Dio: Greek Intellectual and Roman Politician*. (Leiden & Boston): 159–76.
Reinhold, M. (1988) *From Republic to Principate: An Historical Commentary on Cassius Dio's Roman History Books 49–52 (36–29 B.C.)*, Atlanta.
Reinhold, M. & Swan, P. M. (1990) "Cassius Dio's Assessment of Augustus", in K. A. Raaflaub & M. Toher (eds.), *Between Republic and Empire: Interpretations of Augustus and his Principate* (Berkeley): 155–73.
Rich, J. W. (1990) *Cassius Dio: The Augustan Settlement (Roman History 53.1–55.9)*, Warminster.
Steel, C. (2013) *The End of the Roman Republic, 146 to 44 BC: Conquest and Crisis*, Edinburgh.
Swan, P. M. (2004) *The Augustan Succession: An Historical Commentary on Cassius Dio's Roman History Books 55–56 (9 BC–AD 14)*, Oxford.
Syme, R. (1939) *The Roman Revolution*, Oxford.
Urso, G. (forthcoming) "The Origin of the Empire in Cassius Dio's Roman History", in J. M. Madsen & G. Hinge (eds.), *Cassius Dio and the Principate* (Leiden & Boston).

CHAPTER 14

Towards the Conceptualization of Cassius Dio's Narration of the Early Career of Octavian

Konstantin V. Markov

This paper deals with Cassius Dio's narrative of the early career of Caesar Octavianus ("Octavian" hereafter) and the conceptions that lie behind it. Dio's views appear more complex but at the same time more consistent than has been suggested by scholars. The inconsistency that does sometimes characterize Dio's judgments can be explained both by the use of different sources and the ambiguity of his views. The concept of human nature as one of the main driving forces of history, predetermining in particular Octavian's participation in the struggle for power as well as the struggle's methods, is evident in the text. His activities are also shown as corresponding to Dio's general concept of political leaders' behavior at the time of the civil wars (48.29.3). In the "Augustan" books Dio continues to emphasize the pragmatism of the founder of the principate and simultaneously pays attention to certain flaws of his rule and his person.

It is standard among scholars to regard Dio's account of Rome's transition from the Republic to the principate as a special segment of the narrative, "the heart" of Dio's *History*, which occupies around one-third of the entire work.[1] Little less than half of this section belongs to the Augustan account (Books 45–56, covering 44 BCE to 14 CE). The proportions themselves indicate the author's special interest in the period and, specifically, in the activities of the founder of the principate. It has, nevertheless, been shown that Dio's intention was not to explore the historical personality of Augustus, but rather to adapt the sources to present his own historical views.[2] This raises the question of how Dio conceived of the end of the civil wars, and Octavian's role in them. Some scholars have argued that the portrait of an ambitious and hypocritical Octavian before Actium contrasts significantly with the paradigmatic representation of his achievements after the victory over Antony, which is explained by usage of different sources or by different perceptions the author might have

---

1 Twenty-nine of Dio's eighty books (28–56) cover 104 years, from 91 BCE to 14 CE.
2 Swan 2004, 15; Pelling 1997, 135–44; Osgood 2006, 10.

had.³ According to a different opinion, the purpose of Dio was to reveal and expose the "true nature" of Octavian's motives, rather than to provide moral evaluations of the statesman's struggle for power; such a pragmatic and realistic portrait could be intended as a comment on the rulers of Dio's own day.⁴ Kemezis questions these paradigmatic conceptions⁵ and comes to the conclusion that Dio's narrative in Books 45 to 50 depended largely on the scheme of narrative modes, with Octavian as a "dynast" and Augustus as a monarch/ *princeps* belonging to different "narrative domains."⁶ Contrary to this idea of the distinctive division of Dio's Augustan narrative, Madsen, in a contribution to the present volume, has suggested that the conception of Dio's treatment of Octavian was determined primarily by emphasizing his status as heir to the power of Julius Caesar. This shaped to a considerable extent the author's representation of Caesar the Younger as a "legitimate ruler" who stood out "as someone who had justice on his side but also as one who was surrounded by enemies and therefore had to act unscrupulously in order to avenge his great-uncle and follow in his footsteps."⁷

This paper aims at reconsidering the late republican narrative of Dio in order to answer the following questions. What was Dio's general attitude to Octavian's activities in 44–31 BCE? What were the author's criteria for judging the young politician on his way to supreme power? Is Dio's vision consistent, or what could be the reasons for the apparent ambiguity of his evaluations? Is there any general conception detectable behind Dio's narrative on Octavian's early career? In order to answer these questions I start with a re-examination of some of Dio's controversial statements on Octavian's early political activities, particularly his participation in triumviral policies, with special attention being paid to young Caesar's attitudes to his political opponents as well as elements of continuity and consistency with Dio's Augustan narrative. I then finish with an analysis of some indications that Dio's account of Octavian's struggle for power serves a paradigmatic function.

---

3   Manuwald 1979, 70–5; Reinhold 1988, 13–14; Hose 1994, 431; Escribano 1999, 184. The idea of contrasting periods of Octavian's political career affects to some extent the portrayals of the principate's founder provided by modern scholars. See Stahl 2011, 87–105.
4   Wiedemann 1981, 202; Rich 1990, 14; Gowing 1992, 257–9; Swan 2004, 17; Swan 1997, 2525.
5   The idea that Augustus was not inevitably seen as a paradigm in the first centuries of the principate is expressed by Swan (2004, 14–15).
6   Kemezis 2014, 98.
7   Cf. Madsen 2016, 146–9.

1   *Vitia Caesaris*: Exposure or Justification?

It should be noted that insistence on the inconsistency of Dio's evaluations, which is entrenched in the literature, goes back to the work of Manuwald (*Cassius Dio und Augustus*), whose detailed analysis of the Augustan books had an impact on the subsequent scholarship. Manuwald finds it surprising that Dio comments positively on the behavior of Octavian in the time of the proscriptions (47.7–8.1).[8] Dio blames mostly Antony and Lepidus for the killings. As for young Caesar, he got involved in the proscriptions because of his "sharing the authority," but he was not inclined to murder people because he "was not by nature cruel" (τῇ τε γὰρ φύσει οὐκ ὠμὸς ἦν) and he was brought up in the manner of his father. Also, since Octavian just started a career in politics, he had not yet amassed a lot of enemies; on the contrary, he wanted to obtain popularity among the citizens (47.7.1–2). The following expression is the most remarkable here: "A proof of this is that from the time he broke off his joint rulership with his colleagues and held the power alone he no longer did anything of the sort" (σημεῖον δὲ ὅτι, ἀφ' οὗ τῆς πρὸς ἐκείνους συναρχίας ἀπηλλάγη καὶ τὸ κράτος μόνος ἔσχεν, οὐδὲν ἔτι τοιοῦτον ἔπραξεν, 47.7.3).[9] In this passage Dio doesn't make any distinction between Octavian before and after coming to supreme power. The author points to the peculiarity of the politician's policy, which can be observed already in the earliest period of his career. Such a generalization appears to be something more than just echoes of "the official version," as was suggested by Manuwald for this and some other positive evaluations of Octavian's activities (48.54.2, 49.14–16).[10]

Dio is critical of Octavian at a number of points in the history (47.15.2, 48.5.3, 48.8.5, 48.29, 48.34.3, 48.36.1, 48.44, 50.3.4). One of the passages is devoted to the distribution of Italian lands to veterans in 41 BCE, which resulted in a conflict between the soldiers as recipients of lands and senators as land-owners. Octavian had to act in favor of one or the other party, so he might avoid the wrath of both sides. Because of this experience, he recognized the impossibility of obtaining popularity among citizens by the use of force and refrained from depriving senators of their property (48.8.4–5). Dio supplements this statement with the following remark (48.8.5):

---

8   Manuwald 1979, 70.
9   The translation of E. Cary in the Loeb Classical Library is used here and below.
10   Manuwald 1979, 71–2.

> ... πρότερον γὰρ καὶ τὰ ἐκείνων πάντα κατανεῖμαι ἠξίου, διερωτῶν σφας "πόθεν οὖν τὰ γέρα τοῖς ἐστρατευμένοις ἀποδώσομεν;" ὥσπερ τινὸς αὐτῷ πολεμεῖν ἢ καὶ τοσαῦτά σφισιν ὑπισχνεῖσθαι κεκελευκότος.

> ... for previously he used to think it right to distribute anything that was theirs [senators'], asking them: "From what other source, then, are we to pay the veterans their prize money?" – as if anyone had commanded him to wage war or to make his large promises to the soldiers.

Indeed, if we look at Dio's explanation, given parenthetically, we will easily see the disapproval of the actions of Octavian, which is exactly what has been remarked on by researchers. However, if we consider this remark not out of context, but given the circumstances outlined above, the relationship of Dio to young Caesar appears in a different light. Octavian is the statesman who is able to learn from his mistakes, demonstrates relative flexibility, and, already in the period of the civil wars, begins to recognize the importance of public approval of his activities, promoted later so much in the speech of Maecenas.[11] The fact that the decision on the concessions to the citizens was taken by Octavian with great difficulty becomes clear if we pay attention to the content of chapter 9 describing the indignation of the soldiers, who become mutinous, kill many of the centurions, and even threaten Octavian for rejecting confiscations (48.9.1–2). Moreover, if we compare the text of the *History* with Appian's account of those events,[12] it appears that Dio to some extent idealizes the behavior of Octavian. According to Appian (*B Civ.* 5.15), Octavian was primarily concerned with receiving support from soldiers, even at the expense of the interests of the Italian population. Thus, Dio, who claims exactly the opposite, either deliberately distorts the facts, or employs only the evidence that appeals to his own vision of Octavian and creates an opportunity for reasoning about paradigms of proper leadership.

Manuwald points to some critical remarks related to the private life of the future *princeps*. For example, chapter 44 of Book 48 is dedicated to Octavian's marriage to Livia. As we learn from Tacitus, those who were Octavian's opponents among his contemporaries rebuked Octavian for "taking" Nero's wife and for the farce of asking the high priests if she was allowed to enter into a second marriage when being pregnant (Tac. *Ann.* 1.10). But, even if the story belongs to the narrative of critics of Augustus, does it necessarily mean that Dio shared

---

11   De Blois 1998–1999, 272.
12   According to Gowing 1992, Dio's triumviral narrative is less dramatic than the one of Appian.

their evaluations? The author might refer to a number of well-known anecdotes associated with this story, apparently with the aim to amuse his readers, but he does not express assessments. He represents Nero as bringing Livia himself to Octavian, while the request to the pontifices has nothing to do with "mockery." Octavian really hesitated about getting married to Livia when she was pregnant. As Dio writes (48.44.2–3):

> At any rate, when Caesar was in doubt (διστάζοντος γοῦν τοῦ Καίσαρος) and enquired of the pontifices whether it was permissible to wed her while pregnant, they answered that if there was any doubt whether conception had taken place the marriage should be put off, but if this was admitted, there was nothing to prevent its taking place immediately. Perhaps they really found this among the ordinances of the forefathers, but certainly they would have said so, even had they not found it. Her husband himself gave the woman in marriage just as a father would (ἐξέδωκε δὲ αὐτὴν αὐτὸς ὁ ἀνὴρ ὥσπερ τις πατήρ).

There is another story which deals with the private affairs of Octavian, where notes of criticism are again hardly noticeable. This is the first marriage of Octavian, or rather, its dissolution. Octavian could not withstand the bad temper of his mother-in-law (Fulvia), and, therefore, brought her daughter back, solemnly assuring that she was still a virgin, not fearing other people's witty remarks on that (48.5.3). Thus, Dio merely gives the facts without expressing his own evaluations, as he also does when describing the divorce of Octavian and Scribonia (48.34.3). In addition, if we take the context into account, the actions of Octavian as well as the characterization of his mother-in-law appear to be justified. It is Fulvia who, according to Dio, was really the initiator of the conflict (48.5.2). She and Lucius Antonius sought to seize power, ostensibly doing it for Marcus Antonius (Antony), but in actual fact guided by their own vested interests (48.5.3). According to a preliminary agreement, they intended to receive their own share in lands designated for the soldiers of Caesar and Antony (48.5.1–2, 6.1–2). It is noteworthy that the characterization differs from that of Appian, according to whom Lucius and Fulvia had really acted as agents of Antony in order to prevent the veterans from being grateful exclusively to Octavian for receiving lands (*B Civ.* 5.14).

Dio describes Octavian's hypocritical behavior repeatedly (45.12.2, 47.2.2, 47.13.2–4, 47.14.1, 48.2.1, 49.18.7).[13] Some of the examples refer to all the

---

[13] Manuwald 1979, 70. According to Rich (1990, 13), Dio points to Octavian's duplicity at every opportunity.

triumvirs (47.2.2, 47.13.2–4, 47.14.1, 48.2.1), but, as we have already seen in chapter 7 of Book 47, Octavian could refrain from supporting the policy of his colleagues, and, therefore, at least in some cases Dio might make a distinction between the Triumvirate's agenda and Octavian's own course. For instance, when he writes that the triumvirs kept receiving various honors as the saviors and benefactors of the state and did not allow any charges to be made against them in connection with the proscriptions, but rather "wished to be praised because the number of their victims was not greater" (47.13.2–4), it can be regarded as a demonstration of the triumvirs' hypocrisy. But does it refer to Octavian? According to the previous chapters of the book, as we have already seen, Octavian not only refrains from adding to the killings, but saves many people (47.7.3, 47.8.1). Consequently, if we follow Dio's text and recognize its coherence and integrity, Octavian's behavior in the matter of the honors does appear to be less hypocritical than his colleagues'. In two other passages we do actually find examples of the hypocritical behavior of Octavian highlighted. He pretended to be a friend of Antony when expressing his condolences on the disasters inflicted by the Parthians (49.18.7). And when Octavian was gathering troops in Campania in 44 BCE, he covered over his lust for power by alleging a desire to avenge his father (45.12.2). From other passages, it also follows that Octavian could be hypocritical and ambitious (45.4–5, 46.46.3–4, 47.15.2). But the author's formulations are generally quite neutral. Basically, he regards hypocrisy as typical for the majority of people (53.24.1).[14] Here, Dio is very close to the "pragmatic historiography" which can be traced back to Polybius and Thucydides.[15] Octavian's activities are represented in accordance with this basic approach, and this, in turn, allows Dio to reveal the "true" motives of the younger Caesar's undertakings. For instance, the beginning of chapter 36 of Book 49 reads (49.36.1):

> ἐπεὶ δ᾽ οὖν οὗτοί τε ἀπωλώλεσαν καὶ οἱ ἄλλοι κατεστράφατο μηδὲν ἀξιόλογον πράξαντες, ἐπὶ Παννονίους ἐπεστράτευσεν, ἔγκλημα μὲν οὐδὲν αὐτοῖς ἐπιφέρων οὐδὲ γὰρ οὐδ᾽ ἠδίκητό τι ὑπ᾽ αὐτῶν, ἵνα δὲ δὴ τοὺς στρατιώτας ἀσκῇ τε ἅμα καὶ ἐκ τῶν ἀλλοτρίων τρέφῃ, πᾶν τὸ τῷ κρείττονι τοῖς ὅπλοις ἀρέσκον δίκαιον ἐς τοὺς ἀσθενεστέρους ποιούμενος.

---

14   Concerning Cornelius Gallus' suicide: "and the insincerity of the majority of people (τὸ δὲ δὴ τῶν πολλῶν κίβδηλον) was again proved by his case" (48.29.3).
15   Hose 1994, 381, 433, 436. For Thucydides as a model for Dio's descriptions of civil war violence, see Lange 2018 and Lange forthcoming, as well as Lange's paper in this volume.

When these, then, had perished and the rest had been subdued without performing any exploit of note, Caesar made a campaign against the Pannonians. He had no complaint to bring against them, not having been wronged by them in any way, but he wanted both to give his soldiers practice and to support them at the expense of an alien people, for he regarded every demonstration against a weaker party as just, when it pleased the man who was their superior in arms.

This passage echoes the thoughts that Thucydides put into the mouths of the Athenian ambassadors pragmatically reasoning that "in human disputation justice is then only agreed on when the necessity is equal; whereas they that are superior exact as much as they can, and the weak yield to such conditions as they can get" (δίκαια μὲν ἐν τῷ ἀνθρωπείῳ λόγῳ ἀπὸ τῆς ἴσης ἀνάγκης κρίνεται, δυνατὰ δὲ οἱ προύχοντες πράσσουσι καὶ οἱ ἀσθενεῖς ξυγχωροῦσιν, Thuc. 5.89).

But, in addition to making such general judgments about human nature, Dio emphasizes the specific behavior of military leaders in times of civil wars. A good example of the latter is given in the account of the reconciliation of Octavian and Antony at Brundisium in later 40 BCE (48.29). Octavian and Antony divided up the empire anew and jointly undertook the war against Sextus Pompey, although Antony had previously taken oaths to side with Sextus and fight against Octavian. The latter, for his part, declared a general amnesty and received those who had once been adversaries of himself and Antony, including assassins of Caesar and supporters of Brutus and Cassius.[16] It was done in order to attract those who took Antony's side (48.29.1–2). Dio comments on the situation in the following way (48.29.3):

> τοσοῦτος μὲν δὴ καὶ τῶν στάσεων καὶ τῶν πολέμων παράλογός ἐστι, δίκῃ μὲν οὐδὲν τῶν τὰ πράγματα ἐχόντων νομιζόντων, πρὸς δὲ δὴ τάς τε ἀεὶ χρείας καὶ τὰ συμφέροντά σφων τό τε φίλιον καὶ τὸ πολέμιον ἐξεταζόντων, καὶ διὰ τοῦτο τοὺς αὐτοὺς τότε μὲν ἐχθροὺς τότε δὲ ἐπιτηδείους σφίσι πρὸς τὸν καιρὸν ἡγουμένων.

> So great, indeed, is the perversity that reigns in factional strife and war; for men in power take no account of justice, but determine on friend and foe according as their own interests and advantage at the time dictate,

---

[16] This shows that Dio was, as Madsen has suggested in this volume, less concerned with emphasizing Octavian's thirst for revenge as a justification of his role in the civil wars. Further evidence for this is the previously mentioned passage (45.12.2) where the idea of avenging Julius Caesar appears as a pretext for collecting soldiers.

and accordingly they regard the same men, now as their enemies, now as their friends, according to the occasion.

Here, the activities of Octavian are represented as an example of the general rule.[17] Consequently, Dio highlights the trends in the behavior of military and political leaders in times of civil wars. Similar patterns can be found in other sections of the *Roman History* where civil discord is described. Examples are the dramatic story of the treacherous conspiracy of Otho, who betrays Galba (63.5.2–3);[18] or the brief remark on how Valens murdered the decurion who had previously saved his life (64[65].1.1–2). Another possible parallel, which belongs to the narrative on πόλεμοι καὶ στάσεις of 193–197 CE, is Severus' attitude to Albinus. According to Dio, Albinus was granted a rank of Caesar, because Severus "understood in advance that after Julianus had been deposed the three would clash and fight against one another for the empire, and he therefore determined to win over the rival who was nearest to him" (74[73].15.1). But later "Severus would no longer give him even the rank of Caesar, now that he had got Niger out of the way and had settled other matters in that part of the world to his satisfaction" (76[75].4.1). As such material shows, there is an explanatory model that determines what the author focuses on when writing about civil discord in any part of his work.

2 The Limits of Augustan Ruthlessness and Clemency

There is an opinion among some scholars that Dio represents the "ruthlessness" of young Caesar in dealing with his political opponents (47.49.4, 48.13.6, 48.14.3, 49.12.44, 51.2.4–6).[19] Let us consider the cases. When Brutus was defeated, some of his colleagues committed suicide; others were captured and executed (47.49.4). Having taken Nursia, Octavian imposed a fine on the residents, which forced them to leave their territory (48.13.6). Octavian executed many senators and equestrians from among Lucius Antonius' supporters (48.14.3). Lepidus was deprived of authority and forced to live in Italy under guard.

---

17 According to an alternative interpretation suggested by Lange, the idea of the passage is that "individuals and warring groups naturally aimed to emerge on the winning side" (Lange in this volume). Nevertheless, Dio's comment, as can be concluded from the context, refers primarily to the decisions of such "men in power" as Octavian and Antony: both let their former "foes" become their "friends," because it corresponded to their interests at some point.

18 This is a version which is quite different from what Plutarch reports (*Galb.* 24.2).

19 Reinhold & Swan 1990, 155–73; Swan 2004, 17.

Of those who were recruited in Sextus' troops, the senators and equestrians, with the exception of some, were punished;[20] soldiers from among the free citizens joined the legions of Caesar; and the former slaves were returned to their owners. Those who surrendered voluntarily received a pardon, but those who resisted were punished (49.12.4). After the battle of Actium many of the senators and equestrians were punished by a fine (χρήμασιν ἐζημίωσε), many were executed, but some were spared (51.2.4–6).

Thus, Octavian's methods of dealing with political adversaries are marked by a certain flexibility and discretion. As we have seen, he not only punishes, but also bestows forgiveness.[21] As for the punishments, he employs different types of penalties. Despite this, modern scholars discern a contradiction between the clemency which Octavian showed in the time of the proscriptions (47.7.3), and the "ruthlessness" with which he would deal with his political opponents.[22] But there could be no contradiction, since, as the contents of the speeches of Maecenas and Livia underscore, Dio makes clear distinctions between the opposition from civilians and military leaders rendering armed resistance. It is essential to show mercy to the former, while the latter should be pursued as "enemies of the people" (52.31.10, 55.18.5). In addition, it should be noted that Dio considers senators themselves to be the main culprits in all the bloodshed of the civil wars after Caesar's death, as can be concluded from the author's introduction to his narration on the battle of Mutina (46.33–4). Having mentioned a series of grim omens foretelling a high number of casualties among senators and equestrians on that occasion, Dio then raises the question of who was responsible for all those fatalities (46.33.6–34.1):

> τοῦτο μὲν γὰρ αἱ μάχαι, τοῦτο δὲ καὶ οἱ οἴκοι σφαγαὶ τὸν Σύλλειον τρόπον αὖθις γενόμεναι πᾶν ὅ τι περ ἦν ἄνθος αὐτῶν, ἔξω τῶν δρώντων σφᾶς, ἔφθειραν. αἴτιοι δὲ τῶν κακῶν τούτων αὐτοὶ ἑαυτοῖς οἱ βουλευταὶ ἐγένοντο. δέον γὰρ αὐτοὺς ἕνα τινὰ τὸν τὰ ἀμείνω φρονοῦντα προστήσασθαι καὶ ἐκείνῳ διὰ παντὸς συνάρασθαι, τοῦτο μὲν οὐκ ἐποίησαν, ὑπολαβόντες δὲ δή τινας καὶ ἐπὶ τοὺς ἑτέρους ἐπαυξήσαντες ἔπειτα καὶ ἐκείνους ἀντικαθελεῖν ἐπεχείρησαν, κἀκ τούτου φίλον μὲν οὐδένα, ἐχθροὺς δὲ πάντας ἔσχον.

---

20 Dio uses the word ἐκολάσθησαν and doesn't specify what the punishment was.
21 Also, Dio's account of the siege and capture of Perusia (48.14.1–6) appears "surprisingly brief and subdued in tone." See Westall 2016, 57–8.
22 Manuwald 1979, 71; Swan 2004, 17.

> For in the first place the battles, and in the second place the murders at home which occurred again as in the Sullan regime, destroyed all the flower of the citizens except those who perpetrated the murders. **The responsibility for these evils rested on the senators themselves.** For whereas they ought to have set at their head some one man who had their best interests at heart and to have cooperated with him continually, they failed to do this, but took certain men into their favor, strengthened them against the rest, and later undertook to overthrow these favorites as well, and in consequence gained no friend but made everybody enemies.

Even though Dio does not mention the name of the "man who had senators' best interests at heart," the reader might have had little doubt that the author hinted at his "young favorite" Octavian here.[23] Dio's position is expressed even more clearly in a brief summary of Augustus' rule. According to the author, the main merit of the founder of the principate was that he put an end to all strife and made the state stronger, so that if he committed any violence, as usually happens in extraordinary situations, then the blame should lie with the circumstances and not him (56.44.1–2). As we can see, Dio, when giving an overall evaluation of Octavian, cannot forget what his path to power was. He acknowledges that violence actually took place, but it appears to be inevitable in civil wars. In addition, the author outlines the most relevant criteria for evaluation, namely the strengthening of the state, as well as the efficiency measured by results – not the means by which the goal is achieved.

The books dedicated to Augustus' sole rule do provide us with a number of passages where Dio demonstrates the difference between the words and the real intentions of the founder of the principate.[24] In 27 BCE, the declaration of laying down his powers was no more than a trick intended by Octavian to strengthen the legitimacy of his authority (53.2.5). When Augustus agrees to rule only a part of the provinces and only for a limited period, he wants to seem "democratic" and does not want to be regarded by subjects as an all-powerful monarch, but in fact he grants the Senate with the weaker provinces, allegedly to spare the senators from the hassle and dangers, but in reality to keep the control over the army (53.12.2–3). The picture Dio draws even leads to a distortion of the facts (in order, as might be suggested, to enhance the contrast between what Augustus said and what he did); the historian never mentions

---

23 Madsen in this volume.
24 According to Manuwald (1991, 416), there is no evident changing modality of Dio's evaluations of the activities of Octavian before and after 31 BCE.

that the legions were initially deployed in the senatorial provinces (53.12.3).[25] Some further points in Dio should be taken into account. Octavian cheats when reporting to senators that all Antony's letters had been burned (52.42.8). Nominally, he separates the public funds from his own, but in reality he is the master of all the funds (53.16.1). If we flip through the pages of Dio's work, we recognize the same "good old" Octavian in all this, but Dio's Augustus, as a mature and experienced politician, might seem surprisingly "worse" than young Caesar entering the political arena. Of course, we cannot find anything similar to the proscriptions in the mature Augustus' record, as was pointed out by Dio at 47.7, but the *princeps* appears to be assertive when eliminating potential political threats for himself and his regime. But having described the purge of the senatorial body by Augustus in 18 BCE and mentioned those who were dissatisfied with being, as they believed, unjustly expelled from the Senate, Dio offers the following passage (54.15.1–4):

τούτων οὖν οὕτω γενομένων συχνοὶ μὲν εὐθὺς συχνοὶ δὲ καὶ μετὰ τοῦτο καὶ ἐκείνῳ καὶ τῷ Ἀγρίππᾳ ἐπιβουλεῦσαι, εἴτ' οὖν **ἀληθῶς εἴτε καὶ ψευδῶς**, αἰτίαν ἔσχον ... ἐν δὲ δὴ τῷ τότε παρόντι ὁ Αὔγουστος ἄλλους μέν τινας ἐδικαίωσε, τὸν δὲ δὴ Λέπιδον ἐμίσει μὲν διά τε τἆλλα καὶ ὅτι ὁ υἱὸς αὐτοῦ καὶ ἐπεφώρατο ἐπιβουλεύων αὐτῷ καὶ ἐκεκόλαστο, οὐ μέντοι καὶ ἀποκτεῖναι ἠθέλησεν, ἀλλ' ἐν τρόπῳ τινὶ ἄλλοτε ἄλλῳ προεπηλάκιζεν.

After these events, many immediately and many later were accused, **whether truly or falsely**, of plotting against both the emperor and Agrippa ... As for the time of which we are speaking, Augustus executed a few men; in the case of Lepidus, however, although he hated the man, among other reasons, because his son had been detected in a plot against him and had been punished, yet he did not wish to put him to death, but kept subjecting him to insult from time to time in various ways.

According to this, the number of suspected plotters could be high under Augustus, with Dio expressing doubts about the truth of the allegations and the justice of the measures taken in response (54.15.2–3). The author mentions the execution of several men, as a personal action of Augustus, and proceeds to the case of Lepidus, which is one more example of Octavian's discretion in dealing with political adversaries. According to Dio, Augustus forced Lepidus to attend the Senate's meetings "in order that he might be subjected to the utmost to jeering and insults, so that he might realize his loss of power

---

25   Rich 1990, 15.

and dignity" (ὅπως ὅτι πλείστην καὶ χλευασίαν καὶ ὕβριν πρός τε τὴν τῆς ἰσχύος καὶ πρὸς τὴν τῆς ἀξιώσεως μεταβολὴν ὀφλισκάνῃ) (54.15.5). The next chapter informs us of Augustus' hypocrisy regarding the "matrimonial laws" (54.16.3–5). The account of the adoption of the laws is followed by Dio's statement on Augustus' passionate love for Maecenas' wife, which is mentioned a few chapters later (54.21.3–8). As we learn from Book 55, Augustus' temper could be "more or less uncontrollable" and he needed Maecenas to help him master his anger: "he had found him of especial service on occasions when his own temper was more or less uncontrollable. For Maecenas would always banish his anger and bring him to a gentler frame of mind" (... μάλιστα δὲ ὁσάκις ἀκρατοτέρῳ τῷ θυμῷ ἐχρῆτο· τῆς τε γὰρ ὀργῆς αὐτὸν ἀεὶ παρέλυε εὐθὺς ἐξαναστῆναι..., 55.7.1).[26] He also needed Livia to convince him, as an old man, to refrain from executing potential conspirators (55.22.1).

3   Pragmatism as a Paradigm

Do all these imperfections of Augustus preclude us from seeing the late republican and Augustan narrative of Dio as paradigmatic? Is there any paradigm of political leadership in all this? To answer the question, we should consider the specifics of Dio's own criteria for the evaluation of politicians. The peculiarity of Dio's attitude to Octavian is especially detectable, when he is compared to the assassins of Caesar.[27] Brutus and Cassius, as well as their companions-in-arms, are characterized as "freedom fighters,"[28] supporters of ἰσονομία – "equality before the law" or "political equality" (47.42.3) – and "friends of the people" (47.38.3).[29] Dio's account of the battle of Philippi is especially

---

26   Cf. Sen. *Ben.* 6.32.2. See further Swan 2004, 69.
27   Some scholars state that the positive portrayal of Brutus and Cassius in Dio's work proves the author's pro-republican sympathies as well as the critical attitude to Octavian. See Manuwald 1979, 70; Kuhn-Chen 2002, 193.
28   According to some scholars, the famous slogan *rem publicam in libertatem vindicare* (Cic. *Brut.* 212, *Fam.* 2.5.2, *Epist.* fr. 4.14) was no more than a bargaining chip for various political forces in late republican times (Welwei 2004, 217; Mouritsen 2001, 9–10; an alternative point of view: Tokarev 2011, 70). Dio not only demonstrates the commitment of the republicans to this principle but also refers to "liberty and popular government" as the issues of the struggle (47.39.1).
29   A similar vision can be found in the work of Appian, according to whom Brutus and Cassius were distinguished by their nobility, fame, and undeniable prowess and fought for their ideals sincerely (*B Civ.* 4.132). Apparently, Dio might follow a certain literary cliché. But the recognition of the republicans' commitment to ideals of freedom and democracy doesn't prevent him from blaming them for murdering Julius Caesar and demonstrating

important to us as a pattern that opposes representatives of the two camps and their means of political propaganda. Dio depicts the republicans as upholders of equality (ἰσονομία) who believed sincerely that they had struggled for the Romans' best interests. Their adversaries seem to be more practical. They "urged their army to take vengeance on the assassins of Caesar, to get the property of their antagonists, to be filled with a desire to rule all the men of their own race, and – the thing which heartened them most – they promised to give them twenty thousand sesterces apiece" (47.42.4). The slogans of Brutus' associates, though captivating, are too abstract in comparison with Caesar's appeal to material benefits, which proved to be more attractive to soldiers and therefore more efficient in Dio's view. In actual fact, at Philippi both parties may have acted pragmatically. According to Appian, Brutus and Cassius "completed the payment of the promised donatives still due to the soldiers. They had provided themselves with an abundant supply of money in order to propitiate them with gifts" (*B Civ.* 4.89).

The difference between Dio and Appian may cast light on Dio's approach. His main purpose here was not only to give an impartial account of events, but to give typical portrayals of the republicans and their rivals. The republicans are depicted by Dio as idealists who fail to understand the real state of affairs and stand for the legendary Republic of Scipios and Catos. On the contrary, the language of Octavian and his supporters is of practical value and efficiency. Such is the focus of the author, which can be traced from the moment when he introduces Octavian as a politician. Dio acknowledges that young Caesar was impelled by thirst for power and acted at first boldly and recklessly. Dio does make a discount for Octavian's young age, and marks Octavian's ability to overcome hardships and achieve results. The brief characterization ends with the following words: "In this way he who was formerly called Octavius, but already by this time Caesar, and subsequently Augustus, took a hand in public affairs; and he managed and dealt with them more vigorously (νεανικώτερον) than any man in his prime, more prudently (φρονιμώτερον) than any graybeard" (45.3–5.1). As the material above shows, this is probably the basic dialectical framework for Dio's treatment of Octavian. Indeed, the author is accurate in choosing the epithets for this key characterization of the younger Caesar, whose style of managing public affairs is represented as a surprising

---

the fallaciousness of their political course (44.1.1–2.1). According to Dio's pragmatic view, "monarchy is a most practical form of government to live under" (χρησιμώτατον δὲ ἐμπολιτεύσασθαι ἐστί, 44.2.1), even though the author recognizes some positive sides of democracy, such as freedom of speech (παρρησία, 47.39.2) and free access to any information concerning the political life of Rome (53.19.2). On παρρησία as a recurring theme in Dio's *Roman History*: Mallan 2016.

combination of two opposites. The prudence of Octavian, in which he would surpass any elderly person, is complemented by what has been rendered in English as "vigor." Perhaps, a more suitable alternative reading of νεανικώτερον (as an antonym for φρονιμώτερον) would be "exceedingly bold, as characteristic of a young person." This extraordinary combination of dialectically interrelated traits would fit well a person who was fated, according to Dio, to solve extraordinary tasks – to break through the wars and civil discord, obtain the supreme power, and establish a new political system.

In sum, Dio's view of young Caesar's public career is more complex and more consistent than has been suggested by scholars. Following traditions of "pragmatic historiography," Dio aimed at providing some keys to understanding how Rome was once capable of overcoming a period of wars and *staseis* and achieving stability and security in its political system. Paying special attention to the causal factors of that process,[30] Dio is accurate enough in revealing and exposing the true motives of the most influential politicians of the time. The author frequently refers to the concept of human nature as one of the main driving forces of history. This is what lurks behind Octavian's quest for power, with his activities corresponding to Dio's general idea of what political leaders do whenever civil wars occur.

At the same time, it can be agreed with Madsen in this volume that Octavian from the very beginning is favored by the narrator as the successor to "the name, authority, and sovereignty" of Julius Caesar (45.1.2), whom Dio regarded as a founder of the new hereditary monarchy and *imperator* in a renovated meaning of the word. Dio refers to Julius Caesar as μόναρχος (43.45.1–3) and "possessing absolute public power" (πᾶν τὸ τοῦ δήμου κράτος ἔχοντι), which is similar to how the author occasionally describes Octavian's authority (51.1.1–2). The opening five chapters of Book 45, devoted exclusively to Octavian, mark a transition: this is an introduction to a new Caesar, which sets a pattern for Dio's introduction of subsequent emperors.[31] Consequently, Dio viewed and represented the period of transition from the late Republic to principate not only as a change of systems of government but also as a period of establishment of the new Julian dynasty. Dio's Octavian is definitely one of the "dynasts," but, on the other hand, he is also a representative of the emerging dynasty. Therefore, the Augustan narrative appears to be an

---

30 One of Dio's generalizations on the political instructiveness of history can be found in the above-mentioned introduction to the battle of Mutina (in particular, 46.35.1). See Hose 1994, 424.

31 For extended introductory and concluding sections in Dio's account of Roman emperors: Questa 1957, 37–53; Coltelloni-Trannoy 2016, 358.

eclectic combination of different historiographical approaches: a biographical technique[32] and a Thucydidean conception of history in which human nature is a constant.

It can be also agreed with Madsen that Dio was particularly interested in explaining why the younger Caesar chanced to be more successful than his predecessor. As the material above shows, Octavian is distinguished from contemporary political leaders. For instance, though not a paragon of traditional republican virtues, he is less responsible for the civil wars' bloodshed and is less hypocritical, if compared to other triumvirs, but more pragmatic, if compared to the republicans. The republicans appeal to basically ethical justification of their causes while Octavian and his supporters rely on language of practical value and efficiency. In this respect young Caesar is represented as one of the warlords of Dio's era of *dynasteiai*, but, also, he is singled out for his overall performance. Dio demonstrates Octavian's purposefulness and commitment to achieving results, regardless the means, as specific features of his personal style of managing public affairs at different stages of his career. Such a narrative appears to be paradigmatic. In the Augustan section of the work, Dio continues emphasizing the statesman's pragmatism and efficiency, as well as finding faults with him at minor points. Accentuating the utility of political activities and admitting their supremacy over traditional virtues, Dio, it appears, came close to finding a path that would lead European political thinking to the Machiavellian idea of separation of politics and morality.[33]

Bibliography

Coltelloni-Trannoy, M. (2016) "Les temporalités du recít impérial dans l'Histoire romaine de Cassius Dion", in V. Fromentin *et al.* (eds.), *Cassius Dion: nouvelles lectures* (Bordeaux): 335–62.

Coudry, M. (2016) "Figures et récit dans les livres républicains (livres 36 à 44)", in V. Fromentin *et al.* (eds.), *Cassius Dion: nouvelles lectures* (Bordeaux): 287–301.

De Blois, L. (1998–1999) "The Perception of Emperor and Empire in Cassius Dio's Roman History", *Ancient Society* 29, 267–81.

Escribano, M. V. (1999) "Estrategias retoricas y pensamiento politico en la Historia Romana de Cassio Dion", *L'antiquité classique* 68, 171–90.

Gowing, A. M. (1992) *The Triumviral Narratives of Appian and Cassius Dio*, Ann Arbor.

---

32 Coudry 2016, 287.
33 I am grateful to Josiah Osgood and Christopher Baron for comments on a draft of this chapter.

Hose, M. (1994) *Erneuerung der Vergangenheit: die Historiker im Imperium Romanum von Florus bis Cassius Dio*, Stuttgart.

Kemezis, A. (2014) *Greek Narratives of the Roman Empire under the Severans: Cassius Dio, Philostratus and Herodian*, Cambridge.

Kuhn-Chen, B. (2002) *Geschichtskonzeptionen griechischer Historiker im 2 und 3. Jahrhundert n. Chr.: Untersuchungen zu den Werken von Appian, Cassius Dio und Herodian*, Frankfurt am Main.

Lange, C. H. (2018) "Cassius Dio on Violence, *Stasis*, and Civil War: the Early Years", in C. Burden-Strevens & M. Lindholmer (eds.), *Cassius Dio's Forgotten History of Early Rome: The 'Roman History' Books 1–21* (Leiden & Boston), 165–89.

Lange, C. H. (forthcoming) "Cassius Dio on Perusia: A Study in Human Nature During Civil War", in J. M. Madsen & C. H. Lange (eds.), *Cassius Dio the Historian: Methods and Approaches* (Leiden & Boston).

Madsen, J. M. (2016) "Criticising the Benefactors: The Severans and the Return of Dynastic Rule", in C. H. Lange & J. M. Madsen (eds.), *Cassius Dio: Greek Intellectual and Roman Politician.* (Leiden & Boston): 136–58.

Mallan, C. (2016) "*Parrhêsia* in Cassius Dio" in C. H. Lange & J. M. Madsen (eds.), *Cassius Dio: Greek Intellectual and Roman Politician* (Leiden & Boston): 258–75.

Manuwald, B. (1979) *Cassius Dio und Augustus: philologische Untersuchungen zu den Büchern 45–56 des dionischen Geschichtswerkes*, Wiesbaden.

Manuwald, B. (1991) Review of M. Reinhold, *From Republic to Principate: An Historical Commentary on Cassius Dio Roman History Books 49–52 (36–29 B.C.)*, *American Journal of Philology* 112/3, 413–17.

Markov, K. V. (2013) "The Concepts of 'Democracy' and 'Tyranny' in the Speech of Agrippa in Cassius Dio 52.1–13: Conventional Rhetoric or Political Theory?", in A. Mehl *et al.* (eds.), *Ruthenia classica aetatis novae: A Collection of Works by Russian Scholars in Greek and Roman History* (Stuttgart): 215–31.

Mouritsen, H. (2001) *Plebs and Politics in the Late Roman Republic*, Cambridge.

Osgood, J. (2006). *Caesar's Legacy: Civil War and the Emergence of the Roman Empire*, Cambridge.

Pelling, C. B. R. (1997). "Biographical History? Cassius Dio on the Early Principate", in M. J. Edwards & S. Swain (eds.), *Portraits: Biographical Representation in the Greek and Latin Literature of the Roman Empire* (Oxford): 117–44.

Questa, C. (1957) "Tecnica biographica e tecnica annalistica nei libri LIII–LXIII di Cassio Dione", *Studi urbinati* 31, 37–53.

Reinhold, M. (1988) *From Republic to Principate: An Historical Commentary on Cassius Dio Roman History Books 49–52 (36–29 B.C.)*, Atlanta.

Reinhold, M. & Swan, P. M. (1990) "Cassius Dio's Assessment of Augustus", in K. A. Raaflaub & M. Toher (eds.), *Between Republic and Empire: Interpretations of Augustus and his Principate* (Berkeley): 155–73.

Rich, J. W. (1990) *Cassius Dio: The Augustan Settlement (Roman History 53.1–55.9)*, Warminster.

Stahl, M. (2011) "Vom 'kalten Terroristen' zum Friedenkaiser? Über die Wende im politischen Wirken von Octavian zu Augustus", *Potestas* 4, 87–105.

Swan, P. M. (1997) "How Cassius Dio Composed his Augustan Books", *Aufstieg und Niedergang der römischen Welt* 2.34.3, 2524–57.

Swan, P. M. (2004) *The Augustan Succession: An Historical Commentary on Cassius Dio's Roman History Books 55–56 (9 BC–AD 14)*, Oxford.

Tokarev, A. N. (2011) *Formation of the Official Ideology of the Emperor Augustus' Principate* (in Russian), Kharkov.

Welwei, K. W. (2004) "Augustus als vindex libertatis. Freiheitsideologie und propaganda im frühen Prinzipat", in *Res publica und Imperium. Kleine Schriften zur römischen Geschichte* (Stuttgart): 217–29.

Westall, R. (2016) "The Sources for Cassius Dio for the Roman Civil Wars of 49–30 BC", in C. H. Lange & J. M. Madsen (eds.), *Cassius Dio: Greek Intellectual and Roman Politician* (Leiden & Boston): 51–75.

Wiedemann, T. E. J. (1981) Review of B. Manuwald, *Cassius Dio und Augustus*, *Journal of Roman Studies* 71, 201–3.

Index

Notes: (1) except for major writers and emperors, Romans are always referred to by their *nomen*; (2) for Cassius Dio's views on topics also treated historically in this book (e.g., bribery or Sibylline oracles), refer to relevant entry (e.g. "bribery" or "Sibylline oracles")

Achaia   249
Acilius Glabrio, M.' (*cos.* 67 BCE)   76, 77
Actium, war of   4, 19, 116, 163, 282, 290
Aelius Tubero, Q.   73, 190
Aemilius Lepidus, M. (*cos.* 46, 42 BCE)   51, 243, 244–56, 271, 273, 274, 284, 289, 292
Aemilius Paulus, L. (*cos.* 182, 168 BCE)   99–100
Aemilius Scaurus, M. (*pr.* 56 BCE)   162
Afranius, L. (*cos.* 60 BCE)   264
Africa   64, 69, 161
Alexander Severus   232
Alexander the Great   29, 63, 110, 161
Alexandria   109, 197–8, 199, 207, 211
Allobroges   26, 44, 184
Annius Milo, T. (*pr.* 55 BCE)   1, 162, 185, 211, 217, 226–30
Antonius, L. (*cos.* 40 BCE)   69, 286, 289
Antonius, M. (*cos.* 44, 34 BCE)   10, 11, 45, 51, 69, 108–9, 111–18, 138, 160, 163–4, 187–90, 242, 244–56, 270–7, 284–9
Antonius Creticus, M. (*pr.* 74 BCE)   78, 188
Antonius Hybrida, C. (*cos.* 63 BCE)   179, 185, 188
Appian   24 n. 14, 29, 30 n. 41, 36, 39, 41, 44, 74, 75, 78, 84, 86, 87, 88, 102 n. 21, 104, 114, 115, 122, 132–4, 148, 149, 184, 187–8, 237, 241, 248–55, 262, 285, 286, 293 n. 29, 294
Appuleius Saturninus, L. (*tr. pl.* 103, 100 BCE)   43
Arabia   60
Archelaus   207
Aretas III   60
Artavasdes II   116
Asconius   38, 39, 132
Asia   61, 63, 90, 199
Asinius Pollio, C. (*cos.* 40 BCE)   69, 73, 191, 244, 248 n. 29
Aufidius Bassus   73

augurium salutis   62
Augustus   4, 8, 10, 11, 12, 13, 32, 41, 51, 56–7, 65, 67, 68, 98, 117–23, 134, 140, 151–5, 160, 162, 165–8, 173, 201, 238–56, 259–79, 282–96
Aurelius Cotta, L. (*cos.* 65 BCE)   180–1
Autronius Paetus, P. (*cos. desig.* 65 BCE)   180–1

Bellum Alexandrinum   3, 218 n. 2, 219–24
Berenice IV   207
Bithynia   8, 163–4, 168
Blossius of Cumae   97–8
bribery   1, 4, 7, 8, 10, 37–42, 46–8, 85–6, 131, 206–11
Britain   29
Brundisium, peace of   251, 252, 288

Caecilius Bassus, Q.   53
Caecilius Metellus Creticus, Q. (*cos.* 69 BCE)   4, 21, 24
Caecilius Metellus Nepos, Q. (*cos.* 57 BCE)   44–5, 176–9
Caecilius Metellus Pius Scipio, Q. (*cos.* 52 BCE)   64
Caelius Rufus, M. (*pr.* 48 BCE)   7, 12, 217, 224–30, 227–8, 231–3
Caesetius Flavus, L. (*tr. pl.* 44 BCE)   229
Caligula   166, 171, 172
Calpurnius Bestia, L. (*tr. pl.* 62 BCE)   176–9, 187
Calpurnius Bibulus, M. (*cos.* 59 BCE)   132, 148, 155, 159
Calpurnius Piso Caesoninus, L. (*cos.* 58 BCE)   114, 187–8
Campania   225, 226, 287
Caninius Gallus, L. (*tr. pl.* 56 BCE)   203
Cappadocia   77
Caracalla   6, 160, 166, 169–73, 227 n. 28
Carthage   67–8, 103

Cassius Dio   5–6, 8, 11, 42, 91, 98, 120, 121, 159–60, 164, 168–73, 212–13, 230–3, 283 (*see also Roman History* of Cassius Dio)
Cassius Longinus, C. (*pr.* 44 BCE)   51, 52–6, 276, 288, 293–4
Cassius Longinus, Q. (*tr. pl.* 49 BCE)   3, 45, 217–21
Catilinarian conspiracy, *see* Sergius Catilina, L.
Cilicia   77, 163, 203
civil war   7–9, 12–13, 27–32, 36, 41–2, 45, 107, 143, 161, 162–4, 201, 211–13, 217–33, 236–56, 259–79, 282–96
Claudius, emperor   171
Claudius Marcellus, M. (*cos.* 222 etc. BCE)   99–100, 103
Claudius Marcellus Aeserninus, M. (*quaest.* 48 BCE, likely *cos.* 22 BCE)   7, 12, 217–24, 230, 232–3
Claudius Pulcher, Ap. (*cos.* 54 BCE)   131, 132
Claudius Quadrigarius   103
clemency   64, 67–8, 107–11, 117, 120, 153, 264, 267, 289–90
Cleopatra VII   116, 118, 163–4
Clodius Pulcher, P. (*tr. pl.* 58 BCE)   1, 40–1, 44–5, 75, 76–7, 162, 179, 185, 187, 188, 204, 211
Commodus   6, 160, 166, 170–3, 230–2
Corinth   67
Cornelius, C. (*tr. pl.* 67 BCE)   38
Cornelius Cinna, L. (*cos.* 87–84 BCE)   108
Cornelius Cossus Arvina, A. (*cos.* 343, 332 BCE)   139
Cornelius Dolabella, P. (*cos.* 44 BCE)   53
Cornelius Lentulus Spinther, P. (*cos.* 57 BCE)   198, 202–5
Cornelius Lentulus Sura, P. (*cos.* 71 BCE)   11, 44, 47, 178–9, 184, 185, 186, 187, 188, 189, 199
Cornelius Rufinus, P. (*cos.* 290, 277 BCE)   139
Cornelius Scipio Aemilianus, P. (*cos.* 147, 134 BCE)   10, 99–101, 102, 103–4
Cornelius Scipio Africanus, P. (*cos.* 205, 194 BCE)   10, 99–100, 103
Cornelius Sulla, Faustus (*quaest.* 54 BCE) 160
Cornelius Sulla, L. (*cos.* 88, 80 BCE)   4, 67, 68, 108, 133, 138–55, 249, 261, 273

Cornelius Sulla, P. (*cos. desig.* 65 BCE)   178–9, 180–1
Corsica   249
Cremutius Cordus   73, 120
Cyzicus   8, 163–4

Dacia   7
Dellius, Q.   240
dictatorship   3, 4, 11, 13, 41, 67–8, 115, 131–55, 260–8
Didius Julianus   231
Didius, Q.   163–4
Diodorus Siculus   103, 183, 190, 191
Dionysius of Halicarnassus   90, 136–9, 140, 149, 154, 190
Domitian   166, 172
Domitius Ahenobarbus, L. (*cos.* 54 BCE)   131–2, 212
Domitius Calvinus, Cn. (*cos.* 53, 40 BCE)   69, 131, 133
dynasteiai   4–5, 8, 9, 13, 20, 27, 31, 46, 205, 209–10, 225, 227–8, 237–8, 239–40, 276, 283, 295–6

Elagabalus   231, 232
Epidius Marullus, C. (*tr. pl.* 44 BCE)   229
Etruria   183, 254

Fabius Maximus Rullianus, Q. (*cos.* 322 etc. BCE)   99
Fabius Maximus Verrucosus, Q. (*cos.* 233 etc. BCE)   140
Fabricius Luscinus, C. (*cos.* 282, 278 BCE)   99–100, 101, 121
Favonius, M. (*pr.* 49 BCE)   148
Fenestella   204
Florus   74
Fufius Calenus, Q. (*cos.* 47 BCE)   111–16, 122, 184, 185–90
Fulvia   69, 286
Furius Camillus, M. (*dict.* 396 etc. BCE)   99, 102, 123, 140, 263

Gabinius, A. (*cos.* 58 BCE)   12, 43, 78–83, 146, 198, 205–11
Galba   289
games   6, 11, 64–6, 158–73

Gaul   1, 7, 21, 26, 27, 29, 40, 108, 184, 189, 200, 246, 251, 273
giraffes   7, 64, 170
gladiators   1, 6, 11, 158–73
greed   42, 54, 198, 224 (*see also pleonexia*)

Hadrian   168, 171
Hannibal   10, 100, 101, 105, 107 n. 48, 140
Herod the Great   164
Herodian   171
Herodotus   57
hostis publicus   2, 28, 43, 46, 243

Ilerda, battle of   264
imperator   67, 154, 269, 295

Jews   7, 60
Julia (daughter of Caesar the dictator)   158–9, 212
Julia (mother of M. Antonius)   188
Julius Caesar, C. (*cos.* 59, 48, 46–44 BCE)   1, 3, 4, 5, 7, 8, 9, 10, 13, 21, 24, 26, 27–32, 36, 41, 45–6, 51, 61–8, 76, 89–91, 106–11, 112, 122–3, 131, 133, 134, 138–9, 140, 141, 153–5, 158–9, 163, 164, 169, 172, 177, 178, 179, 185, 187, 188, 191, 200, 206, 209, 217–30, 232, 242, 243, 246, 259–79
Junius Brutus, L. (*cos.* 509 BCE)   149–51
Junius Brutus, M. (*pr.* 44 BCE)   51, 52–6, 149–51, 185, 188, 190, 276, 288, 289, 293–4
Junius Brutus Albinus, D. (*cos. desig.* 42 BCE)   189, 273, 276
Junius Pera, M. (*cos.* 230 BCE)   140

Labienus, Q.   69
Lartius, T. (*cos.* 501, 498 BCE)   135–8, 141
lex Antonia (abolishing dictatorship)   137–9, 151, 155
lex Calpurnia de ambitu   38
lex Gabinia de imperio Cn. Pompeii   1, 5, 10, 21, 37–8, 47, 78–83, 90, 141–5, 153, 208–9
lex Julia de ambitu (of Augustus)   41
lex Julia de provinciis (of Julius Caesar)   30
lex Manilia de imperio Cn. Pompeii   62, 79, 145, 267
lex Pompeia de ambitu   41
lex Tullia de ambitu   39, 85–6

Licinius Crassus, M. (*cos.* 70, 55 BCE)   1, 21, 24, 30, 36, 43, 45, 53, 63, 131, 188, 191, 204, 206, 209, 210, 211, 237, 252
Licinius Lucullus, L. (*cos.* 74 BCE)   10, 21, 24, 25, 29, 39, 53, 74–8, 191, 264, 267
Livia   69, 285–6, 290, 293
Livy   20, 24, 26, 27, 30 n. 40, 73, 74, 75, 78, 84, 89, 90, 136–9, 154, 190, 218 n. 2, 219, 223–4, 227–30
Luca, conference of   8, 36, 45
Lucceius, L.   190
Lucian   91
Lucilius Hirrus, C. (*tr. pl.* 53 BCE)   131, 146
Lutatius Catulus, Q. (*cos.* 78 BCE)   37–8, 79–83, 141–5, 151, 154, 155, 191

Macrinus   231
Maecenas, C.   293 (*see also Roman History* of Cassius Dio, speech of Maecenas in)
Manlius, C.   183
Manlius Torquatus, L. (*cos.* 65 BCE)   180–1
Manlius Torquatus, L. (*pr.* 49 BCE)   178–9, 181
Marcius Rex, Q. (*cos.* 68 BCE)   77
Marcus Aurelius   168, 170
Marius, C. (*cos.* 107, 104–100, 86 BCE)   108, 142, 144, 261
Massinissa   101
Memmius, C. (*pr.* 58 BCE)   131
Menas   240, 253
Misenum, pact of   12, 58, 243, 245, 247–55
Mithridates VI   21, 25, 29, 60, 63, 74–8, 207, 249, 264, 267
Munda, war of   65, 243
Mutina, war of   187, 189, 241, 245, 272–3, 276, 290

Naulochus, battle of   243–4
Nero   166, 172, 201, 212
Numantia, war of   104

Octavian, *see* Augustus
Otho   289

paideia   102, 103
Panaetius   97–8, 104
Papirius Cursor, L. (*cos.* 326 etc. BCE)   99, 139

Parthia 7, 21, 25, 30, 53, 68, 69, 116, 200, 252, 287
Pertinax 230–1
Perusia, war of 58, 69, 251, 278, 290 n. 21
Pharnaces 30
Pharsalus, battle at 30, 53, 190, 217, 224, 228, 230, 232
Philippi, war of 51, 52, 56, 247, 293–4
Philiscus 47, 105–6, 118, 184
Plato 3
Plautius, A. (*pr.* 51 BCE) 203
pleonexia 25 (*see also* greed)
Plutarch 29, 30 n. 41, 32 n. 47, 36, 41, 44, 74, 75, 76, 78, 79, 80–2, 84, 86, 88, 122, 132–4, 148, 177, 180, 182, 187
Polybius 7, 20, 51, 103, 104, 287
Pompeius Magnus, Cn. (*cos.* 70, 55, 52 BCE) 1, 3, 7, 8, 11, 21, 24, 25, 26, 27–9, 36, 37–8, 41, 43, 45, 58–63, 65, 75, 76, 78–83, 91, 123, 131–5, 137, 141–55, 161, 162, 172, 178, 191, 198, 203–12, 217–30, 237, 245, 246, 256, 261, 264, 266, 267
Pompeius Magnus, Cn. (son of preceding) 65, 244
Pompeius (Magnus Pius), Sex. 12, 160, 236–56, 276, 288, 290
Pomponius Atticus, T. 190, 243
Pomptinus, C. (*pr.* 63) 1, 26, 212
Porcius Cato, C. (*tr. pl.* 56 BCE) 3, 202–5
Porcius Cato, M. ("Uticensis") (*pr.* 54 BCE) 4, 61, 64, 81, 88, 105 n. 37, 132, 148, 155, 178, 188, 191, 210, 219
Posidonius 98, 103–4, 120
principate 8, 42, 120–2, 143, 151–5, 259, 275, 277, 295
proscriptions 243, 246, 261, 273–6, 284, 287, 290, 292
Ptolemy XII 3, 12, 197–213

Quinctius Cincinnatus, L. (*dict.* 458 BCE) 99, 102, 139–40

Rabirius, C. 1, 36, 43, 46–7, 179
Rhine 29
Roman History of Cassius Dio
  annalistic framework of 6, 9, 10, 20, 21–4, 28, 39–40, 51, 55–8, 69–70, 229–30
  "biostructuring" in 8, 31–2, 51, 67 n. 28
  chronology in 6–7, 10, 28, 47–8, 51–70, 90, 179, 207–8, 228, 229, 233
  on forms of government 3–5, 7, 10, 19, 30, 31–2, 37–8, 41, 68, 90–1, 97–8, 121, 134, 143, 153–5, 172, 239–40, 259–65, 270, 275, 277–9 (*see also* dynasteiai)
  on imperialism 4, 7, 8, 9, 20–32, 143–5
  on individuals 4–5, 10, 20, 24, 72–93, 227–8
  sources of 3, 72–4, 82, 88–93, 103–4, 109–11, 114, 120, 122–3, 134, 162, 190–2, 208–13, 218, 233, 260, 279
  speech of Maecenas in 11, 19, 31, 41–2, 73 n. 10, 154–5, 167–8, 265, 278–9, 285, 290
  speeches in 3, 7, 29, 37–8, 47, 87–8, 105–23, 141–5, 185–90, 290
  on virtues 3, 10, 97–123
Roscius Otho, L. (*pr.* 63 BCE) 162
Rutilius Rufus, P. (*cos.* 105 BCE) 98, 104

Sallust 3, 11, 25 n. 18, 27, 39, 44, 47, 73, 74, 83–4, 86, 90, 179, 180, 181, 183, 184, 185, 191, 241
Sardinia 249, 251
Scribonia 286
Scribonius Curio, C. (*tr. pl.* 50 BCE) 36
Scribonius Libo, L. 190
Sempronius Gracchus, Ti. (*tr. pl.* 133 BCE) 103, 104, 263–4
Senate 3, 4, 5, 10, 12, 28, 36–48, 79, 81–2, 86, 89–90, 132, 147, 152, 164–6, 199, 200, 202–5, 210, 266–8, 273, 278–9, 292
senatus consultum ultimum (SCU) 2, 43, 45, 182, 191
Seneca the Elder 248 n. 29
Septimius Severus 68, 230–2, 289
Sergius Catilina, L. (*pr.* 68 BCE) 3, 5, 10, 11, 39, 43–5, 47, 60, 83–9, 176–92, 206, 242
Sertorius, Q. (*pr.* 83 BCE) 244, 246
Servilius Vatia Isauricus, P. (*cos.* 48, 41 BCE) 69, 225–6
Sibylline oracles 3, 12, 197–213
Sicily 58, 69, 243, 246, 250, 251, 253
Spain 12, 29, 63, 65, 217–24, 243–5
Suetonius 32 n. 47, 74, 143 n. 52, 152, 159, 212
Sulpicius Rufus, Ser. (*cos.* 51 BCE) 132
Syria 53, 56, 60, 163–4, 198, 207, 209

Tacitus   155, 212, 285
Tanusius Geminus   190
Thapsus, battle of   64, 107
Thorius, T.   220
Thucydides   5, 9, 13, 51, 102, 236–8, 243, 276, 287–8, 296
Tiberius   42, 69, 121–2, 165, 201
Tigranes II   75, 267
Trebonius, C. (*cos.* 45 BCE)   211, 225–6
triumph   23, 64, 67, 68, 161, 162, 165, 169, 212, 244, 249
Triumvirate   32, 41, 51, 237–56, 271, 273–7, 284–9
Tullius Cicero, M. (*cos.* 63 BC)   3, 8, 10, 11, 26 n. 22, 37, 39–40, 44–5, 46–7, 67, 74, 83–9, 98, 104, 105–6, 109–10, 111–16, 120, 122–3, 132–4, 137–9, 140, 144–51, 154, 161, 176–92, 198, 204–8, 210, 244
tumultus   44, 45, 182, 191

Valerius Antias   103
Valerius Messalla, M. (*monetal.* 53 BCE, likely *cos.* 32 BCE)   147–9

Valerius Messalla Corvinus, M. (*cos.* 31 BCE)   164, 240
Valerius Messalla Rufus, M. (*cos.* 53 BCE)   131, 133, 147
Vatinius, P. (*cos.* 47 BCE)   188
Velleius Paterculus   41, 44, 74, 75, 76, 78, 79, 80–2, 84, 86, 87, 90, 110, 152, 227–30
Ventidius, P. (*cos.* 43 BCE)   68
Vergil   192
violence   1, 37, 40–2, 81–2, 162–3, 178, 209–12, 217, 224–30, 233
Vipsanius Agrippa, M. (*cos.* 37, 28, 27 BCE)   10, 118–20, 122–3, 162, 252, 292
Viriathus   101, 105
Vitellius, emperor   165
Vitellius, Q.   165

Xiphilinus   172

Zonaras   135, 139–40, 172, 200

Printed in the United States
By Bookmasters